Global Governance and the International Law of the Sea

This book conducts an examination of the international legal regime of the continental shelf through the lens of international relations (IR), with a primary focus on global governance theory.

Presenting a new perspective within the field of IR and international law, the book offers new insights into the rules, principles, practices, and actors that establish and govern social interactions and the management of common affairs at the transnational level. The governance framework within the continental shelf can encompass a wider scope than legal laws alone, incorporating informal rules or potentially disregarding formal "black letter" rules that may not be effectively applied in practice. To exemplify how governance theory and other IR theories contribute to the analysis of the legal regime concerning the continental shelf, the book conducts an in-depth examination of three significant issues: (i) the demarcation and delimitation of the continental shelf, (ii) the rights and obligations of coastal States in the continental shelf, and (iii) procedural matters related to the continental shelf and international maritime adjudication.

This book will be of interest to students and scholars in the field of the law of the sea, international law, global governance, and international relations.

Shani Friedman has a PhD degree from the Faculty of Law, Hebrew University of Jerusalem, and is a member of the Israeli Bar Association. In addition, Shani has an LLB from the Hebrew University of Jerusalem; MA in international relations from the Hebrew University of Jerusalem; and BA in political science and Middle Eastern studies, Ben-Gurion University, Beer-Sheva. Shani researches various topics within the field of the law of the sea, which is her main field of expertise, and international institutions and the interaction between international law and international relations, including theoretical aspects.

Acknowledgements

This book is based on my PhD dissertation at the Law Faculty, the Hebrew University of Jerusalem. I wish to thank Prof. Moshe Hirsch, my PhD supervisor, for his generosity, patience, and kindness and continuous support for over a decade, which made the completion of the dissertation and this book not only possible but also pleasant and enjoyable.

Very special thanks also go to Prof. Jeffrey Dunoff and Prof. Arie Kacowicz, who served as my PhD advisory committee members. I am particularly grateful for their comments on my research proposal that helped improve my theoretical framework, which is the basis for this book. Special thanks also go to Prof. Ruth Lapidoth for her advice and continuous support in my research. I'm also thankful for the guidance and support of Prof. Yuval Shany and Prof. Tomer Broude in developing my knowledge and research skills.

Both the PhD dissertation and this book would not have been possible without external financial support. I would like to thank the Aharon Barak Center for Interdisciplinary Legal Research and the Cheshin Center for Advanced Legal Studies for the doctoral scholarship and research grant that enabled my research. I also wish to thank the Fineberg Fund for supporting this book project.

Lastly, I want to thank my family – my parents and brothers. Thank you for your love and endless support. Special thanks go also to all my friends who were part of this journey.

Introduction

The book analyzes the international legal rules applying to the continental shelf from the perspective of international relations (IR) theories, primarily global governance theory. The existing literature on the continental shelf essentially examines this significant topic from a legal perspective, dominated by a positivist legal analysis of the formal legal rules and institutions. This study offers an innovative and broader IR approach that sheds new light on this well-researched legal field. This approach assists in exposing hidden or underexplored interactions between legal regimes and other institutional arrangements. As we expose these patterns of behavior, we learn more about the international system and the roles each actor plays within the system. Such analysis generates new insights and explanations regarding past evolution and current developments of legal rules and institutions in this sphere. Furthermore, this perspective may also facilitate some forecasts of future trends or developments, such as possible emergence of new rules, actors, and institutional design, as well as generating proposals for better legal mechanisms to cope with new challenges arising in this significant sphere of international law.

The term "global governance" generally refers to activities of various actors backed by shared goals undertaken in the absence of formal political authority or police powers at the international level. The term "governance" refers here to a network: a system of formal and informal (i.e., non-governmental or non-legal) bundles of rules, norms, roles, institutions, and practices that define and regulate social interactions and management of common affairs at the transnational level. The term "global" indicates that this approach examines not only states but also a wide range of non-state actors, such as multinational corporations, non-governmental organizations (NGOs), and individuals. From this perspective, the prevailing global order (or "world politics") encompasses every region, country, social movement, and private organization that engages in activities across national boundaries or beyond national jurisdictions.[1]

The disciplines of international law (IL) and governance theory interact and overlap, and political scientists and international lawyers draw from each other's work with increasing frequency. The concept of "global governance" constitutes a theoretical framework that bridges the gap between mainstream IR theories and international law scholarship.[2] Governance system analysis often employs legal elements to explain the regulation of global society, while international legal

DOI: 10.4324/9781003479772-1

analysis is often comprised of governance frameworks. Consequently, each field of IL can be analyzed as a particular governance framework with its own set of explicit and implicit rules, norms, roles, actors, and institutions.

Scholarship in both disciplines helps to explain the construction and distribution of norms in the international system through various types of institutional arrangements. However, governance theory's examination of formal and informal relationships and instruments that define and regulate international social practices highlights the importance of implicit or informal elements, such as non-legally binding rules (i.e., "soft law") in international law. In addition, while institutions may not always possess competence to create rules or enforce them, they often guide actors' behavior and contribute to the implementation of existing formal rules.[3]

The IR "governance" is a broader concept than "legal regime" in international *legal* literature. The book will use the term "legal regime" in reference to the formal legal rules, principles, and institutions that govern the continental shelf, enshrined mostly in the UN Convention on the Law of the Sea (hereinafter: UNCLOS or the Convention).[4] The term "governance framework" is used to describe and analyze the IR perspective of the formal legal regime. The governance framework includes formal and informal, explicit and implicit, rules, norms, principles, institutions, processes, and a broad range of actors that affect and govern the subject-area of the continental shelf.

This broader global governance perspective, it is submitted, assists international legal scholars to conceive and explain certain developments and trends in the narrower "legal regime". The governance approach sheds light on commonly underexplored interactions and effects to provide more meaningful explanations for well-researched questions regarding the continental shelf; in certain cases, this broader approach may better explain developments that the legal perspective (i.e., the law of the sea) alone cannot adequately explain.

For example, the decisions of international judicial bodies can be better understood from a broader governance perspective. One of the most significant questions in the law of the sea concerns the delimitation of overlapping maritime zones between states. The legal literature on the delimitation process mostly focuses on the result: to achieve an "equitable solution".[5] However, there is no legal rule clarifying how to determine the location of an "equitable" boundary. Governance theory suggests examining the factors that judges employ in practice (such as security, economic, or geographical variables) to determine the location of a maritime boundary and clarifying how and why adjudicators choose to rely on different factors in setting the boundary. This method offers a better understanding of the interpretation of legal rules governing the process of continental shelf delimitation, thus allowing actors to better coordinate their expectations.

Governance theory not only broadens the scope of analysis but, in some cases, also narrows the range of factors to be considered when analyzing the legal regime. For example, analysis of the governance framework often ignores formal "black letter" legal rules enshrined in the legal convention that have no significant influence on states' behavior or that are not implemented in practice. For example, as discussed in Chapter 3, the governance framework of the continental shelf downplays certain obligations during the process of delimitation.

To illustrate the contribution of governance theory and other IR theories to the analysis of the continental shelf's legal regime, the book will analyze in depth three significant issues: (i) demarcation and delimitation of the continental shelf; (ii) the rights and obligations of coastal States in the continental shelf; and (iii) procedural issues regarding the continental shelf and international maritime adjudication (such as the roles and procedures of UNCLOS's institutions, the influence of third-parties, and the evaluation of scientific evidence). The analysis of each topic will show how the governance framework broadens or narrows the legal regime of the continental shelf and how such analysis can produce different answers to significant questions in this significant sphere of international law.

Governance theory literature is not homogenous, and different theoretical streams in IR generate somewhat different perspectives in governance scholarship. As elaborated in Chapter 1, the *realist* approach contends that power relations between actors are essential for understanding the international system. States are the main actors in the international system and, generally, rational actors seeking to maximize their interests (mainly material interests).[6] The *constructivist* approach highlights the social characteristics of the international system; from this perspective, actors shape international relations and are also shaped by these relations. In addition, this approach emphasizes cognitive structures that give meaning to the material world and mold the international system.[7] The *institutional* approach, like realism, views state behavior as rational. However, unlike realism that assume constant conflictual relations, the institutional approach acknowledges that international institutions can affect states' behavior and recognizes that there are conditions that facilitate institutional arrangements for the benefit of all actors – despite the obstacles that hinder international cooperation.[8]

Each of these major theoretical streams in IR offers different insights on the construction of *legal* regime and its development. Thus, for example, each stream provides different explanations for the development of new rules concerning the continental shelf, focuses on different types of actors within the continental shelf's governance system, or highlights different considerations in maritime adjudication.

1. Demarcation and delimitation of the continental shelf

Coastal States have two types of rights in the continental shelf: (i) inherent rights that apply to all coastal States in the area up to 200 nm;[9] and (ii) special rights that apply beyond 200 nm, only to states that can prove they have a wider continental shelf.[10] One of the main legal issues relating to the continental shelf is the establishment of the zone's outer limit. Since the continental shelf reflects important economic interests for states, it is essential to determine the breadth of the zone and set boundaries vis-à-vis other states.

The discussion on delimitation of the continental shelf is divided into two parts: continental shelf demarcation (that is, setting the outer limit unilaterally, up to and beyond 200 nm); and delimitation of the continental shelf *between* states with opposite or adjacent coasts (that is, when two or more continental shelves overlap). Coastal States must define the breadth of the zone before determining whether neighboring continental shelves overlap; if they are found to overlap, delimitation becomes necessary.

1.1 Demarcation of the outer limit of the continental shelf

1.1.1 The outer limit of the continental shelf up to 200 nm

Article 76(1) provides two possibilities for the outer limit of the continental shelf: a geological criterion (the outer edge of the continental margin) or a distance criterion (200 nautical miles [nm]).[11] The formal rule stipulates that the geological criterion is the *primary* option for the limit, while the distance of 200 nm is a *secondary* demarcation option if the physical outer edge is less than 200 nm from the coast. In practice, the distance criterion essentially became the accepted outer limit of the continental shelf. Almost all coastal States have claimed a 200 nm continental shelf, regardless of the configuration of the seabed.[12] The informal norms concerning the limit of the continental shelf have mainly developed through state practice, often overlooking the formal legal rules included in the Convention.

In addition, under the formal legal regime, the basis for entitlement to a continental shelf is the connection to the land territory ("natural prolongation"), regardless of whether the outer limit is at the edge of the margin or at 200 nm from the coast. However, the employment of the distance criterion ensures that coastal States have a continental shelf regardless of the geological circumstances. Thus, there is a difference between the *legal* regime and the *governance* perspective concerning the entitlement and criteria for the breadth of the continental shelf.

This example illustrates how governance theory employs informal rules and practices when analyzing the development of legal rules. In this case, the governance framework downplays the formal legal rule. This perspective not only highlights the difference between the legal regime and the governance framework but can also explain the development of legal norms.

1.1.2 The outer limit of the continental shelf beyond 200 nm

UNCLOS permits coastal States to extend their continental shelf up to 350 nm from the coast when the breadth of the continental shelf is more than 200 nm.[13] To substantiate their claims, states must collect and interpret data in accordance with Article 76. This process is not only complicated and expensive but also makes it difficult for other states to verify the claims according to the Convention's criteria. This is probably a result of the drafters' intent to limit coastal States' claims to an extensive continental shelf.[14] Article 76 requires coastal States to submit information supporting a claim for an extended continental shelf to the UN Commission on the Limits of the Continental Shelf (hereinafter: CLCS or the Commission).[15]

The Commission has a significant role in this process: While the Convention assigns it a technical role of reviewing scientific data and issuing non-binding recommendations, in practice, the CLCS has significantly more influence and competences than conferred to it in the formal legal regime. For example, there is a high level of cooperation of states with the Commission that cannot be exclusively explained by the formal legal regime.

Furthermore, even though the Commission is formally a scientific expert body, states treat it like a semi-judicial body. For example, since most of the terms in Article 76 are technical and vague, the Commission has created guidelines for interpreting Article 76, which is essentially a legal function. Furthermore, since the CLCS is the only institution to create such guidelines, states have an interest in relying on its interpretation – even though they are not obligated to do so.[16] In addition, the Commission is the sole body involved in the process of extending the continental shelf, thus, no external undermining influences. This strengthens the CLCS's practical authority and legitimacy.[17]

Thus, while the CLCS has limited competences under the formal legal regime, it has greater significance within the governance framework in influencing boundaries in disputed areas. In addition, despite the Commission's lack of legally binding powers, coastal States often regard these recommendations seriously.

1.1.2.1 CURRENT PRACTICE OF THE CLCS

Today, there is an extensive practice of coastal States' submissions to the CLCS to demarcate their continental shelf beyond 200 nm. Russia was the first to make such submission in 2001.[18] As of December 2023, the Commission had received 104 full, partial, joint, or revised submissions concerning the outer limits of the continental shelf.[19] So far, the CLCS has issued 40 recommendations, including some that requested additional information[20] and others that recommended the final location of the outer limit.[21]

Reviewing all the submissions and recommendations, one can detect some patterns in the CLCS's work: In its first few years, the Commission presented its recommendations within several months of submission. However, since 2007, the process has slowed due to an increased workload; in some cases, the Commission has taken several years to submit its recommendations.[22] For example, while the Commission issued its recommendation on Russia's initial submission regarding the Arctic Ocean within several months, it took the Commission approximately eight years to issues recommendations on the revised submission submitted by Russia in 2015.[23] The CLCS issued its latest recommendation on March 2023.[24]

The main streams of IR theory highlight different elements in the governance framework and give different interpretations to explain the development of rules. For example, the realist approach, which emphasizes actors' relative power and interests, is likely to prefer a legal interpretation that allocates larger areas (and thus more material resources) to coastal States. On the other hand, the institutional approach, which focuses on conditions for cooperation through institutions, is less likely to support extension of the shelf, as it might encourage unilateral action and hinder international cooperation. The institutional approach is more inclined to support an interpretation that balances the interests of coastal States with those of other states (and non-state actors) or to promote rules that motivate cooperation (e.g., through allocating authority to multilateral institutions).

1.2 Delimitation of overlapping continental shelves (within and beyond 200 nm)

The Convention establishes a mechanism for delimiting overlapping areas between neighboring states. As mentioned, delimitation is a separate process from demarcation of the outer limit (whether up to 200 nm or beyond). Essentially, the question of delimitation arises when the breadth between coastal States is less than 400 nm. In other words, the shelves overlap, and each state cannot claim the full breadth of the zone due to claims of neighboring states.[25]

In such cases, UNCLOS provides a two-stage mechanism for delimitation. Article 83 reflects the primary rule regarding delimitation, which obligates coastal States to delimit their overlapping continental shelves through a bilateral agreement in accordance with international law, with the aim of achieving an "equitable solution".[26] The Convention refers the parties to delimitation through a judicial process only if they cannot reach such agreement themselves within a reasonable period.[27]

One of the significant questions in judicial delimitation relates to the definition of the informal rule of "relevant circumstances" in the process of delimitation. The formal legal regime stipulates only that the final line should reflect an "equitable solution" but does not specify how to reach such result. International tribunals have developed informal principles concerning the considerations that should be taken into account to implement the formal rules.

The governance perspective can explain or interpret the term "relevant circumstances" employed in the delimitation process, and each of the major IR theoretical streams suggests a different set of factors that tribunals should consider when delimiting overlapping continental shelves between neighboring states. For example, realists are likely to emphasize security and economic considerations, or the balance of power between the parties, thus granting more weight to the stronger party in the delimitation process. The institutional approach is likely to highlight the role of mathematical calculations (such as median points), as they are perceived as more "objective" (and less susceptible to power relations), thus promoting greater cooperation and compliance with judicial decisions. The constructivist approach is likely to emphasize that a provisional line generates greater certainty and knowledge in the delimitation process than the possibility of shifting the final line and thus better promotes stability and mutual trust between the parties involved. This stream might also consider the role of social norms (such as "distributive justice") in the process of delimitation, as it conceived to influence the legitimacy of the process.

2. The rights and obligations of coastal States in the continental shelf

UNCLOS confers upon states various rights regarding the continental shelf and its natural resources and imposes obligations regarding disputed areas. The formal legal regime cannot explain the fact that, in practice, judicial institutions practically downplay certain obligations codified in the Convention. For example, Article

83(3) provides that states must avoid actions that might jeopardize reaching a final delimitation agreement. However, international adjudication has rarely addressed this provision, even though it reflects a significant interest, and when they have address it, tribunals generally have tended to interpret the obligation narrowly.[28] Furthermore, state practice seems to circumvent this provision completely. Thus, the governance framework essentially narrows the legal regime, while broadening the rights of coastal States by establishing new informal practices.[29]

The analysis of the application of Article 83(3) illustrates the significant role of informal actors, such as the International Law Commission (ILC), in the development of informal norms that are not part of the Convention. For example, the Arbitral Tribunal in the *Arctic Sunrise* case[30] noted that UNCLOS contains no explicit provision empowering coastal States to enforce laws regarding non-living resources in the exclusive economic zone (EEZ)[31] (i.e., resources in the seabed of the continental shelf). However, the Tribunal relied on UNCLOS Article 77 that regulates non-living resources in the continental shelf, as well as the ILC's commentary, to determine that coastal States have law-enforcement jurisdiction over non-living resources in the EEZ, despite rejection of such notion during the Convention's negotiations.[32]

3. Procedural questions

The contribution of governance theory can also be illustrated by the analysis of procedural questions, such as those pertaining to dispute-settlement procedures, the role and procedures of UNCLOS's institutions, and specific questions in the context of judicial dispute-settlement (such as the influence of third parties and the evaluation of scientific evidence in maritime boundary disputes). In each of these procedural questions, the governance framework can explain the development and application of the legal rules.

Within a governance system, the main IR theoretical streams highlight different elements of UNCLOS's procedural rules. For example, each theoretical approach provides a different explanation for the structure of the Convention's dispute-settlement mechanism. Realists emphasize actors' self-interests and are likely to reject the idea of compulsory judicial dispute-settlement, preferring diplomatic means that are more likely to promote states' individual material interests. In contrast, the institutional and constructivist approaches are more likely to embrace compulsory mechanism since it generates knowledge, certainty, and predictability regarding the parties' behavior and judicial decisions, which in turn can enhance cooperation.

Notes

1 For example, James N. Rosenau, *Governance, Order, and Change in World Politics, in* Governance Without Government: Order and Change in World Politics 1, 4–5, 12–13 (James N. Rosenau and Ernest-Otto Czempiel (eds.), 1992); Kenneth W. Abbott and Duncan Snidal, *International "Standards" and International Governance*, 8(3) J. Eur. Public Policy 345, 346 (2001); John Gerard Ruggie, *Global Governance and "New Governance Theory": Lessons from Business and Human Rights*, 20(5) Glob. Gov. 5

(2014); Anthony McGrew, *Globalization and Global Politics*, *in* Globalization of World Politics, An Introduction to International Relations 19, 31 (John Baylis, Steve Smith and Patricia Owens (eds.), 8th ed., 2020).

2 For example, Oran R. Young, International Governance: Protecting The Environment in A Stateless Society 12 (1994); Anne-Marie Slaughter-Burley, Andrew S. Tulumello and Stepan Wood, *International Law and International Relations Theory: A New Generation of Interdisciplinary Scholarship,* 92(3) Am. J. Int. Law 367, 367 (1998); McGrew, *supra* note 1, p. 31.

3 Slaughter-Burley et al., *supra* note 2, p. 371.

4 1982 UN Convention on the Law of the Sea, 1833 UNTS 397 (UNCLOS).

5 For example, Robin Churchill, Vaughan Lowe and Amy Sander, The Law of the Sea (4th ed., 2022).

6 Robert Powell, *Anarchy in International Relations Theory: The Neorealist-Neoliberal Debate*, 48(2) Int. Org. 313 (1994); Patricia Owens, John Baylis, and Steve Smith, *Introduction: From International Politics to World Politics*, *in* Globalization of World Politics, An Introduction to International Relations 5, 9 (John Baylis, Steve Smith and Patricia Owens (eds.), 8th ed., 2020).

7 For example, Stephan Walt, The Origins of Alliances (1987); Emanuel Adler, *Seizing the Middle Ground: Constructivism in World Politics*, 3(3) Eur. J. Int. Relat. 319, 319, 322 (1997); Alexander Wendt, Social Theory of International Politics 122 (1999); Michael Barnett, *Social Constructivism*, *in* Globalization of World Politics, An Introduction to International Relations 192, 195 (John Baylis, Steve Smith and Patricia Owens (eds.), 8th ed., 2020).

8 For example, Jonathan W. Kuyper, *Global Democratization and International Regime Complexity*, 20(3) Eur. J. Int. Relat. 620 (2014); Daniel Drezner, *The Power and Peril of International Regime Complexity*, 7(1) Perspectives On Politics 65 (2009).

9 UNCLOS, *supra* note 4, Articles 76(1), 77.

10 Ibid., Article 76(4)-76(7)

11 Yoshifumi Tanaka, The International Law of the Sea 163 (3rd ed., 2019).

12 Ibid.

13 UNCLOS, *supra* note 4, Article 76(4)-(6).

14 Anna Cavnar, *Accountability and the Commission on the Limits of the Continental Shelf: Deciding Who Owns the Ocean Floor* 42(3) Cornell Int. l. J. 387, 399–400 (2009).

15 UNCLOS, *supra* note 4, Article 76(8); Churchill et al., *supra* note 5, p. 230.

16 Cavnar, *supra* note 14, p. 403–404.

17 Ibid., p. 406.

18 Ted L. McDorman, *The Continental Shelf*, *in* The Oxford Handbook of the Law of the Sea 181, 194 (Donald R. Rothwell, Alex G. Oude Elferink, Karen N. Scott and Tim Stephens (eds.), 2015); CLCS, 10th Sess, UN Doc CLCS/32 (12 April 2002).

19 See Division for Ocean Affairs and the Law of the Sea (DOALOS) website, submissions to the Commission on the Limits of the Continental Shelf, pursuant to article 76, paragraph 8, available at www.un.org/Depts/los/clcs_new/commission_submissions.htm.

20 For example, the recommendation to Russia, see CLCS, 11th Sess, UN Doc CLCS/34 (1 July 2002).

21 For example, the recommendation to Norway, in the Northeast Atlantic and the Arctic, see CLCS, 23rd Sess, UN Doc CLCS/62 (20 April 2009).

22 For example, Japan submitted information in 2008 and received recommendations in 2012, see CLCS/62, *supra* note 21; CLCS, 29th Sess, UN Doc CLCS/74 (30 April 2012). Since 2009, the mark of the ten-year time limit for submitting information set in the Convention, the workload of the CLCS has increased, which led to significant delays in issuing recommendations. For example, Uruguay and the Cook Islands submitted information in 2009 and received recommendations in 2016, see CLCS, 24th Sess, UN Doc CLCS/64 (1 October 2009); CLCS, 41st Sess, UN Doc CLCS/95 (21 September 2016).

23 For the first submission, see CLCS/32, *supra* note 18; CLCS/34, *supra* note 20. For the second submission, see CLCS, 40th Sess, UN Doc CLCS/93 (18 April 2016); CLCS, 57th Sess, UN Doc CLCS/57/2 (3 April 2023). Russia made a third submission concerning the Arctic Ocean on 14 February 2023. See DOALOS website, *supra* note 19.
24 The latest recommendations were concerning the joint submission by France and South Africa and submission by Kenya, CLCS/57/2, *supra* note 23.
25 See Malcolm D. Evans, *Maritime Boundary Delimitation*, *in* The Oxford Handbook of the Law of the Sea 254, 261 (Donald R. Rothwell, Alex G. Oude Elferink, Karen N. Scott and Tim Stephens (eds.), 2015); Massimo Lando, Maritime Delimitation as a Judicial Process 24, 30 (2019).
26 UNCLOS, *supra* note 4, Article 83(1).
27 Ibid., Article 83(2), Chapter XV; LANDO (2019), *supra* note 25, p. 17.
28 For example, it was determined that resources exploitation in a particular contentious area did not violate Article 83, thus allowing states to protect their economic interests. For example, Guyana v. Suriname, Award, case no. 2004–04, 17 September 2007, Permanent Court of Arbitration [PCA], paras. 467, 470; Dispute Concerning Delimitation of the Maritime Boundary between Ghana and Côte d'Ivoire in the Atlantic Ocean (Ghana/Côte d'Ivoire), Judgment, ITLOS Reports 2017, p. 4, paras. 592, 627, 629.
29 This might also explain coastal States' reluctance to submit delimitation disputes to international adjudication. See declarations and reservations, United Nations Convention on the Law of the Sea, Chapter XXI, UN treaty collection (UNTC) website, available at https://treaties.un.org/Pages/ViewDetailsIII.aspx?src=TREATY&mtdsg_no=XXI-6&chapter=21&Temp=mtdsg3&clang=_en.
30 While this case does not directly relate to the continental shelf, it does address the question of non-living resources and artificial installations, both connected to the seabed, meaning the continental shelf. In addition, the Tribunal does refer to rules regulating the continental shelf. Thus, the case has also indirect relevance to the development of rules and principles concerning the continental shelf and understanding of such developments and, therefore, is significant in the analysis of this book.
31 The EEZ is an area beyond and adjacent to the territorial sea, which extends up to 200 nm. The EEZ includes both the seabed and the waters superjacent to it. UNCLOS, *supra* note 4, Articles 55, 56(1)(a); Churchill et al., *supra* note 5, p. 253. While the continental shelf up to 200 nm is part of the EEZ, these are two separate legal regimes regulated under different parts. See UNCLOS, ibid., Articles 56(3), 78(1). See also e.g., McDorman (2015), *supra* note 18, p. 199. On the other hand, the *Arctic Sunrise* case reflects the position that the continental shelf regime has incorporated into the EEZ legal regime, although the reasoning was unclear. See Churchill et al., ibid., p. 260, 264.
32 The Arctic Sunrise Arbitration (Netherlands v. Russia), Award on the Merits, case no. 2014–02, 14 August 2015, Permanent Court of Arbitration [PCA], paras. 281, 283–284.

1 Global governance and International Relations Theories

Governance theory and similar theories discussed in this book predominantly stem from the institutional approach.[1] Thus, the book focuses on this approach. However, other streams of thought address governance theory at least in some way. For example, realists examine power relations and different actors' gains or losses within global governance frameworks. A constructivist approach explores questions such as the normative parameters in the discourse on global governance and defines the terms of global governance debates.[2] Therefore, the book also addresses other IR streams of thought to demonstrate the contribution of the broader IR perspective to the analysis of the legal regime of the continental shelf.

1. Main streams of thought in IR

Three main streams of thought have shaped IR's theoretical literature: realism, cognitivism, and liberalism. Realism identifies power relations between actors as a key factor. States are the main actors in the international system; they are rational actors that seek to maximize their interests (mainly material interests). "Anarchy" (the lack of central enforcement)[3] in the international system generally hinders cooperation, but the need to survive may encourage states to cooperate. In such cases, hard material power shapes interstate relations.[4] Neo-realism, a substream of realism developed in the 1970s and 1980s, emphasizes the influence of the international system's structure (i.e., anarchy and lack of hierarchy among sovereign states) on states' behavior.[5]

Cognitivism emphasizes elements such as knowledge, communication, and social identities. Actors in the international system retain knowledge through rules, principles, and norms, which help define actors' interests. A substream of cognitivism, known as constructivism, emphasizes the social and normative characteristics of international relations, such as legitimacy. Actors shape international relations but are also shaped by it. This approach views international reality as constructed by cognitive structures that lend meaning to the material world.[6]

Liberalism emphasizes both liberal values of individualism and the stability of the community. Like realists, liberals agree that the international system is anarchic. However, unlike realism, liberalism does not view anarchy as a cause of conflict. Proponents of the liberal approach underline the need for cooperation to

DOI: 10.4324/9781003479772-2

ensure collective interests and overcome common problems, between states as well as other transnational actors.[7]

A substream of liberalism is neoliberalism (also known as "institutional theory"). This approach also perceives states as the main actors and as rational actors seeking to maximize their interests. However, unlike realism, this approach acknowledges that international institutions can affect states' behavior independently.[8] The institutional approach views institutions as frameworks that guide interactions, created to mitigate problems of coordination and cooperation resulting from actors' unilateral actions by establishing interdependencies between different actors and activities. This approach maintains that despite barriers to international cooperation (e.g., anarchy, uncertainty, and military power), institutional arrangements benefit all actors. It emphasizes the mutual gains from cooperation that cannot be achieved otherwise.[9]

2. Global governance theory

The rise of liberal IR theories such as the institutional theory reflects broader intellectual movements in social sciences discipline, influenced by globalization and other changes in the international arena. Since the 1990s, the international socio-political order has changed; national powers have been weakened by transnational processes such as economic interdependency and technological development.[10] While governments are still sovereign and important actors, these developments influenced a shift in their authority; some governmental functions are now performed by subnational or supranational entities.[11] These theories also reflect a shift in IR literature from international institutions to global governance, which bridges the gap between IR, political science, and international law.[12]

Globalization and increasing interdependency in the international system have led to the emergence of transnational problems, which require cooperation and coordination among individual actors to enhance international social welfare. Such coordination can be achieved when cost-benefit calculations lean more toward cooperation than unilateral action. Global governance establishes frameworks that facilitate cooperation and collective action.[13] The book employs this innovative perspective to analyze the continental shelf's legal regime, exposing underexplored practices and interactions that influence the formal legal regime.

Global governance is the process or framework by which the international community, on the basis of shared values and interests, collectively manages resources, issues, and conflicts in a world that is increasingly interconnected (i.e., global).[14] In an increasingly interdependent world, where authority and power relocate constantly in the absence of central authority at the international level, states and other actors must develop mechanisms that enhance their capacity to address problems that can no longer be dealt with by states individually or domestically.[15]

The term "global" indicates that this governance framework considers not only states[16] but also a wide range of non-state actors such as multinational corporations, domestic social groups, intergovernmental organizations (IGOs), and non-governmental organizations (NGOs). The global order, or "world politics", is perceived as all-encompassing – embracing every region, country, social movement, and private organization that engages in activities across national boundaries. The purposes and scope of these activities may be limited to specific issues, but as such, they are nonetheless a part of the prevailing global order.[17]

Global governance is a network or system of formal and informal (i.e., non-governmental or non-legal) bundles of rules, norms, roles, institutions, relationships, and practices that define and regulate social interactions and the management of common affairs of states and non-state actors globally. Governance is a system that works through consent since it is not endowed with formal authority.[18]

2.1 The formation of governance frameworks

One of the prominent questions in global governance literature is the formation of governance systems: how and why actors establish such institutional arrangements despite the constraints they place on their own behavior.[19] The three main streams of thought in IR emphasize different sets of driving forces in the governance formation process. For example, the formation of some social arrangements can be viewed as a spontaneous process – that is, a system that emerges through the convergence of expectations influenced by social practices, without conscious efforts by those who expect to become members of the regime.[20] Neo-realism emphasizes imposed processes – arrangements favored by powerful actors who succeed to compel others to accede to their institutional preferences.[21]

As mentioned, governance theory is predominantly embedded within institutional theory. This approach views the formation of governance frameworks as a bargaining process designed to establish sets of rules, norms, procedures, and institutions to guide actors' behavior concerning a given common issue.[22] The bargaining process is essentially divided into three stages: (i) the pre-negotiation stage, a process of formulating an issue as a sufficiently prominent subject for the international agenda, justifying negotiation of a governance system to regulate the issue; (ii) the negotiations stage, which begins with the initiation of direct and focused negotiations and ends with concluding a legally binding instrument accepted by all parties; and (iii) the post-negotiation stage, which covers all of the steps and implementation procedures needed to transform a treaty into an actual institutional arrangement or governance framework. In practice, it is not always easy to identify and distinguish between the stages since they often overlap.[23]

All three IR streams of thought identify five essential factors that play a causal role in the process of governance formation: interests, power, norms and principles, custom, and knowledge.[24] The term *interests* (sometimes *self-interest*) emphasizes actors' desire to maximize their gains. Despite competition and conflict, actors will choose cooperation when it yields gains that cannot be achieved otherwise.[25] *Power* may be viewed as an instrument to achieve optimal outcomes or as an instrument that enhances the value of specific actors within the system (i.e., desired characteristic).[26] Bargaining processes are influenced by the distribution of power among participants through the interaction of different interest-groups, which leads to development of governance frameworks that meet the basic needs of major interest-groups.[27]

Norms and principles define the basic characteristics of a governance framework. Principles are "beliefs of fact, causation, and rectitude", while norms are "standards of behavior defined in terms of rights and obligations".[28] Norms and principles are viewed as both independent and dependent variables; they comprise an element within governance systems but also influence their formation.[29] *Custom* refers to patterns of behavior based on certain practices. These patterns, along with actors' shared expectations, are likely to become normatively significant and legitimate. *Knowledge* lays the basis for cooperation by illuminating complex interactions that were not previously understood. This increases prospect of convergence of actors' behavior and may help to overcome disputes and obstacles to cooperation.[30]

2.2 How governance frameworks operate

Governance is the process by which global society manages resources, problems, and conflicts on the basis of shared values.[31] Governance systems embrace different types of actors, along with formal and informal bundles of rules, norms, values, social practices, and institutions in international affairs.[32] To influence actors' behavior and encourage compliance with these bundles that prescribe action, governance systems must have some kind of legitimate authority.[33] Governance frameworks come with transaction costs, such as constraints on unilateral action or monetary contributions. Legitimacy mitigates these costs, allowing actors to make concessions. In other words, governance frameworks can function if actors agree that they are needed. Legitimacy helps governance systems gain actors' support – not just for strategic self-interest but also for moral reasons, even when there is no immediate gain or if others gain more.[34]

Legitimacy of governance systems can stem from different sources – for example, from popular public attitude,[35] tradition, or personal charisma.[36] Another source for legitimacy is "legal legitimacy", which means exercising authority at the international level in accordance with legal principles. This is the mechanism that links the governance framework's authority to its original basis of consent. Governance systems are composed of institutional arrangements established by a legal mechanism, usually a founding treaty or agreement, based on the participants' consent.[37]

The legitimacy of a governance framework can also stem from expertise. The underlying assumption is that decisions by experts lead to better outcomes. Similarly, decision-making processes that take place within expert institutions are more likely to yield desirable results.[38] For example, though the mandate of the CLCS, an expert body established in UNCLOS, is to issue non-binding recommendations concerning the outer limit of the continental shelf beyond 200 nm, in practice, it enjoys a high level of legitimacy. This, in turn, leads to greater compliance with its recommendations.

Legitimacy serves as an important basis for the effectiveness of governance. The more an institutional arrangement is perceived as legitimate, the more stable and effective it is likely to be. For example, the perceived legitimacy of an institutional arrangement can affect its ability to adopt decisions, the strength of those decisions, and the ability of the members to implement and comply with the decisions in the absence of coercion or rational persuasion.[39]

In addition, governance systems facilitate transparency, reducing the influence of uncertainty and information deficit. Actors wishing to join a governance framework are generally required to supply information regarding the resources at their disposal, formal negotiating positions, and intentions and preferences and to express their willingness to adhere to agreements.[40] Governance frameworks help members to assess the reputations of others by establishing standards of behavior against which performance can be measured and by providing forums for such evaluations. Thus, governance systems affect actors' reputation by raising the costs associated with non-compliance.[41]

Governance may operate in part through "institutional deference". This concept refers to situations where one institution accepts the authority of another institution. Deference occurs when one institution formally adopts rules, decisions, or recommendations established by another institution from a different subject-area or by other institutions operating in the same domain or dealing with the same problems.[42] For example, while there is no doctrine of judicial precedence in international law, the ICJ's decisions have significant precedential value.[43] The presence of multiple institutions governing a single issue often leads to legal overlap and inconsistencies. Governance frameworks mitigate this problem by coordinating rulemaking via institutional deference. Institutions often selectively accept the authority of other institutions, which allows them to avoid adopting conflicting rules and increase efficiency through division of labor.[44]

2.3 Assessing the effectiveness of governance frameworks

Governance systems are established to address problems that require coordination and collective action, and they influence actors' behavior. Thus, to understand the function of governance frameworks, it is essential to examine not only the elements of these frameworks (e.g., norms, rules, and institutions) but also their outcomes, mostly in terms of compliance.[45]

Earlier scholarship focused mainly on whether governance systems were effective in resolving the problems that motivated the parties to create them in the first place.[46] Some approaches examined the goals attained, while others focused on the ways in which these frameworks altered participants' behavior.[47] However, outcome-based analysis of governance systems has its limitations. For example, the disappearance of a problem following the formation of a governance system is not sufficient proof of the significance of that governance system.

These limitations prompted recent scholarship to focus on the behavioral consequences of governance frameworks as a measure of effectiveness. From this perspective, the significance of a governance framework is measured by its ability to influence behavior on the international level.[48] Generally, an effective governance system facilitates cooperation and collective-action – despite contradictory short-term interests and obstacles imposed by the anarchic international system – by establishing mutual expectations about others' behavior and by creating opportunities for actors to demonstrate credibility.[49] Governance frameworks also facilitate effective multilateral cooperation by formulating unified rules and standards of behavior and by harmonizing rules through institutional deference, which promotes compliance and reduces transaction costs.[50]

There are several criteria for assessing the performance of governance systems. An economic criterion stresses efficiency and cost-benefit analysis of behavior, while a political criterion directs attention to the fairness of the results of institutional arrangements.[51] A more legal approach measures effectiveness by how domestic legal and political systems implement and comply with the governance framework's rules and requirements.[52] This approach emphasizes the question of compliance in the absence of coercion, meaning the capacity to influence actors' behavior without using intimidation or force.[53] For example, as discussed in Chapter 2, while in practice the rules concerning the breadth of the continental shelf are somewhat different from what is prescribed in UNCLOS, they were shaped by noncoercive processes.[54]

Governance systems also produce side effects – that is, results that were not intended or foreseen at the time of their establishment. Sometimes side effects take the form of unforeseen distributive consequences, such as the profits gained through fishing licenses. In other cases, side effects involve the operation of an institutional arrangement itself; for example, the participation of various actors may change the nature and operation of the system. These side effects have greater influence and often initiate chain reactions of considerable magnitude that may affect future institutional design and the assessment of their performance.[55] Essentially, scholars view governance frameworks as public goods that enhance the welfare of all members.

2.4 Governance dynamics

Governance frameworks are complex and dynamic social entities; once a framework is in place, it operates through constant interactions that often develop and change it.[56] The literature addresses several exogenous and endogenous factors that shape and sustain governance frameworks and may influence transformation. Endogenous factors arise from the operation of the frameworks themselves – that is, internal forces associated with governance frameworks' function, as opposed to external forces that impact the operation of governance systems.[57]

Numerous endogenous factors, including the system's own success or failure, can give rise to governance change. The success of a governance system can lead to the disappearance of the problem it is designed to solve, which in turn affects the existence of the system. In contrast, failure to achieve its designed goals can influence institutional change.[58] For example, transnational problems such as environmental protection, currency crises, terrorism, crime, and disease pose collective-action challenges that require cooperation. This heightens the need for new institutional arrangements to replace the global order that reigned until the 1990s.[59]

Governance dynamics or change can also derive from institutional contradictions.[60] For example, the governance framework regulating marine living resources seeks to conserve fish stocks while also regulating utilization.[61] As discussed in Chapter 3, the continental shelf's governance framework regulates the utilization of non-living resources but also broadens coastal States' jurisdiction to conserve the marine environment and resources in the continental shelf. Conflicts can also occur between different actors within the same governance framework. For example, as discussed in Chapter 2, the CLCS and international tribunals sometimes clash.

Some exogenous conditions relate to material resources and interests. For example, widening economic discrepancies among members may create pressure for change, which may lead to a new order. Economic discrepancies sometimes derive from a disparity in the actors' technological advancement, which affects the distribution of power.[62] Essentially, this was the underlying process in the inception and construction of UNCLOS: coastal States began to extend their national jurisdiction beyond their territorial waters after 1945 in accordance with the "exploitation ability" criterion, which gave an advantage to developed states with advanced technology. The gap in exploitation abilities led developing states to lobby for defined maritime limits based on a fixed distance (200 nm), regardless of capabilities or presence in the area.[63]

Governance literature differentiates between a change *of* the governance system (that is, changing the norms and principles that provide the system's defining characteristics) and a change *within* the governance system (that is, changing the rules and decision-making procedures that comprise the system's operational or implementation mechanisms). Changing the principles and norms constitutes a change of the governance system itself. This type of change indicates either the emergence of a new system or the disappearance of the existing system (or the disappearance of the problem it was designed to address).[64]

The dynamics of governance systems, like those involved in their formation, include spontaneous or self-generating change, negotiated change, and imposed change. Spontaneous processes of change feature outcomes that arise from the self-interested activities of many actors but are not specifically planned by anyone. Many changes start as spontaneous processes, which then codified more formally at later stages.[65] For example, the continental shelf's legal regime began spontaneously as coastal States began extending their national jurisdiction beyond the agreed territorial waters.[66] Negotiated changes are processes in which self-interested actors discuss proposed amendments in the existing governance framework.[67] Some governance systems require unanimity or at least a strong majority to implement institutional changes.[68]

Imposed changes may occur when self-interested actors seek to promote or resist institutional changes. Actors' material power may influence processes of governance transformation, although it does not always yield the optimum result for the powerful actor.[69] For example, the United States objected Part XI on the International Seabed Area. Despite the opposition, the draft convention was adopted. However, this led to the establishment of the implementation agreement relating to part XI, which the United States is not a party to.[70]

3. Governance theory and other institutional arrangements

IR literature addresses several social mechanisms similar to governance frameworks. It is important to identify and understand the differences between these mechanisms and how they interact with each other. The first distinction is between *governance frameworks* and *international regimes*. International regimes are a subcategory of governance frameworks relating to specific issue-areas or defined geographical areas. Regimes can be perceived as particular mechanisms for solving governance problems.[71]

The terms "governance" and "regimes" both refer to arrangements for managing and regulating activities across national boundaries, encompassing both governmental and non-governmental actors interested in cooperating to promote shared interests. Such cooperation justifies adherence to shared principles, norms, and procedures. However, governance is a broader concept, connecting more than one regime, bridging the gaps between them, and prevailing when two or more regimes overlap or conflict.[72]

In recent years, IR literature has focused not only on specific single regimes but also on "regime complexes" – networks of specific and relatively narrow regimes characterized by the absence of hierarchy among them.[73] Regime complexity examines how the growing density of international institutions and actors influence global governance.[74] Thus, IR scholarship has shifted from a specific regime analysis to broader concepts that are equivalent to frameworks of global governance.[75]

As in the discussion of governance formation, a prominent explanation for the establishment of regime complexes is the distribution of interests and power. When actors share similar interests and objectives, the benefits of cooperation can be achieved through a singular regime. However, when actors have different interests, it is more beneficial to create a complex regime that links several specific regimes to balance concessions. This linkage enlarges the scope for dealmaking, increases gains from cooperation, and strengthens incentives for compliance. Like governance frameworks, complex arrangements allow actors to "shop" or shift forums to best serve their individual interests while remaining part of the complex regime.[76]

Regime complexes and governance frameworks enhance the role of experts, lawyers, and NGOs that help actors manage confusion about rules and institutions. These institutional arrangements contribute to rule ambiguity and allow for cross-institutional strategies, thus creating opportunities for political actors to shift framings.[77] This flexibility can also support and accommodate changes in actors' interests, power, information, and beliefs. When there are several forums and institutions in the same issue-area that vary in their level of obligations and interests, having an alternative that deals with the same problems in a different way can allow actors to continue to participate despite change of preference.[78]

While the concept of regime complexes is very similar to the concept of global governance, the two concepts differ in the way they frame and treat the interaction between multiple institutional arrangements. Typically, regime complex theory views the coexistence of multiple institutional arrangements with overlapping mandates as "fragmentation" that threatens the effectiveness of governance through redundancy, inconsistency, and conflict.[79] In contrast, governance theory offers to solve this problem by coordination through institutional deference[80] or treats this overlap as part of the normal operation and significance of global governance.[81]

Competition between institutions is not necessarily detrimental; it can sometimes enhance cooperation and the effectiveness and significance of the governance framework.[82] For example, as discussed in Chapter 2, the jurisdictional competition between international tribunals and the CLCS influenced the legal rules and norms and promoted compliance with the legal regime in general. In contrast, as discussed in Chapter 3, the interplay between domestic environmental and tort policies and international conservation obligations may inhibit compliance with the legal regime. Both examples are part of governance frameworks operation: Sometimes they broaden the legal regime, adding informal rules and practices, and sometimes they narrow the legal regime, downplaying rules that are not implemented in practice. Thus, the governance perspective shifts the focus from non-compliance to broader social practices that reflect better international interactions.

4. Governance theory and international law

The IR global governance is broader than "legal regimes" in international legal literature. Legal regimes mainly comprise international legal instruments and international judicial institutions. Governance frameworks, however, contain informal rules, norms, processes, and actors, in addition to formal legal rules and institutions.[83]

Governance theory and international law (IL) interact and overlap, with political scientists and international lawyers drawing from each other's work.[84] Global governance is a theoretical framework that bridges the gap between IR's main streams of thought and IL.[85] Governance systems include and employ IL's rules and institutions to regulate global society, and IL is also a significant part of many governance frameworks. Each field of IL constitutes a governance framework with its own set of explicit and implicit rules, norms, roles, actors, and institutions.[86]

International legal scholars emphasize the role of law in explaining the structure and functions of the international system. For example, some IL experts highlight the "legalization" of international institutions.[87] In addition, legal scholars view legal norms as playing a constitutive role in the formation of actors' identities and interests and in the structure of the international system itself. Through their dynamic impact on actors' interests, legal rules and norms continually reshape the purposes for which power is exercised. IL scholarship also employs IR theories to explain the meaning and function of international agreements, procedures, and institutions.[88] IL scholars and practitioners use the language of governance theory to describe the institutional arrangements established in treaties, as well as the practices that have evolved more informally in international society.[89]

At the same time, IR scholars have developed a research design that relates also to the IL approach to international rules. For example, IR scholars have sought to analyze the "causes and consequences of the 'legalization' of international politics".[90] IL is significant for analysis of the conditions for international cooperation.[91]

Scholarship in both disciplines has helped to explain the creation and distribution of norms in the international system through various types of institutional arrangements and has investigated the consequences of legalization on participants, on political and legal processes, and on the international system.[92]

The study of legalization unites both perspectives in a genuinely collaborative venture. Law is viewed as deeply embedded in politics. It is affected by political interests, power, and institutions but also affects international affairs through communication based on norms and values. International law cannot be understood in isolation from politics. Conversely, law and legalization affect political processes and political outcomes. The relationship between law and politics is reciprocal, mediated by institutions.[93]

However, some scholars argue that the strictly legal perspective of IL has largely failed to deal with today's significant global challenges and that IR governance literature can better contribute to the examination and evaluation of IL's institutional arrangements and practices.[94] As mentioned earlier, globalization processes in the 1990s – such as the emergence and growing importance of non-state actors and increasing international economic and political interdependence – engendered global problems that require coordinated responses. In this increasingly complicated environment, IR scholars have embraced governance theory, which provides alternative explanations for global affairs. Governance theory offers a broader perspective that includes a wide range of non-state actors and not only states, as in classic IL discipline.[95] In addition, as discussed, governance perspective considers formal legal regimes (i.e., IL) but also informal elements that affect the creation and development of legal rules.

For example, the definition of a governance framework highlights the importance of "soft" law (i.e., non-binding rules) in both the organization of global society and the construction of international law. Institutional arrangements may not always be able to enforce law, but they can and do frequently generate norms that promote social change.[96]

IR scholars also highlight the advantages of "soft" law over "hard" law.[97] Softer legalization is often easier to achieve, especially since binding rules pose a challenge to actors' autonomy (and states' sovereignty). In addition, soft law mitigates the influences of uncertainty since it initiates processes that allow actors to learn about the impact of agreements over time. Lastly, soft law facilitates compromise and mutually beneficial cooperation between actors that have different interests and values and different degrees of power.[98]

The contribution of the interaction between governance theory and IL is also reflected in the interdependency of negotiations and outcomes.[99] Negotiation processes influence not only the final institutional arrangement but also members' compliance. As discussed in Chapter 2, the UNCLOS III negotiation process between two major interest-groups created an institutional design that favored one group (developed states with broad continental shelves). This can explain the gap between the legal regime and the governance framework since the deviant practice was established by the opposing group (developing states with narrow continental shelves).

Governance theory has also contributed to the discourse on legitimacy in IL. Scholars in both disciplines essentially view legitimacy as a basis for compliance and effectiveness.[100] For example, as discussed in Chapter 2, the CLCS has a significant role in establishing legitimate and stable maritime boundaries that also influence the effectiveness and stability of the CLCS itself.

The relations between global governance and IL can illustrate another role of governance frameworks: creating norms that govern actors' behavior and disseminating them in the international system. Governance systems define and regulate international social practices, guiding actors' actions through norms, principles, and institutions.[101] A governance analysis of IL addresses the conditions for establishing legalized institutional frameworks and how legalized constraints influence actors' behavior; for example, such legalization can facilitate cooperation or construct a stable order on the basis of norms rather than power politics.[102] Governance literature emphasizes the benefits of legalized arrangements – for example, in forging credible commitments and reducing transactions costs – in comparison to non-legalized institutions.[103] This approach focuses on the interaction of interests, norms, and legalization as an explanation for the creation of governance systems.[104]

Considering the earlier contributions and others discussed throughout the book, the governance theory perspective exposes hidden or underexplored interactions between legal regimes and other institutional arrangements. As we expose these patterns of behavior, we learn more about the international system and the roles each actor plays within the system. Such understanding may generate new insights and explanations regarding past evolution and current developments of international legal rules and institutions.

4.1 The continental shelf's governance framework

Governance theory or governance perspective is the methodology, the analytical tool of this book. "Governance framework" is the term used to describe existing arrangements and interactions in practice. As explained earlier, governance frameworks are networks of formal and informal bundles of rules, norms, roles, institutions, relationships, and practices that regulate global problems. The governance framework of the continental shelf includes the formal legal regime, as well as the informal or implicit elements addressed later.

To understand why the following elements are informal and part of the broader governance framework, we need to understand the characteristics and structure of international law because the continental shelf's legal regime is embedded within this body of law. The international legal system differs from domestic legal systems; it has no legislative body, no system of courts with defined hierarchy, no enforcement powers, and no executive authority.[105] Formally, the international legal system consists of all states, equal in power. States are both the lawmakers and the principal subjects of IL.[106]

Article 38(1) of the Statute of the International Court of Justice (ICJ) specifies the formal sources of IL: treaties, customary law, and general principles recognized by civilized nations.[107] These are the sources that provide legally binding norms based on states' consent. On the other hand, non-binding instruments such as recommendations,[108] decisions, declarations, guidelines, and codes of conduct are not formal elements of IL but can be viewed as informal soft law instruments that affect actors' behavior as part of the governance framework.[109]

The continental shelf regime is a good example of governance dynamics and the evolvement of a governance framework. For example, changing circumstances, such as the advancement of marine science and technology, have influenced the broader governance framework since UNCLOS entered into force.[110] The following sections analyze some of the more prominent informal or implicit elements that have influenced the development of the governance framework of the continental shelf.

4.1.1 Historical documents and treaty negotiation processes

While multilateral treaties are generally part of the formal legal regime,[111] the negotiation process and the documents it produces can also be viewed as part of the broader governance framework of the continental shelf. As discussed in Chapter 2, UNCLOS was negotiated within a multilateral diplomatic conference that was primarily political in nature.[112] UNCLOS III is an example of modern international law-making, facilitated by the interaction of states and non-state actors. As such, it reflects a broader governance framework.[113] Furthermore, the continental shelf regime was constructed within a unique geo-political structure. For example, the growing international political power of certain coalitions, interest-groups, and negotiation blocs influenced the construction and development of the legal regime.[114] In addition, the complexity of issues, which were in part technical and scientific issues that required expertise, created an opportunity for informal actors (such as IGOs) to influence the law-making process.[115]

While other fields of IL have witnessed a decrease in the establishment of multilateral treaties in recent years, several such treaties have been negotiated and adopted regarding the law of the sea.[116] This trend can contribute to the evolvement of the governance framework since there are more opportunities for institutional overlap, and this creates more opportunities for institutional deference to sustain the governance framework. In addition, this trend may generate new informal legal instruments that are exogenous to the continental shelf regime yet can influence its development.

4.1.1.1 THE INTERNATIONAL LAW COMMISSION (ILC)

The ILC is a body of experts established by the UN General Assembly to promote the development and codification of IL. The ILC has promoted the establishment and adoption of many international treaties, including the 1958 Geneva Convention on the Continental Shelf (CSC).[117] The ILC did not facilitate the inception of UNCLOS and is not part of the current formal legal regime of the continental shelf. However, the ILC's interpretation of the CSC's provisions influenced states' positions during the negotiations on UNCLOS.[118] In addition, the jurisprudence on the continental shelf has assimilated the ILC's interpretation of the CSC's delimitation provisions into UNCLOS's rules of delimitation, which eventually gained the status of customary law.[119] Thus, the ILC is an informal actor within the broader governance framework concerning the continental shelf. As such, it has significant influence on the construction and development of the continental shelf's legal regime.

4.1.2 Judicial decisions

As mentioned earlier, while states are the principal actors within the legal regime of the continental shelf, the governance framework also includes a wide range of non-state actors.[120] Some scholars and jurists perceive international law as a process rather than a mere collection of rules. Thus, international courts and tribunals do not just apply legal rules but also engage in the decision-making process itself.[121] International judicial bodies are an important element in the governance framework of the continental shelf; they are formal actors that establish informal legal norms and provide guidance for other international institutions.[122]

Judicial decisions are not a formal and binding source of international rules but are considered a secondary means of determining rules of law.[123] Essentially, international tribunals only indicate what the rules are, in the context of settling disputes; they do not create binding rules of IL.[124] In practice, international judicial bodies have an informal law-making role, which has influenced the construction and development of the continental shelf's legal regime.

For example, although formally there is no doctrine of precedence in international law,[125] in practice, tribunals cite others, mostly the ICJ, and their own past decisions. Thus, international courts essentially develop and create new rules within a broader governance framework through the process of institutional deference.[126] The three-stage method of delimitation was established by the ICJ and endorsed by other tribunals. Thus, the "equidistance/relevant circumstances" method became the primary rule in the context of judicial dispute-settlement concerning maritime delimitation, regardless of UNCLOS's formal rules.[127]

Furthermore, interpretation and application of the continental shelf's legal regime in the context of dispute-settlement significantly contributed to the development of the continental shelf's governance framework beyond the formal original instrument.[128] For example, as discussed in Chapter 2, international tribunals interpreted UNCLOS's vague formal obligation concerning delimitation and established new informal rules and methods of delimitation, sometimes contrary to the formal legal regime. This process reflects institutional preferences for clear and simple rules for allocating property rights, despite the vague formal rules in UNCLOS.[129] This is another example of the informal function of international tribunals as "legislators" within the broader continental shelf's governance framework.

In addition, international lawyers and academic scholars tend to have great respect for international judicial decisions and attribute significant weight to them.[130] Such interaction between informal actors within the broader governance framework can also influence the creation and distribution of norms in international law. Thus, international judicial bodies, as non-state actors, and the jurisprudence itself are part of the broader governance framework concerning the continental shelf.

4.1.3 State practice

State practice is one of the required components for establishing customary international law – one of the formal sources of IL – and is thus part of the formal legal regime.[131] However, when there is insufficient practice to meet the requirements for establishing customary rules or when state practice is not accompanied by *opinio juris* (i.e., the belief that a practice is legally binding), state practice can be considered an informal element of a governance framework.

Unilateral actions by states have influenced the development of the legal regime concerning the continental shelf,[132] and such actions can create informal norms within the broader governance framework. For example, even if states practice (e.g., domestic law and bilateral agreements) does not necessarily meet the required conditions for becoming customary law, they still have significance from a governance perspective, indicating patterns of behavior that create informal rules and norms within the broader continental shelf's governance framework.

5. Concluding remarks

The term governance framework refers to the actual situation that governance theory analyzes. A governance framework is a network of formal and informal bundles of rules, norms, actors, institutions, and practices that define and regulate social interactions and the management of common affairs. Governance systems are formed to address challenges and collective-action problems caused by the increasing interdependence of the international system and to enhance international social welfare. These frameworks facilitate cooperation to solve transnational problems through various political and legal mechanisms. The governance framework of the continental shelf includes the formal legal regime, enshrined mostly in UNCLOS, and informal elements such as political processes, judicial decisions, and state practice.

This broader IR perspective may help international legal scholars to better understand and explain certain developments and trends concerning the continental shelf, especially the developments and trends that the formal legal regime fails to address. The governance perspective exposes underexplored interactions and developments that the legal regime alone cannot adequately explain – for example, the creation of new informal norms and the non-implementation of formal rules.

Notes

1 See also Karen J. Alter, *The Promise and Perils of Theorizing International Regime Complexity in an Evolving World*, 17 Rev. Int. Organ. 375, 390 (2022).
2 Ibid., p. 391, 393.
3 What Rosenau refers to as "governance without government", see James N. Rosenau, *Governance, Order, and Change in World Politics*, *in* Governance Without Government: Order and Change in World Politics 3 (James N. Rosenau and Ernest-Otto Czempiel (eds.), 1992).
4 Jonathan W. Kuyper, *Global Democratization and International Regime Complexity*, 20(3) Eur. J. Int. Relat. 620 (2014); Stephan Walt, The Origins of Alliances (1987); Patricia Owens, John Baylis, and Steve Smith, *Introduction: From International*

Politics to World Politics, *in* Globalization of World Politics, An Introduction to International Relations 5, 5 (John Baylis, Steve Smith and Patricia Owens (eds.), 8th ed., 2020).

5 Robert Powell, *Anarchy in International Relations Theory: The Neorealist-Neoliberal Debate*, 48(2) Int. Org. 313 (1994); Owens et al., *supra* note 4, p. 5.

6 For example, Emanuel Adler, *Seizing the Middle Ground: Constructivism in World Politics*, 3(3) Eur. J. Int. Relat. 319, 319, 319, 322 (1997); Alexander Wendt, Social Theory of International Politics 122 (1999); Michael Barnett, *Social Constructivism*, *in* Globalization of World Politics, An Introduction to International Relations 192, 195–198 (John Baylis, Steve Smith and Patricia Owens (eds.), 8th ed., 2020).

7 Owens et al., *supra* note 4, p. 5; Tim Dunne, *Liberalism*, *in* Globalization of World Politics, An Introduction to International Relations 116, 117, 122 (John Baylis, Steve Smith and Patricia Owens (eds.), 7th ed., 2017).

8 Powell, *supra* note 5; Kuyper, *supra* note 4; Daniel Drezner, *The Power and Peril of International Regime Complexity*, 7(1) Perspectives on Politics 65 (2009).

9 Kuyper, *supra* note 4; Drezner, *supra* note 8.

10 The term "interdependency" in this context essentially means that actors' actions affect the welfare of others. See for example Oran R. Young, International Governance: Protecting the Environment in a Stateless Society 1, 4, 15 (1994); Moshe Hirsch, *Compliance with International Norms in the Age of Globalization: Two Theoretical Perspectives*, *in* The Impact of International Law on International Cooperation: Theoretical Perspectives 166, 168 (Eyal Benvenisti and Moshe Hirsch (eds.), 2009).

11 Rosenau, *supra* note 3, p. 2–3; Mark W. Zacher, *The Decaying Pillars of the Westphalian Temple: Implications for International Order and Governance*, *in* Governance Without Government: Order and Change in World Politics 58 (James N. Rosenau and Ernest-Otto Czempiel (eds.), 1992); Klaus Dingwerth and Philipp Pattberg, *Global Governance as a Perspective on World Politics*, 12 Glob. Gov. 185, 191, 193 (2006).

12 Young (1994), *supra* note 10, p. 12; Anthony McGrew, *Globalization and Global Politics*, *in* Globalization of World Politics, An Introduction to International Relations 19, 31–32 (John Baylis, Steve Smith and Patricia Owens (eds.), 8th ed., 2020).

13 Young (1994), *supra* note 10, p. 15–16.

14 Rosenau, *supra* note 3, p. 4–5; Marcel Brus, *Bridging the Gap Between State Sovereignty and International Governance: The Authority of Law*, *in* State, Sovereignty, and International Governance 3, 5 (Gerard Kreijen, Marcel Brus, Jorri Duursma, Elisabeth De Vos and John Dugard (eds.), 2002); John Gerard Ruggie, *Global Governance and "New Governance Theory": Lessons from Business and Human Rights*, 20 Glob. Gov. 5, 5 (2014); McGrew, *supra* note 12, p. 31.

15 Brus, *supra* note 14, p. 18; Oran R. Young, Governance in World Affairs 2 (1999); Ruggie, *supra* note 14, p. 8–9.

16 The term "international" usually indicates an institutional arrangement composed of states or governments. See for example Young (1999), ibid., p. 11. For more refined distinction, see e.g., Dingwerth and Pattberg, *supra* note 11, p. 196–197; McGrew, *supra* note 12, p. 31.

17 For example, Rosenau, *supra* note 3, p. 12–13; McGrew, *supra* note 16; Arie M. Kacowic, *Regional Governance and Global Governance: Links and Explanations* 24 Glob. Gov. 61, 62 (2018).

18 Rosenau, *supra* note 3, p. 4–5; Kenneth W. Abbott and Duncan Snidal, *International "Standards" and International Governance*, 8(3) J. Eur. Public Policy 345, 346 (2001); Brus, *supra* note 14, p. 19; Dingwerth and Pattberg, *supra* note 11, p. 189, 191, 193 (2006); Ruggie, *supra note* 14, p. 5.

19 Young (1994), *supra* note 10, p. 81.

20 This process does not involve social or institutional design. Stephen D. Krasner, *Structural Causes and Regime Consequences: Regimes as Intervening Variables*, 36(2) Int. Org. 185, 196 (1982); Andreas Hasenclever, Peter Mayer and Volker Rittberger, *Interests, Power, Knowledge: The Study of International Regimes*, 40(2) Mershon Int. Stud.

Rev. 177, 198 (1996). Although not advocated by a specific IR theoretical stream, some argue that realism might accept such approach, see Oran R. Young, *Review: International Regimes: Toward a New Theory of Institutions*, 39(1) World Politics 104, 119 (1986). Some liberal scholars also support this approach, see Friedrich A. Hayek's research in Oran R. Young, *Regime Dynamics: The Rise and Fall of International Regimes*, 36(2) Int. Org. 277, 282 (1982).

21 This approach also known as "hegemonic stability theory", see e.g., Roger K. Smith, *Explaining the Non-Proliferation Regime*, 41(2) Int. Org. 253 (1987); Marc A. Levy, Oran R. Young and Michael Zurn, *The Study of International Regimes*, 1(3) Eur. J. Int. Relat. 267 (1995).

22 For example, Oran R. Young (1994), *supra* note 10, p. 44, 84–86, 87. International treaty negotiation is a bargaining process in the context of governance formation, see discussion sections 3 and 4 later and in the following chapters.

23 Young (1994), *supra* note 10, p. 27, 83.

24 The scholarship recognizes that single-factor explanations are limited and thus focuses on multivariate models of governance formation. See ibid., p. 28.

25 Krasner, *supra* note 20, p. 195; Young (1994), *supra* note 10, p. 42–43. Some scholars treat governance systems as a solution for "market-failure" – situations where interactions that meant to yield gains lead to unwanted outcomes. Governance frameworks supposed to rectify these defects and promote and enhance efficiency. See e.g., Robert O. Keohane, *The Demand for International Regimes*, 36(2) Int. Org. 325, 334–336 (1982); Richard Little, *International Regimes*, *in* The Globalization of World Politics, An Introduction to International Relations 299, 307 (John Baylis and Steve Smith (eds.), 2001); Abbott and Snidal (2001), *supra* note 18, p. 346.

26 Krasner, *supra* note 20, p. 197–200 (1982); Young (1994), *supra* note 10, p. 118–119.

27 Young (1994), *supra* note 10, p. 38. See also discussion in Chapters 2 and 4.

28 Keohane (1982), *supra* note 25, p. 341–342. Norms are specific type of standard, which is a term that is used to guide and judge behavior. Actors create standards to promote their collective welfare by coordinating and constraining individual behavior. Abbott and Snidal (2001), *supra* note 18, p. 345.

29 Krasner, *supra* note 20, p. 187, 202.

30 Krasner, ibid., p. 202–203; Young (1994), *supra* note 10, p. 39–40.

31 When actors do not share the same values, it can create conflicts. See Brus, *supra* note 14, p. 5.

32 Young (1994), *supra* note 10, p. 15–16; Brus, *supra* note 14, p. 5; Kacowic, *supra* note 17.

33 "Legitimacy" means that actors perceive that the governance framework has "a right" to prescribe action, see Allen Buchanan and Robert O. Keohane, *The Legitimacy of Global Governance Institutions* 20(4) Ethics & Int. Aff. 405 (2006); Daniel M. Bodansky, *The Legitimacy of International Governance: A Coming Challenge for International Environmental Law?* 93 Am. J. Int. Law 596, 601 (1999).

34 Buchanan and Keohane, *supra* note 33, p. 407–409, 411.

35 Buchanan and Keohane, *supra* note 33; Bodansky, *supra* note 33.

36 See Max Weber, Essays in Economic Sociology Chapter 6 (Richard Swedberg (ed.), 1999).

37 Bodansky, *supra* note 33, p. 605. See also Weber, ibid., p. 99. See also *supra* notes 18 and 22.

38 Bodansky, *supra* note 33, p. 619–620.

39 Ibid., p. 603–604.

40 Keohane (1982), *supra* note 25, p. 346.

41 While reputational costs do not guarantee compliance, they hinder opportunism of rational egoist actors sensitive to their longer-term interests. See Hasenclever et al. (1996), *supra* note 20, p. 186.

42 Tyler Pratt, *Deference and Hierarchy in International Regime Complexes*, 72 Int. Org. 561, 562 (2018).

43 See discussion in Section 4.1.2 later.

44 Pratt, *supra* note 42.
45 K.J. Holsti, *Governance Without Government: Polyarchy in Nineteenth-century European International Politics*, *in* Governance Without Government: Order and Change in World Politics 30, 44 (James N. Rosenau and Ernest-Otto Czempiel (eds.), 1992); Oran R. Young, *The Effectiveness of International Institutions: Hard Cases and Critical Variables*, *in* Governance Without Government: Order and Change in World Politics 160, 161 (James N. Rosenau and Ernest-Otto Czempiel (eds.), 1992); Barbara Koremenos, Charles Lipson and Duncan Snidal, *The Rational Design of International Institutions*, 55(4) Int. Org. 761 (2001).
46 For example, Levy et al., *supra* note 21, p. 291–292; Andreas Hasenclever, Peter Mayer and Volker Rittberger, Theories of International Regimes 2–3 (1997); Oran R. Young, Institutional Dynamics: Emergent Patterns in International Environmental Governance 2 (2010).
47 Young (1994), *supra* note 10, p. 144–145.
48 See e.g., Holsti, *supra* note 45, p. 44; Young (1999), *supra* note 15, p. 109–110.
49 Keohane (1982), *supra* note 25, p. 331–334, 338; Young (1994), *supra* note 10, p. 30; Buchanan and Keohane, *supra* note 33, p. 407. The concept of "reciprocity" also helps mitigating cooperation problems. See e.g., Keohane (1982), ibid., p. 342; Robert O. Keohane, *International Institutions: Can Interdependence Work?* 110 Foreign Policy 82 (1998). See also "legitimacy", *supra* note 39, and "transparency", *supra* notes 40 and 41.
50 See also Pratt, *supra* note 42, p. 566.
51 Young (1999), *supra* note 15, p. 12.
52 Young (1994), *supra* note 10, p. 146, and Chapter 6 for other approaches to effectiveness; Levy et al., *supra* note 21, p. 291–292; Hasenclever et al. (1997), *supra* note 46, p. 2–3.
53 See *supra* note 18 and text connected to it.
54 See also James Harrison, Making the Law of the Sea, A Study in the Development of International Law 36–37 (2011).
55 Young (1994), *supra* note 10, p. 151–152; Young (1999), *supra* note 15, p. 16.
56 For example, Rosenau, *supra* note 3, p. 19–20; Young (2010), *supra* note 46, p. 4–5.
57 Young (1999), *supra* note 15, p. 149; Jean-Frédéric Morin and Laura Gomez-Mera, *The Evolution of Governance Systems: The Case of the Trade Regime*, 22 Int. Stud. Rev. 1022 (2020).
58 Young (1999), *supra* note 15, p. 149; Michael Barnett and Liv Coleman, *Designing Police: Interpol and the Study of Change in International Organizations*, 49 Int. Stud. Q. 593, 594 (2005); Morin and Gomez-Mera, *supra* note 57, p. 1026. Some scholars view failure as an exogenous factor, see e.g., Rosenau, *supra* note 3, p. 21–22.
59 Rosenau, ibid.
60 Thomas Gehring and Benjamin Faude, *The Dynamics of Regime Complexes: Microfoundations and Systemic Effects*, 19 Glob. Gov. 119 (2013); Kenneth W. Abbott, Jessica F. Green and Robert O. Keohane, *Organizational Ecology and Institutional Change in Global Governance*, 70(2) Int. Org. 247, 259, 261 (2016); Morin and Gomez-Mera, *supra* note 57, p. 1026.
61 Young (1999), *supra* note 15, p. 148–149.
62 Rosenau, *supra* note 3, p. 21; Young (1999), *supra* note 15, p. 147–148, 151; Barnett and Coleman, *supra* note 58, p. 594.
63 See detailed discussion in Chapter 2.
64 Krasner, *supra* note 20, p. 187–189; Rosenau, *supra* note 3, p. 22; Young (1999), *supra* note 15, p. 136.
65 Young (1999), *supra* note 15, p. 144; Barnett and Coleman, *supra* note 58, p. 594. This process is similar to the development of customary law at the international level. See Vaughan Lowe, International Law Chapter 2.1 (2007). See also discussion in Section 4 later.

66 In 1945, United States President Harry Truman proclaimed jurisdiction over the continental shelf. Harry S. Truman, "Proclamation 2667 – Policy of The United States with Respect to the Natural Resources of the Subsoil and Sea Bed of the Continental Shelf", 28 September 1945. See also D. P. O'Connell, The International Law of the Sea, VOL. 1 470–471 (I.A Shearer (ed.), 1982); Robin Churchill, Vaughan Lowe and Amy Sander, The Law of the Sea 22 (4th ed., 2022); Ted L. McDorman, *The Continental Shelf, in* The Oxford Handbook of the Law of the Sea 181, 183 (Donald R. Rothwell, Alex G. Oude Elferink, Karen N. Scott and Tim Stephens (eds.), 2015).

67 Young (1999), *supra* note 15, p. 145–146; Barnett and Coleman, *supra* note 65.

68 Young (1999), ibid., p. 145–146. For example, UNCLOS encourage agreeing on amendments be consensus or unanimity, see UNCLOS, *supra* note 4, Articles 312–313.

69 Young (1999), *supra* note 15, p. 146; Barnett and Coleman, *supra* note 65.

70 Harrison, *supra* note 54, p. 46–47, 86–87. See Table recapitulating the status of the Convention and of the related Agreements, DOALOS website, available at www.un.org/depts/los/reference_files/status2019.pdf.

71 Rosenau, *supra* note 3, p. 9; Young (1999), *supra* note 15, p. 3, 5, 10. An international regime is defined as "a set of implicit or explicit principles, norms, rules, and decision-making procedures, around which actors' expectations converge in a given area of international relations". See Krasner, *supra* note 20.

72 Rosenau, *supra* note 3, p. 4, 8–9; Young (1994), *supra* note 10, p. 26.

73 Kal Raustiala and David G. Victor, *The Regime Complex for Plant Genetic Resources*, 58 Int. Org. 277, 279 (2004); Karen J. Alter and Sophie Meunier, *The Politics of International Regime Complexity*, 7(1) Perspectives on Politics 13, 13 (2009); Robert Keohane and David Victor, *The Regime Complex for Climate Change*, 9(1) Perspectives on Politics 7 (2011); John Gerard Ruggie, *supra* note 14; Jonathan W. Kuyper, *supra* note 4.

74 Alter (2022), *supra* note 1, p. 375–376.

75 See for example the discussion in Rosenau, *supra* note 3, p. 8–9; Young (1994), *supra* note 10; Raustiala and Victor, *supra* note 73, p. 278. For review of "regime complexity" and current literature on global governance, see Alter (2022), *supra* note 1, p. 379–384.

76 Keohane and Victor, *supra* note 73, p. 8–9. See also Raustiala and Victor, *supra* note 73, p. 277, 299; Drezner, *supra* note 8, p. 66.

77 Alter and Meunier, *supra* note 73, p. 17–18.

78 Keohane and Victor, *supra* note 73, p. 13. See for example interaction between the CLCS and international judicial bodies, in Chapter 2, Section 1.2.3.

79 For example, Raustiala and Victor, *supra* note 73, p. 297; Alter and Meunier, *supra* note 73, p. 16; Pratt, *supra* note 42, p. 562, 564. This view is similar to international law analysis on "fragmentation". See detailed explanation in ILC, *Fragmentation* of *International Law: Difficulties arising from the Diversification and Expansion* of *International Law*, Report of the Study Group of the International Law Commission, Finalized by Martti Koskenniemi, A/CN.4/L.682 (2006); Tomer Broude and Yuval Shany, Multi-Sourced Equivalent Norms in International Law (2011); Malcolm N. Shaw, International Law 54–55 (9th ed., 2021). See also Kal Raustiala, *Institutional Proliferation and the International Legal Order, in* Interdisciplinary Perspectives on International Law and International Relations: The State of the Art 293, 294–295 (Jeffrey L. Dunoff and Mark A. Pollack (eds.), 2013).

80 See discussion earlier in Section 2.2. Although some "regime complexes" scholars address the concept of "institutional deference", see Pratt, *supra* note 42, p. 562, 564.

81 See discussion earlier in Section 2.3; Drezner, *supra* note 8, p. 65; Ruggie, *supra* note 14, p. 14.

82 Drezner, *supra* note 8, p. 66; Alter and Meunier, *supra* note 73, p. 14, 19.

83 See for example *supra* notes 18 and 32 and discussion in Section 3.

84 Although for several decades after World War II, both IR and IL scholarship developed separately, rarely interacting. See e.g., Jeffrey L. Dunoff and Mark A. Pollack, *International Law and International Relations: Introducing an Interdisciplinary Dialogue, in* Interdisciplinary Perspectives on International Law and International Relations: The State of the Art 3 (Jeffrey L. Dunoff and Mark A. Pollack (eds.), 2013).

85 Young (1994), *supra* note 10, p. 12; Anne-Marie Slaughter-Burley, Andrew S. Tulumello and Stepan Wood, *International Law and International Relations Theory: A New Generation of Interdisciplinary Scholarship,* 92(3) Am. J. Int. Law 367, 367 (1998); McGrew, *supra* note 12, p. 31–32.

86 See examples in Alan Boyle and Christine Chinkin, The Making of International Law 19–20, 50 (2007).

87 "Legalization" refers to the degree in which institutional arrangements reflect legal characteristics. In more recent scholarship, it also refers to "the process of adding to, changing, or subtracting from the body of law and the legal system over time", see Kenneth W. Abbott and Duncan Snidal, *Law, Legalization, and Politics: An Agenda for the Next Generation of IL/IR Scholars, in* Interdisciplinary Perspectives on International Law and International Relations: The State of the Art 33, 34 (Jeffrey L. Dunoff and Mark A. Pollack (eds.), 2013).

88 Slaughter-Burley et al., *supra* note 85, p. 367–368, 370, 375, 381; Judith Goldstein, Miles Kahler, Robert O. Keohane and Anne-Marie Slaughter, *Introduction: Legalization and World Politics*, 54(3) Int. Org. 385, 385–386, 390 (2000); Kenneth W. Abbott and Duncan Snidal, *Hard and Soft Law in International Governance*, 54(1) Int. Org. 421, 425 (2000); Raustiala and Victor, *supra* note 73, p. 295; Dunoff and Pollack, *supra* note 84, p. 6–7.

89 For example, Donald R. Rothwell and David L. VanderZwaag, *The Sea Change Towards Principled Ocean Governance, in* Towards Principled Ocean Governance, Australian and Canadian Approaches and Challenges 1 (Donald R. Rothwell and David L. VanderZwaag (eds.), 2006); Barbara Woodward, Global Civil Society in International Lawmaking and Global Governance: Theory and Practice 62 (2010); Dunoff and Pollack, *supra* note 84, p. 7. See IL scholars that employ IR explanations, for example, Boyle Chinkin, *supra* note 86, p. 98–99; Eyal Benvenisti, *Customary International Law as a Judicial Tool for Promoting Efficiency, in* The Impact of International Law on International Cooperation: Theoretical Perspectives 85 (Eyal Benvenisti and Moshe Hirsch (eds.), 2009); Shaw, *supra* note 79, p. 6–7.

90 Dunoff and Pollack, *supra* note 84, p. 3.

91 For example, Barbara Koremenos, *Institutionalism and International Law, in* Interdisciplinary Perspectives on International Law and International Relations: The State of the Art 59, 59 (Jeffrey L. Dunoff and Mark A. Pollack (eds.), 2013). See also discussion on "legal legitimacy" in Section 2.2 earlier.

92 Goldstein et al., *supra* note 88, p. 386. See discussion on international regimes in Section 3 earlier.

93 Slaughter-Burley et al., *supra* note 85, p. 379; Goldstein et al., *supra* note 88, p. 387; Abbott and Snidal (2013), *supra* note 87, p. 34.

94 See for example Goldstein et al., *supra* note 88, p. 388; Ruggie, *supra* note 14, p. 8.

95 For example, James Crawford, The Creation of States in International Law (2nd ed., 2006); Shaw, *supra* note 79, p. 181.

96 Slaughter-Burley et al., *supra* note 85, p. 370–371; Goldstein et al., *supra* note 88, p. 388; Abbott and Snidal (2000), *supra* note 88, p. 421, 427; Abbott and Snidal (2013), *supra* note 87, p. 36. An example of "soft law" is the rules concerning conservation of the continental shelf. See discussion in Chapter 3, Section 1.1.

97 The term "hard law" refers to legally binding obligations that are precise and delegate authority for interpreting and implementing the law. "Soft law" refers to legal arrangements that are weakened in the level of obligation, precision, and delegation. These arrangements vary in degrees of each dimension and in the combinations across dimensions. See Abbott and Snidal (2000), *supra* note 88, p. 421–422.

98 Ibid., p. 423.
99 Koremenos, *supra* note 91, p. 65.
100 Nele Matz-Lück, *Norm Interpretation Across International Regimes: Competences and Legitimacy*, *in* Regime Interaction in International Law: Facing Fragmentation 201 (Margaret A. Young (ed.), 2012); Daniel Bodansky, *Legitimacy in International Law and International Relations*, *in* Interdisciplinary Perspectives on International Law and International Relations: The State of the Art 321, 322, 328 (Jeffrey L. Dunoff and Mark A. Pollack (eds.), 2013). See discussion on "legitimacy" in governance theory earlier in Section 2.2, and discussion on "legitimacy" in IL in Boyle and Chinkin, *supra* note 86, p. 24.
101 Slaughter-Burley et al., *supra* note 85, p. 371; Woodward, *supra* note 89, p. 35.
102 Abbott and Snidal (2000), *supra* note 88, p. 427; Goldstein et al., *supra* note 88, p. 391–393. A corresponding legal theory is "international legal process" school. This approach emphasizes law and legal reasoning as forms of social control. See Slaughter-Burley et al., *supra* note 85, p. 380–381.
103 Goldstein et al., *supra* note 88, p. 396–397; Abbott and Snidal (2000), *supra* note 88, p. 428, 430; Abbott and Snidal (2013), *supra* note 87, p. 37–38.
104 See for example Anne-Marie Slaughter, *International Law and International Relations Theory: A Prospectus*, *in* The Impact of International Law on International Cooperation: Theoretical Perspectives 16, 46 (Eyal Benvenisti and Moshe Hirsch (eds.), 2009); Abbott and Snidal (2013), *supra* note 87, p. 47; Koremenos, *supra* note 91, p. 68–69.
105 Shaw, *supra* note 79, p. 2–3. See also discussion earlier on the "anarchic" characteristics of the international system, text connected to *supra* note 3.
106 Woodward, *supra* note 89, p. 109; Shaw, *supra* note 79, p. 1, 5.
107 Statute of the International Court of Justice, San Francisco, 24 October 1945, Article 38(1); Woodward, ibid., p. 112.
108 For example, the CLCS's recommendations, see discussion in Chapter 2, Section 1.2.
109 Woodward, *supra* note 89, p. 112, 122.
110 Zhang Hua, *The Development of International Law of the Sea by International Courts and Tribunals, A Case Study of Due Diligence Obligation*, 9 Korean J. Int. & Comp. L. 132, 133 (2021).
111 Multilateral treaties can also be implicit part of the governance framework, for example, formal treaties that are exogenous to the continental shelf legal regime. These instruments can also be considered as "soft law", which is an element of the governance framework. See Section 4.1 earlier; Boyle and Chinkin, *supra* note 86, p. 211.
112 See also Boyle and Chinkin, *supra* note 86, p. 98, 103, 144–145, 159–160. See also discussion on decolonization, politics, maritime boundaries, and entitlements, Surabhi Ranganathan, *Decolonization and International Law: Putting the Ocean on the Map*, 23 J. Hist. Int. Law 161, 169 (2021).
113 See also Boyle and Chinkin, *supra* note 86, p. 98–100.
114 Boyle and Chinkin, *supra* note 86, p. 103; Ranganathan, *supra* note 112, p. 170; Andreas Motzfeldt Kravik, *An Analysis of Stagnation in Multilateral Law-making – And Why The Law of the Sea Has Transcended the Stagnation Trend*, 34(4) Leiden J. Int. Law 935, 953–954 (2021).
115 Boyle and Chinkin, *supra* note 86, p. 145. See e.g., the influence of the American petroleum industry and the International Hydrographic Organization (IHO) during UNCLOS III, in Chapter 3.
116 Kravik, *supra* note 114, p. 935–936.
117 Boyle and Chinkin, *supra* note 86, p. 171–172; Shaw, *supra* note 79, p. 101. In 1958, the UN General Assembly convened the first UN Conference on the Law of the Sea (UNCLOS I), with the participation of 86 states. UNCLOS I established four conventions rather than a single legal instrument: the CSC, the convention for the territorial sea and the contiguous zone, the convention for the high sea, and the convention for fishery rights and natural resources. In addition, the conference formulated an optional protocol for dispute settlement. See Tullio Treves, *Historical Development of the Law*

of the Sea, *in* The Oxford Handbook of the Law of the Sea 1, 13–14 (Donald R. Rothwell, Alex G. Oude Elferink, Karen N. Scott, and Tim Stephens (eds.), 2015); Lawrence Juda, International Law and Ocean Use Management, the Evolution of Ocean Governance 138 (1996).

118 For example, UNCLOS III, 2nd, Sess, 3rd Committee, 9th Mtg, UN Doc A/CONF.62/C.3/SR.9 (19 July 1974), paras. 21, 72; UNCLOS III, 2nd, Sess, 2nd Committee, 30th Mtg, UN Doc A/CONF.62/C.2/SR.31 (7 August 1974), paras. 55–56.

119 Boyle and Chinkin, *supra* note 86, p. 204. See detailed analysis in Chapter 2, Section 2.

120 See also Michael Zürn, A Theory of Global Governance: Authority, Legitimacy, and Contestation 31 (2018).

121 As reflects in Neil B. Nucup, *Infallible or Final?: Revisiting the Legitimacy of the International Court of Justice as the "Invisible" International Supreme Court*, 18 Law Prac. Int. Courts Trib. 145, 156–157 (2019).

122 For example, Goldstein et al., *supra* note 88, p. 389; Brus, *supra* note 14, p. 15; Karen J. Alter, *The Multiple Roles of International Courts and Tribunals: Enforcement, Dispute Settlement, Constitutional and Administrative Review*, *in* Interdisciplinary Perspectives on International Law and International Relations: The State of the Art 345, 357 (Jeffrey L. Dunoff and Mark A. Pollack (eds.), 2013). From a purely legalistic point of view, while judicial decisions are considered subsidiary sources of IL, international judicial bodies' legal interpretation may influence the evolution of the rules over time in accordance with the formal rules of treaty interpretation in IL. However, if this practice is not consistent or coherent, then the evolution of the law may not follow the rules of treaty interpretation and can be considered an informal element within the governance framework.

123 *Supra* note 107; Boyle and Chinkin, *supra* note 86, p. 2; Hua, *supra* note 110, p. 134, 150.

124 For example, Woodward, *supra* note 89, p. 111, 116, 122; Alter (2013), *supra* note 122, p. 350, 354; Shaw, *supra* note 79, p. 92. See also Article 59 of the ICJ Statute determining that "the decision of the Court has no binding force except between the parties and in respect of that particular case". Statute of the ICJ, *supra* note 107, Article 59. See also further discussion on the structure of international adjudication in Moshe Hirsch, Invitation to the Sociology of International Law 4 (2015).

125 Judicial bodies' decision binds only the parties to the specific dispute. See *supra* note 124.

126 For example, Boyle and Chinkin, *supra* note 86, p. 293; Woodward, *supra* note 89, p. 122–123; Hua, *supra* note 110; Shaw, *supra* note 79, p. 93.

127 Since 2009, the ICJ has employed a three-stage method of delimitation: The first stage is to draw a provisional delimitation line, usually an equidistance line, unless there are compelling reasons to use other methods. The second stage is to consider whether there are relevant factors that mandate adjusting the provisional equidistance line to achieve equitable results. In the final stage, the Court verifies that the delimitation line (provisional or adjusted) does not lead to an inequitable result, e.g., disproportion between the parties' coastal lengths and the area allocated to them. Maritime Delimitation in the Black Sea (Romania v. Ukraine), Judgment, ICJ Reports 2009, p. 61, para. 122; Maritime Dispute (Peru v. Chile), Judgment, ICJ Reports 2014, p. 3, para. 180; Territorial and Maritime Dispute (Nicaragua v. Colombia), Judgment, ICJ Reports 2012, p. 624, paras. 190–193; Massimo Lando, Maritime Delimitation as a Judicial Process 22 (2019).

128 For example, Boyle and Chinkin, *supra* note 86, p. 244; Joost Pauwelyn and Manfred Elsig, *The Politics of Treaty Interpretation: Variations and Explanations across International Tribunals*, *in* Interdisciplinary Perspectives on International Law and International Relations: The State of the Art 445, 446 (Jeffrey L. Dunoff and Mark A. Pollack (eds.), 2013); Niels M. Blokker, *Governance of the International Tribunal of the Law*

of the Sea: The Role of the Meeting of States Parties to the Law of the Sea Convention, *in* Interpretations of the United Nations Convention on the Law of the Sea by International Courts and Tribunals 81, 81–82 (Angela- Del Vecchio and Roberto Virzo (eds.), 2019).

129 Benvenisti, *supra* note 89, p. 91.

130 Woodward, *supra* note 89, p. 122–123; Hua, *supra* note 110, p. 134.

131 See also Boyle and Chinkin, *supra* note 86, p. 105; Benvenisti, *supra* note 89, p. 88; Shaw, *supra* note 79, p. 59, 61.

132 See also Slaughter, *supra* note 104, p. 46.

2 Demarcation and delimitation of the continental shelf

The research assumption of this book is that analysis of legal regimes should focus not only on formal legal elements but also on informal elements such as processes and non-state actors. This broader perspective sheds new light on the construction of the formal regime and explains the differences between the legal regime and the actual practice in this sphere.

This chapter analyzes the governance perspective's contribution to the formation and development of the continental shelf's legal regime and specifically to the questions of demarcation and delimitation of the continental shelf. Within the governance framework, political considerations, state practice, and judicial decisions have influenced the establishment of informal rules and principles governing the breadth and delimitation of the continental shelf.

1. Demarcation of the outer limit of the continental shelf

The legal scholarship on delimitation of the continental shelf is divided into two separate spheres: continental shelf demarcation (i.e., unilaterally setting the outer limit up to or beyond 200 nm) and delimitation of overlapping continental shelves between states with opposite or adjacent coasts. This section analyzes the legal regime for demarcating the outer limit of the continental shelf from the perspective of governance theory.

The legal regime provides two *alternative* possibilities for the location of the outer limit of the continental shelf: one based on geology (the outer edge of the continental margin) and the other based on geography (a distance of 200 nm).[1] The formal legal rule emphasizes the primacy of geological features (i.e., the physical edge) in determining the outer limit, while the distance of 200 nm is an ancillary option.[2] However, in practice, the distance criterion has primacy over geological circumstances.

This gap between the formal rule and actual practice highlights the difference between the legal regime and the governance framework concerning the continental shelf. As elaborated later, state practice and international adjudication, both informal elements in the governance framework,[3] have essentially downplayed the formal legal rule, influencing change in the concept of the continental shelf from

DOI: 10.4324/9781003479772-3

a geological component to a legal concept based on the distance criterion, thus detaching it from its geological origins.[4]

For example, coastal States with broad continental shelves (i.e., beyond 200 nm) contributed to the creation of a new informal rule concerning the breadth of the continental shelf. Instead of directly establishing the outer limit at the edge of the continental margin, these states demarcated the outer limit by first adopting the 200 nm distance criterion and then extending it later on, essentially dividing their continental self into two parts: up to 200 nm and beyond 200 nm.[5] In addition, some states defined their continental shelf in terms of the 200 nm EEZ.[6] This is more prominent in light of the fact that some broad-shelf states applied the "edge of the margin" option.[7] Still, most broad-shelf states have employed the 200 nm standard, regardless of the geographical situation, which contributed to the primacy of the distance criterion contrary to the formal legal rule.

Thus, the two *alternative* options for the outer limit in the formal rule became *complementary* criteria in the governance framework: Where the outer edge of the continental margin does not reach 200 nm, the "natural prolongation" is defined by distance, irrespective of the geological circumstances.[8] Within the governance framework, the distance criterion eventually prevailed as the outer limit of the continental shelf.[9] The following section analyzes the processes and influences that contributed to the establishment of the broader governance framework for demarcation of the continental shelf.

1.1 The governance framework for the continental shelf up to 200 nm

The governance perspective of the continental shelf can help to explain the formation of the formal rule by analyzing the influence of informal actors and processes, such as technological developments,[10] domestic non-state actors,[11] international organizations,[12] and individuals.[13] The governance perspective can also shed light on the significant differences between the legal regime and the governance framework in practice. For example, informal elements can explain broad-margin states' division of the continental shelf into two parts, though no such requirement exists in the legal regime.[14]

This section analyzes the definition of the continental shelf's breadth from a governance perspective, highlighting the role of informal actors, principles, and processes that influenced the change in the balance between the geological criterion and the geographical criterion in the legal regime.

1.1.1 Article 76(1) as a political compromise

The institutional approach views governance formation as a bargaining process. An examination of UNCLOS's negotiation process and the compromise reached concerning Article 76(1) can help to explain the differences between the legal regime and the governance framework for demarcating the continental shelf and the dominance of geography (the distance criterion) over geology (natural prolongation).[15]

During UNCLOS III, most states supported the 200 nm distance criterion as the standard outer limit and the edge of the continental margin for states with wider continental shelves.[16] However, despite this broad support, the outcome of the negotiations reversed this formula: The edge of the continental margin was adopted as the primary rule for the breadth of the shelf, with distance as an alternative option.[17] The gap between the formula supported by the majority of states and the final text is the result of a political compromise between various conflicting interest-groups. Most notably, the negotiations reflected a conflict between broad-margin coastal States, which sought to expand the breadth of the continental shelf and advocated the "edge of the margin" criterion, and geographically disadvantaged coastal States, which advocated for a fixed limit of 200 nm.[18]

The competing positions reflect the main approaches of IR. For example, broad-margin states sought to maximize their interests and material power, which reflects the realist approach, while other states' positions reflect more liberal approaches, supporting ideas of distributive justice, equality, knowledge-sharing, and resources-sharing for the benefit of all.

The final text of Article 76(1) combines both limits, supposedly to accommodate the interests of all major interest-groups,[19] but the emphasis is on geology to the advantage of broad-margin coastal States. The parties reached a compromise, accepting the extension of the continental shelf beyond 200 nm in exchange for a revenue-sharing system that protects the interests of geographically disadvantaged states.[20] This system essentially created linkage between the geological criterion (edge of the continental margin) and the rights of landlocked and geographically disadvantaged states, primarily developing states.[21] In practice, the final text of Article 76(1) mostly reflects the interests of broad-margin states due to the primacy of geology rather than the interests of all states; indeed, the majority of states supported an opposite formula.[22] This anomaly, as elaborated later, helps to explain the gap between the legal regime and the governance framework.

1.1.2 The structure of negotiations as an informal institution

A structural analysis of the formation of the legal regime can also help to explain the differences between the legal regime and the governance framework for demarcation of the continental shelf. UNCLOS III negotiations were an informal element within the broader governance framework.[23] Such underexplored interactions, both during and after the conference, influenced development of informal norms that contributed to the gap between the legal regime and the actual practice.

As discussed earlier, the negotiations established linkage between several, sometimes conflicting, issues concerning the definition of the continental shelf. This bargaining process resulted in a rule that favored one group (broad-margin coastal States), despite general support for a different formula.[24] The revenue-sharing system allowed the extension of the continental shelf in return for monetary compensation. This ensured elimination of any opposition to expanding the sovereign rights of broad-margin coastal States beyond 200 nm to include an area recognized until then as part of the international seabed (hereinafter: the Area).[25]

Another structural element that influenced the informal norms concerning the outer limit of the continental shelf was the relationship between three significant bodies during the negotiations; the Seabed Committee[26] and UNCLOS III's first and second committees.[27] The dynamics within and between these committees contributed to the adoption of the formal rule in favor of broad-margin states, despite overall support for an opposite rule.

The drafting process created linkage between the continental shelf and the Area; the definition of one zone affected the definition of the other zone.[28] Thus, the proposals regarding the outer limit of the continental shelf and the final text of Article 76(1) reflect broad-margin states' proposals for the baseline of the Area rather than the outer limit of the continental shelf.[29] This allows coastal States to extend the continental shelf without breaching areas beyond national jurisdiction. Since these proposals emphasized the physical characteristics of the continental shelf, Article 76(1) emphasized geological features rather than the fixed-distance criterion.[30]

Despite this linkage, each committee represented different interests. Thus, the outcome does not reflect the majority's position. Broad-margin states wanted to "push" the baseline of the Area as far as possible seaward, so a larger area could potentially fall under their national jurisdiction. This was not the same as setting the limit at 200 nm and then allowing these states to extend their zones into the international zone as an exception to the rule. The latter scenario, in theory, would involve greater international supervision and demand for more compensation to developing countries for infringement of the Area. In the first scenario, there is no infringement of the Area and thus no need for strict regulation.[31]

The transfer of proposals from the Seabed Committee and the first committee to the second committee changed the balance of interests in the negotiation process. These proposals did not account for the interests of geographically disadvantaged states, except for the revenue-sharing system.[32] Yet the prospect of monetary compensation ensured that there would be no significant opposition to the extension of the continental shelf beyond 200 nm.[33] Consequently, Article 76(1) reflects mostly the interests of broad-margin states. The reluctance of geographically disadvantaged states to agree to the final text, and the fact that this provision does not serve their interests can explain why most states have implemented the opposite formula in practice.

1.1.3 The conflict between geography and geology in defining the continental shelf

The conflict between geography (the 200 nm distance criterion) and geology (natural prolongation) in continental shelf's demarcation and tribunals' interpretation of concepts such as "adjacency", "natural prolongation", and "the coast" can also explain the difference between the legal regime and the application of Article 76(1) within the governance framework.

The continental shelf is a geological component connected to the land mass, as reflected through the concept of natural prolongation.[34] Despite the formal rule, which is based on geology, tribunals employed geographical criteria such as adjacency to the coast and fixed distance (200 nm), thus developing the continental shelf as a legal concept. While Article 76(1) establishes entitlement based on geology (natural prolongation), the ICJ acknowledged that geography (i.e., adjacency or proximity) is a better criterion for establishing coastal States' entitlement to the continental shelf.[35]

This approach confers greater significance to the distance principle.[36] The ICJ adopted the position that the distance principle defines the continental shelf, irrespective of the natural prolongation of the land territory.[37] Thus, the distance criterion, which is a measure of breadth, also became the basis for entitlement to the continental shelf.[38] The primacy of distance in practice, irrespective of the geological situation, contradicts the legal regime: it favors geographically disadvantaged states, granting them a continental shelf of at least 200 nm, unlike the formula of Article 76(1).

While judicial bodies have stressed that this approach is not intended to compensate or protect the interests of geographically disadvantaged states,[39] the 200 nm distance principle is not always objective in practice and essentially reflects considerations of distributive justice or compensation.[40] As discussed later, the conflict between geography and geology also led to the conflation of entitlement and delimitation.[41]

The interactions between the legal regimes of the continental shelf and the EEZ also influenced the primacy of the distance criterion, contrary to the formal legal rule.[42] While the continental shelf refers only to the seabed, the EEZ includes both the seabed and superjacent waters.[43] Since the continental shelf is part of the EEZ, the 200 nm limit of the EEZ strengthened the distance criterion in Article 76(1). It thus became the standard for all coastal States, with the exception that broad-margin states are allowed to extend the outer limit beyond 200 nm.[44]

International tribunals also facilitated the influence of the EEZ regime on the demarcation of the continental shelf by treating the two legal regimes as parallel or even overlapping.[45] For example, the ICJ maintained that the distance principle should apply to the continental shelf due to its link to the EEZ.[46] This shifted the balance between geology and geography, weakening the role of "natural prolongation" and strengthening the primacy of distance as the criterion for determining both entitlement and the breadth of the continental shelf.[47] The link between the EEZ and the continental shelf significantly contributed to the informal primacy of the distance criterion, as well as the conflation of distance as both a measure of the continental shelf's breadth and a legal basis for entitlement to it.[48]

1.1.4 The effect of delimitation on the breadth of the continental shelf

The preceding section demonstrates the contribution of jurisprudence to the emergence of the informal rule concerning the breadth of the continental shelf. The governance perspective can also help to explain the contribution of judicial bodies through a structural analysis of dispute-settlement. Structural analysis is an analytical tool that examines judicial bodies themselves – that is, their structure and rules and not just their decisions. The operation of these institutions influences their decisions, which also explains the formation of informal rules and principles.

Judicial bodies are institutions – that is, social structures with specific organizing principles.[49] These institutions are also agents of international law, exercising power and jurisdiction in certain contexts.[50] Judicial bodies interpret and apply formal legal rules within a specific structure of dispute-settlement (e.g., delimitation disputes).[51] This structure is significant to the development of the informal rule for demarcating the continental shelf because this framework links questions of entitlement and breadth to delimitation; the division of the zone between two states defines the extent of the continental shelf.[52]

Despite the differences between entitlement, breadth, and delimitation, the structure of dispute-settlement makes it difficult for judicial bodies to separate these issues.[53] For example, the process of delimitation affects the definition of the disputed area, irrespective of the actual physical situation. Judicial bodies "delimit" the relevant area for examination, defined in terms of distance, before delimiting the overlapping zones. This informal process essentially modifies the disputed areas, which can affect the zone allocated to each party. For example, the allocated zone would be broader if tribunals considered the full breadth of the parties' maritime zones.[54]

The structure of delimitation also influenced the primacy of the distance principle by applying the concept of a single boundary line, developed through state practice, when delimiting both the continental shelf and the EEZ.[55] This method draws one boundary line for both zones, essentially prescribing that the continental shelf cannot extend beyond 200 nm, contrary to Article 76(1).[56] Thus, the structure of delimitation facilitated the formation of an informal norm that gives priority to the distance criterion in order to establish unified rules for both zones.

The social cognition approach in IR provides further insight on how judicial bodies have contributed to the gap between the legal regime and the governance framework.[57] The ICJ does not only settle delimitation disputes. It also exercises influence by producing "schemata" – generalized knowledge structures and abstract guidelines that represent objects or events and provide default assumptions about their characteristics and relationships. Under conditions of incomplete information, schemata can help people better understand the world. Schemata represent existing knowledge and serve as information-processing mechanisms for new knowledge, providing a framework for understanding decisions and outcomes that seem unpredictable or unlikely.[58] In our example, the ICJ produces schemata defining the continental shelf in the context of dispute-settlement, thus reinforcing the conflation of entitlement, breadth, and delimitation.

1.2 The governance framework for the continental shelf beyond 200 nm

As analyzed earlier, Article 76(1) primarily reflects the interests of broad-margin states, allowing them to extend their continental shelf up to the edge of the continental margin. Article 76 contains conditions and scientific formulas regulating the extension of the continental shelf beyond 200 nm.[59] In practice, as discussed earlier, broad-margin states do not directly demarcate the outer limit at the edge of the margin, as permitted in the legal regime. Rather, they demarcate their continental shelves in two stages: first, they automatically demarcate the zone up to

200 nm and then demarcate an area beyond 200 nm in accordance with the relevant provisions.[60]

The governance perspective can explain the formation of the formal rules by analyzing the contribution of informal processes and actors, such as international organizations[61] and individuals.[62] In addition, within the governance framework, each of the principal IR theories highlights different elements of the legal regime, providing different explanations for the development of the rules and norms.[63]

The governance perspective can also provide explanations for informal norms and principles developed in practice, sometimes contrary to the legal regime.[64] For example, informal powers of formal actors beyond what the legal regime prescribes. As discussed earlier, Article 76(1) reflects the interests of broad-margin states. However, other sections within Article 76 supposedly mitigate this imbalance by imposing limitations on the extension of the continental shelf beyond 200 nm.[65]

1.2.1 The role of the CLCS

The Commission's formal mandate is to issue non-binding recommendations concerning the outer limit of the continental shelf beyond 200 nm.[66] The definition of the Commission's role in Article 76(8), like the definition of the continental shelf in Article 76(1), reflects a conflict between broad-margin states and geographically disadvantaged states; the latter wanted the CLCS to exercise broad competence and to essentially function as a "boundary commission",[67] while the former preferred to assign only recommendatory powers to the CLCS.[68]

Earlier versions of Article 76(8) indicated that the drafters did not intend the CLCS to have a significant role in determining the outer limit of the continental shelf beyond 200 nm.[69] Broad-margin states perceived the CLCS as eroding coastal States' sovereignty, interpreting Article 76(8) as giving the Commission the competence to determine the outer limits of the continental shelf, contrary to Article 76(1). These states wanted the CLCS to be a supervisory body assigned to ensure compliance with Article 76.[70] In contrast, geographically disadvantaged states viewed the Commission as a mitigating factor for what they perceived as the "adverse effects" of Article 76(1) – that is, its protection of the interests of broad-margin states. Therefore, they wanted the CLCS's recommendations to be binding.[71]

Article 76(8) reflects a compromise: It limits the claims of broad-margin states without imposing any legal consequences if a state establishes an outer limit that does not comply with the Commission's recommendations or if a state fails to make a submission.[72] Thus, the legal regime treats the CLCS more like a depository of information, ostensibly still reflecting the interests of broad-margin states.

However, as shown later, the CLCS has acquired a broader mandate than the legal regime provides. In practice, the Commission is not just a technical-scientific body. Rather, it functions as a semi-judicial body with considerable competences for determining the outer limit of the continental shelf beyond 200 nm. This analysis of the CLCS is another example of how the governance framework is broader than the legal regime by including informal norms and roles. Coastal States cooperate significantly with the Commission, even non-member states,[73] which cannot be exclusively attributed to the formal legal regime. The significance of the CLCS may also explain why broad-margin states do not act in accordance with the formal rule concerning the outer limits, which is in their favor.

1.2.2 The semi-judicial role of the CLCS

While geographically disadvantaged states succeeded in incorporating their proposals on the Commission's competence in the final text of Article 76(8), this provision still establishes its mandate as technical in nature. However, from a governance perspective, it is apparent that the CLCS has broader informal competences than the legal regime conferred to it.

For example, the CLCS has a significant role in *interpreting* Article 76, which is essentially a legal function. Since most of the terms in Article 76 are technical, subject to multiple interpretations, the Commission cannot evaluate submissions in accordance with Article 76 unless there is a consensus on the meaning of these terms; and indeed, the CLCS has adopted guidelines for interpreting Article 76. Since it is the only relevant institution to do so, states have an interest in relying on its interpretation, even though they are not legally bound to do so.[74]

The Commission interprets various terms included in its own Rules of Procedure (ROP).[75] For example, it determines whether an issue is procedural or substantive to determine whether it affects the rights of coastal States.[76] When interpreting its technical guidelines, the CLCS exercises methods of interpretation employed by international judicial bodies.[77]

The language of Article 76(8) indicates that demarcation of the outer limit beyond 200 nm is a quasi-judicial process in which coastal States must "justify" the extension of their continental shelf to an international body.[78] Thus, despite the Commission's lack of formal legally binding powers, coastal States often take its proceedings and recommendations seriously.[79]

Another prominent example of the CLCS's semi-judicial nature is the *stare decisis* doctrine.[80] Both the CLCS and coastal States maintain that the Commission should adhere to its past practices and decisions, though no such obligation is stipulated in UNCLOS Annex II or in the CLCS's ROP and despite the notion that the CLCS's proceedings are unilateral and supposedly have no effect on other submissions.[81] In their communications with the CLCS, states often maintain that the Commission should exercise its functions in accordance with past decisions in similar cases. For example, in a communication to the CLCS, France and South Africa presented their view on the term "natural prolongation", arguing that the Commission's view derogates from its own past practices.[82] This implies that the CLCS should be bound by past decisions rather than a case-by-case analysis, which is a common feature of judicial bodies.

Coastal States' communications with the UN Secretary-General (UNSG) support this argument. For example, in 2011 the United Kingdom submitted a communication to the UNSG conveying its disappointment with the CLCS's final recommendations and questioning whether its approach was consistent with UNCLOS. The United Kingdom also implied that it would rely on the outcome of future submissions which raise similar questions of legal interpretation, in particular, those involving entitlement to a continental shelf beyond 200 nm.[83] It is noteworthy that the question of entitlement is outside the scope of a technical body composed of scientific experts. In addition, the United Kingdom seemed to treat the outcome of the process as if the commission had issued a final decision rather than recommendations.[84]

In 2016, the Cook Islands also expressed its disappointment with the Commission's recommendations to the UNSG.[85] The Cook Islands had raised some concerns regarding the sub-commission during a presentation to the CLCS, despite the fact that the formal legal rules do not allow the presentation of such concerns or complaints.[86] The Cook Islands essentially indicated that it regarded the process as a hearing or complaint mechanism, which is a characteristic of a judicial body.

In another example, South Africa sent a *Note Verbale* to the UNSG in 2017, stating its disappointment and objection to the Commission's recommendations on its submission.[87] South Africa noted that the conduct of the sub-commission was in line with past practice in similar cases and, therefore, "broadly acceptable"[88] but expressed disappointment that the CLCS had not adopted the sub-commission's recommendations – that is, that the Commission had not adhered to precedence.[89]

These examples demonstrate that states regard the CLCS and its sub-commissions as semi-judicial bodies that should defer to past practices and decisions (i.e., the legal doctrine of precedence), which is a common feature of judicial bodies, rather than conduct a case-by-case analysis.

Another judicial feature of the CLCS's proceedings concerns states' "right of rebuttal". While the legal regime views the Commission's proceedings as unilateral, concerning only the submitting states, this is not the case in practice: Submitting states conduct semi-adversarial dialogues with other states on their submissions, through diplomatic communications with the CLCS or the UNSG.[90] In some cases, the submitting state responds to other states' reactions, similar to a rebuttal in court. This essentially turns the proceedings into an adversarial process.

As of December 2023, submitting states had made approximately 40 such "rebuttals" to other states' communications.[91] Most of the rebuttals concerned the ramifications of the submissions on delimitation of overlapping continental shelves between neighboring states, mainly that submissions are without prejudice to delimitation.[92] Other rebuttals pertained to the existence or absence of a dispute over the relevant area.[93]

Ostensibly, if the Commission's proceedings affect only the submitting state and the recommendations are non-binding and without prejudice to delimitation between states, communication with other states is unnecessary. States' reactions to other states' submissions suggest that the CLCS has greater significance than the legal regime intended.

1.2.2.1 SUBMISSIONS CONCERNING DISPUTED AREAS

Article 76(10) provides that demarcation of the outer limit of the continental shelf beyond 200 nm is without prejudice to delimitation of overlapping continental shelves, thus essentially a unilateral process. Article 76 is silent on the involvement of third parties in the CLCS's proceedings. The CLCS, however, determined that it will consider submissions concerning a disputed area only if all parties consent to the process.[94] This is similar to the requirement of consent to the jurisdiction of international tribunals, indicating that the Commission recognizes that its proceedings and rulings affect delimitation in practice.[95]

While the CLCS's ROP do not define what constitutes as "disputes", which might hinder the evaluation of a submission, the CLCS itself refers to an "actual or potential delimitation dispute".[96] This indicates a low threshold, requiring only that other states claim that a dispute exists (even if the submitting state argues that no dispute exists) to prevent the CLCS from evaluating a submission.[97] Both the ROP and state practice reflect the converged expectation that states have a right to "block" the consideration of other states' submission. This underlines the adversarial nature of the Commission's proceedings.[98]

In addition, while the implied threshold for a dispute empowers other states to hinder the CLCS's proceedings, the CLCS has asserted that it makes an independent evaluation regarding the existence of a dispute.[99] For example, regarding Myanmar's submission, the Commission noted that not all the relevant states consented to the proceedings to consider the submission, meaning that it thought that there was a dispute between the parties. The CLCS regarded the proceedings in ITLOS as indicating the existence of a dispute. The CLCS also asked Bangladesh for its position on the existence of a dispute, to which Bangladesh gave a positive answer. The CLCS actively sought to examine whether a dispute exists.[100] This evaluation is essentially a judicial function, indicating that the Commission has greater influence than the legal regime intended, certainly with respect to delimitation.

The CLCS not only decides whether a dispute exists but also assesses the "consent" of relevant states to determine whether it can proceed to consider a submission. Some scholars suggest that the relevant states have no obligation to explicitly object to the Commission's proceedings.[101] In many cases, the affected states do communicate their consent or "non-opposition" to the CLCS's proceedings.[102] However, in some cases, at least one relevant party explicitly refuses to consent to the Commission's proceedings.[103] As in the discussion on identifying disputes, the consent of other states indicates that the CLCS has greater influence than the legal regime provides, especially with respect to delimitation.

When third parties explicitly declare that they give or withhold their consent, there is no conflict concerning the interpretation of consent.[104] However, in some cases, the relevant states offer neither consent nor objection.[105] Since in cases of disputed areas, the consent of relevant states is a precondition for the Commission's proceedings, some argue that the default assumption should be that a state objects unless it expresses its consent.[106] Third states will not consent to consideration of a submission if it affects their rights and interests. This suggests that the CLCS's requirement of consent is similar to that of *locus standi* in judicial dispute-settlement, though the CLCS does not have the same competence or capacity to consider whether a state has sufficient legal interest to be party to a dispute.[107] The requirement of consent is also similar to consent to jurisdiction in judicial dispute-settlement. Thus, the Commission has in practice greater significance than what

UNCLOS confers to it, effectively broadening the governance framework in this context in comparison to the legal regime.

As of December 2023, states had communicated approximately 43 objections to the CLCS's consideration of submissions.[108] It is hard to determine the effect of such objections on the CLCS's proceedings. Generally, it seems that when a third-party objects to the consideration of a submission, the CLCS postpones the proceedings.[109] However, it is difficult to determine whether the postponement is due to the third-party's lack of consent or other factors.[110] If possible, the CLCS considers only the parts of a submission that are not subject to dispute.[111]

In some cases, the objecting state also initiated dispute-settlement proceedings at the ICJ concerning the area to which the submission relates.[112] However, this judicial proceeding does not necessarily lead to postponement of the Commission's proceedings. Thus, it seems that such postponement is more likely attributable to a lack of consent rather than the ICJ's proceedings.[113] In other cases, the CLCS postponed its proceedings and referred the parties to the delimitation mechanism in Article 83(3) concerning provisional arrangements pending a final agreement.[114]

The opportunity of states to react to other states' submissions and the submitting state's option of addressing these responses give the submission process a semi-judicial adversarial character: The CLCS must decide on "pre-trial" questions – such as the existence of a dispute and the consent of relevant states to its proceedings – before considering the submission, essentially exercising semi-judicial functions.[115] These functions are beyond the CLCS's formal technical-scientific competence and are seemingly irrelevant to the unilateral demarcation of the outer edge of the continental margin. Thus, the CLCS has greater significance within the governance framework, which is broader than the legal regime in this context.

1.2.3 The relations between the CLCS and international tribunals

As analyzed, the CLCS exercises semi-judicial functions prior to and during consideration of submissions, thus wielding greater significance than the legal regime explicitly provides. However, while the CLCS can consider whether a dispute exists, it cannot resolve disputes. Therefore, judicial dispute-settlement proceedings influence the CLCS's proceedings with respect to disputed areas.[116] This relation between the CLCS and judicial bodies essentially conflicts with Article 76 and the unilateral nature of demarcation.

However, this influence is not one-sided; the Commission has greater significance not only with respect to the demarcation of the outer limit of the continental shelf beyond 200 nm but also with respect to delimitation of overlapping continental shelves. While judicial proceedings might not postpone the CLCS's proceedings, postponement of proceedings in the CLCS may influence the jurisdiction of judicial bodies vis-à-vis disputed areas beyond 200 nm. The reactions of judicial bodies to the Commission's role in the context of delimitation have contributed to its broader significance.

A review of judicial decisions and the scholarly literature reveals that the relations between international adjudication and the CLCS can be classified into three approaches: exclusive jurisdiction of the CLCS, primary jurisdiction of the CLCS, and parallel jurisdiction.

In some cases, it seems that judicial bodies confer exclusive jurisdiction to the CLCS with respect to the continental shelf beyond 200 nm, even in the context of delimitation. Despite the legal regime's distinction between demarcation of the outer limit of the continental shelf beyond 200 nm and delimitation of overlapping continental shelves, tribunals have abstained from delimiting the area beyond 200 nm when the CLCS is not involved.[117]

The ICJ has asserted its competence to decide on the delimitation of the maritime boundary without specifying a precise endpoint; however, it has clarified that the line should not extend beyond 200 nm since claiming rights beyond 200 nm must be in accordance with Article 76 and reviewed by the CLCS.[118] This indicates that submissions to the CLCS and its recommendations are prerequisites for judicial delimitation beyond 200 nm.[119] In addition, some judges have maintained that the authority to examine scientific data concerning the outer limits of the continental shelf lies exclusively with the CLCS. Thus, the task of delimitation becomes more complicated if judicial bodies delimit the continental shelf beyond 200 nm before the Commission has issued recommendations on the outer limit.[120]

In other cases, judicial bodies have indicated that the CLCS has primary jurisdiction with respect to the continental shelf beyond 200 nm even in the context of delimitation and that judicial bodies have secondary or complementary jurisdiction. In other words, judicial bodies only exercise jurisdiction in cases where the Commission has not exercised its jurisdiction. For example, in the Bay of Bengal case, the Annex VII Arbitral Tribunal concluded that it would decide on delimitation in the absence of recommendations from the CLCS, when the latter does not exercise its functions (e.g., postponement of proceedings). The Tribunal argued that such cases would be inconsistent with the object and purpose of UNCLOS.[121]

In several cases, judicial bodies claimed jurisdiction to delimit the continental shelf beyond 200 nm irrespective of the CLCS, essentially maintaining parallel jurisdiction. This approach is based on the distinction between demarcating the outer limit of the continental shelf and delimitation of overlapping continental shelves. For example, while in the 2012 *Nicaragua/Colombia* case, the Court indicated that a submission to the CLCS is necessary to prove entitlement,[122] it maintained its competence to delimit the continental shelf beyond 200 nm in the absence of the CLCS's recommendations when Nicaragua made a submission in 2016.[123] The ICJ essentially maintained that it had parallel jurisdiction with the CLCS in the same case.

Although these decisions might seem to create procedural incoherency concerning the role of the CLCS in continental shelf delimitation beyond 200 nm,[124] the Court explained its decisions by distinguishing between delimitation and delineation. According to the ICJ, the CLCS's proceedings relate to the demarcation of the outer limits of the continental shelf, which is distinct from the delimitation of the continental shelf.[125] Therefore, the recommendations of the CLCS are not a prerequisite for delimitation. The ICJ also distinguishes between making a submission to the CLCS and receiving its recommendations. While submitting information is a prerequisite for delimitation, recommendations are not.[126]

This reasoning, which emphasizes the need for information on the outer limit of the continental shelf beyond 200 nm before proceeding with delimitation, is also reflected in the decisions of the International Tribunal for the Law of the Sea (ITLOS). While ITLOS has mostly employed the parallel jurisdiction approach,[127] it has also implied that the CLCS has "primary jurisdiction" in some cases.[128] ITLOS emphasized that it will not proceed with delimitation beyond 200 nm in cases of "significant uncertainty" concerning the continental margin.[129] This indicates that judicial bodies will not proceed with delimitation without the CLCS's recommendations when there is scientific uncertainty concerning the continental margin. Thus, the ICJ indicated a new "case-by-case" approach to the role of the CLCS based on the test of "scientific certainty".[130]

At first glance, a review of the case law shows that judicial bodies treat the role of the CLCS in maritime delimitation inconsistently. However, a more thorough analysis reveals that there are three different approaches with respect to the CLCS in the delimitation of the continental shelf beyond 200 nm: the CLCS has exclusive jurisdiction (recommendations are a prerequisite), the CLCS has primary jurisdiction, and the CLCS and judicial bodies have parallel jurisdiction. The parallel jurisdiction approach has been adopted in most delimitation cases beyond 200 nm. However, it seems that judicial bodies have exercised parallel jurisdiction only in "appropriate circumstances" – that is, when there is scientific certainty concerning the continental margin beyond 200 nm.[131]

While delimitation is distinct from delineation, in practice, judicial bodies need to know the extent of the parties' continental shelves before delimiting the boundary between them. In the absence of the CLCS's recommendations and in cases of significant scientific uncertainty, some argue that a decision on delimitation based on the parties' claims is hypothetical and reversible, which can undermine the legitimacy and stability of judicial boundaries.[132] This indicates that the Commission has greater significance than initially intended.

The perception concerning the CLCS's role contributes to the conflation of entitlement, breadth, and delimitation of the continental shelf. For example, ITLOS maintained that it must settle the question of entitlement before it can delimit the continental shelf and that the absence of a precise limit beyond 200 does not preclude a decision on entitlement and then delimitation.[133] This position is problematic since there is no need to determine entitlement unless the continental shelf extends beyond 200 nm and overlaps with another state's continental shelf.[134] However, delineating the continental shelf beyond 200 nm is a unilateral state action based on the CLCS's recommendation; it is not on a judicial decision.[135] Similar to the continental shelf up to 200 nm, the structure and schemata of international tribunals in the context of delimitation affect the role and significance of the CLCS beyond 200 nm.[136]

2. Delimitation of overlapping continental shelves within and beyond 200 nm

The primary rule concerning delimitation of overlapping continental shelves between neighboring states, found in Article 83, obligates coastal States to delimit their overlapping maritime zones through a bilateral agreement to achieve an "equitable solution".[137] However, UNCLOS does not define what constitutes an equitable solution. This section analyzes the rules concerning delimitation of overlapping continental shelves between neighboring states from the governance perspective, demonstrating the contribution of IR theories to the construction and implementation of the legal regime.

2.1 The governance framework for the delimitation of overlapping continental shelves

The governance perspective can help to explain the construction of the formal rules concerning delimitation of the continental shelf by analyzing the contribution of informal actors, such as the Conference's president[138] and chairmen of the negotiating groups.[139] In addition, as discussed later, each of the main IR theoretical streams can highlight different elements and interpretations to explain the construction process of the formal legal rules.

The governance perspective also highlights the informal norms and principles developed in practice, mainly by international tribunals, whose decisions are an informal element within the governance framework.[140] This section analyzes how the governance framework broadens the legal regime, essentially establishing informal norms and principles to interpret and implement the formal legal rules.

2.1.1 "Equitable solution" and "equidistance"

As in the case of demarcation, the legal rule of delimitation reflects a conflict between broad-margin states and geographically disadvantaged states. However, while the formal method of delimitation, which became the customary rule, reflects the interests of broad-margin states, in practice, judicial bodies have essentially created new informal rules concerning delimitation that reflect the interests of geographically disadvantaged states, thus broadening the governance framework of the continental shelf in this context.

UNCLOS III negotiations featured two interrelated but competing principles or methods concerning the delimitation of overlapping continental shelves. One method is the objective principle of "equidistance" (or a "median line"), and the other is the subjective principle of "equity" or an "equitable solution".[141] The latter is more flexible since it considers all relevant factors to reach an equitable result. Different interest-groups supported different methods in the UNCLOS III negotiations: Broad-margin states promoted equity,[142] while geographically disadvantaged states preferred the equidistance method.[143] Although some proposals for Article 83 that included references to equidistance gained wide support,[144] the final text emphasized the goal of reaching an equitable solution.[145]

While Article 83 does not define what constitutes an equitable solution, it stipulates that states should resolve delimitation disputes primarily through an agreement based on international law.[146] Although this obligation is mainly directed to states, Article 83 was drafted with international judicial bodies in mind, establishing their competence to employ *existing* legal rules.[147] Thus, international tribunals have applied the equidistance method in line with the existing principles of international law,[148] despite the formal regime prescribed otherwise.

It is noteworthy that the ICJ's earlier practice was incoherent and highly criticized for its unpredictable results.[149] With the increase of maritime disputes deferred to international adjudication, tribunals tried to develop clearer rules for delimitation based on existing norms.[150] Thus, they interpreted the relatively clearer equidistance principle as an expression of an equitable solution – that is, as a convenient basis for the application of equity.[151] The Court determined that equidistance is *prima facie* the appropriate method for delimitation. In addition, it reiterated the need to examine all *relevant* circumstances to achieve equitable results since they may influence the equity of the boundary line.[152]

Thus, the Court reverted to the previous method of delimitation but with a slight difference, maintaining that the "equidistance/relevant circumstances" method is the practical implementation of equity rather than an independent rule. The ICJ thus combined the two competing principles, ostensibly to clarify the vagueness of Article 83, and essentially established a new informal formula for delimitation: "equitable principles/relevant circumstances". This method involves first drawing and equidistance line, contrary to the legal regime expressed in Article 83.[153] Although the Court's justification lacked coherence,[154] it continued to apply this approach in subsequent cases, maintaining that this formula reflects customary international law.[155] Hence, the governance framework is again broader than the formal legal regime in this context.

2.1.2 Relevant circumstances

As discussed earlier, "relevant circumstances" are not part of the formal method of delimitation of the continental shelf under UNCLOS.[156] Nevertheless, the jurisprudence developed this concept as part of a "three-stage method" of delimitation aimed at achieving an equitable solution.[157] This became customary international law for international judicial bodies, contrary to the legal regime.

Arguably, the practice of international tribunals in the application of the formal rules is part of international law concerning treaty interpretation,[158] which influences the evolution of the law of the sea over time. Thus, the three-stage method could be considered part of the formal legal regime. However, the practice and reasoning of international tribunals may not be consistent enough for the interpretation to develop the law.[159] In this sense, the practice of international tribunals can be viewed as informal elements in the broader governance framework.[160]

While the term equitable solution does not prescribe a closed list of considerations, the ICJ clarified that it will consider only those that are pertinent to the continental shelf, developed in international law, and reflect "equitable principles".[161]

The Court must then identify and weigh the factors that constitute "relevant circumstances" in determining the delimitation line.

The development of the concept of relevant circumstances in the jurisprudence can be explained by examining informal considerations such as the desire for predictability[162] and the composition of the bench.[163] In addition, the governance perspective can help explain the choice of the relevant factors employed in specific cases, out of seemingly endless possibilities. The main theoretical streams in IR highlight different factors that tribunals should consider in the process of delimitation.

For example, the realist stream is likely to emphasize security and economic considerations or the balance of power between the parties, assigning greater weight to the more powerful party when determining the location of the boundary line.[164] Therefore, one can assume that the final location will be different from the provisional equidistance line determined in the first stage of the delimitation process. The institutional approach is likely to highlight the role of mathematical calculations (e.g., measuring the length of the coast or the distance from the coast), perceiving them to be more objective and less susceptible to power relations, thus promoting greater cooperation and compliance. Here, the final boundary will be much closer to the provisional equidistance line. The constructivist approach might downplay the role of relevant circumstances or the need to adjust the provisional boundary line, emphasizing that the provisional equidistance line generates greater certainty and knowledge regarding the delimitation process and is thus more likely to promote stability and mutual trust between the parties. This stream is also more inclined to consider the role of accepted social norms such as "equal distribution" in the delimitation process, which might be seen as more legitimate. Thus, scientific precision or geological factors are liable to receive less weight than other values.[165]

In practice, as described later, the decisions of international tribunals mainly reflect elements of the institutional approach and some elements of the constructivist stream, focusing mostly on geographical factors. This focus is perceived as more objective and more likely to promote predictability and stability,[166] as opposed to an approach focusing on security and economic factors. Indeed, international judicial bodies have accorded less weight to security and economic factors in determining the final boundary line.[167]

2.1.2.1 GEOGRAPHICAL FACTORS

In the context of judicial delimitation, tribunals employ mostly geographical factors as relevant circumstances. Most of these factors relate to the coast: for example, the "relevant coasts" (i.e., those whose projections overlap) and the "relevant area" (i.e., the maritime area generated by projections from the relevant coasts).[168] However, tribunals have also employed other geographical factors, such as the effect of islands,[169] and the location and direction of the land boundary terminus.[170]

Judicial bodies perceive geographical factors as significant because sovereignty over the coast (a geographical feature) is the basis of entitlement.[171] In addition, these factors are considered more equitable than others. Non-geographic considerations, such as economic factors, are perceived as diverging from the core issue of delimitation; employing these considerations is thus viewed as a discretionary decision-making process, rather than one strictly based on law.[172]

Since the continental shelf is a geological component, one might assume that geological factors are relevant for delimitation. However, contrary to state practice,[173] judicial bodies have rejected geological factors as relevant to delimitation in most cases,[174] even beyond 200 nm.[175] It seems that the conflation of entitlement and delimitation,[176] the primacy of the distance criterion, and the concept of a "single shelf"[177] all contributed to diminishing the role of geology also in the context of delimitation, despite the geological origin of the continental shelf.[178]

2.1.2.1.1 The "cut-off effect"

The "cut-off effect" is another example of the gap between the legal regime and the governance framework concerning the delimitation of the continental shelf. This geographical factor is not mentioned in the CSC or UNCLOS; rather, it was first introduced in the *North Sea Continental Shelf* case. The ICJ determined that the continental shelf, as the natural prolongation of a state's land territory, must not encroach upon or "cut off" the natural prolongation of another state.[179]

The "cut-off" effect is often treated as a factor that can lead to an inequitable result. Thus, a provisional boundary may be adjusted if its initial location cuts off a party's entitlement or affects the seaward projection of its coast.[180] In practice, this factor has influenced the location of the boundary line only in cases where the cut-off effect was significant, preventing a coastal State from extending its maritime claims as far seaward as international law permits, in a way that impedes an equitable solution.[181] In some cases, the concavity of the coast influenced the significance of the cut-off effect.[182]

This factor is another example of an informal rule developed in jurisprudence. The increased significance of the coast for delimitation and entitlement also influenced the "non-cut-off" principle because a delimitation line that "cuts off" areas belonging to other states, preventing their coasts from producing their effects, would not be an equitable solution.[183]

Despite conflicting with the core purpose of delimitation, the cut-off effect became a principle of delimitation, employed in every case of judicial dispute-settlement involving the delimitation of the continental shelf. This principle "avoids" the essence of delimitation, which entails dividing (cutting off) the continental shelf as a compromise between equal entitlements. This only makes sense if we accept that delimitation means allocating entitlements rather than the division of geographical areas between equally entitled parties.[184] Such interpretation is contrary to the legal regime, which asserts that entitlement to the continental shelf is inherent, based on geology, and does not depend on any procedural action.[185]

The ICJ rationalized the non-cut-off principle as "the negative expression of the positive principle that coastal States enjoy sovereign rights in the full extent of the continental shelf as authorized in international law".[186] This is a problematic view since sovereign rights are linked to entitlement, while the non-cut-off principle ostensibly relates to delimitation. Thus, this principle perpetuates the conflation of entitlement and delimitation vis-à-vis the continental shelf, especially since distance is not actually the basis for entitlement but a criterion for the breadth of the continental shelf.[187]

The non-cut-off principle and the jurisprudence's inclination to treat entitlement and delimitation as interchangeable concepts influenced another misguided interpretation concerning entitlement to maritime zones: the notion of "overlapping entitlements" – meaning the perception that one state's entitlement to a certain maritime zone limits another state's entitlement in the same area.[188] The concept of overlapping entitlements assumes that both parties have entitlement to the disputed continental shelf, while avoiding geological examination of the zone.[189]

This principle essentially maintains that delimitation negates or cuts off entitlement to the continental shelf rather than its seaward projection. There is no rule in international law that supports such interpretation. On the contrary, state practice and the legal regime suggest that coastal States are entitled to the maximum extent of the continental shelf allowed under international law. Thus, the entitlements of states do not "overlap"; they merely have overlapping claims in a particular area. That is, one state's entitlement does not exclude another state's entitlement in the same zone, and delimitation does not affect their respective entitlement. Rather, delimitation is a process of compromise through an agreement or judicial decision that determines how entitlements are divided.[190] States would still have entitlement to the full extent even after delimitation.

The notions of "non-cut-off" and "overlapping entitlements" are even more problematic in delimitation of the continental shelf beyond 200 nm since in this area, coastal projections (i.e., distance) are not relevant. Entitlement beyond 200 nm is based on "natural prolongation" rather than the coast.[191] The notion of "overlapping entitlements" essentially ensures that delimitation through adjudication will not include the continental shelf beyond 200 nm, even if it exists.[192]

The non-cut-off principle has no relevance for delimitation even in its original context. It is noteworthy that the *North Sea Continental Shelf* case involved unique circumstances: due to the concavity of the coast, employing the equidistance method in this situation would have "locked" Germany's maritime zones between those appertaining to Denmark and the Netherlands.[193] In other words, the equidistance line would allocate a smaller area to Germany than other methods, thus creating disparity between the maritime zones that justifies recourse to the equity principle. However, even in these unique circumstances, Germany's entitlement was not affected, only the division of the continental shelf between the three states.

Even if the unique geographical circumstances of this case might justify employing the non-cut-off principle, there is no justification for employing this principle in other situations.[194] However, despite the incoherency, judicial bodies continue to employ this principle, essentially creating "zero-sum" situations, where one state's entitlement limits the entitlement of another, contrary to the legal regime and the purpose of delimitation.[195]

2.1.2.1.2 Length of the coasts

Another often utilized geographical factor is the ratio or disparity between the length of the relevant coast and the breath of the continental shelf. This factor emphasizes the significance of the coast and its seaward projections in the process of delimitation.[196] Judicial bodies have determined that there should be a reasonable degree of proportionality between a state's continental shelf and the length of its coastline.[197]

The underlying assumption is that longer coasts generate a more substantial presence in the disputed area. Thus, the disparity between the length of the coasts might justify adjusting the provisional equidistance line, especially in cases where the line creates a negative ratio between the length of the relevant coasts – that is, when it allocates a smaller area to the party with the longer coast.[198] However, tribunals have indicated that they would employ this factor only in cases where the provisional equidistance line generates a substantially disproportionate ratio that produces inequitable results.[199] In practice, judicial bodies adjust the provisional equidistance line in favor of the party with the longer relevant coast, though this does not necessarily mean it has a broader continental shelf. While judicial bodies have emphasized that delimitation does not reflect "distributive justice" considerations, judicial bodies have sometimes adjusted the provisional line as a corrective measure in situations they perceive as inequitable.[200]

This geographical factor is an example of an informal rule developed within the governance framework that promotes the primacy of geography (distance) over geology as the governing principle of delimitation.[201] This informal rule contributed to the conflation of entitlement and delimitation. The inconsistent treatment of delimitation in the jurisprudence and the reliance on geographical circumstances increased the significance of the coast in delimitation.[202] Thus, the coast became not only a relevant circumstance in delimitation but also the basis for entitlement to the continental shelf, contrary to the legal regime.[203]

2.1.2.2 NON-GEOGRAPHICAL FACTORS

While judicial bodies usually focus on geographical circumstances when adjusting the provisional equidistance line, they are sometimes willing to consider non-geographical factors as relevant circumstances when examining the boundary line in maritime delimitation.[204] For example, tribunals have addressed claims to historic rights, especially in the context of fishing rights. "Historic rights" or "historic title" are justifications for extending maritime jurisdiction based on historic circumstances, not necessarily in accordance with existing rules of international law.[205] In the context of delimitation, "historic circumstances" may justify adjusting the provisional equidistance line when it does not produce equitable results.[206] However, the jurisprudence has set a high threshold for the application of this non-geographical factor.[207] Although judicial bodies have recognized the importance of historic circumstances, in most cases, they rejected this factor as justification for the adjustment of the provisional delimitation line.[208]

Another example of non-geographic circumstances that judicial bodies are willing to consider is economic factors, which are significant especially when delimitation disputes involve also disputes over resources.[209] However, while tribunals have addressed these considerations, they have treated them cautiously and inconsistently. In some cases, the ICJ maintained that economic considerations are not relevant for delimitation as they are unpredictable and extraneous.[210] In other cases, the Court recognized the need to consider the delimitation's effects on the parties' respective fishing activities and to ensure that the boundary line would not have catastrophic repercussions on the livelihood and economic well-being of their population.[211] Nonetheless, the *Jan Mayen* case is the only case where resource-related factors have directly influenced the location of the boundary line.[212] In most cases, judicial bodies have not considered resource-related circumstances as relevant for the adjustment of the provisional line.[213]

It seems that judicial bodies have not completely rejected the role of economic factors in delimitation but have restricted the application of these factors to cases where the provisional boundary line is inequitable and may lead to catastrophic results.[214] This judicial downplaying of the importance of economic circumstances in the context of delimitation is paradoxical because the goal of the continental shelf's legal regime is to regulate the exploration and exploitation of natural resources, and delimitation often involves disputes over natural resources.[215] This is parallel to the paradoxical decline of geological factors and principles, despite the geological origin of the continental shelf.

3. Concluding remarks

This chapter analyzes the construction and development of the legal regime for demarcating and delimiting the continental shelf, within and beyond 200 nm, from the perspective of governance theory. Each section highlights the differences between the legal regime and the governance framework.

The discussion in the first part focuses on how the governance framework downplays formal rules that are not applicable in practice, such as the "natural prolongation" principle. In contrast, it adds informal rules, such as the primacy of the "distance" principle, which are not included in the legal regime. These informal rules developed by considering actors, norms, interests, roles, and institutions outside the narrow legal regime of the continental shelf.

Informal factors can help explain the gap between the legal regime and the governance framework. For example, these factors enabled Article 76(1) to be drafted in a way that favors a particular interest-group, contrary to the position of most states. In practice, states have acted in conformity with their interests and claimed a continental shelf up to 200 nm, in accordance with judicial decisions that supported such practice. Other prominent explanations include the influence of the EEZ and the structure of judicial delimitation, which also influenced the rules concerning the extension of the continental shelf beyond 200 nm and the informal principles of delimitation.

The second part of the analysis also demonstrates how the governance perspective adds informal rules, interpretations, roles, and practices to the formal legal regime. Primarily, the governance framework has conferred greater significance to the CLCS than initially intended in the legal regime, thus making it a formal actor with broader informal powers. The legal regime established the Commission with limited competence, possibly to correspond with the formulation of Article 76(1).[216] However, the implementation of Article 76(1) has favored geographically disadvantaged states due to the primacy of the distance principle and the enhanced significance of the CLCS, reflecting the general desire to limit the claims of broad-margin states.

One explanation for the CLCS's significance is its role in delimitation processes. While the legal regime excludes the CLCS from delimitation, in practice, the Commission affects not only the location of the outer limit of the continental shelf but also delimitation. As discussed, delimitation requires knowledge about the extent of the continental shelf and whether it overlaps with other maritime zones. The extension of the continental shelf beyond 200 nm is based on the CLCS's recommendations. Therefore, it plays an essential role in delimitation, despite its limited formal competences under the legal regime. The CLCS's significance is also influenced by its high level of legitimacy, which promote coastal States' cooperation even if their short-term interests are not maximized.

The chapter also discusses how international tribunals have interpreted the formal but vaguely defined method of delimitation to take into consideration informal methods and factors. This mostly reflects the institutional approach in IR and the constructivist approach to a lesser degree.[217] Judicial bodies are formal actors whose decisions are informal elements within the broader governance framework. They add informal rules, contrary to their competence under the formal legal regime.

Annex A

Broad-margin coastal States legislation

	State	*CS legislation*	*CLCS submission*[218]	*Ref to Art. 77*
1	Argentine	The seabed and the subsoil . . . that extend beyond its territorial sea throughout the natural prolongation of its land territory **to the outer edge of the continental margin or to a distance of 200 nm . . .** where the outer edge of the continental margin does not extend up to that distance.[219]	2009	yes[220]
2	Brazil	The seabed and subsoil . . . that extend beyond its territorial sea throughout the natural prolongation of its land territory **to the outer edge of the continental margin or to a distance of 200 nm** . . . where the outer edge of the continental margin does not extend up to that distance. . . . The outer limits of the continental shelf will be established in accordance with article 76 of UNCLOS.[221]	2004	yes[222]
3	Mexico	The seabed and subsoil . . . extend beyond the territorial sea throughout the natural prolongation of national territory **to the outer edge of the continental margin or to a distance of 200 nm** . . . where the outer edge of the continental margin does not extend up to that distance.[223] In places where the outer edge of the continental margin of the continental shelf . . . does not extend 200 nm . . . the outer limit of these shelves shall coincide exactly with the outer limit of the subsoil of the exclusive economic zone.[224] **However**, the Mexican maritime zones shall not extend beyond the median line every point of which is equidistant from the nearest points on the baselines from which the breadth of the territorial sea of a neighboring state is measured, unless otherwise agreed with that state.[225]	2007/2011	–

(*Continued*)

(Continued)

	State	*CS legislation*	*CLCS submission*[218]	*Ref to Art. 77*
4	Trinidad and Tobago	The seabed and subsoil . . . that extend beyond the territorial sea throughout the natural prolongation of national territory **to the outer edge of the continental margin or to a distance of 200 nm** . . . where the outer edge of the continental margin does not extend up to that distance[226]	2009	–
5	Nicaragua	200 nm EEZ + undefined CS (natural prolongation).[227]	2013	–
6	Chile	"The exclusive jurisdiction and sovereignty over the maritime zone indicated (up to a **distance of 200 nautical miles**) also include exclusive sovereignty and jurisdiction over the soil and subsoil thereof".[228] However, "Article 76, paragraph 6 of the above-mentioned Convention stipulates that notwithstanding the provisions of paragraph 5, on submarine ridges, the outer limit of the continental shelf shall not exceed 350 nautical miles from the baselines from which the breadth of the territorial sea is measured".[229]	2020	yes
7	Ecuador	Declared a 200 nm continental shelf but also extended the zone per Article 76.[230]	2020	–
8	Costa Rica	"The State exercises complete and exclusive sovereignty over the airspace above its territory, its territorial waters for a distance of 12 miles from the low-water line along its coasts, its continental shelf and its insular sill, in accordance with the principles of international law. Furthermore, it exercises special jurisdiction over the seas adjacent to its territory for an **extent of 200 miles** from the aforesaid line, in order to protect, conserve, and utilize on an exclusive basis all natural resources and riches existing in the waters, soil and sub-soil of those zones, in conformity with the aforesaid principles".[231]	2020	–
9	Guyana	The seabed and subsoil . . . that extend beyond the limit of the territorial sea throughout the natural prolongation of the land territory of Guyana **to the outer edge of the continental margin or to a distance of 200 nm** . . . where the outer edge of the continental margin does not extend up to that distance.[232]	2011	–

	State	*CS legislation*	*CLCS submission*[218]	*Ref to Art. 77*
10	Bahamas	**CSC** formula[233]	2014	–
11	Australia	**Formula of Art. 76(1)** + the governor-general may, from time to time by proclamation, declare, not inconsistently with article 76 of the Convention or any relevant international agreement to which Australia is a party, the limits of the whole or any part of the continental shelf of Australia.[234]	2004	yes[235]
12	New Zealand	In 1977 and 1980, establish only EEZ,[236] the 1964 Act – **formula of Art. 76.**[237] In 2018, there was a CS order, defining the CS as 200 nm or the outer edge of New Zealand's continental margin, the greater of the two.[238]	2006/2012	–
13	Tonga	200 nm EEZ[239] + according to UNCLOS but the law is according to **CSC.**[240]	2009	–
14	Fiji	**CSC formula**[241]	2009	–
15	Palau	**No information, ostensibly 200 nm.**[242]	2009	–
16	Canada	The seabed and subsoil . . . that extend beyond the territorial sea of Canada throughout the natural prolongation of the land territory of Canada . . . **to the outer edge of the continental margin** . . . **to a distance of 200 nm** . . . where the outer edge of the continental margin does not extend up to that distance.[243]	2013/2019	yes[244]
17	USA	**No specific limit**[245]	–	–
18	Russia	Throughout the natural prolongation of its land territory **to the outer edge of the continental margin** . . . **the outer edge of the continental shelf is situated at a distance of 200 nm** . . . provided that the outer edge of the continental margin does not extend for a distance of more than 200 nm. If the continental margin extends for a distance of more than 200 nm, . . . the outer edge of the continental shelf coincides with the outer edge of the continental margin determined in accordance with the rules of international law[246] (before 1995 according to CSC).	2001/2013/ 2015	yes[247]
19	Denmark	1958 CSC[248] + **200 CS**[249] and EEZ[250]	2009/2010/ 2012/2014	yes[251]
20	UK	**CSC** + as defined in continental shelf orders or in accordance with agreed upon boundaries[252]	2006/2008/ 2009	–
21	Ireland	**200 nm CS**[253] – only in 2014, though in its submission, there are more details concerning the extension of the CS from 1974[254]	2005/2006/ 2009	–
22	Portugal	**Exploitation** criterion[255]	2009	yes[256]

(*Continued*)

(Continued)

	State	*CS legislation*	*CLCS submission*[218]	*Ref to Art. 77*
23	Spain	Only 200 nm EEZ[257]	2006/2009/2014	–
24	France	1958 CSC + 200 nm EEZ[258]	2006/2007/2009/2012	yes[259]
25	Iceland	The seabed and subsoil . . . that extend beyond the territorial sea throughout the natural prolongation of the land territory **to the outer edge of the continental margin or to a distance of 200 nm** . . . where the outer edge of the continental margin does not extend up to that distance.[260]	2009	yes[261]
26	Norway	the seabed and substrata outside the Norwegian territorial sea, **as far as it may be regarded as a natural prolongation of the Norwegian land territory but no less than 200 nm** . . . and not beyond the median line in relation to other states[262]	2006/2009	yes[263]
27	India	The seabed and subsoil . . . that extend beyond the limit of its territorial waters throughout the natural prolongation of its land territory **to the outer edge of the continental margin or to a distance of 200 nm** . . . where the outer edge of the continental margin does not extend up to that distance.[264]	2009	–
28	Bangladesh	The seabed and subsoil . . . adjacent . . . but beyond the limits of the territorial waters up **to the outer limits of the continental margin bordering on the ocean basin or abyssal floor**.[265]	2011	–
29	Indonesia	Establish 200 nm EEZ which seems to include the CS.[266]	2008	–
30	Malaysia	Law reflects the 1958 CSC + 200 nm EEZ.[267]	2019	–
31	Myanmar	(1977) The seabed and subsoil . . . that extend beyond the territorial sea throughout the natural prolongation of its land territory **to the outer edge of the continental margin or to a distance of 200 nm** . . . where the outer edge of the continental margin does not extend up to that distance.[268] (2017) The seabed and subsoil . . . that extends beyond the territorial sea throughout the natural prolongation of its land territory **to the outer edge of the continental margin**.[269]	2008	–

	State	*CS legislation*	*CLCS submission*[218]	*Ref to Art. 77*
32	Sri Lanka	The seabed and subsoil . . . that extend beyond the territorial sea of Sri Lanka throughout the natural prolongation of the land territory of Sri Lanka **to the outer edge of the continental margin or to a distance of 200 nm** . . . where the outer edge of the continental margin does not extend up to that distance.[270]	2009	–
33	The Philippines	200 nm EEZ[271] + **exploitation** criterion to CS.[272]	2009	–
34	Japan	200 nm CS + adjacent [extended] zone established in accordance with Art. 76.[273]	2008	–
35	China	The seabed and subsoil . . . that extend beyond its territorial sea throughout the natural prolongation of its land territory **to the outer edge of the continental margin or to a distance of 200 nm** . . . where the outer edge of the continental margin does not extend up to that distance.[274]	2012	–
36	Maldives	No CS.[275]	2010	–
37	Micronesia	No information but ostensibly 200 nm CS.[276]	2009/2013	yes[277]
38	Madagascar	The seabed and its subsoil beyond the territorial sea **to a distance of 200 nm** . . . **or to the limit determined by agreement** with adjacent States **or else to 100 nautical miles from the 2,500-meter isobaths**.[278]	2011	yes[279]
39	Côte d'Ivoire	200 nm EEZ.[280]	2009	–
40	Ghana	The seabed and subsoil . . . that extend beyond the territorial sea throughout the natural prolongation of its land territory **to a distance of 200 nm**.[281]	2009	–
41	Kenya	Its legislation includes **only the EEZ**, no reference to the CS at all, certainly not beyond 200 nm.[282]	2009	–
42	Somalia	The continental shelf of Somalia extends throughout the natural prolongation of its land territory **to the outer edge of the continental margin**.[283]	2014	–
43	Nigeria	Established 200 nm EEZ but not CS[284]	2009	–
44	Gabon	Established 200 nm EEZ but not CS[285]	2012	–
45	Namibia	According to the Convention[286]	2009	–
46	South Africa	Art. 76[287]	2009	–
47	Mozambique	The seabed and subsoil . . . that extend beyond its territorial sea throughout the natural prolongation of its land territory **to the outer edge of the continental margin or to a distance of 200 nm** . . . where the outer edge of the continental margin does not extend up to that distance.[288]	2010	–

(*Continued*)

(Continued)

	State	*CS legislation*	*CLCS submission*[218]	*Ref to Art. 77*
48	Mauritius	The seabed and subsoil . . . that extend beyond its territorial sea throughout the natural prolongation of its land territory **to the outer edge of the continental margin or to a distance of 200 nm** . . . where the outer edge of the continental margin does not extend up to that distance.[289]	2008/2009	–
49	Seychelles	The seabed and subsoil . . . that extend beyond its territorial sea throughout the natural prolongation of its land territory **to the outer edge of the continental margin or to a distance of 200 nm** . . . where the outer edge of the continental margin does not extend up to that distance.[290]	2008/2009	–
50	Tanzania	No information on CS[291]	2012	–
51	Liberia	200 nm CS[292]	2018	–
52	Pakistan	The seabed and subsoil . . . that extend beyond the limit of the territorial waters of Pakistan throughout the natural prolongation of the land territory of Pakistan **to the outer edge of the continental margin or** where the outer edge of the continental margin does not extend **up to a distance of 200 nm**.[293]	2009	–
53	Oman	Art. 76[294]	2017	ipso facto/ ab initio

Annex B

List of states making "rebuttals" to communications from other states concerning their submissions to the CLCS

	State	*Rebuttal*
1	New Zealand	1. Responded to Tonga's note communication concerning its submission. Tonga claimed that the EEZ and continental shelf overlap with those of New Zealand, while the latter claim that there is no overlap, meaning that there is a dispute. However, Tonga did not object to the Commission's review of the submission.[295] 2. Responded to Japan's claim that the submission conflicts with the Antarctic treaty.[296]
2	Norway	Responded to Spain's communication concerning its submission in the North East Atlantic and the Arctic, clarifying it position on the applicability of the Treaty concerning Spitsbergen 1920 on the submission.[297]
3	Indonesia	Responded to India's communication that maintained that under Article 83 delimitation should be settled by an agreement; thus, the submission should be without prejudice to such agreement.[298] Indonesia expressed its agreement with India's statement and reminded that there is an agreement between the states.[299]
4	Malaysia and Viet Nam in the South China Sea[300]	1. In response to China's communication, Viet Nam claimed its sovereignty over islands in the area.[301] Malaysia reiterated that submissions are without prejudice to the question of delimitation.[302] 2. In response to the Philippines's communication, Viet Nam reiterated that submissions are without prejudice to the question of delimitation.[303] Malaysia offered the Philippines to join the joint submission and referred to previous decision of the ICJ relating to the Philippines's argument concerning historic waters.[304] 3. In response to China and the Philippines's communications, Viet Nam reiterated that certain islands are part of its territory.[305]
5	Viet Nam	1. In response to China's communication, Viet Nam continued to maintain its sovereignty over islands in the area.[306] 2. In response to the Philippines's communication, Viet Nam reiterated that submissions are without prejudice to the question of delimitation and that it has sovereignty over islands in the area.[307] 3. In response to China and the Philippines's communications, Viet Nam reiterated that certain islands are part of its territory.[308]

(*Continued*)

(Continued)

	State	Rebuttal
6	Japan	1. In response to China and Korea's communications, concerning the interpretation of Article 121 by the CLCS, Japan requested the Commission not to consider China and Korea's position in this issue.[309] 2. In response to China's communication, Japan reiterated that since there is no provision governing the issue of interpretation of Article 121 by the Commission, it is not entitled to consider interpretation by individual state party.[310] 3. In response to China's communication, Japan argue that there is no dispute with China over islands and that China's arguments have no legal basis.[311] 4. In response to Korea's communication, concerning the Rules of Procedures, Japan maintain that the rules did not envision a situation where the Commission does not take action on parts of the recommendations made by the sub-commission.[312]
7	Fiji	In response to Vanuatu's communication, Fiji notified the Commission that it will submit a comprehensive response in the future.[313]
8	Argentina	In response to United Kingdom's communication, Argentina argued that the Malvinas Islands, South Georgia Islands, South Sandwich Islands, and those archipelagos and the surrounding maritime areas are an integral part of the national territory of the Argentine Republic and that, being illegally occupied by the United Kingdom, they are the subject of a sovereignty dispute between the two countries.[314]
9	Pakistan	In response to Oman's communication, Pakistan referred to potential overlap with Oman's continental shelf and that it will be resolved bilaterally. The submission is not prejudice to the potential delimitation question.[315]
10	Kenya	1. In response to Sri Lanka's communication, Kenya explained its method of determining the edge of the continental margin.[316] 2. In response to Somalia's communication, Kenya stated that it has indicated to the Commission that pending further negotiations, a mechanism will be established to finalize the maritime boundary negotiations with Somalia. Thus, the Commission decided to revert to the consideration of the submission by way of a sub-commission to be established at a future session. The parties agreed to delimit their boundaries after the Commission will issue its recommendations. Kenya raised its objection, claiming that Somalia acted unilaterally despite such agreement, and thus, the CLCS did not consider Kenya's submission.[317]
11	Palau	In response to the Philippines's communication, Palau maintains that both parties' submission does not create a dispute for the purpose of Article 76(10).[318]
12	Portugal	In response to the Spain's communication, Portugal clarified the scope of its submission and confirmed the absence of a dispute with Spain.[319]
13	Guyana	In response to Venezuela's communication, Guyana argued that there is no territorial dispute with Venezuela in accordance with the Arbitral award and the ICJ's decision.[320]

	State	*Rebuttal*
14	China	1. In response to Japan's communication, China claims that Japan's occupation and claim of sovereignty over Diaoyu Dao is illegal and invalid.[321] 2. In response to Japan's communication, China rejected Japan's argument that a state cannot extend its continental shelf beyond 200 nm when the distance between two states is less than 400 nm. Delimitation does not affect the submission, as Japan maintains.[322] 3. In response to the Philippines's communication, China maintains that there is a dispute in the South China Sea and that the Arbitral Tribunal asserted jurisdiction *ultra vires*.[323]
15	Republic of Korea	In response to Japan's communication, Korea also rejected the argument that establishing the outer limit beyond 200 nm when the distance between two states is less than 400 nm cannot be accomplished. The submission is without prejudice to delimitation, and thus, the Commission should consider its partial submission next in line.[324]
16	Nicaragua	1. In response to Colombia, Costa Rica, and Panama's communications, Nicaragua reiterated Article 76(10), referred to Costa Rica's practice, to the ICJ's decisions and that its submission does not relate to areas appertain to Panama.[325] 2. In response to Colombia's communications, Nicaragua reiterated Article 76(10) that the submission does not affect bilateral delimitation in accordance with ICJ's decisions.[326] 3. In response to Costa Rica's communications, Nicaragua reiterated its positions earlier.[327] 4. In response to Jamaica's communications, Nicaragua argues that its submission does not affect Jamaica's rights and it does not include areas appertain to Jamaica.[328] 5. In response to Panama's communications, Nicaragua reiterated its positions earlier.[329]
17	Canada/ France	During its proceedings with the Commission, Canada rejected France's submission to areas beyond the boundary decided in the 1992 Saint Pierre and Miquelon Arbitration since its prejudice to Canada's rights.[330] In response, France argued that the arbitral decision did not include a determination of the continental shelf beyond 200 nm from Saint Pierre and Miquelon because the Court of Arbitration declared that that question did not fall within its competence. The overlap between the parties constitute as an obstacle to the consideration of the Canadian submission relating to that region, although France is in favor of a mutually agreed solution.[331]
19	Spain	1. In response to Portugal's communication, Spain maintain that the area in the partial submission is not the subject of any dispute with any other coastal State or States nor does the partial submission prejudice matters relating to the delimitation of boundaries between States and that the partial submission neither prejudges nor prejudices the fixing of the outer limits of the continental shelf resulting from Portugal's submission nor the rights of third parties which may be claimed in the future. Spain communicates to the Commission its willingness to undertake, in agreement with Portugal.[332] 2. In response to Morocco's communication, Spain emphasized that the partial submission does not constitute a unilateral delimitation of its maritime areas.[333]

(*Continued*)

(Continued)

	State	*Rebuttal*
20	Bangladesh	1. In response to Myanmar's communication, Bangladesh communicated its views on the measurement of the outer limit and the role of the CLCS vis-à-vis ITLOS's decision.[334] 2. In response to India's communication, Bangladesh communicated its views on the question of "grey areas" and the role of the CLCS vis-à-vis the Arbitral Tribunal's decision.[335]
21	Micronesia	In response to Indonesia's communication, Micronesia maintains that there is no dispute with Indonesia and that the partial submission does not prejudice matters relating to the delimitation of boundaries between other states.[336]
22	Malaysia	In response to the Philippines's communication, Malaysia rejected the Philippines's claims in the area of its submission.[337]

Annex C

List of states objections to consideration of other states' submissions

	The states	*Effects of the objections*
1	US, Russia, and Japan concerning Australia's submission	On the basis of the Antarctic Treaty 1959 (not explicit opposition).[338] Based on these communications, the Commission decided not to consider the part of the submission referred to as region 2 in the executive summary of the Australian submission.[339]
2	Japan concerning New Zealand's submission	Similarity, Japan did not recognize New Zealand's submission on the Antarctic, though not explicitly objected to the submission.[340] The Commission decided that, in accordance with its rules of procedure, it was not in a position to consider and qualify those parts of the submission that are subject to dispute.[341]
3	Iceland and Denmark concerning Hatton-Rockall Area submitted by Ireland	No recommendations, no sub-commission established.[342] No sub-commission established since there was no indication of consent of all the states involved.[343]
4	Iceland and Denmark concerning Hatton-Rockall Area submitted by UK	No recommendations.[344] No sub-commission established since there was no indication of consent of all the states involved.[345]
5	UK, US, Russia, India, and Japan concerning Argentina's submission	Recommendations given.[346] The Commission decided that, in accordance with its rules of procedure, it was not in a position to consider and qualify those parts of the submission that are subject to dispute.[347]
6	Japan concerning Norway's submission	Recommendations given.[348]
7	China and Philippines concerning Malaysia/ Viet Nam	No recommendations, no sub-commission established.[349]

(*Continued*)

(Continued)

	The states	Effects of the objections
8	Somalia concerning Kenya's submission[350]	In 2014, Somalia objected to the consideration of Kenya's submission. In addition, Somalia had instituted proceedings against Kenya at the ICJ with regard to a dispute concerning maritime delimitation in the Indian Ocean. Kenya observed that the actions of the Commission would not prejudice matters relating to the delimitation of boundaries between States and that the Commission was not stopped from considering Kenya's submission; otherwise, Kenya would be prejudiced with respect to time and resources and its rights under the Convention. The Commission, in keeping with its practice, reiterated its decision to defer further consideration of the submission and the communications from Kenya and Somalia.[351] In 2015, after receiving communication from Somalia, the Commission established a sub-commission to consider Kenya's submission,[352] which means that Somalia granted its consent to the proceedings.
9	China and Philippines concerning Viet Nam's submission	No recommendations, no sub-commission established.[353]
10	Philippines concerning Palau's submission	No recommendations issued.[354] After recalling a note verbale dated 4 August 2009 from the Permanent Mission of the Philippines addressed to the Secretary-General, in which the Philippines had objected to Palau's submission of 8 May 2009, and the note verbale dated 22 July 2010, in which Palau had responded, stating that its submission areas were "submitted without prejudice to the question of delimitation", Mr. Rechebei noted that the Philippines had not filed an objection to the partial amended submission of Palau in respect of the North Area. In that connection, he noted that the objection of the Philippines to Palau's submission of 8 May 2009 could only apply to the West Area since according to Palau, there was no possible connection from the North Area to any part of the 200-mile limit of the Philippines or to any potential claim for a continental shelf of the Philippines. Therefore, he stated, there was no need to further defer the consideration of those parts of the submission, as amended, which related to the North Area. The Commission then continued its meeting in private. Addressing the modalities for the consideration of the submission and in the light of the statements by Palau in connection with the communications, the Commission decided that, as provided for in article 5 of annex II to the Convention and in rule 42 of its rules of procedure, it would proceed with the examination of the partial amended submission in respect of the North Area by way of a sub-commission to be established at a future session, taking into account the order of submissions in the queue.[355]

	The states	*Effects of the objections*
11	Argentina concerning UK's submission	No recommendations, no sub-commission established.[356]
12	UK concerning Argentina's submission[357]	Argentina asserted "its legitimate and imprescriptible sovereignty over Islas Malvinas, Georgias del Sur and Sandwich del Sur and the corresponding island and maritime areas as they are part of the national territory". The United Kingdom had sent a note verbale in this regard.[358] Consequently, the Commission decided that, in accordance with its Rules of Procedure, it was not in a position to consider and qualify those parts of the submission that were subject to dispute and was not in a position to consider and qualify the part of the submission that related to the continental shelf appurtenant to Antarctica either.[359]
13	Bangladesh to India's submission	Bangladesh objected to the consideration of the submission.[360] No recommendations made yet,[361] but a sub-commission has been established.[362]
14	Iceland concerning Denmark's submission	No recommendations, no sub-commission established.[363]
15	Japan concerning China's submission	No recommendations, no sub-commission established.[364] The Commission decided to defer further consideration of the submission and the notes verbales until such time as the submission was next in line for consideration, as queued in the order in which it was received. The Commission took the decision to take into account any further developments that might occur throughout the intervening period, during which states may wish to take advantage of the avenues available to them, including the provisional arrangements of a practical nature outlined in annex I to its rules of procedure.[365]
16	Japan concerning Korea's submission	No recommendations, no sub-commission established.[366] The Commission also took note of the views expressed in the presentation by the Republic of Korea in connection with the notes verbales. Taking into account the notes verbales and the presentation made by the delegation, the Commission decided to defer further consideration of the submission and the notes verbales until such time as the submission was next in line for consideration, as queued in the order in which it was received. The Commission took this decision to take into account any further developments that might occur throughout the intervening period, during which States may wish to take advantage of the avenues available to them, including the provisional arrangements of a practical nature outlined in annex I to its rules of procedure.[367]

(*Continued*)

(Continued)

	The states	*Effects of the objections*
17	Korea and China concerning Japan's submission	China objected to the consideration of part of the submission.[368] However, the CLCS decided to consider the full submission but maintained that it will not take action with respect to the part under dispute.[369] Korea made the same objection later on,[370] but the CLCS made its recommendations.[371]
18	Panama concerning Nicaragua's submission	No recommendations, no sub-commission established.[372] In its communication to the Commission, Panama quoting the ICJ decision in the *Nicaragua v. Colombia* case, which recognized the right of the Republic of Panama over its maritime areas and the role of third states in delimitation process and defining the "relevant areas of entitlements". In addition, Panama argued that the result of the decision (of the CLCS) resolving the maritime and territorial conflict between Nicaragua and Colombia may not compromise the law protecting Panama's maritime territorial extension, just like the decision of the Court has no binding effect on third parties.[373] Costa Rica also rejected Nicaragua's claims raised in its submission, instituting proceedings against Nicaragua before the ICJ, requesting it to determine the complete course of a single maritime boundary of the maritime areas appertaining to Costa Rica and Nicaragua.[374] The Commission decided to defer further consideration of the submission and the communications until such time as the submission was next in line for consideration in order to take into account any further developments that might occur throughout the intervening period, during which States may wish to take advantage of the avenues available to them, including the provisional arrangements of a practical nature outlined in annex I to its rules of procedure.[375]
19	Congo and Gabon concerning Angola's submission	No recommendations, no sub-commission established.[376] The Government of the Democratic Republic of the Congo requests that the Commission on the Limits of the Continental Shelf, in compliance with paragraph 5 of annex I of its rules of procedure, prohibit consideration of the submission made by the Republic of Angola before the two states have settled their border dispute.[377] The Gabonese Republic requested the Commission not to examine the part of Angola's submission that overlaps with Gabon's continental shelf.[378]
20	US concerning Bahamas's submission	The US changed its position. However, no recommendations, no sub-commission established.[379]

	The states	*Effects of the objections*
21	Canada concerning France's submission	No recommendations, no sub-commission established.[380] The area of continental shelf covered by the submission was subject to a dispute. In that regard, he recalled that the maritime boundary between France and Canada in the area had been settled by an arbitral award dated 10 June 1992, noting that, however, the Arbitral Tribunal declined to delimit the continental shelf beyond 200 nautical miles owing to a lack of competence. He also recalled the note verbale dated 2 September 2014, by which Canada had objected to the consideration of the submission by the Commission, and the note verbale dated 17 December 2014, which contained the response by France. The Commission took the decision in order to take into consideration any further developments that might occur throughout the intervening period during which States might wish to take advantage of the avenues available to them, including provisional arrangements of a practical nature, as set out in article 83, paragraph 3, of the Convention and implemented through relevant provisions of annex I to the rules of procedure.[381]
22	Yemen and Kenya concerning Somalia's submission	But changed their position. However, no recommendations, no sub-commission established.[382] Somalia elaborated on unresolved issues in relation to the bilateral delimitation of the continental shelf of Somalia with Kenya and Yemen. Somalia recalled that the case *Maritime Delimitation in the Indian Ocean (Somalia v. Kenya)* was pending before the ICJ. In addition, in its communication, dated 30 June 2015, the Government of Kenya had consented to the consideration of the submission by the Commission. Somalia expressed the view that the Commission could make recommendations concerning the outer limits of the continental shelf off the coasts of Somalia and Kenya and that consideration of the submission would not prejudice matters relating to the delimitation of boundaries between Somalia and any other state. With respect to the dispute between Somalia and Yemen, Somalia indicated that it looked forward to engaging with Yemen to reach an arrangement acceptable to both countries that would allow the Commission to consider and make recommendations on their respective submissions.[383] The Commission decided to defer further consideration of the submission and the communications until such time as the submission was next in line for consideration as queued in the order in which it had been received. At that time, the Commission will take into account any further developments that might occur throughout the intervening period, during which the States concerned might wish to take advantage of the avenues available to them, including the provisional arrangements of a practical nature as set out in article 83, paragraph 3, of the Convention and implemented through relevant provisions of annex I to the rules of procedure.[384]

(*Continued*)

(Continued)

	The states	*Effects of the objections*
23	China concerning Malaysia's submission	No recommendations, no sub-commission established.[385]
24	Bangladesh concerning Myanmar's submission	Bangladesh objected to the consideration of the submission.[386] The Commission decided to defer further consideration of the submission and not to establish a sub-commission.[387]
25	Vanuatu concerning Fiji's submission	Vanuatu objected to the consideration of the submission. The Commission decided to defer further consideration of the submission.[388]
26	India concerning Sri Lanka's submission	India objected to the consideration of the submission.[389]
27	UK and Argentina concerning Chile's submission	UK and Argentina objected to consideration on the basis of the Antarctic Treaty 1959.[390]
28	The Maldives and UK concerning Mauritius's submission	The Maldives maintained that "it does not consider it appropriate to respond to the 2022 Partial Submission", although it did not explicitly object to consideration.[391] The UK objected to the consideration of the submission.[392]

Notes

1 1982 UN Convention on the Law of the Sea, 1833 UNTS 397 (UNCLOS), Article 76(1). See also Continental Shelf (Tunisia/Libyan Arab Jamahiriya), Judgment, ICJ Reports 1982, p. 18, para. 47 and Separate Opinion of Judge Jiménez De Aréchaga, at para. 51; Continental Shelf (Libyan Arab Jamahiriya/Malta), Judgment, ICJ reports 1985, p. 13, Dissenting Opinion of Judge Oda, para. 61.

2 UNCLOS III, UN Doc A/CONF.62/C.2/L.17 (23 July 1974), para. 3; Tunisia v. Libya, *supra* note 1, Dissenting Opinion of Judge Oda, p. 157, para. 100.

3 See Chapter 1, Section 4.1.

4 The ICJ acknowledged that there is a difference between practice and the law, Libya v. Malta, *supra* note 1, para. 43 and Separate Opinion of Judge Mbaye, p. 94; Stephen Fietta and Robin Cleverly, A Practitioner's Guide to Maritime Boundary Delimitation 19–20 (2016).

5 For example, Canada's position during the negotiations, UNCLOS III, 9th Sess, 125th Plen Mtg, UN Doc A/CONF.62/SR.125 (2 April 1980), p. 8, para. 20. Canada claimed a 200 nm continental shelf but made a submission to extend the continental shelf to the CLCS several years later. See Oceans Act of 18 December 1996, DOALOS website, available at www.un.org/Depts/los/LEGISLATIONANDTREATIES/PDFFILES/CAN_1996_Act.pdf; Canada's page, DOALOS website, available at www.un.org/Depts/los/LEGISLATIONANDTREATIES/STATEFILES/CAN.htm. See also analysis in Tunisia v. Libya, *supra* note 1, Dissenting Opinion of Judge Oda p. 157, para. 101. See also domestic laws, Annex A, e.g., Argentina, Brazil, Trinidad and Tobago, Mexico, and Russia.

6 See Annex A. For example, Spain, Nicaragua, and Indonesia established a 200 nm EEZ, which seems to include the continental shelf.

7 See Annex A, e.g., Somalia, Bangladesh, and Myanmar. The latter changed its law to establish a limit up to the edge of the continental margin, replacing a law that referred to both options.

8 For example, Maritime Delimitation in the Black Sea (Romania v. Ukraine), Judgment, ICJ Reports 2009, p. 61, para. 136; UNCLOS III, 2nd Sess, 30th Plen Mtg, UN Doc A/CONF.62/SR.30 (4 July 1974), para. 38. States perceived distance as more precise criterion, allowing narrow-margin states to claim areas as continental shelf that scientifically may not be part of the continental margin, extending their jurisdiction. UNCLOS III, 9th Sess, 128th Plen Mtg, UN Doc A/CONF.62/SR.128 (3 April 1980), paras. 79, 104; Tunisia v. Libya, *supra* note 1, Separate Opinion of Judge Jiménez De Aréchaga, para. 41. However, some states objected to this position. See e.g., UNCLOS III, 9th Sess, 126th Plen Mtg, UN Doc A/CONF.62/SR.126 (2 April 1980), p. 15, para. 60; A/CONF.62/SR.128, ibid., paras. 104, 187.

9 Even for broad-margin states, see Libya v. Malta, *supra* note 1, separated opinion of Vice-President Sette-Camara, p. 69. The area up to 200 nm is also considered as the "the full" breadth, or the "normal continental shelf". For example, Maritime Delimitation in the Area between Greenland and Jan Mayen, Judgment, ICJ Reports 1993, p. 38 (The Jan Mayen case), paras. 19, 64, Dissenting Opinion of Judge Fischer, para. 9, Separated Opinion of Judge Oda, paras. 45–46, Separated Opinion of Judge Shahabuddeen, p. 135, 191. However, "natural prolongation" remains relevant beyond 200 nm, see for example ibid., Separated Opinion of Judge Shahabuddeen, p. 166.

10 Modern technology enabled utilization of vaster areas of the continental shelf and its natural resources. This influenced coastal States' interests and contributed to the development of the law of the sea, specifically the precise definition of the continental shelf. For example, UNGAOR, 25th Sess, UN Doc A/RES/2749 (XXV) (1970); UNCLOS III, 1st Sess, 1st Plen Mtg, UN Doc A/CONF.62/SR.1 (3 December 1973), para 5; L. D. M. Nelson, *The Emerging New Law of the Sea*, 42(1) Mod. L. Rev. 42, 42–43 (1979).

11 For example, the American petroleum industry contributed to the development of the legal regime by influencing US policy concerning national jurisdiction over the entire continental margin. Since petroleum resources exist not only in the continental shelf itself but also in the continental slope and margin beyond, it influenced the demand to widen the breadth of the continental shelf. See e.g., Tunisia v. Libya, *supra* note 1, Dissenting Opinion of Judge Oda, paras. 91, 95–96, 98; James K. Sebenius, Negotiating the Law of the Sea 7, 76–77 (1984).

12 For example, the International Hydrographic Organization (IHO) participated in the Conference. The IHO provided information, such as charts that assisted in defining limits and evaluating morphological factors, which was the basis for the definition of the maritime zones and their limits. See UNCLOS III, 2nd Sess, 22nd Plen Mtg, UN Doc A/CONF.62/SR.22 (28 June 1974), paras. 52–53. For the contribution of other organizations, see Final Act, UNCLOS III, Resumed 11th Sess, UN Doc A/CONF.62/121 (27 October 1982).

13 For example, the Chairman of the 2nd committee influenced the drafting of the Convention. The Chairman was a driving force that promoted bargaining and compromise while reducing some of the tensions and uncertainties in negotiations, he provided incentives to delegations to initiate compromises, and provided crucial source of momentum sufficiently to produce an agreed single text. The Chairman drafted the text that would become Article 76(1). Barry Buzan, *Negotiating by Consensus: Developments in Technique at the United Nations Conference on the Law of the Sea*, 75 Am. J. Int. Law 324, 334–335, 337 (1981).

14 For example, the fact that the CLCS established only in 1997, 3 years after UNCLOS entered into force. See UN press release, UN Doc SEA/2047 (6 March 2017);

SPLOS, 6th Mtg, UN Doc SPLOS/20 (20 March 1997). One might assume that broad-margin states would have delineated the outer limit of the continental shelf beyond 200 nm before 1997, however, in practice, these states waited to make a submission to the CLCS to extend their continental shelf. The first submission was of Russia in the Arctic Ocean in 2001, see e.g., Ted L. McDorman, *The Continental Shelf*, *in* The Oxford Handbook of the Law of the Sea 181, 194 (Donald R. Rothwell, Alex G. Oude Elferink, Karen N. Scott and Tim Stephens (eds.), 2015); CLCS, 10th Sess, UN Doc CLCS/32 (12 April 2002).

15 See also Chapter 1, sections 2.1 and 4.1.1.

16 For example, UNCLOS III, 2nd Sess, 2nd Committee, 17th Mtg, UN Doc A/CONF.62/C.2/SR.17 (26 July 1974), para. 28; UNCLOS III, 2nd Sess, 2nd Committee, 18th Mtg, UN Doc A/CONF.62/C.2/SR.18 (29 July, 1974), paras. 11, 25; UNCLOS III, UN Doc A/CONF.62/C.2/L.47 (8 August 1974), Article 22.

17 Following proposals were similar to the final text of Article 76(1), for example, informal single negotiating text, UNCLOS III, 3rd Sess, UN Doc A/CONF.62/WP.8/PART II, Article 62.

18 See for example Reynaldo Galindo Pohl, *Latin America's Influence and Role in the Third Conference on the Law of the Sea*, 7 Ocean Dev. & Int. Law 65 (1979); Shunmugam Jayakumar, *The Continental Shelf Regime under the UN Convention on the Law of the Sea: Reflections after Thirty Years*, *in* The Regulation of Continental Shelf Development, Rethinking International Standards 1 (Myron H. Nordquist, John Norton Moore, Aldo Chircop and Ronán Long (eds.), 2013). See also analysis of the different interest-groups in Surabhi Ranganathan, *Decolonization and International Law: Putting the Ocean on the Map*, 23 J. Hist. Int. Law 161, 176–177 (2021).

19 For example, UNCLOS III, 2nd Sess, 2nd Committee, 22nd Mtg, UN Doc A/CONF.62/C.2/SR.22 (31 July 1974), para. 28; UNCLOS III, 11th Sess, 159th Plen Mtg, UN Doc A/CONF.62/SR.159 (30 March 1982), para. 36. For such proposals, see e.g., UNCLOS III, 2nd Sess, 23rd Plen Mtg, UN Doc A/CONF.62/SR.23 (1 July 1974), at para. 51.

20 UNCLOS obligates coastal States to make payments to the international community in respect of resources' exploitation beyond 200 nm. UNCLOS, *supra* note 1, Article 82. See also e.g., UNCLOS III, 2nd Sess, 2nd Committee, 5th Mtg, UN Doc A/CONF.62/C.2/SR.5 (16 July 1974), at para. 3; Tommy T. B. Koh, *Negotiating a New World Order for the Sea*, 24 Va. J. Int. L. 761, 772 (1984). The focus of the analysis is the influence of Article 82 on the definition of the continental shelf, rather than the practical implementation of Article 82.

21 To facilitate coordination to reduce the costs of competitive unilateral actions, UNCLOS III adopted procedures such as the "consensus" rule and a tacit agreement to deal with all subjects as a "package". See e.g., Buzan (1981), *supra* note 13, p. 329, 331, 339; Sebenius, *supra* note 11, p. 13; Suezett V. Suarez, The Outer Limits of the Continental Shelf, Legal Aspects of Their Establishment 42 (2008). Thus, negotiations on Articles 76 and 82 conducted as a "package", balancing the rights of both interests-groups. Many states reluctantly accepted this compromise to regulate the extension of the continental shelf beyond 200 nm and to gain some benefits. See e.g., UNCLOS III, 7th Sess, 103rd Plen Mtg, UN Doc A/CONF.62/SR.103 (18 May 1978), para. 9; UNCLOS III, 9th Sess, UN Doc A/CONF.62/WS/4 (10 April 1980), para. 14; UNCLOS III, 9th Sess, UN Doc A/CONF.62/WS/6 (10 April 1980), para. 10; Libya v. Malta, *supra* note 1, Dissenting Opinion of Judge Oda, para. 57.

22 *Supra* note 16. The final formula maintained the primacy of geology (natural prolongation). See e.g., UNCLOS III, 2nd Sess, 2nd Committee, 25th Mtg, UN Doc A/CONF.62/C.2/SR.25 (5 August 1974), para. 46; UNCLOS III, UN Doc A/CONF.62/L.4 (26 July 1974), Article 19. Russia implied that other interests were at stake, that the linkage essentially imposes a unilateral point of view, and that landlocked states supported

the opposite formula for Article 76(1). For example, A/CONF.62/SR.103 *supra* note 21, para. 22; UNCLOS III, 11th Sess, 165th Plen Mtg, UN Doc A/CONF.62/SR.165 (1 April 1982), para. 3.

23 See Chapter 1, Section 4.1.1. The Conference is a social structure with specific organizing principles or "rules of the game". Alexander Wendt, *The Agent-Structure Problem in International Relations Theory*, 41(3) Int. Org. 335, 337–338 (1987); Barry Buzan, From International to World Society?: English School Theory and the Social Structure of Globalisation 165 (2004).

24 *Supra* note 22 and text connected to it.

25 UNCLOS III, 2nd Sess, 2nd Committee, 26th Mtg, UN Doc A/CONF.62/C.2/SR.26 (5 August 1974), para. 96; UNCLOS III, 5th Sess, UN Doc A/CONF.62/L.17 (16 September 1976), paras. 38–39. States did not want to reopen discussion on rules already agreed upon, for example, A/CONF.62/C.2/SR.25, *supra* note 22, para. 73; UNCLOS III, 11th Sess, 166th Plen Mtg, UN Doc A/CONF.62/SR.166 (1 April 1982), paras. 33–34, 40.

26 The General Assembly adopted resolution, creating a permanent Committee on the Peaceful Uses of the Sea-Bed and the Ocean Floor Beyond the Limits of National Jurisdiction ("Seabed Committee"), see H. Gary Knight, *Issues Before the Third United Nations Conference on the Law of the Sea*, 34 LA. L. Rev. 155, 160–161 (1974).

27 The 1st committee dealt with the Area, essentially replacing the Seabed Committee, while the 2nd committee dealt with various issues, including the continental shelf. UNCLOS III, 1st Sess, 2nd Plen Mtg, UN Doc A/CONF.62/SR.2 (7 December 1973), para. 1; Penelope Simoes Ferreira, *The Role of African States in the Development of the Law of the Sea at the Third United Nations Conference*, 7 Ocean Dev. & Int. Law 89, 123 (1979).

28 For example, UNCLOS III, 2nd Sess, 17th Plen Mtg, UN Doc A/CONF.62/SR.17 (26 June 1974), para. 4; UNCLOS III, 3rd Sess, UN Doc A/CONF.62/C.2/L.89/Rev.1 (15 July 1975), para. 2; Thomas M. Franck and Evan R. Chesler, *An International Regime for the Sea-Bed Beyond National Jurisdiction*, 13(2) Osgoode Hall L. J. 579, 580 (1975). Proposals concerning the Area essentially defined it through the limit of the continental shelf, while proposals concerning the continental shelf defined it through the baseline of the Area. For example, UNCLOS III, 2nd Sess, 2nd Committee, 16th Mtg, UN Doc A/CONF.62/C.2/SR.16 (26 July 1974), para. 4; UNCLOS III, 1st Committee, UN Doc A/CONF.62/C.1/L.3 (5 August 1974), Article 1. Some proposals in the 2nd committee were based on proposals submitted to the Seabed Committee. For example, informal working paper no. 3, submitted to the Seabed Committee, was the basis for the working paper in the 2nd committee regarding formulas for the continental shelf. For example, A/CONF.62/C.2/SR.18, *supra* note 16, paras. 16, 21, 23–25, 42; UNCLOS III, 2nd Committee, UN Doc A/CONF.62/C.2/L.86 (28 August 1974); UNCLOS III, 2nd Sess, 1st Committee, 11th Mtg, UN Doc A/CONF.62/C.1/SR.11 (6 August 1974), para. 2; UNCLOS III, UN Doc A/CONF.62/L.8/REV.1 (17 October 1974), p. 107 and p. 117, provision 68.

29 See *supra* note 28; A/CONF.62/WP.8/PART II, *supra* note 17; A/CONF.62/C.2/L.47, *supra* note 16; Franck and Chesler, *supra* note 28, p. 581–582. Some of the proposals suggested a gap between the two zones; the baseline of the Area would not begin immediately from the outer limit of the continental shelf but at a further point. See e.g., United States' proposal to the Seabed Committee, A. V. Lowe, *The International Seabed and the Single Negotiating Text*, 13 San Diego L. Rev. 489, 498, 502 (1976); Sebenius, *supra* note 11, p. 77.

30 For example, Mexico and Venezuela's proposals included geological elements such as the "lower edge of the continental margin which adjoined the abyssal plains", UNCLOS III, 2nd Sess, 1st Committee, 7th Mtg, UN Doc A/CONF.62/C.1/SR.7 (17 July 1974), paras. 11, 79.

31 For example, John R. Stevenson and Bernard H. Oxman, *The Preparations for the Law of the Sea Conference*, 68 Am. J. Int. Law 1, 18 (1974); Barbara Kwiatkowska, *Creeping Jurisdiction beyond 200 Miles in the Light of the 1982 Law of the Sea Convention and State Practice*, 22 Ocean Dev. & Int. Law 153, 154 (1991). See early proposals to "push" the international seabed further seaward, e.g., Knight, *supra* note 26, p. 166–167; F. M. Auburn, *The 1973 Conference on the Law of the Sea in the Light of Current Trends in State Seabed Practice*, 50 Can. B. Rev. 87, 92–93 (1972). In addition, the terminology during negotiations and the final text do not frame the extended area as beyond national jurisdiction, only that it is beyond 200 nm. However, some states argued, at least in the beginning, that the Area begins at 200 nm and that the International Seabed Authority (ISA)'s powers depend on the 2nd committee's decisions on the breadth of the EEZ. See *supra* note 28; UNCLOS III, 2nd Sess, 1st Committee, 10th Mtg, UN Doc A/CONF.62/C.1/SR.10 (30 July 1974), para. 24. Scholars suggest that these scenarios reflect two competing concepts; broad-margin states argued that the area beyond 200 nm is *res nullius*, while developing states argued that it is *res communis* ("common heritage of mankind"). The language of Article 76(1) implies that the area beyond 200 nm is *res nullius*. Jonathan I. Charney, *United States Interests in a Convention on the Law of the Sea: The Case for a Continued Efforts*, 11 Vand. J. Transnat'l L. 39, 54 (1978); Knight, ibid., p. 170.

32 For example, UNCLOS III, 2nd Sess, 33rd Plen Mtg, UN Doc A/CONF.62/SR.33 (9 July 1974), paras. 30–33; A/CONF.62/C.1/L.3, *supra* note 28, Article 1; Lowe, *supra* note 29, p. 512.

33 *Supra* note 25; Stevenson and Oxman (1974), *supra* note 31, p. 19.

34 North Sea Continental Shelf, Judgment, ICJ Reports 1969, p. 3, para. 23; UNCLOS, *supra* note 1, Article 76(1).

35 Delimitation of the Maritime Boundary in the Gulf of Maine Area, Judgment, ICJ reports 1984, p. 246, para. 103; Barbados v. Trinidad and Tobago, Award, case no. 2004–02, 11 April 2006, Permanent Court of Arbitration [PCA], para. 239. Some argued that "natural prolongation" was a measure for breadth rather than the basis for entitlement. Tunisia v. Libya, *supra* note 1, Separate Opinion of Judge Jiménez De Aréchaga, para. 59; Suarez, *supra* note 21, p. 139. For support for "natural prolongation" as the basis for entitlement, see Tunisia v. Libya, *supra* note 1, Dissenting Opinion of Judge Oda, para. 41. In the *North Sea Continental Shelf* cases, the Court coined the "the land dominates the sea" principle; non-submerged land is the legal basis for jurisdiction over submerged land. While this principle reflects "natural prolongation", it also emphasizes the coast, paving the way for "distance" as the governing principle. For example, Libya v. Malta, *supra* note 1, Separated opinion of Vice-President Sette-Camara, p. 63, 68; Land, Island and Maritime Frontier Dispute (El Salvador/Honduras: Nicaragua intervening), Judgment, ICJ Reports 1992, para. 420.

36 The Court use "adjacency" and "distance" interchangeably. For example, Gulf of Maine Area case, *supra* note 35, para. 104. See also states' position during the negotiations, although some maintained the need to consider geomorphological characteristics. For example, UNCLOS III, 2nd Sess, 21st Plen Mtg, UN Doc A/CONF.62/SR.21 (28 June 1974), paras. 11–12; A/CONF.62/SR.23, *supra* note 19, para. 10. However, see UNCLOS III, 3rd Sess, 3rd Committee, 19th Mtg, UN Doc A/CONF.62/C.2/SR.19 (30 July 1974), para. 26, indicating the Court's conflation between "natural prolongation" and "adjacency".

37 For example, Gulf of Maine Area case, *supra* note 35, Dissenting opinion of judge Gros, para. 11; The Jan Mayen case, *supra* note 9, Separated Opinion of Judge Shahabuddeen, p. 166. Other judges maintained that the distance principle supplemented the "natural prolongation" criterion, see Libya v. Malta, *supra* note 1, Separated opinion of Vice-President Sette-Camara, p. 68; Suarez, *supra* note 21, p. 141, 143–144.

38 Nuno Marques Antunes and Vasco Becker-Weinberg, *Entitlement to Maritime Zones and Their Delimitation: In the Doldrums of Uncertainty and Unpredictability*, *in* Maritime Boundary Delimitation: The Case Law: Is It Consistent and Predictable? 62, 68 (Alex G. Oude Elferink, Tore Henriksen and Signe Veierud Busch (eds.), 2018). The Court interpreted "natural prolongation" as only relevant for the outer limit beyond 200 nm. Libya v. Malta, *supra* note 1, Separate Opinion of Judge Mbaye, p. 98–99.

39 Judicial bodies maintained that delimitation does not reflect "distributive justice" considerations. For example, Tunisia v. Libya, *supra* note 1, para. 71; Dispute Concerning Delimitation of the Maritime Boundary between Ghana and Côte d'Ivoire in the Atlantic Ocean (Ghana/Côte d'Ivoire), Judgment, ITLOS Reports 2017, p. 4, para. 452. Judicial bodies also maintained that delimitation is not "refashioning nature", i.e., judges may not alter the factual geographical situation. See Gulf of Maine Area case, *supra* note 35, Dissenting Opinion of Judge Gros, p. 360, para. 33; Libya v. Malta, *supra* note 1, para. 46.

40 For the "objectivity" of the distance principle, see Maritime Delimitation in the Caribbean Sea and the Pacific Ocean (Costa Rica v. Nicaragua) and Land Boundary in the Northern Part of Isla Portillos (Costa Rica v. Nicaragua), Judgment, ICJ Reports 2018, p. 139, Declaration of Judge Ad Hoc Al-Khasawneh, p. 278. See "distributive justice" consideration, for example, access to resources, Gulf of Maine Area case, *supra* note 35, para. 237; or substantive disparity between the parties' coasts, Romania v. Ukraine, *supra* note 8, para. 164.

41 This might be the result of interpreting the question of entitlement in the context of delimitation rather than demarcation. Libya v. Malta, *supra* note 1, Dissenting Opinion of Judge Oda, paras. 54, 61; Fietta and Cleverly, *supra* note 4, p. 27–28. See also discussion in Section 1.1.4 later and Chapter 5, Section 1.5.

42 Libya v. Malta, *supra* note 1, para. 34 and Separated opinion of Vice-President Sette-Camara, p. 69; Suarez, *supra* note 21, p. 36; Yoshifumi Tanaka, The International Law of the Sea 163 (3rd ed., 2019).

43 UNCLOS, *supra* note 1, Articles 56–57.

44 For example, A/CONF.62/C.2/SR.22, *supra* note 19, para. 63. See earlier drafts of Article 76 referring to the limits of the continental shelf beyond the 200 nm EEZ. UNCLOS III, 8th Sess, UN Doc A/CONF.62/WP.10/REV.1 (28 April 1979), Article 76(7); UNCLOS III, 9th Sess, UN Doc A/CONF.62/WP.10/Rev.2 (11 April 1980), Article 76.

45 See examples of state practice, Libya v. Malta, *supra* note 1, para. 34; UNCLOS III, 9th Sess, 127th Plen Mtg, UN Doc A/CONF.62/SR.127 (3 April 1980), p. 28–29, para. 53. State practice influenced the Court. For example, Tunisia v. Libya, *supra* note 1, Dissenting Opinion of Judge Oda, paras. 126, 146 and Separate Opinion of Judge Jiménez De Aréchaga, paras. 54–55; The Jan Mayen case, *supra* note 9, para. 46, Separated Opinion of Judge Oda, paras. 5, 62, 70 and Separated Opinion of Judge Shahabuddeen, p. 167. In the latter, the Court adopted completely the notion that the continental shelf absorbed into the EEZ regime.

46 The Court explained that common elements of both concepts, such as the distance criterion, should be attributed greater importance. For example, Libya v. Malta, *supra* note 1, at para. 33 and Separate Opinion of Judge Mbaye, p. 94; Tunisia v. Libya, *supra* note 1, Separate Opinion of Judge Jiménez De Aréchaga, paras. 54–55, Dissenting opinion of Judge Evensen, paras. 8–9.

47 Tunisia v. Libya, *supra* note 1, Dissenting opinion of Judge Evensen, para. 10; The Jan Mayen case, *supra* note 9, Separated Opinion of Judge Oda, paras. 36–37, 72.

48 Libya v. Malta, *supra* note 1, Dissenting Opinion of Judge Oda, paras. 2–3.

49 *Supra* note 23.

50 Barry Buzan, The Logic of Anarchy: Neorealism To Structural Realism 103 (1993).

51 Judicial bodies do not conduct an independent legal study concerning legal questions; rather, their jurisdiction is constraint by the context of an existing dispute. Statute of

the International Court of Justice, San Francisco, 24 October 1945, Article 36. Buzan defines this as "structural constraints", see Buzan (1993), *supra* note 50, p. 107. In practice, tribunals deal with the breadth or outer limits of the continental shelf only in the context of delimitation disputes.

52 The constructivist approach would argue that the Court, through delimitation, constructed the *a priori* definition of the continental shelf. See e.g., Timothy Dunne, *The Social Construction of International Society*, 1(3) Eur. J. Int. Relat. 367, 371–372 (1995). For further reading on social structures, see Alexander Wendt, Social Theory of International Politics 122 (1999).

53 For example, Libya v. Malta, *supra* note 1, paras. 27, 34, and Separate Opinion of Judge Mbaye, p. 96–97.

54 Ibid., para. 68, and Dissenting Opinion of Judge Oda, paras. 8–9, 11–13, 16. See also Section 2.1.2.1 on the "relevant area".

55 Maritime Delimitation and Territorial Questions between Qatar and Bahrain, Merits, Judgment, ICJ Reports 2001, p. 40, para. 173. See for example Gulf of Maine Area case, *supra* note 35, paras. 106, 192–194, and Dissenting opinion of judge Gros, paras. 5, 15, 19; Guyana v. Suriname, Award, case no. 2004–04, 17 September 2007, Permanent Court of Arbitration [PCA], para. 334; Jonathan I. Charney, *Progress in International Maritime Boundary Delimitation Law*, 88(2) Am. J. Int. Law 227, 246 (1994). In some cases, the parties themselves asked the Court to establish a single boundary line. For example, The Jan Mayen case, *supra* note 9, para. 41. See also the *Qatar/Bahrain* case, although Bahrain did not refer to "single maritime boundary" in its submissions. Qatar v. Bahrain, ibid., para. 168, and Separate Opinion of Judge Oda, para. 12; Land and Maritime Boundary between Cameroon and Nigeria (Cameroon v. Nigeria: Equatorial Guinea intervening), Judgment, ICJ Reports 2002, p. 303, para. 286.

56 Gulf of Maine Area case, *supra* note 35, Dissenting opinion of judge Gros, paras. 6, 8, 12, 18.

57 Social cognition is a branch of social psychology that focuses on understanding the processes and structures that influence concepts and beliefs. Susan T. Fiske and Shelley E. Taylor, Social Cognition: From Brain to Culture 7–28 (3rd ed., 2017); Ziva Kunda, Social Cognition: Making Sense of People 4 (2nd ed., 2000).

58 Karen A. Cerulo, *Mining the Intersections of Cognitive Sociology and Neuroscience*, 38 Poetics 115, 125–126 (2010); Paul DiMaggio, *Culture and Cognition*, 23 Annual Review of Sociology 263, 269 (1997).

59 UNCLOS, *supra note* 1, Article 76. Article 76(4)(a) contains two formulas for the outer limit. Article 76(5)-(6) determines the maximum limit of the extended continental shelf. See e.g., Robert W. Smith and George Taft, *Legal Aspects of the Continental Shelf*, *in* Continental Shelf Limits, The Scientific and Legal Interface 17, 19–20 (Peter J. Cook and Chris M. Carleton (eds.); *Glossary of Technical Terms*, *in* Continental Shelf Limits, The Scientific and Legal Interface 321, 329 (Peter J. Cook and Chris M. Carleton (eds.), 2000).

60 This is strengthened by the fact that earlier drafts of Article 76 did not refer to the "outer continental shelf" beyond 200 nm or to conditions for extension, only to the revenue-sharing system. A/CONF.62/WP.8/PART II, *supra* note 17, Articles 62, 69; UNCLOS III, 4th Sess, UN Doc A/CONF.62/WP.8/REV.1/Part II, Articles 64, 70; UNCLOS III, 6th Sess, UN Doc A/CONF.62/WP.10 (15 July 1977), Articles 76, 82.

61 For example, the Intergovernmental Oceanographic Commission (IOC) and the IHO. See *supra* note 12; UNCLOS III, 7th Sess, 2nd Committee, UN Doc A/CONF.62/C.2/L.98 AND ADD.1–3 (18 April 1978); UNCLOS III, 8th Sess, 2nd Committee, UN Doc A/CONF.62/C.2/L.99 (9 April 1979), paras. 8–10, 13, 16.

62 For example, the chairman of the 2nd committee also had an essential role in drafting the conditions for extending the continental shelf beyond 200 nm by proposing a compromised between the competing formulas. See e.g., UNCLOS III, 8th Sess, UN Doc A/CONF.62/L.37 (26 April 1979); Bernard Oxman, *The Third United Nations*

Conference on the Law of the Sea: The Eighth Session (1979), 74 Am. J. Int. Law 1, 19–20 (1980).

63 For example, realists might support the revenue-sharing system since it allows allocating larger maritime zones to developed coastal States, maximizing their self-interests in exchange for relative lower costs. Realists would also support norms that limit the powers of the international institution governing the allocation of resources. See Knight, *supra* note 26, p. 166; Franck and Chesler, *supra* note 28, p. 583, 585. Geographically disadvantaged states' position reflects the institutional approach; supporting the revenue-sharing system due to the presence of an international institution (the ISA) that would ensure an equitable division of the resources, curb broad-margin states' claims, and promote cooperation rather than a unilateral action. For example, UNCLOS III, Resumed 11th Sess, 193rd Plen Mtg, UN Doc A/CONF.62/SR.193 (10 December 1982), para. 48; John R. Stevenson and Bernard H. Oxman, *The Third United Nations Conference on the Law of the Sea: The 1975 Geneva Session*, 69(4) Am. J. Int. Law 763, 771 (1975). As discussed, the final text of these articles reflects better the realist approach.

64 The gap between the formal legal rules and the practice could be explain through the institutional structure established in UNCLOS and specifically the work of the CLCS, which became operational 15 years after the adoption of UNCLOS and 3 years after it entered into force. *Supra* note 14; Donald R. Rothwell, *Issues and Strategies for Outer Continental Shelf Claims*, 23 Int. J. Marine Coastal L. 185, 187 (2008).

65 The scientific formulas create a complicated and expensive process to establish the outer limit. This might be the result of the drafters' intent to limit broad-margin states' claims to extensive areas. For example, *supra* notes 59 and 63; A/CONF.62/L.17, *supra* note 25, para. 38; A/CONF.62/C.2/L.99, *supra* note 61, the annexes. These formulas restrict claims through another "distance" criterion, see e.g., UNCLOS III, 6th Sess, 2nd Committee, 50th Mtg, UN Doc A/CONF.62/C.2/SR.50 (23 June 1977), paras. 6–7, 13, 21, 25, 28; A/CONF.62/SR.103 *supra* note 21, para. 21. However, geographically disadvantaged states still argued that Article 76 is not equitable.

66 Ostensibly, the CLCS's recommendations are binding. See UNCLOS, *supra* note 1, Article 76(8). However, since demarcation is a unilateral process, the accepted interpretation of the article is that the limit binds only the coastal State that made the submission. This is strengthened by Article 76(10), provided that the CLCS's conduct should be "without prejudice" to delimitation, to protect other states' rights. Thus, the term "final and binding" does not apply to other states, especially in cases of overlapping maritime zones. Alex G. Oude Elferink and Constance Johnson, *Outer Limits of the Continental Shelf and "Disputed Areas": State Practice Concerning Article 76(10) of the LOS Convention* 21(4) Int. J. Mar. Coast. L. 461, 464 (2006).

67 For example, A/CONF.62/SR.125, *supra* note 5, para. 31; UNCLOS III, Resumed 9th Sess, UN Doc A/CONF.62/WS/11 (2 October 1980), para. 10. The term "final and binding" was included in Article 76 to strengthen the CLCS's authority and its recommendations' legal status and to decrease challenges from other states. Suarez, *supra* note 21, p. 214–215.

68 For example, A/CONF.62/SR.126, *supra* note 8, para. 97; A/CONF.62/SR.127, *supra* note 45, para. 15; A/CONF.62/SR.128, *supra* note 8, para. 50.

69 According to earlier drafts, states should "take into account" the CLCS's recommendations, rather than establish limits "on the basis" of these recommendations. Some states suggested that the limit should be "in accordance" with the CLCS's recommendations, allowing coastal States to deviate from such recommendations in consultation with the Commission. A/CONF.62/WP.10/Rev.2, *supra* note 44, Article 76(8); UNCLOS III, Resumed 8th Sess, UN Doc A/CONF.62/91 (19 September 1979), p. 107. The Chairman of the committee contributed to the final text, UNCLOS III, 9th Sess, UN Doc A/CONF.62/L.51 (29 March 1980), para. 6 and p. 84; UNCLOS III, 9th Sess, UN Doc A/CONF.62/WP.10/Rev.2/Corr.2 (9 May 1980).

70 A/CONF.62/WS/4, *supra* note 21, para. 15; UNCLOS III, Resumed 9th Sess, UN Doc A/CONF.62/WS/14 (3 October 1980), para. 9.

71 A/CONF.62/SR.128, *supra* note 8, para. 64; UNCLOS III, 11th Sess, 168th Plen Mtg, UN Doc A/CONF.62/SR.168 (15 April 1982), para. 43. See also UNCLOS III, 11th Sess, 170th Plen Mtg, UN Doc A/CONF.62/SR.170 (16 April 1982), para. 6.

72 In addition, if a state makes a submission to the CLCS, but the latter cannot examine it, that state is considered to comply *prima facie* with Article 76(8) in good faith. See Alex G. Oude Elferink, *The Continental Shelf of Antarctica: Implications of the Requirement to Make a Submission to the CLCS under Article 76 of the LOS Convention*, 17(4) Int. J. Marine Coastal L. 485, 498, 515 (2002); Suarez, *supra* note 21, p. 212–213.

73 Some argue that non-parties cannot participate in the CLCS's proceeding. This is based on the link between submissions to the CLCS and UNCLOS's ratification, which indicates that non-parties cannot make a submission. UNCLOS, *supra note* 1, Annex II, Article 4. Some argue that non-parties cannot invoke Article 76's benefits since not all the article is customary law. A/CONF.62/SR.193, *supra* note 63, para. 48; Ted L. McDorman, *The Role of the Commission on the Limits of the Continental Shelf: A Technical Body in a Political World,* 17(3) Int. J. Mar. Coast. L. 301, 303 (2002). In practice, non-parties participate in the CLCS's proceedings, communicating with it and the UN Secretary-General. For example, although the United States is not a party to UNCLOS, it perceives Article 76 as customary law, including provisions concerning the continental shelf beyond 200 nm and the CLCS. The United States made communications in response to Russia's submission in the Arctic Ocean. See e.g., Ted L. McDorman, *The Continental Shelf beyond 200 nm: Law and Politics in the Arctic Ocean*, 18(2) J. Transnat'l Law & Pol. 155, 164 (2009).

74 Anna Cavnar, *Accountability and the Commission on the Limits of the Continental Shelf: Deciding Who Owns the Ocean Floor* 42(3) Cornell Int. l. J. 387, 403–404 (2009); Suarez, *supra* note 21, p. 122. There was a debate concerning the CLCS's competence to interpret UNCLOS or seek legal advice on such matters. Some states argued that legal certainty is necessary for the CLCS to function properly. Others maintained that it should refrain from examining or seeking advice on legal matters. Yet the general notion is that the CLCS has competence to interpret Article 76. CLCS, 28th Sess, UN Doc CLCS/72 (16 September 2011), para. 39; CLCS, 29th Sess, UN Doc CLCS/74 (30 April 2012), para. 52. However, the CLCS generally tend to avoid such questions, see e.g., CLCS, 23rd Sess, UN Doc CLCS/62 (20 April 2009), paras. 54, 59.

75 For example, the CLCS interprets what constitute as dispute or if relevant states have given their consent to the proceedings. See detailed discussion in Section 1.2.2.2. For the CLCS's competence to create ROP, see Signe Veierud Busch, *More Disputes ahead for the CLCS? CLCS Practice on Rule 46 of its Rules of Procedure*, *in* New Knowledge and Changing Circumstances in the Law of the Sea 232, 234 (Tomas Heidar (ed.), 2020).

76 For example, the CLCS interpreted the ROP to determine whether the choice of two or more states to make a joint submission concerning a disputed area is procedural in nature. This is important since if it is procedural issue, it does not affect their rights under Article 76. In some cases, an issue that the CLCS presented as a procedural issue was a substantial question that affected coastal States' rights. For example, The CLCS concluded that the total area of continental shelf in a joint submission could not be larger than the sum of the individual areas if each state would have made separate submission. The CLCS presented this as a procedural issue, while in practice, it affects coastal States' rights. CLCS, 20th Sess, UN Doc CLCS/56 (4 October 2007), paras. 27–28.

77 For example, referring to "ordinary reading" (i.e., meaning) like the rules concerning treaty interpretation. CLCS, 31st Sess, UN Doc CLCS/78 (1 April 2013), paras. 52–53.

78 The CLCS's guidelines essentially establish a review process for submissions. See Suarez, *supra* note 21, p. 131; Rothwell, *supra* note 64, p. 188.

79 While there is no enforcement mechanism or compelling obligation for states to accept the CLCS's recommendations, there is an expectation that coastal States at least determine the outer limit based on the Commission's work. *Supra* notes 66 and 72; Rothwell, *supra* note 64, p. 188.

80 A policy of following rules or principles laid down in previous judicial decisions. See "Stare decisis", Merriam-Webster dictionary, available at www.merriam-webster.com/dictionary/stare%20decisis. See also Chapter 1, Section 4.1.2.

81 *Supra* note 77; SPLOS, 18th Mtg, UN Doc SPLOS/184 (21 July 2008), para. 95. Some members maintained that the interpretation of the guidelines should be in accordance with past practices. Under UNCLOS Article 76(10), the CLCS's recommendations are without prejudice to dispute-settlement. See Section 1.2.2.2 later.

82 Joint Submission by the French Republic and the Republic of South Africa: General Principles of Natural Prolongation, DOALOS website, available at www.un.org/Depts/los/clcs_new/submissions_files/frazaf34_09/frazaf_clcs34_2018.pdf.

83 Note Verbale no. 08/11, 11 January 2011, DOALOS website, available at www.un.org/Depts/los/clcs_new/submissions_files/gbr08/gbr_nv_11jan2011.pdf.

84 Note Verbale no. 08/11, ibid., last paragraph in the first page.

85 Cook Islands' Note Verbale no. 108/2016–17, 30 November 2016, DOALOS website, available at www.un.org/Depts/los/clcs_new/submissions_files/cok23_09/2016_11_30_COK_NV_UN_037_16-00919.pdf.

86 According to the CLCS's ROP, presentations can include technical information such as charts; the provisions of Article 76 which were applied; information regarding the location of the foot of the continental slope; and information regarding any disputes related to the submission. Presentations can also address communications from other states regarding the submission. The term "any disputes related to the submission" refers to disputes between states, not disputes with the Commission itself. See Rules of Procedure of the Commission on the Limits of the Continental Shelf, CLCS, 21st Sess, UN Doc CLCS/40/Rev.1 (17 April 2008), Rule 46, Annex III, Section II, para. 2(a), Annex III, Section III, para. 7.

87 Note Verbale no. 270/2017, 13 September 2017, DOALOS website, available at www.un.org/Depts/los/clcs_new/submissions_files/zaf31_09/2017_09_14_zaf_nv_un_030_17_00683.pdf.

88 Ibid., p. 2.

89 Ibid.

90 For example, Suarez, *supra* note 21, p. 202; Signe Veierud Busch, Establishing Continental Shelf Limits Beyond 200 Nautical Miles By The Coastal State 99, 113–114 (2016). See also Section 1.2.2.1 later.

91 Ron Macnab, *Third-Party Reactions to Continental Shelf Submissions, and their Treatment by the CLCS*, Law of the Sea Conference, Trinity College Dublin 1, 17 (2010); Annex B concerning list of "rebuttals".

92 For example, China and Korea's rebuttals to Japan's communications, See annex B.

93 See Annex B. For example, Japan's response to China's communication, Portugal's rebuttal, and Micronesia's rebuttal. Some rebuttals referred to sovereignty disputes, e.g., Argentina and China's rebuttals.

94 The CLCS's ROP, *supra* note 86, rule 46 and Annex I, paragraph 5(a). It is noteworthy that UNCLOS's provisions referred to *delimitation* disputes, while the CLCS's ROP included also other types of disputes. Thus, the CLCS broadened the scope of Article 76(10). Busch (2020), *supra* note 75, p. 235.

95 Suarez, *supra* note 21, p. 202; Busch (2016), *supra* note 90, p. 96, 98–99.

96 CLCS, 3rd Sess, UN Doc CLCS/7 (15 May 1998), para. 5.

97 Clive R. Symmons, *The Irish Partial Submission to the Commission on the Limits of the Continental Shelf in 2005: A Precedent for Future Such Submissions in the Light of*

the "Disputed Areas" Procedures of the Commission?, 37 Ocean Dev. & Int. Law 299, 300–301 (2006); Busch (2020), *supra* note 75, p. 235.

98 See earlier discussion on other states' reactions to submissions. Other states' communications become an element in the CLCS's considerations, especially their position on the existence of a dispute or consent to the CLCS's proceedings. Rothwell, *supra* note 64, p. 190–191; Busch (2016), *supra* note 90, p. 100–101, 112. The previous version of the ROP allowed other states to submit communications even if there is no dispute between the relevant states. Thus, e.g., the CLCS considered communication concerning the Russian submission from states that did not have a direct dispute with Russia in that area. CLCS/32, *supra* note 14, paras. 14–18; Busch, ibid., p. 102. The ROP was amended so the CLCS considers other states' communications only in cases of existing disputes. Thus, the CLCS did not consider a letter from the United States concerning Brazil's submission. CLCS, 14th Sess, UN Doc CLCS/42 (14 September 2004), para. 17.

99 Oude Elferink, *supra* note 72, p. 502.

100 CLCS, 24th Sess, UN Doc CLCS/64 (1 October 2009), paras. 37, 39; Bangladesh's Note Verbale no. PMBNY-UNCLOS/2009, available at www.un.org/Depts/los/clcs_new/submissions_files/mmr08/clcs16_2008_mmr_bgd_e.pdf; CLCS/78, *supra* note 77, para. 47.

101 Busch (2016), *supra* note 90, p. 114.

102 Macnab, *supra* note 91, p. 17. For example, France, Suriname and Guyana *consented* to the proceedings concerning Barbados' submission, CLCS, 22nd Sess, UN Doc CLCS/60 (26 September 2008), at para. 25. See also "non-objections" to the proceedings concerning Suriname's submission, CLCS/64, *supra* note 100, para. 33.

103 See discussion further later in this section.

104 Some argue that "non-objection" can be regarded as an implied consent, which should be sufficient for the CLCS to consider a submission, see Busch (2016), *supra* note 90, p. 113–114.

105 Some states made a general statement, reiterating the text of Article 76(10). See e.g., Canada's reaction to Russia's submission concerning the Arctic Ocean. Canada stated that its lack of comment should not be interpreted as agreement or acquiescence to the Russian submission. However, Canada did not explicitly object to the consideration of Russia's submission. See Canada's notification to the CLCS, DOALOS website, available at www.un.org/Depts/los/clcs_new/submissions_files/rus01/CLCS_01_2001_LOS__CANtext.pdf.

106 *Supra* note 104. For example, Vanuatu disputed France's sovereign claim over Matthew and Hunter Islands but did not explicitly object to the CLCS's consideration of France's submission, see Vanuatu's Note Verbale, DOALOS website, available at www.un.org/Depts/los/clcs_new/submissions_files/fra07/van_0701306.pdf. The CLCS interpreted Vanuatu's position as objection. CLCS/56, *supra* note 76, para. 40.

107 Busch (2016), *supra* note 90, p. 105. See also *supra* notes 97 and 98.

108 Macnab, *supra* note 91, p. 17. See also Annex C concerning the list of objections. In most cases, the lack of consent was due to the existence of potential *delimitation* disputes. Some states argued that the CLCS should prohibit proceedings before states have settled their disputes. See Congo's position concerning Angola's submission, the Government of the Democratic Republic of the Congo's Note Verbale, DOALOS website, available at www.un.org/Depts/los/clcs_new/submissions_files/ago69_2013/1430662E.pdf and at www.un.org/Depts/los/clcs_new/submissions_files/ago69_2013/cod_re_ago_oct_2015e.pdf. Some objections concerned sovereignty claims in the disputed area. See United Kingdom's communication concerning Argentina's submission, Annex C, no. 12.

109 In most cases, the CLCS did not establish a sub-commission nor issued recommendations. See Annex C. However, see proceedings concerning India and Japan's submissions. Annex, no. 13 and 17.

110 For example, the backlog in the CLCS's work. See e.g., Bahamas's submission; even though the United States changed its position and consented, no sub-commission was established. See Annex C, no. 20. Only in few cases, postponement of proceedings was explicitly caused by lack of consent, see Annex C, e.g., Iceland and Denmark's objections to Ireland's submission concerning Hatton-Rockall Area, no. 3; China's submission, no. 15.

111 Only parts of Australia's submission were considered due to other states' objections. See Annex C, no. 1. See also e.g., New Zealand and Argentina's submissions, Annex C, no. 2, 5.

112 For example, Costa Rica instituted proceedings in the ICJ against Nicaragua, see Annex C, no. 18; Costa Rica v. Nicaragua (2018), *supra* note 40. In addition, Somalia instituted proceedings in the ICJ against Kenya, see Kenya's submission Annex C, no. 8 and 22; Maritime Delimitation in the Indian Ocean (Somalia V. Kenya), Application, Instituting Proceedings, ICJ (28 August 2014).

113 For example, in 2014 Somalia objected to the consideration of Kenya's submission. Somalia had instituted proceedings against Kenya at the ICJ. Annex C, no. 8; Somalia V. Kenya (2014), *supra* note 112. Despite the ongoing judicial proceedings, in 2015, both parties consented to the CLCS's proceeding concerning the other's submission. The Commission established a sub-commission to consider Kenya's submission. Thus, states' objections or consent influenced the Commission rather than judicial proceedings. See Annex C, no. 8 and 22. However, Nicaragua's submission might have been postponed partially due to the ICJ's proceedings, although it is hard to determine what influenced the Commission more, the ICJ or third parties' objections. See Maritime Delimitation in the Caribbean Sea and the Pacific Ocean (Costa Rica v. Nicaragua), Application instituting proceedings, ICJ 2014; Colombia, Costa Rica and Panama objections, Note Verbale, available at www.un.org/Depts/los/clcs_new/submissions_files/nic66_13/col_cri_pan_re_nic_2014_02_05_e.pdf; CLCS, 34th Sess, UN Doc CLCS/83 (31 March 2014), para. 83.

114 See e.g., France and Somalia's submissions, Annex C, no. 21, 22. See discussion on Article 83(3) in Chapter 3.

115 Although some judges, in the context of judicial dispute-settlement, argued that the Commission's proceedings are neither adjudicative nor adversarial. Dispute concerning delimitation of the maritime boundary between Bangladesh and Myanmar in the Bay of Bengal (Bangladesh/Myanmar), Judgment, ITLOS Reports 2012, p. 4, Joint Declaration of Judges *Ad Hoc* Mensah and Oxman, p. 147. See also Section 1.2.3.

116 For example, submission made by Mauritius concerning the southern Chagos Archipelago region. Chagos's representative recalled the ICJ's advisory opinion concerning the status Chagos Archipelago, elaborating in detail on Mauritius's views on the implications of the advisory opinion for the Commission. CLCS, 50th Sess, UN Doc CLCS/50/2 (5 September 2019), para. 66. Another example is Côte d'Ivoire's submission, where the sub-commission referred to ITLOS's decision, which led the sub-commission to declare that its conclusions regarding the test of appurtenance would need to be reexamined, based on that decision. CLCS, 45th Sess, UN Doc CLCS/101 (15 December 2017), para. 30.

117 In the 1992 *Canada-France* Arbitration, the Tribunal abstained from delimitation beyond 200 nm, noting that without a CLCS recommendation or agreement between the parties, entitlements beyond 200 nm were merely hypothetical. See Giovanny Vega-Barbosa, *The Admissibility of Outer Continental Shelf Delimitation Claims Before the ICJ Absent a Recommendation by the CLCS*, 49(2) Ocean Dev. & Int. Law 103, 105 (2018). Although, it is noteworthy that this decision was prior to the CLCS's establishment in 1997, see *supra* note 14.

118 Territorial and Maritime Dispute between Nicaragua and Honduras in the Caribbean Sea (Nicaragua v. Honduras), Judgment, ICJ Reports 2007, p. 659, para. 319. The ICJ

reaffirmed this observation in the *2012 Nicaragua/Colombia* Case, where it rejected Nicaragua's claim beyond 200 nm since it only submitted "preliminary information" to the CLCS, falling short of a formal submission. Since Nicaragua failed to prove that its continental shelf extends beyond 200 nm, it could not delimit the boundary in the area. For example, Territorial and Maritime Dispute (Nicaragua v. Colombia), Judgment, ICJ Reports 2012, p. 624, paras. 126–129; Jianjun Gao, *The Delimitation Method for the Continental Shelf Beyond 200 Nautical Miles: A Reflection on the Judicial and Arbitral Decisions*, 51(2) Ocean Dev. Int. & Law 116, 117–118 (2020).

119 However, this might not apply if one party is not a party to UNCLOS, see Nicaragua v. Colombia (2012), *supra* note 118, Declaration of Judge Ad Hoc Mensah, paras. 3, 6. This opinion establishes a dangerous precedent where a state that is not a party to UNCLOS has no guidance on establishing the outer limit if its continental shelf extends beyond 200 nm, especially since non-parties do engage with the Commission. *Supra* note 73; Signe Veierud Busch, *The Delimitation of the Continental Shelf beyond 200 nm: Procedural Issues, in* Maritime Boundary Delimitation: The Case Law: Is It Consistent and Predictable? 319, 338 (Alex G. Oude Elferink, Tore Henriksen and Signe Veierud Busch (eds.), 2018); Vega-Barbosa, *supra* note 117, p. 108.

120 Bangladesh v. Myanmar, *supra* note 115, Separate Opinion of Judge Tafsir M. Ndiaye, paras. 60–61, 87.

121 The Arbitral Tribunal argued that when the CLCS does not exercise its functions, in cases of disputes, for example, the outer limits of the continental shelf of the parties would remain unresolved and they will not be able to exercise their rights fully. See Bay of Bengal Maritime Boundary Arbitration between Bangladesh and India, Award, case no. 2010–16, 07 July 2014, Permanent Court of Arbitration [PCA], para. 82; Helmut Tuerk, *Questions Relating to the Continental Shelf Beyond 200 Nautical Miles: Delimitation, Delineation, and Revenue Sharing*, 97 Int. Law Stud. 232, 240–241 (2021). See also the ICJ's position in the *Indian Ocean* case that delimitation should be in "appropriate circumstances", *infra* note 130.

122 *Supra* note 118.

123 Question of the Delimitation of the Continental Shelf between Nicaragua and Colombia beyond 200 Nautical Miles from the Nicaraguan Coast (Nicaragua v. Colombia), Preliminary Objections, Judgment, ICJ Reports 2016, p. 100, paras. 112, 114. However, see individual judges' position on the contribution of the CLCS, ibid., Declaration of Judge Gaja, p. 202 and Declaration of Judge Bhandari, p. 204.

124 Nicaragua v. Colombia (2016), *supra* note 123, Joint Dissenting Opinion of Vice-President Yusuf, Judges Cançado Trindade, Xue, Gaja, Bhandari, Robinson and Judge Ad Hoc Brower, p. 154 and paras. 49, 58.

125 Nicaragua v. Colombia (2016), ibid., paras. 112, 114.

126 Ibid., paras. 85, 105, 114.

127 ITLOS reiterated the distinction between demarcation and delimitation, arguing that a decision on delimitation does not infringes on the CLCS's exercise of functions or exclude it from considering a submission and issuing recommendations. See Bangladesh v. Myanmar, *supra* note 115, paras. 363, 370, 374–377, 379, 393; Ghana v. Côte d'Ivoire (2017), *supra* note 39, paras. 494–495.

128 For example, the Tribunal implied that delimitation requires a proof of entitlement to a continental shelf beyond 200 nm, which confers significance to the CLCS. Ghana v. Côte d'Ivoire (2017), *supra* note 39, para. 491; Edwin E. Egede and Lawrence Apaalse, *Dispute Concerning Delimitation of the Maritime Boundary between Ghana and Cote D'Ivoire in the Atlantic Ocean – Lessons from Another Maritime Delimitation Case Arising from the African Region*, 29 Ind. Int. & Comp. L. Rev. 55, 85 (2019).

129 In the *Bay of Bengal* cases, there was information on the continental margin since both Parties made submissions to the CLCS, while in the ICJ's *Nicaragua/Colombia* cases, there was no such information, although the Court did not employ this reasoning. See Vega-Barbosa, *supra* note 117, p. 107–109, 110.

130 In the *Indian Ocean* case, the Court clarified that the CLCS's recommendations would not be prerequisite in every case. In some "appropriate circumstances", scientific uncertainty regarding the outer limits beyond 200 nm would not necessarily prevent the Court from proceeding with delimitation before the CLCS has made its recommendations, although the Court did not specify what would constitute such circumstances. Maritime Delimitation in the Indian Ocean (Somalia v. Kenya), Preliminary Objections, Judgment, ICJ Reports 2017, p. 3, para. 94; Vega-Barbosa, *supra* note 117, p. 111.

131 *Supra* note 130. However, in the *Somalia/Kenya* case, there were doubts whether the Court had enough information on the outer limits beyond 200 nm, see Maritime Delimitation in the Indian Ocean (Somalia v. Kenya), Judgment, ICJ Reports 2021, p. 206, Separate opinion of President Donoghue, paras. 4, 8.

132 Vega-Barbosa, *supra* note 117, p. 111.

133 ITLOS noted that since the question of the parties' entitlement to a continental shelf beyond 200 nm in the Bay of Bengal raised legal questions, it could and should determine the entitlements of the parties. Although in this case, the parties agreed that both had entitlement in the area. Bangladesh v. Myanmar, *supra* note 115, paras. 397–398, 409–410, 413; Øystein Jensen, *The Delimitation of the Continental Shelf beyond 200 nm: Substantive Issues, in* Maritime Boundary Delimitation: The Case Law: Is It Consistent and Predictable? 351, 354–355 (Alex G. Oude Elferink, Tore Henriksen and Signe Veierud Busch (eds.), 2018).

134 The continental shelf is an inherent right of coastal States. See North Sea continental shelf, *supra* note 34, paras. 19, 39. The legal basis for entitlement to the continental shelf is that it is the submerged continuity of the land mass (i.e., "natural prolongation"). Since entitlement stems from a preexisting *geological* feature, it does not depend on any action. UNCLOS, *supra* note 1, Article 77(3).

135 UNCLOS, *supra* note 1, Article 76. While there is no law that excludes judicial bodies from determining the endpoint beyond 200 nm, there is also no rule that grants them such competence.

136 See Section 1.1.4 earlier.

137 UNCLOS, *supra note* 1, Article 83(1).

138 During UNCLOS III, some states criticized the "equidistance" method as being too rigid. Since states could not agree on the text, the president suggested removing all reference to equidistance, leaving only the goal of achieving "equitable solution", which states accepted as suitable compromise. While the final formula avoided any controversial term, it lacked substantive content. See for example Malcolm D. Evans, *Maritime Boundary Delimitation, in* The Oxford Handbook of the Law of the Sea 254, 258 (Donald R. Rothwell, Alex G. Oude Elferink, Karen N. Scott and Tim Stephens (eds.), 2015); Massimo Lando, Maritime Delimitation as a Judicial Process 15–17 (2019).19).

139 The Chairman of negotiation group 7 in constructing the formal method of delimitation, UNCLOS III, Resumed 9th Sess, 130th Plen Mtg, UN Doc A/CONF.62/SR.130 (28 July 1980), paras. 59–60.

140 See discussion in Chapter 1, Section 4.1.2.

141 These competing methods also reflected in state practice (i.e., bilateral agreements). UNCLOS III, 8th Sess, 2nd Committee, 57th Mtg, UN Doc A/CONF.62/C.2/SR.57 (24 April 1979), at para. 27; Gerard J. Tanja, The Legal Determination of International Maritime Boundaries xix, 28, 151–153, 296–297 (1990); *Glossary of Technical Terms, supra* note 59, p. 326.

142 UNCLOS III, Resumed 9th Sess, 138th Plen Mtg, UN Doc A/CONF.62/SR.138 (26 August 1980), para. 138.

143 UNCLOS III, Resumed 9th Sess, 135th Plen Mtg, UN Doc A/CONF.62/SR.135 (25 August 1980), para. 79. See other proposals in UNCLOS official records, Platzoder, vol. IX 393–396 (1986). Some geographically disadvantaged states supported

the "equity" principle, claiming that geographical factors were not the only considerations, even though "equidistance" might accord those states wider areas. See for example UNCLOS III, Resumed 9th Sess, 140th Plen Mtg, UN Doc A/CONF.62/SR.140 (27 August 1980), at para. 30.

144 UNCLOS III, 9th Sess, UN Doc A/CONF.62/L.47 (24 March 1980), p. 78; A/CONF.62/SR.126, *supra* note 8, para. 48.

145 States recognized that there are cases where employing the median line would be inequitable, see A/CONF.62/SR.138, *supra* note 142, para. 6; UNCLOS III, Resumed 9th Sess, 139th Plen Mtg, UN Doc A/CONF.62/SR.139 (27 August 1980), at para. 171. For many states, "equity" became the "the general rule in international law in delimitation matters", see A/CONF.62/SR.138, ibid., para. 73.

146 UNCLOS, *supra* note 1, Article 83(1); Tunisia v. Libya, *supra* note 1, Dissenting Opinion of Judge Oda, p. 240 and para. 144.

147 See e.g., A/CONF.62/L.47, *supra* note 144, para. 4; A/CONF.62/SR.127, *supra* note 45, paras. 37, 74. It seems that "equity" meant to replace dispute-settlement mechanisms, employing existing legal norms and principles in accordance with Article 38 of the ICJ's Statute. See *supra* note 146; A/CONF.62/WP.8/REV.1/Part II, *supra* note 60, introductory note, para. 12; Bernard H. Oxman, *The Third United Nations Conference on the Law of the Sea: The 1976 New York Sessions*, 71(2) Am. J. Int. Law 247, 267 (1977).

148 Reference to existing legal norms essentially means that the interpretation of the term "equitable solution" relies on the CSC, see Gulf of Maine Area case, *supra* note 35, para. 106; Libya v. Malta, *supra* note 1, Dissenting opinion of Judge Mosler, p. 120, part VI. However, the CSC contains the "equidistance/*special* circumstances" formula, as opposed to "equitable principles/*relevant* circumstances". See 1958 Geneva Convention on the Continental Shelf, 499 UNTS 311 (CSC), Article 6; North Sea continental shelf, *supra* note 34, paras. 69, 101(c)(1). While the latter formula is broader, in practice, they are the same. See the Jan Mayen case, *supra* note 9, Separate Opinion of Judge Shahabuddeen, p. 147, 151; Malcolm Evans, *Relevant Circumstances*, *in* Maritime Boundary Delimitation: The Case Law: Is It Consistent and Predictable? 222, 226, 228 (Alex G. Oude Elferink, Tore Henriksen and Signe Veierud Busch (eds.), 2018).

149 Since UNCLOS was not yet in force, the Court analyzed the term "equitable solution" in light of the CSC. However, it did not employ the "equidistance" method in either the *Tunisia/Libya* or the *Gulf of Maine* cases, despite it being the applicable norm at the time. In the *Tunisia/Libya* case, the Court seems to decide based on "relevant circumstances" rather than "special circumstances", disregarding relevant geographical factors. This seems closer to an *ex aequo et bono* decision-making process, rather than a process based on international law. For example, Libya v. Malta, *supra* note 1, Dissenting opinion of Judge Oda, p. 123, p. 140; The Jan Mayen case, *supra* note 9, Separated Opinion of Judge Ajibola, p. 297; David A. Colson, *The Delimitation of the Outer Continental Shelf between Neighboring States* 97(1) Am. J. Int. Law 91, 100–101 (2003).

150 The ICJ clarified that "equity" should be implemented according to the rule of law to achieve consistency and predictability. See e.g., Colson, *supra* note 149, p. 99–100; Lando (2019), *supra* note 138, p. 19–20.

151 Tunisia v. Libya, *supra* note 1, Dissenting Opinion of Judge Evensen, p. 292, 294, and Dissenting Opinion of Judge Oda, para. 165; Gulf of Maine Area case, *supra* note 35, Dissenting Opinion of Judge Gros, para. 10. See also the Jan Mayen case, *supra* note 9, Separated Opinion of Judge Ajibola, p. 295.

152 Libya v. Malta, *supra* note 1, para. 65 and Dissenting opinion of Judge Oda, paras. 64–65. Although, some argue that in this case, the Court began by drawing a median line, without giving a reason. See ibid., Dissenting Opinion of Judge Schwebel, p. 178–179.

153 The Jan Mayen case, *supra* note 9, Separate Opinion of Judge Schwebel, p. 128, and Dissenting Opinion of Judge Fischer, para. 5; Cameroon v. Nigeria, *supra* note 55, para. 288, and Separate Opinion of Judge Mbaye, para. 132. This approach also reflects in states' positions during UNCLOS III, e.g., NG7/2, UNCLOS official records, Platzoder, vol. IX 399 (1986); A/CONF.62/SR.135, *supra* note 143, para. 51.

154 In some cases, the Court relied on similarity to the equidistance/*special* circumstances method in UNCLOS Article 15 regarding the territorial sea, as it set the baseline from which the continental shelf is measured. In other cases, the relationship between continental shelf and EEZ and the notion of "single delimitation line" influenced the employment of the equidistance method. See Davor Vidas, *The Delimitation of the Territorial Sea, the Continental Shelf, and the EEZ: A Comparative Perspective*, *in* Maritime Boundary Delimitation: The Case Law: Is It Consistent and Predictable? 33 (Alex G. Oude Elferink, Tore Henriksen and Signe Veierud Busch (eds.), 2018); Evans (2018), *supra* note 148. See discussion on "single delimitation line" in Section 1.1.4.

155 Qatar v. Bahrain (2001), *supra* note 55, para. 230; however, see the critique in the Separated Opinion of Judge Oda, p. 127, 133; Cameroon v. Nigeria, *supra* note 55, para. 290.

156 In fact, many states opposed this notion since it is very vague, for example, A/CONF.62/SR.135, *supra* note 143, para. 17; UNCLOS III, Resumed 9th Sess, 136th Plen Mtg, UN Doc A/CONF.62/SR.136 (26 August 1980), para. 96.

157 See also Mark B. Feldman, Sang-myon Rhee, Jonathan I. Charney and Ted L. Stein, *ICJ Decision in the Libya-Tunisia Continental Shelf Case*, 76 Proceedings of the Asil Annual Meeting 150, 151–153 (1982). For the three-stage method see Chapter 1, Section 4.1.2.

158 See 1969 Vienna Convention on the Law of Treaties, 1155 UNTS 331 (VCLT), Article 31(3)

159 See *supra* notes 149 and 154.

160 See Chapter 1, Section 4.1.2

161 See Section 2.1.1. See also Libya v. Malta, *supra* note 1, paras. 48, 62, 73; The Jan Mayen case, *supra* note 9, Dissenting Opinion of Judge Fischer, para. 11; Evans (2018), *supra* note 148, p. 227.

162 *Supra* note 150. See also a statement of the former president of the Court, Gilbert Guillaume, concerning the unpredictability of the *Tunisia/Libya* judgment. Alex G. Oude Elferink, Tore Henriksen, and Signe Veierud Busch, *The Judiciary and the Law of Maritime Delimitation: Setting the Stage*, *in* Maritime Boundary Delimitation: The Case Law: Is It Consistent and Predictable? 1, 21 (Alex G. Oude Elferink, Tore Henriksen and Signe Veierud Busch (eds.), 2018).

163 The composition of the judges influences the development of the jurisprudence on maritime delimitation. See analysis in Oude Elferink et al., *supra* note 162, p. 21, 23–24.

164 Since security interests influenced the formulation of Article 76, one might assume that this factor will also be relevant in delimitation of the continental shelf. For the relevance of security considerations see for example UNCLOS III, 2nd Sess, 29th Plen Mtg, UN Doc A/CONF.62/SR.29 (4 July 1974), at para. 20; A/CONF.62/C.2/SR.16, *supra* note 28, para. 8; Sebenius, *supra* note 11, p. 74.

165 Suarez, *supra* note 21, p. 13, 15.

166 See also discussion in Chapter 5. Although see opposite opinions, e.g., Qatar v. Bahrain (2001), *supra* note 55, Separate Opinion of Judge Oda, para. 25.

167 See Section 2.1.2.2. Judicial bodies recognized the relevance of security interests in the context of delimitation. For example, Nicaragua v. Colombia (2012), *supra* note 118, para. 222. However, in most cases, such considerations were not accepted as relevant circumstances that justify adjusting the provisional boundary line. See e.g., Romania v. Ukraine, *supra* note 8, para. 204; Somalia v. Kenya (2021), *supra* note 131. Conduct of the parties or third parties' rights in the area were not considered as

relevant circumstances at all, although some judges argued that the latter is relevant for delimitation. Tunisia v. Libya, *supra* note 1, Dissenting Opinion of Judge Oda, p. 250–251. For more details, see Chapter 3, Section 2; Evans (2018), *supra* note 148, p. 235–236, 244; Lando (2019), *supra* note 138, p. 205–209, 210. In contrast, states refer to security considerations in bilateral agreement. See e.g., Treaty between the Republic of Venezuela and the Kingdom of the Netherlands (1978), DOALOS website, available at www.un.org/Depts/los/LEGISLATIONANDTREATIES/PDFFILES/TREATIES/VEN-NLD1978BD.PDF, Article 4; Treaty between the State of Barbados and the Republic of Guyana (2003), 55 Law of the Sea Bulletin 36 (2004), Article 7. See also discussion in Chapter 3, Section 2.1.2.1.

168 Romania v. Ukraine, *supra* note 8, paras. 77, 106. See detailed analysis in *infra note* 196. These factors are part of the general factor of the "configuration of the coast". See Libya v. Malta, *supra* note 1, paras. 56–57, 79B; Ghana v. Côte d'Ivoire (2017), *supra* note 39, paras. 286, 421, 452; Romania v. Ukraine, ibid., at paras. 169, 178. Other related factors in this category will be discussed in detail later.

169 See detailed analysis on the influence of islands in maritime delimitation, Evans (2015), *supra* note 138, p. 273; Lando (2019), *supra* note 138, p. 178–192.

170 Lando (2019), ibid., p. 193.

171 Arbitration between Newfoundland and Labrador and Nova Scotia concerning portions of the limits of their offshore areas as defined in the Canada-Nova Scotia Offshore Petroleum Resources Accord Implementation Act and the Canada-Newfoundland Atlantic Accord Implementation Act, Award of the Tribunal in the second phase, 26 March 2002, available at www.cnsopb.ns.ca/sites/default/files/resource/phaseii_award_english.pdf, p. 22.

172 For example, Tunisia v. Libya, *supra* note 1, para. 71, and Dissenting Opinion of Judge Evensen, p. 278, p. 290; The Jan Mayen case, *supra* note 9, Separated Opinion of Judge Schwebel, p. 119.

173 Many maritime boundary agreements refer to geological factors that might affect the boundary line, e.g., Treaty between the Republic of Lithuania and the Russian Federation (1997), DOALOS website, available at www.un.org/Depts/los/LEGISLATIONANDTREATIES/PDFFILES/TREATIES/LTU-RUS1997CS.PDF; Treaty Between the Republic of Vanuatu and the Solomon Islands (2016), DOALOS website, available at www.un.org/Depts/los/LEGISLATIONANDTREATIES/PDFFILES/TREATIES/vut_slb_wsm_2016.pdf, Article 5.

174 Lando (2019), *supra* note 138, p. 221. Although in the *Jan Mayen* case, the Court considered the presence of ice in the waters of the region, see The Jan Mayen case, *supra* note 9, para. 77.

175 Antunes and Becker-Weinberg, *supra* note 38, p. 66–68, 86–88. This position is even more critical since entitlement to the continental shelf beyond 200 nm depends on geology, rather than geography. UNCLOS, *supra* note 1, Article 76(4).

176 As discussed earlier, tribunals treated "natural prolongation" as both the basis for entitlement and a measure of breadth, conflating between "entitlement" and "delimitation", which possibly reduced the relevancy of geology in delimitation. See e.g., Bangladesh v. Myanmar, *supra* note 115, paras. 429,434; Antunes and Becker-Weinberg, *supra* note 38, p. 67.

177 The language of Article 83 influenced the "single shelf" approach since it does not distinguish between the continental shelf up to and beyond 200 nm in the context of delimitation. Antunes and Becker-Weinberg, *supra* note 38, p. 88; Busch (2018), *supra* note 119, p. 323.

178 Some argued that considering geological factors would "introduce a new element of difficulty and uncertainty into the process of maritime delimitation", see Bangladesh v. Myanmar, *supra* note 115, Joint Declaration of Judges *Ad Hoc* Mensah and Oxman, para. 11.

179 North Sea Continental Shelf, *supra* note 34, para. 85(c). For different forms of distorting and cut-off effects, see Yunus Emre Acikgonul, *Reflections on the Principle of Non-Cut Off: A Growing Concept in Maritime Boundary Delimitation Law*, 47(1) Ocean Dev. & Int. Law 52, 55 (2016); Bangladesh v. Myanmar, *supra* note 115, paras. 297, 324.

180 Acikgonul, *supra* note 179, p. 54; Evans (2015), *supra* note 138, p. 269; Lando (2019), *supra* note 138, p. 168–169.

181 Acikgonul, ibid., p. 54–55; Bangladesh v. India, *supra* note 121, p. 119, para. 417, and Concurring and Dissenting Opinion of Dr. P.S. RAO, para. 16. The "cut-off effect" was significant enough to justify the adjustment of the provisional equidistance line in several cases, e.g., Nicaragua v. Colombia (2012), *supra* note 118, para. 215; Costa Rica v. Nicaragua (2018), *supra* note 40, paras. 193–194.

182 In the *Bangladesh/India* arbitration, the Tribunal stated that a concave coastline is typical configuration to cut-off of a state located between two states, which warrants the adjustment of the provisional equidistance line, as in the *North Sea Continental Shelf* cases. Bangladesh v. India, *supra* note 121, paras. 402, 418. See also Bangladesh v. Myanmar, *supra* note 115, paras. 292–294. See also Somalia v. Kenya (2021), *supra* note 131, para. 162, although separate opinions disagreed with the Court's application of the "concavity" test in this case, see e.g., Somalia v. Kenya (2021), ibid., Separate Opinion of Judge Yusuf, para. 4.

183 Evans (2018), *supra* note 148, p. 250; Acikgonul, *supra* note 179, p. 52. This principle originally linked to "natural prolongation", which was the basis for entitlement. Over time, "distance" became the basis for entitlement, at least within 200 nm, which emphasize the role of the coast. See *supra* note 176; The Jan Mayen case, *supra* note 9, Separated Opinion of Judge Ajibola, p. 290. Some argue that this change influenced the shift from "non-cut-off upon the natural prolongation of another state" to "non-cut-off of the seaward projection of the coasts of another state", see Acikgonul, ibid., at p. 53.

184 Ostensibly, delimitation is the process of setting boundary lines to divide the overlapping continental shelves. UNCLOS, *supra* note 1, Articles 76(10), 83. Some cases reflect this position, i.e., that delimitation is "a process which involves establishing the boundaries of an area already, in principle, appertaining to the coastal State and not the determination de novo of such an area", see The Jan Mayen case, *supra* note 9, para. 64. However, some judges viewed delimitation as a process of allocating entitlements, see e.g., Libya v. Malta, *supra* note 1, Separate Opinion of Judges Ruda, Bedjaoui and Jiménez De Aréchaga, para. 40; Land, Island and Maritime Frontier Dispute, *supra* note 35, p. 351, Separate Opinion of Judge Torres Bernardez, at para. 192; The Jan Mayen case, *supra* note 9, Separate Opinion of Judge Shahabuddeen, p. 159–160; Bangladesh v. India, *supra* note 121, para. 410. These examples demonstrate the incoherency concerning the definition of delimitation. In the author's opinion, the question is not only whether delimitation is a process that allocates entitlements or divides an overlapping area but, if it is the former, also whether judicial bodies have the competence to do so.

185 *Supra* note 134.

186 Libya v. Malta, *supra* note 1, para. 46.

187 For detailed discussion on this misinterpretation, see Shani Friedman, *The Concept of Entitlement to an Exclusive Economic Zone as Reflected in International Judicial Decisions*, 53(1) ISR. Law Rev. 101, 104 (2020).

188 The Jan Mayen case, *supra* note 9, Separated Opinion of Judge Oda, paras. 45–46, 97; Nicaragua v. Colombia (2012), *supra* note 118, p. 678; Ghana v. Côte d'Ivoire (2017), *supra* note 39, para. 591; Friedman, *supra* note 187, p. 123. The notion of "overlapping entitlements" also linked to the concept of "relevant area"; only the maritime spaces that generate potential "overlap of entitlements" of the parties would be considered in

the process of delimitation, rather than all areas to which a coastal State is entitled. See e.g., *supra* note 168; Evans (2015), *supra* note 138, p. 267; Lando (2019), *supra* note 138, p. 65, 83–84, 91.

189 See Section 2.1.2.1. Establishing the distance criterion as the basis of entitlement negates the need to establish the natural prolongations of the parties. See Friedman, *supra* note 187. This is more prominent concerning the EEZ.

190 For example, The Jan Mayen case, *supra* note 9, Separated Opinion of Judge Ajibola, p. 290. For further discussion, see also *supra* note 184; Friedman, *supra* note 187.

191 Some argue that the coast is necessary element for asserting rights beyond 200 nm, although tribunals did not consider coastal lengths as relevant circumstance beyond 200 nm. Lando (2019), *supra* note 138, p. 173, 177.

192 See e.g., Maritime Dispute (Peru v. Chile), Judgment, ICJ Reports 2014, p. 3, para. 189.

193 Lando (2019), *supra* note 138, 168–169.

194 Tunisia v. Libya, *supra* note 1, Dissenting Opinion of Judge Oda, para. 62. The principle was employed in the *St. Pierre et Miquelon* case despite revolving two opposite coasts. The standard of "significant 'cut-off effect'" strengthens the argument that the true reasoning behind the 1969 judgment was equity rather than a true effect on geological circumstances. *Supra* note 181; Lando (2019), *supra* note 138, p. 169–170. See also the *Somalia/Kenya* case, where the ICJ employed the "cut-off" principle, despite Tanzania not being part of the proceedings and despite having no actual concavity of the coast, Somalia v. Kenya (2021), *supra* note 131.

195 For example, Evans (2015), *supra* note 138, p. 257–258; Lando (2019), *supra* note 138, p. 14–15. In the *Bangladesh/India* arbitration, the Tribunal stated that the jurisprudence does not recognize coastal States' general right to the maximum breadth of their entitlements, irrespective of the geographical situation and other coastal States' rights. Bangladesh v. India, *supra* note 121, para. 469.

196 Tribunals determined that the coast is the decisive factor for entitlement. Thus, it is important to identify the areas of the coasts that generate rights; those areas that produce "overlapping projections". The parts of the coasts that do not generate overlap are not considered. See e.g., Romania v. Ukraine, *supra* note 8, paras. 77, 99; Barbados v. Trinidad and Tobago, *supra* note 35, para. 239; Peru v. Chile, *supra* note 192, paras. 140–141. The coast is also significant for delimitation since it is the starting point from which the continental shelf is measured. See Tunisia v. Libya, *supra* note 1, para. 74. For the concept of "relevant coasts", see Yurika Ishii, *Relevant Coasts and Relevant Area in the Maritime Delimitation of the EEZ and Continental Shelf*, 51(4) Ocean Dev. & Int. Law 307 (2020).

197 Not to be confused with the test of disproportionality in the third stage of delimitation, Lando (2019), *supra* note 138, p. 173. See e.g., The Jan Mayen case, *supra* note 9, paras. 61, 64–65; Nicaragua v. Colombia (2012), *supra* note 118, paras. 208–211.

198 For example, The Jan Mayen case, *supra* note 9, Separate Opinion of Judge Schwebel, p. 125; Barbados v. Trinidad and Tobago, *supra* note 35, paras. 236–238, 327; Bangladesh v. Myanmar, *supra* note 115, para. 185; Evans (2015), *supra* note 138, p. 269; Lando (2019), *supra* note 138, p. 173.

199 For example, The Jan Mayen case, *supra* note 9, para. 65; Nicaragua v. Colombia (2012), *supra* note 118, para. 211; Lando (2019), *supra* note 138, p. 176.

200 For example, Thomas Cottier, Equitable Principles of Maritime Boundary Delimitation: The Quest for Distributive Justice in International Law 190–191 (2015); Andrea Insolia, *The Law of Maritime Delimitation in the Croatia/Slovenia Final Award, in* Interpretations of the United Nations Convention on the Law of the Sea by International Courts and Tribunals 225 (Angela Del Vecchio and Roberto Virzo (eds.), 2019).

201 Antunes and Becker-Weinberg, *supra* note 38. Since only those parts of the coasts that generate overlapping projections are relevant for delimitation, this does not reflect the

physical reality of the disputed area. *Supra note* 196; Evans (2018), *supra* note 148, p. 233.

202 *Supra* note 184; The Jan Mayen case, *supra* note 9, Separate Opinion of Judge Shahabuddeen, p. 162–163, 164–165. In the *Jan Mayen* case, some judges criticized the Court for "rewarding" Greenland for the length of its coast and "penalizing" Jan Mayen for having shorter coast since Denmark claimed a 200 nm continental shelf, while Norway did not. They argued that such decision might encourage immoderate claims in future. See ibid., Separate Opinion of Judge Oda, paras. 45–46.

203 *Supra* note 196. The ICJ implied that a claim for the entire 200 nm continental shelf might be a claim for entitlement. The Jan Mayen case, *supra* note 9, Separate Opinion of Judge Ajibola, p. 290–291, and Dissenting Opinion of Judge Fischer, para. 9; Costa Rica v. Nicaragua (2018), *supra* note 40, para. 134. This seems to perceive delimitation as affecting the parties' entitlements, rather than a division of the disputed area.

204 For example, Evans (2018), *supra* note 148, p. 252.

205 It essentially attributes coastal States areas that would not normally be allocated to them under international law. Zou Keyuan, *Historic Rights in International Law and in China's Practice*, 32(2) Ocean Dev. & Int. Law 149, 150–151 (2001); Christopher Mirasola, *Historic Waters and Ancient Title: Outdated Doctrines for Establishing Maritime Sovereignty and Jurisdiction*, 47 J. Mar. L. & Com. 29, 41 (2016). There are several types of "historic" arguments; some refer to questions of sovereignty over land, while others, such as "historic waters" and "historic bays", address specifically access to maritime areas. For example, Fisheries Case, Judgment, ICJ Reports 1951, p. 116, p. 130; Dispute between the Government of the State of Eritrea and the Government of the Republic of Yemen, Award of the Arbitral Tribunal in the Second Stage of the Proceedings (Maritime Delimitation), case no. 1996–04, 17 December 1999, Permanent Court of Arbitration [PCA], para. 31; The South China Sea Arbitration (The Republic of Philippines v. The People's Republic of China), Award, case no. 2013–19, 12 July 2016, Permanent Court of Arbitration [PCA], paras. 225, 257, 261.

206 In earlier cases, the ICJ maintained that "historic titles" must be respected and preserved and that it might be relevant circumstance since the boundary line should not encroach upon such rights, see Tunisia v. Libya, *supra* note 1, paras. 100, 102, 105 and Separate Opinion of Judge Jiménez De Aréchaga, para. 100. However, other judges rejected this position; see ibid., Dissenting Opinion of Judge Gros, paras. 20–22.

207 The South China Sea Arbitration (2016), *supra* note 205, para. 223; Vidas, *supra* note 154, p. 46.

208 For example, Eritrea v. Yemen, *supra* note 205, para. 109; Qatar v. Bahrain (2001), *supra* note 55, paras. 36, 98, and Separate Opinion of Judge Kooijmans, para. 3. In contrast, some states addressed historic rights in their bilateral agreement, also as a justification for adjustment of the boundary line. See e.g., Ecuador and Peru's Joint Declaration (2012), DOALOS website, available at www.un.org/Depts/los/LEGISLATIONANDTREATIES/PDFFILES/TREATIES/ECU_PER_1617143(E).pdf; Agreement between Sri Lanka and India (1974), DOALOS website, available at www.un.org/Depts/los/LEGISLATIONANDTREATIES/PDFFILES/TREATIES/LKA-IND1974BW.PDF; Agreement between the Solomon Islands and Papua New Guinea (2004), available at www.fao.org/faolex/results/details/fr/c/LEX-FAOC067017/.

209 For example, The Jan Mayen case, *supra* note 9, Separate Opinion of Judge Schwebel, p. 118; Guyana v. Suriname, *supra* note 55, paras. 383–389; Romania v. Ukraine, *supra* note 8, para. 198. See also Chapter 3.

210 For example, Tunisia v. Libya, *supra* note 1, para. 107. Although the ICJ examined the economic conduct of the parties to determine the existence of a *de facto* maritime limit, ibid., at para. 82–96, 117; Lando (2019), *supra* note 138, p. 196. See discussion in Chapter 3.

211 In the *Fisheries* case, the Court established the "long usage" tests to determine whether the delimitation line should be adjusted due to historical fishing practices. Fisheries case, *supra* note 205, p. 133, 142. In the *Gulf of Maine* case, the Court established the "catastrophic" test; the provisional line might be adjusted if it's "radically inequitable". However, in this case, the ICJ did not adjust the line since there were no serious economic repercussions to the parties. Although this was before UNCLOS entered into force, the Court implied that the underlined principle is "equity". Gulf of Maine Area case, *supra* note 35, paras. 237–238. The Arbitral Tribunal also employed the "catastrophic test", see Eritrea v. Yemen, *supra* note 205, paras. 49–50; Barbados v. Trinidad and Tobago, *supra* note 35, para. 241.

212 The Court adjusted the provisional median line since it was too far in one party's zone, where the other party would not have equitable access to the fishing stock. Some argued that such approach, which reflects distributive justice ideas, departed from the accepted law. The Jan Mayen case, *supra* note 9, paras. 72, 75–76, Separate Opinion of Judge Schwebel, p. 120, and Dissenting Opinion of Judge Fischer, para. 14; Lando (2019), *supra* note 138, p. 200.

213 For example, Qatar v. Bahrain (2001), *supra* note 55, para. 236; Barbados v. Trinidad and Tobago, *supra* note 35, paras. 241, 277, 279, 289; Nicaragua v. Colombia (2012), *supra* note 118, para. 223. Tribunals still maintained that delimitation does not reflect "distributive justice", e.g., Bangladesh v. India, *supra* note 121, para. 397; Somalia v. Kenya (2021), *supra* note 131, para. 159.

214 For example, Barbados v. Trinidad and Tobago, *supra* note 35, paras. 241, 267; Ghana v. Côte d'Ivoire (2017), *supra* note 39, paras. 452, 455; Evans (2018), *supra* note 148, p. 244, 255.

215 Evans (2018), *supra* note 148, p. 244, 254. States claim entitlement to maritime zones to utilize the resources in these zones, which is why delimitation is an important interest of coastal States.

216 The area beyond 200 nm is part of national jurisdiction, rather than a part of the international seabed. Thus, ostensibly broad-margin states needed only to submit information to the CLCS, as an advisory non-binding institution, since they have complete jurisdiction up to the edge of the continental margin.

217 The institutional approach would explain the emphasis on geographical factors, which perceived as more objective, promoting stability and predictability. Constructivism might underline generating practical and convenient knowledge to promote legitimacy. See also discussion in Chapter 5.

218 See Division for Ocean Affairs and the Law of the Sea (DOALOS) website, submissions to the Commission on the Limits of the Continental Shelf, pursuant to article 76, paragraph 8, available at www.un.org/Depts/los/clcs_new/commission_submissions.htm

219 Act No. 23.968 of 14 August 1991, DOALOS website, available at www.un.org/Depts/los/LEGISLATIONANDTREATIES/PDFFILES/ARG_1991_23968.pdf, Article 6

220 Argentine's submission to the Commission, available at www.un.org/Depts/los/clcs_new/submissions_files/arg25_09/arg2009e_summary_eng.pdf, p. 3

221 Law No. 8.617 of 4 January 1993, on the territorial sea, the contiguous zone, the exclusive economic zone and the continental shelf(1), DOALOS website, available at www.un.org/Depts/los/LEGISLATIONANDTREATIES/PDFFILES/BRA_1993_8617.pdf, Article 11

222 Partial revised Submission by Brazil in respect of the Brazilian Oriental and Meridional Margin, available at www.un.org/Depts/los/clcs_new/submissions_files/bra02_rev18/BR-OMM-ExecutiveSummary.pdf, at p. 4

223 Federal Act relating to the Sea, 8 January 1986, DOALOS website, available at www.un.org/Depts/los/LEGISLATIONANDTREATIES/PDFFILES/MEX_1986_Act.pdf, Article 62

224 *Ibid.*, Article 65

225 *Ibid.*, Article 9

226 Continental Shelf (Amendment) Act, 1986 (Act No. 23 of 1986), DOALOS website, available at www.un.org/Depts/los/LEGISLATIONANDTREATIES/STATEFILES/TTO.htm; Trinidad and Tobago's submission to the Commission, available at www.un.org/Depts/los/clcs_new/submissions_files/tto49_09/tto2009executive_summary.pdf, p. 3
227 Act No. 205 of 19 December 1979 on the Continental Shelf and Adjacent Sea, DOALOS website, available at www.un.org/Depts/los/LEGISLATIONANDTREATIES/PDFFILES/NIC_1979_Act.pdf
228 Declaration by the Ministry of Foreign Affairs, 14 September 1985, DOALOS website, available at www.un.org/Depts/los/LEGISLATIONANDTREATIES/PDFFILES/CHL_1985_Declaration.pdf, Article 2; Decree no. 95 Determining the Maritime Zones from Punta Puga to Diego Ramírez Islands, 23 August 2021, DOALOS website, available at www.un.org/Depts/los/LEGISLATIONANDTREATIES/PDFFILES/2113525E.pdf, p. 3
229 Declaration by the Ministry of Foreign Affairs, *ibid.*, Article 4
230 Declaration on the continental shelf, 19 September 1985, DOALOS website, available at www.un.org/Depts/los/LEGISLATIONANDTREATIES/PDFFILES/ECU_1985_Declaration.pdf
231 Constitution as amended by Decree No. 5699 of 5 June 1975, DOALOS website, available at www.un.org/Depts/los/LEGISLATIONANDTREATIES/PDFFILES/CRI_1975_Decree5699.pdf, Article 6
232 Maritime Boundaries Act, 1977, Act No. 10 of 30 June 1977, DOALOS website, available at www.un.org/Depts/los/LEGISLATIONANDTREATIES/PDFFILES/GUY_1977_Act.pdf, Article 9
233 Continental Shelf Act, 1970, available at http://laws.bahamas.gov.bs/cms/images/LEGISLATION/PRINCIPAL/1970/1970-0017/ContinentalShelfAct_1.pdf; Fisheries Resources (Jurisdiction and Conservation) Act, 1977, No. 13 of 16 June 1977, DOALOS website, available at www.un.org/Depts/los/LEGISLATIONANDTREATIES/PDFFILES/BHS_1977_13.pdf; Bahamas's submission to the Commission, available at www.un.org/Depts/los/clcs_new/submissions_files/bhs71_14/BHS-ES-DOC.pdf, para. 1–5
234 Seas and Submerged Lands Act 1973, as amended by the Maritime Legislation Amendment Act 1994, DOALOS website, available at www.un.org/Depts/los/LEGISLATIONANDTREATIES/PDFFILES/aus_1994_sea_act.pdf, Article 12
235 Australia's submission to the Commission, available at www.un.org/Depts/los/clcs_new/submissions_files/aus04/Documents/aus_doc_es_web_delivery.pdf, p. 48
236 Territorial Sea and Exclusive Economic Zone Act 1977, Act No. 28 of 26 September 1977 as amended by Act No. 146 of 1980, DOALOS website, available at www.un.org/Depts/los/LEGISLATIONANDTREATIES/PDFFILES/NZL_1980_Act.pdf
237 New Zealand Submission to the Commission on the Limits of the Continental Shelf, Executive Summary, available at www.un.org/Depts/los/clcs_new/submissions_files/nzl06/nzl_exec_sum.pdf, p. 5
238 Continental Shelf Order 2018, DOALOS website, available at www.un.org/Depts/los/LEGISLATIONANDTREATIES/PDFFILES/NZL_2018_Order.pdf, p. 49
239 The Territorial Sea and Exclusive Economic Zone Act, Act No. 30 of 23 October 1978, as amended by Act No. 19 of 1989, DOALOS website, available at www.un.org/Depts/los/LEGISLATIONANDTREATIES/PDFFILES/TON_1989_Act.pdf
240 Tonga's Partial Submission of Data and Information on the Outer Limits of the Continental Shelf Executive Summary, available at www.un.org/Depts/los/clcs_new/submissions_files/ton46_09/ton2009executive_summary.pdf, p. 1–2; CIA's World Factbook, Maritime Claims, available at www.cia.gov/the-world-factbook/field/maritime-claims/
241 Continental Shelf Act, No. 9 (1970), DOALOS website, available at www.un.org/Depts/los/LEGISLATIONANDTREATIES/PDFFILES/FJI_1970_Act.pdf; CIA's World Factbook, Maritime Claims, *ibid*

242 Palau's Page, DOALOS website, available at www.un.org/Depts/los/LEGISLATIONANDTREATIES/STATEFILES/PLW.htm; CIA's World Factbook, *supra* note 240.

243 Oceans Act of 18 December 1996, *supra* note 5, Article 17; Canada's partial submission to the Commission concerning the Atlantic Ocean (2013), available at www.un.org/Depts/los/clcs_new/submissions_files/can70_13/es_can_en.pdf, p. 3

244 Canada's partial submission (2013), ibid; Canada's partial submission to the Commission concerning the Arctic Ocean (2019), available at www.un.org/Depts/los/clcs_new/submissions_files/can1_84_2019/CDA_ARC_ES_EN_secured.pdf, p. 5

245 Public Notice 2237, Exclusive Economic Zone and Maritime Boundaries; Notice of Limits, Federal Register Vol. 60, No. 163 (1995), available at www.un.org/Depts/los/LEGISLATIONANDTREATIES/PDFFILES/USA_1995_eez_public_notice.pdf; CIA's World Factbook, *supra* note 240

246 Federal Law on the Continental Shelf of the Russian Federation, adopted by the State Duma on 25 October 1995, DOALOS website, available at www.un.org/Depts/los/LEGISLATIONANDTREATIES/PDFFILES/RUS_1995_Law.pdf

247 Partial Revised Submission of the Russian Federation in respect of the Continental Shelf of the Russian Federation in the Arctic Ocean, available at www.un.org/Depts/los/clcs_new/submissions_files/rus01_rev15/2015_08_03_Exec_Summary_English.pdf, p. 5

248 Royal Decree of 7 June 1963 concerning the exercise of Danish sovereignty over the Continental Shelf, DOALOS website, available at www.un.org/Depts/los/LEGISLATIONANDTREATIES/PDFFILES/DNK_1963_Decree.pdf, Article 2

249 Amendment made in 1985, see Partial Submission of the Government of the Kingdom of Denmark together with the Government of the Faroes to the Commission concerning The Northern Continental Shelf of the Faroe Islands (2009), available at www.un.org/Depts/los/clcs_new/submissions_files/dnk28_09/dnk2009executivesummary.pdf, p. 5

250 The Jan Mayen case, *supra* note 9, para. 19

251 Partial Submission of the Government of the Kingdom of Denmark together with the Government of the Faroes, *supra* note 249; Partial Submission of the Government of the Kingdom of Denmark together with the Government of the Faroes to the Commission concerning The Southern Continental Shelf of the Faroe Islands (2010), available at www.un.org/Depts/los/clcs_new/submissions_files/dnk54_10/SFM-Executive_Summary_secure.pdf, p. 5; Partial Submission of the Government of the Kingdom of Denmark together with the Government of Greenland to the Commission concerning the Southern Continental Shelf of Greenland, available at www.un.org/Depts/los/clcs_new/submissions_files/dnk61_12/DNK2012_EX_SUM_S_GREENLAND.pdf, p. 5; Partial Submission of the Government of the Kingdom of Denmark together with the Government of Greenland to the Commission concerning the North-Eastern Continental Shelf of Greenland, available at www.un.org/Depts/los/clcs_new/submissions_files/dnk68_13/DNK2013_ES.pdf, p. 5

252 CIA's World Factbook, *supra* note 240.

253 Continental Shelf (Designated Areas) Order 2014, S.I. No. 87 of 2014, DOALOS website, available at www.un.org/Depts/los/LEGISLATIONANDTREATIES/PDFFILES/IRL_2014_Order87.pdf

254 Ireland's submission to the CLCS concerning Hatton-Rockall Area, available at www.un.org/Depts/los/clcs_new/submissions_files/irl09/irl09_exsum.pdf, p. 2

255 Decree-Law No. 49–369 of 11 November 1969, DOALOS website, available at www.un.org/Depts/los/LEGISLATIONANDTREATIES/PDFFILES/PRT_1969_Decree.pdf; CIA's World Factbook, *supra* note 240

256 Portugal's 2009 submission to the Commission, Executive Summary, available at www.un.org/Depts/los/clcs_new/submissions_files/prt44_09/prt2009executivesummary.pdf, p. 3; Portugal's 2017 submission to the Commission, Executive Summary, available at www.un.org/Depts/los/clcs_new/submissions_files/prt44_09/prt2017executivesummary.pdf, p. 2

257 Spain's Page, DOALOS website, available at www.un.org/Depts/los/LEGISLATIONANDTREATIES/STATEFILES/ESP.htm
258 Act No. 68–1181 of 30 December 1968 relating to the exploration of the Continental Shelf and to the exploitation of its natural resources, DOALOS website, available at www.un.org/Depts/los/LEGISLATIONANDTREATIES/PDFFILES/FRA_1968_Act.pdf; Law No. 76–655 of 16 July 1976 relating to the Economic Zone off the coasts of the territory of the Republic, DOALOS website, available at www.un.org/Depts/los/LEGISLATIONANDTREATIES/PDFFILES/FRA_1976_Law.pdf
259 France's partial submission to the Commission in respect of Saint-Pierre-et-Miquelon, available at www.un.org/Depts/los/clcs_new/submissions_files/fra72_14/SPM_Summary_EN_April2014.pdf, p. 3
260 Law No. 41 of 1 June 1979 concerning the Territorial Sea, the Economic Zone and the Continental Shelf, DOALOS website, available at www.un.org/Depts/los/LEGISLATIONANDTREATIES/PDFFILES/ISL_1979_Law.pdf, Article 5
261 The Icelandic Continental Shelf – Partial Submission, available at www.un.org/Depts/los/clcs_new/submissions_files/isl27_09/isl2009executivesummary.pdf, p. 5
262 Act of 22 March 1985 No. 11 Pertaining to Petroleum Activities, DOALOS website, available at www.un.org/Depts/los/LEGISLATIONANDTREATIES/PDFFILES/NOR_1985_Act.pdf; Act of 29 November 1996 No. 72 relating to petroleum activities, which build on article 76 of the Convention. It refers to the seabed and subsoil of the submarine areas that extend beyond the Norwegian territorial sea throughout the natural prolongation of the Norwegian land territory to the outer edge of the continental margin but no less than 200 nautical miles from the baselines, Continental Shelf Submission of Norway in respect of areas in the Arctic Ocean, the Barents Sea, and the Norwegian Sea, Executive Summary, available at www.un.org/Depts/los/clcs_new/submissions_files/nor06/nor_exec_sum.pdf, p. 6
263 Norway's Continental Shelf Submission, *ibid.*
264 The Territorial Waters, Continental Shelf, Exclusive Economic Zone and other Maritime Zones Act, 1976, Act No. 80 of 28 May 1976, DOALOS website, available at www.un.org/Depts/los/LEGISLATIONANDTREATIES/PDFFILES/IND_1976_Act.pdf, Article 6(1)
265 Territorial Waters and Maritime Zones Act 1974, Act No. XXVI of 1974, DOALOS website, available at www.un.org/Depts/los/LEGISLATIONANDTREATIES/PDFFILES/BGD_1974_Act.pdf, Article 7; Bangladesh's submission to the Commission, Executive Summary, available at www.un.org/Depts/los/clcs_new/submissions_files/bgd55_11/Executive%20summary%20final.pdf, para. 1.3
266 Declaration by the Government concerning the Exclusive Economic Zone of Indonesia 21 March 1980, DOALOS website, available at www.un.org/Depts/los/LEGISLATIONANDTREATIES/PDFFILES/IDN_1980_DeclarationEEZ.pdf; Act No. 5 of 1983 on the Indonesian exclusive economic zone, 18 October 1983, DOALOS website, available at www.un.org/Depts/los/LEGISLATIONANDTREATIES/PDFFILES/IDN_1983_Act.pdf
267 Exclusive Economic Zone Act, 1984, Act No. 311, DOALOS website, available at www.un.org/Depts/los/LEGISLATIONANDTREATIES/PDFFILES/MYS_1984_Act.pdf, Articles 1, 3
268 Territorial Sea and Maritime Zones Law, Pyithu Hluttaw Law No. 3 of 9 April 1977, DOALOS website, available at www.un.org/Depts/los/LEGISLATIONANDTREATIES/PDFFILES/MMR_1977_Law.pdf, Article 12
269 Territorial Sea and Maritime Zones Law (Pyidaungsu Hluttaw Law No.14, 2017), DOALOS website, available at www.un.org/Depts/los/LEGISLATIONANDTREATIES/PDFFILES/Myanmar_MZL_2017.pdf, Article 23
270 Maritime Zones Law No. 22 of 1 September 1976, DOALOS website, available at www.un.org/Depts/los/LEGISLATIONANDTREATIES/PDFFILES/LKA_1976_Law.pdf, Article 6

271 Presidential Decree No. 1599 of 11 June 1978 establishing an Exclusive Economic Zone and for other purposes, DOALOS website, available at www.un.org/Depts/los/LEGISLATIONANDTREATIES/PDFFILES/PHL_1978_Decree.pdf
272 Continental Shelf Presidential Proclamation No. 370 (1968), DOALOS website, available at www.un.org/Depts/los/LEGISLATIONANDTREATIES/PDFFILES/PHL_1968_Proclamation.pdf; CIA's World Factbook, *supra* note 240
273 Law on the Exclusive Economic Zone and the Continental Shelf (Act No. 140 of 1996), 33 Law of the Sea Bulletin 36 (1997), Article 2; Law on the Exclusive Economic Zone and the Continental Shelf (Law No. 74 of 1996), 35 Law of the Sea Bulletin 94 (1997), p. 94–95, Article 2.
274 Exclusive Economic Zone and Continental Shelf Act (1998), DOALOS website, available at www.un.org/Depts/los/LEGISLATIONANDTREATIES/PDFFILES/chn_1998_eez_act.pdf, Article 2
275 Maritime Zones of Maldives Act No. 6/96, DOALOS website, available at www.un.org/Depts/los/LEGISLATIONANDTREATIES/PDFFILES/MDV_1996_Act.pdf
276 An act to amend title 18 of the Code of the Federated States of Micronesia by amending sections 101, 102, 103, 104, 105, and 107 and by adding a new Section 108 to establish an exclusive economic zone in the oceans surrounding the Federated States of Micronesia, to expand the size of the Territorial Sea, to make the chapter consistent with the current political status of the Federated States of Micronesia, and for other purposes (16 December 1988), DOALOS website, available at www.un.org/Depts/los/LEGISLATIONANDTREATIES/PDFFILES/FSM_1988_Act.pdf; Micronesia's submission to the Commission concerning the Eauripik Rise, available at www.un.org/Depts/los/clcs_new/submissions_files/fsm67_13/FSM_EAU_Executive_Summary.pdf, paras. 1–3
277 Micronesia's submission to the Commission concerning the Eauripik Rise, ibid, paras. 1–7
278 Ordinance No. 85–013 determining the limits of the maritime zones (territorial sea, continental shelf and exclusive economic zone) of the Democratic Republic of Madagascar, 16 September 1985, as amended and ratified by Law No. 85–013 of 11 December 1985), DOALOS website, available at www.un.org/Depts/los/LEGISLATIONANDTREATIES/PDFFILES/MDG_1985_Ordinance.pdf, Article 7; Madagascar's submission to the Commission, Executive Summary, available at www.un.org/Depts/los/clcs_new/submissions_files/mgd56_11/MDG-DOC-002_EXECUTIVE_SUMMARY_Updated.pdf, p. 7
279 Madagascar's submission to the Commission, *ibid.*, p. 8
280 Law No. 77–926 delimiting the Maritime Zones placed under the National Jurisdiction of the Republic of Ivory Coast of 17 November 1977, DOALOS website, available at www.un.org/Depts/los/LEGISLATIONANDTREATIES/PDFFILES/CIV_1977_Law.pdf, Article 2
281 Maritime Zones (Delimitation) Law, 1986, DOALOS website, available at www.un.org/Depts/los/LEGISLATIONANDTREATIES/PDFFILES/GHA_1986_Law.pdf, Article 6(1)
282 Chapter 371, The Maritime Zones Act 1989, DOALOS website, available at www.un.org/Depts/los/LEGISLATIONANDTREATIES/PDFFILES/KEN_1989_Maritime.pdf; Submission by the Republic of Kenya, Executive summary, available at www.un.org/Depts/los/clcs_new/submissions_files/ken35_09/ken2009_executivesummary.pdf, para. 1–3. However, in its submission to the CLCS, Kenya refers to paragraph 1 of Article 76 of the Convention, asserting that its continental shelf extends beyond its territorial sea throughout the natural prolongation of its land territory to the outer edge of the continental margin, see *ibid.*, para. 2–1
283 Law No. 5 dated 26 January 1989, as mentioned in Maritime Delimitation in the Indian Ocean (Somalia v. Kenya), Application Instituting Proceedings, ICJ (28 August 2014), at para. 7

284 Exclusive Economic Zone Decree No. 28 of 5 October 1978, DOALOS website, available at www.un.org/Depts/los/LEGISLATIONANDTREATIES/PDFFILES/NGA_1978_Decree.pdf
285 Gabon Page, DOALOS website, available at www.un.org/Depts/los/LEGISLATION-ANDTREATIES/STATEFILES/GAB.htm
286 Territorial Sea and Exclusive Economic Zone of Namibia, Act No. 3 of 1990, 30 June 1990, DOALOS website, available at www.un.org/Depts/los/LEGISLATIO-NANDTREATIES/PDFFILES/NAM_1990_Act.pdf, Article 6; Continental shelf submission of Namibia, Executive Summary, available at www.un.org/Depts/los/clcs_new/submissions_files/nam50_09/nam2009executivesummary.pdf, p. 1
287 Maritime Zones Act, No. 15 of 1994, DOALOS website, available at www.un.org/Depts/los/LEGISLATIONANDTREATIES/PDFFILES/ZAF_1994_Act.pdf, Article 8; South Africa's submission to the Commission, available at www.un.org/Depts/los/clcs_new/submissions_files/zaf31_09/zaf2009executive_summary.pdf, p. 1, and at www.un.org/Depts/los/clcs_new/submissions_files/zaf31_09/zaf2013_amended_executive_summary.pdf
288 Mozambique's submission to the Commission, available at www.un.org/Depts/los/clcs_new/submissions_files/moz52_10/moz_2010_es.pdf, p. 1
289 Maritime Zones Act 1977 (Act No. 13 of 3 June 1977), DOALOS website, available at www.un.org/Depts/los/LEGISLATIONANDTREATIES/PDFFILES/MUS_1977_Act.pdf, Article 5; Maritime Zone Act 2005 (Act No. 2 of 2005), 62 Law of the Sea Bulletin 52 (2006), Article 18
290 Maritime Zones Act, 1999 (Act No. 2 of 1999), DOALOS website, available at www.un.org/Depts/los/LEGISLATIONANDTREATIES/PDFFILES/SYC_1999_Act2.pdf, Article 11; Submission by the Republic of Seychelles to the Commission concerning the Northern Plateau Region, Executive Summary, available at www.un.org/Depts/los/clcs_new/submissions_files/syc39_09/syc2009executivesummary.pdf, para. 1–5
291 Territorial Sea and Exclusive Economic Zone Act, 1989, DOALOS website, available at www.un.org/Depts/los/LEGISLATIONANDTREATIES/PDFFILES/TZA_1989_Act.pdf; Tanzania's partial submission to the Commission, available at www.un.org/Depts/los/clcs_new/submissions_files/tza59_12/Executive%20Summary_%20URT-DOC-001_18-01-2012.pdf, p. 3
292 Executive Order No. 48 (10 January 2013), Extension of Executive Order No. 39 Delimiting the Maritime Zones of the Republic of Liberia, DOALOS website, available at www.un.org/Depts/los/LEGISLATIONANDTREATIES/PDFFILES/LBR_10Jan2013_Act_EO48.pdf, Section 6; Liberia's submission to the Commission, available at www.un.org/Depts/los/clcs_new/submissions_files/lib81_18/es_lib81_18.pdf, para. 1.6
293 Territorial Waters and Maritime Zones Act, 1976 (of 22 December 1976), DOA-LOS website, available at www.un.org/Depts/los/LEGISLATIONANDTREATIES/PDFFILES/PAK_1976_Act.pdf, Article 5; Pakistan's submission to the Commission, available at www.un.org/Depts/los/clcs_new/submissions_files/pak29_09/pak2009ex-ecutivesummary.pdf, p. 3
294 Oman's submission to the Commission, available at www.un.org/Depts/los/clcs_new/submissions_files/omn78_17/omn_es.pdf, para. 3
295 Tonga's Note Verbale to the Commission, available at www.un.org/Depts/los/clcs_new/submissions_files/nzl06/tonga_e.pdf; New Zealand's Note Verbale to the Commission, available at www.un.org/Depts/los/clcs_new/submissions_files/nzl06/nzl_2008_e.pdf; CLCS, 21th Sess, UN Doc CLCS/58 (25 April 2008), para. 16
296 Japan's note to the Commission concerning New Zealand's submission, available at www.un.org/Depts/los/clcs_new/submissions_files/nzl06/japan_e.pdf; New Zealand's Note Verbale to the Commission, *ibid*

297 Norway's Diplomatic Note, DOALOS website, available at www.un.org/Depts/los/clcs_new/submissions_files/nor06/note28march2007.pdf; CLCS, 19th Sess, UN Doc CLCS/54 (27 April 2007), para. 45
298 India's Communications received regarding the submission made by Indonesia to the Commission, available at www.un.org/Depts/los/clcs_new/submissions_files/idn08/clcs12_2008_ind_e.pdf
299 Indonesia's Note Verbale, available at www.un.org/Depts/los/clcs_new/submissions_files/submission_idn.htm
300 See also Viet Nam's independent submission to the Commission, DOALOS website, available at www.un.org/Depts/los/clcs_new/submissions_files/submission_vnm_37_2009.htm
301 Viet Nam's Note Verbale no. 86/HC-2009, available at www.un.org/Depts/los/clcs_new/submissions_files/mysvnm33_09/vnm_chn_2009re_mys_vnm_e.pdf
302 Malaysia's Note Verbale no. HA 24/09, available at www.un.org/Depts/los/clcs_new/submissions_files/mysvnm33_09/mys_re_chn_2009re_mys_vnm_e.pdf
303 Viet Nam's Note Verbale no. 240/HC-2009, available at www.un.org/Depts/los/clcs_new/submissions_files/mysvnm33_09/vnm_re_phl_2009re_mys_vnm_e.pdf
304 Malaysia's Note Verbale no. HA 41/09, available at www.un.org/Depts/los/clcs_new/submissions_files/mysvnm33_09/mys_re_phl_2009re_mys_vnm_e.pdf
305 Viet Nam's Note Verbale no. 77/HC-2009, available at www.un.org/Depts/los/clcs_new/submissions_files/mysvnm33_09/vnm_2011_re_phlchn.pdf
306 *Supra* note 301
307 *Supra* note 303
308 *Supra* note 305
309 Japan's Note Verbale no. SC/09/108, available at www.un.org/Depts/los/clcs_new/submissions_files/jpn08/jpn_25mar09.pdf
310 Japan's Note Verbale no. PM/09/735, available at www.un.org/Depts/los/clcs_new/submissions_files/jpn08/jpn_26aug09.pdf
311 Japan's Note Verbale no. SC/11/233, available at www.un.org/Depts/los/clcs_new/submissions_files/jpn08/jpn_09aug11.pdf
312 Japan's Note Verbale no. SC/11/239, available at www.un.org/Depts/los/clcs_new/submissions_files/jpn08/jpn_15aug11.pdf; see also Japan's Note Verbale no. PM/12/078, available at www.un.org/Depts/los/clcs_new/submissions_files/jpn08/jpn_09apr12.pdf
313 Fiji's Note Verbale, available at www.un.org/Depts/los/clcs_new/submissions_files/fji24_09/fji24_fji4apr15.pdf
314 Argentina's Note Verbale, available at www.un.org/Depts/los/clcs_new/submissions_files/arg25_09/arg25_arg_2012e.pdf
315 Pakistan's Note Verbale, available at www.un.org/Depts/los/clcs_new/submissions_files/pak29_09/2014_10_09_PAK_NV_UN_003_14-00794.pdf
316 Kenya's Note Verbale no. 12/34, available at www.un.org/Depts/los/clcs_new/submissions_files/ken35_09/ken_2013_10_29.pdf
317 Kenya's Note Verbale no. 586/14, available at www.un.org/Depts/los/clcs_new/submissions_files/ken35_09/ken_2014_10_24.pdf
318 Palau's Note Verbale, available at www.un.org/Depts/los/clcs_new/submissions_files/plw41_09/clcs_41_2009_los_plw.pdf
319 Portugal's Note Verbale, available at www.un.org/Depts/los/clcs_new/submissions_files/prt44_09/prt_re_esp_2013_09_06_13_14_21_886.pdf
320 Guyana's Note Verbale, available at www.un.org/Depts/los/clcs_new/submissions_files/guy57_11/clcs57_2011_guy_e2012.pdf
321 China's Note Verbale no. CML/001/2013, available at www.un.org/Depts/los/clcs_new/submissions_files/chn63_12/chn_re_jpn07_01_2013e.pdf

322 China's Note Verbale no. CML/017/2013, available at www.un.org/Depts/los/clcs_new/submissions_files/chn63_12/chn_re_clcs63_08_2013_e.pdf
323 China's Note Verbale no. CML 11/2020, available at www.un.org/Depts/los/clcs_new/submissions_files/mys_12_12_2019/China_Philippines_ENG.pdf. See also its communication to Viet Nam, Note Verbale no. CML 42/2020, available at www.un.org/Depts/los/clcs_new/submissions_files/mys_12_12_2019/2020_04_17_CHN_NV_UN_003_EN.pdf; its communication to Indonesia, Note Verbale no. CML 46/2020, available at www.un.org/Depts/los/clcs_new/submissions_files/mys_12_12_2019/2020_06_02_CHN_NV_UN_eng.pdf; its communication to Australis, Note Verbale no. CML 54/2020, available at www.un.org/Depts/los/clcs_new/submissions_files/mys_12_12_2019/20200729_CHN_NV_UN_e.pdf; and its communication to New Zealand, Note Verbale no. CML 32/2021, available at www.un.org/Depts/los/clcs_new/submissions_files/mys_12_12_2019/20210816ChnNvUNen.pdf
324 Korea's Note Verbale no MUN/022/13, available at www.un.org/Depts/los/clcs_new/submissions_files/kor65_12/kor_re_jpn_23_01_2013.pdf; see also Korea's Note Verbale no. MUN/191/13, available at www.un.org/Depts/los/clcs_new/submissions_files/kor65_12/kor_re_jpn_26_08_2013.pdf
325 Nicaragua's Note Verbale, available at www.un.org/Depts/los/clcs_new/submissions_files/nic66_13/nic_2013_12_20_001.pdf
326 Nicaragua's Note Verbale no. MINIC-NU-047–13, available at www.un.org/Depts/los/clcs_new/submissions_files/nic66_13/nic_2013_12_20_002.pdf
327 Nicaragua's Note Verbale no. MINIC-NU-048–13, available at www.un.org/Depts/los/clcs_new/submissions_files/nic66_13/nic_2013_12_20_004.pdf
328 Nicaragua's Note Verbale no. MINIC-NU-049–13, available at www.un.org/Depts/los/clcs_new/submissions_files/nic66_13/nic_2013_12_20_005.pdf
329 Nicaragua's Note Verbale no. MINIC-NU-050–13, available at www.un.org/Depts/los/clcs_new/submissions_files/nic66_13/nic_2013_12_20_006.pdf
330 Canada's Note Verbale, available at www.un.org/Depts/los/clcs_new/submissions_files/can70_13/2014_09_03_can_nv_un_001.pdf
331 France's Note Verbale, available at www.un.org/Depts/los/clcs_new/submissions_files/can70_13/1467831E.pdf
332 Spain's Note Verbale no. 064 MPbcm, available at www.un.org/Depts/los/clcs_new/submissions_files/esp77_14/prt_re_esp77_en.pdf
333 Spain's Note Verbale no. 076 MP/bcm, available at www.un.org/Depts/los/clcs_new/submissions_files/esp77_14/2015_04_22_ESP1_NV_UN_004_15-00366.pdf
334 Bangladesh's Note Verbale, no. PMBNY/CLCS/2021, available at www.un.org/Depts/los/clcs_new/submissions_files/bgd55_11/20210506BgdNvUn009.pdf
335 Bangladesh's Note Verbale, no. PMBNY/CLCS/2021, available at www.un.org/Depts/los/clcs_new/submissions_files/bgd55_11/20210913BgdNvUn010.pdf
336 Micronesia's Note Verbale, no. FSMUN 07–2022, available at www.un.org/Depts/los/clcs_new/submissions_files/fsm67_13/20220426FsmNvUn006.pdf
337 See Malaysia's note verbal no. HA 30/20, available at www.un.org/Depts/los/clcs_new/submissions_files/mys_12_12_2019/2020_08_27_MYS_NV_UN_003.pdf
338 Submission by Australia, DOALOS website, available at www.un.org/Depts/los/clcs_new/submissions_files/submission_aus.htm; See for example Unites States' note to the Commission concerning the Australian submission, available at www.un.org/Depts/los/clcs_new/submissions_files/aus04/clcs_03_2004_los_usatext.pdf; Russian Federation's note to the Commission concerning the Australian submission, available at www.un.org/Depts/los/clcs_new/submissions_files/aus04/clcs_03_2004_los_russiantext.pdf; Japan's note to the Commission concerning the Australian submission, available at www.un.org/Depts/los/clcs_new/submissions_files/aus04/clcs_03_2004_los_jap.pdf
339 CLCS, 15th Sess, UN Doc CLCS/44 (3 May 2005), para. 23

340 Japan's note concerning New Zealand's submission, *supra* note 296
341 CLCS/64, *supra* note 100, para. 77
342 Submission by Ireland, DOALOS website, available at www.un.org/Depts/los/clcs_new/submissions_files/submission_irl1.htm
343 CLCS, 27th Sess, UN Doc CLCS/70 (11 May 2011), para. 42
344 Submission by the United Kingdom of Great Britain and Northern Ireland, DOALOS website, available at www.un.org/Depts/los/clcs_new/submissions_files/submission_gbr1.htm
345 CLCS/70, *supra* note 343, para. 42
346 Submission by the Argentine Republic, DOALOS website, available at www.un.org/Depts/los/clcs_new/submissions_files/submission_arg_25_2009.htm; CLCS/64, *supra* note 100, para. 74
347 CLCS/64, *supra* note 100, para. 76
348 Submission by the Kingdom of Norway, DOALOS website, available at www.un.org/Depts/los/clcs_new/submissions_files/submission_nor_30_2009.htm
349 Joint submission by Malaysia and the Socialist Republic of Viet Nam, DOALOS website, available at www.un.org/Depts/los/clcs_new/submissions_files/submission_mys-vnm_33_2009.htm
350 Submission by the Republic of Kenya, DOALOS website, available at www.un.org/Depts/los/clcs_new/submissions_files/submission_ken_35_2009.htm
351 CLCS, 35th Sess, UN Doc CLCS/85 (24 September 2014), paras. 60, 64; Somalia's Note Verbale, available at www.un.org/Depts/los/clcs_new/submissions_files/ken35_09/2014_09_02_SOM_LET_UN_004_14-00700.pdf
352 CLCS, 38th Sess, UN Doc CLCS/90 (1 October 2015), para. 17
353 Submission by the Socialist Republic of Viet Nam, DOALOS website, available at www.un.org/Depts/los/clcs_new/submissions_files/submission_vnm_37_2009.htm
354 Submission by the Republic of Palau, DOALOS website, available at www.un.org/Depts/los/clcs_new/submissions_files/submission_plw_41_2009.htm; CLCS, 26th Sess, UN Doc CLCS/68 (17 September 2010), para. 30
355 CLCS, 46th Sess, UN Doc CLCS/103 (6 April 2018), para. 68–69
356 Submission by the United Kingdom of Great Britain and Northern Ireland, DOALOS website, available at www.un.org/Depts/los/clcs_new/submissions_files/submission_gbr_45_2009.htm; Argentines' Note Verbale to the Commission, no, N.U. No. 290/09/600, available at www.un.org/Depts/los/clcs_new/submissions_files/gbr45_09/arg_re_gbr_clcs_2009e.pdf
357 Submission by the Argentine Republic, *supra* note 346
358 Paula M. Vernet, *The Work of the Commission on the Limits of the Continental Shelf: Current Accomplishments and Challenges on the Verge of Its 20th Anniversary*, 20(1) Max Planck Unyb 36, 65 (2017); United Kingdom's note verbale to the Commission, no. 84/09, available at www.un.org/Depts/los/clcs_new/submissions_files/arg25_09/clcs_45_2009_los_gbr.pdf
359 Paula M. Vernet, *ibid*
360 Bangladesh's Note Verbale no. PMBNY-UNCLOS/2009-, available at www.un.org/depts/los/clcs_new/submissions_files/ind48_09/bgd_re_ind_clcs48_2009e.pdf
361 Submission by the Republic of India, DOALOS website, available at www.un.org/Depts/los/clcs_new/submissions_files/submission_ind_48_2009.htm
362 CLCS/50/2, *supra* note 116
363 Submission by the Kingdom of Denmark, DOALOS website, available at www.un.org/Depts/los/clcs_new/submissions_files/submission_dnk_54_2010.htm
364 Submission by the People's Republic of China, DOALOS website, available at www.un.org/Depts/los/clcs_new/submissions_files/submission_chn_63_2012.htm
365 CLCS, 32nd Sess, UN Doc CLCS/80 (24 September 2013), para. 61
366 Submission by the Republic of Korea, DOALOS website, available at www.un.org/Depts/los/clcs_new/submissions_files/submission_kor_65_2012.htm

367 CLCS/80, *supra* note 365, para. 68
368 China's Note Verbale no. CML/2/2009, available at www.un.org/depts/los/clcs_new/submissions_files/jpn08/chn_6feb09_e.pdf
369 CLCS/62, *supra* note 74, paras. 54, 59; CLCS/64, *supra* note 100, para. 26
370 Korea's Note Verbale no. MUN/230/11, available at www.un.org/depts/los/clcs_new/submissions_files/jpn08/kor11aug11.pdf
371 See CLCS/74, *supra* note 74
372 Submission by the Republic of Nicaragua, DOALOS website, available at www.un.org/Depts/los/clcs_new/submissions_files/submission_nic_66_2013.htm
373 Panama's Note Verbale to the Commission no. DGPE/DG/665/22013, DOALOS website, available at www.un.org/Depts/los/clcs_new/submissions_files/nic66_13/pan_re_nic_2013_09_30e.pdf; see also Panama's Note Verbale to the Commission no. DGPE/FRONT/082/14, DOALOS website, available at www.un.org/Depts/los/clcs_new/submissions_files/nic66_13/pan_re_nic_2014_02_03_e.pdf
374 UNGAOR, 68th Sess, UN Doc A/68/741 (7 February 2014); CLCS/83, *supra* note 113, para. 82
375 CLCS/83, *supra* note 113, para. 83
376 Submission by Angola, DOALOS website, available at www.un.org/Depts/los/clcs_new/submissions_files/submission_ago_69_2013.htm
377 The Government of the Democratic Republic of the Congo's Note Verbale, *supra* note 108
378 The Gabonese Republic's Note Verbale, available at www.un.org/Depts/los/clcs_new/submissions_files/ago69_2013/gab_re_ago_2014_05_30.pdf
379 Submission by the Commonwealth of The Bahamas, DOALOS website, available at www.un.org/Depts/los/clcs_new/submissions_files/submission_bhs_71_2014.htm; CLCS, 47th Sess, UN Doc CLCS/105 (13 September 2018), paras. 71, 73
380 Submission by the French Republic, DOALOS website, available at www.un.org/Depts/los/clcs_new/submissions_files/submission_fra_72_2014.htm
381 CLCS, 41st Sess, UN Doc CLCS/95 (21 September 2016), para. 83
382 Submission by the Federal Republic of Somalia, DOALOS website, available at www.un.org/Depts/los/clcs_new/submissions_files/submission_som_74_2014.htm
383 CLCS/95, *supra* note 381, para. 86
384 Ibid., para. 87. It's noteworthy that the parties agreed in 2009 that the delimitation of maritime boundaries in the areas under dispute, including the delimitation of the continental shelf beyond 200 nautical miles, shall be agreed between the two coastal States on the basis of international law after the Commission has concluded its examination of the separate submissions made by each of the two coastal States and made its recommendations to two coastal States concerning the establishment of the outer limits of the continental shelf beyond 200 nautical mile, see Memorandum of Understanding between the Government of the Republic of Kenya and the Transitional Federal Government of the Somali Republic to Grant to Each Other No-Objection in Respect of Submissions on the Outer Limits of the Continental Shelf beyond 200 Nautical Miles to the Commission on the Limits of the Continental Shelf 7 April 2009, 70 Law of the Sea Bulletin 52 (2009)
385 Partial Submission by Malaysia in the South China Sea, DOALOS website, available at www.un.org/Depts/los/clcs_new/submissions_files/submission_mys_12_12_2019.html
386 Bangladesh's Note Verbale no. PMBNY/67/UNCLOS/2012, *supra* note 56
387 CLCS/64, *supra* note 100, para. 40
388 Ibid., para. 71. See also Vanuatu's Note Verbale no. PMV/MDB/NY/0712/01, available at www.un.org/depts/los/clcs_new/submissions_files/fji24_09/clcs_24_2009_los_vut2.pdf
389 India's Note Verbale no. 55/DPR/PMI/NY-2022, available at www.un.org/depts/los/clcs_new/submissions_files/lka43_09/20221025IndNvUn002.pdf

390 United Kingdom's Note Verbale no. 095/22, available at www.un.org/depts/los/clcs_new/submissions_files/chl_89_2022/20220422GbrNvUn001.pdf; Argentina's Note Verbale no. ENAUN No. 899/2022, available at www.un.org/depts/los/clcs_new/submissions_files/chl_89_2022/20221101ArgNvUn001Eng.pdf

391 The Maldives Note Verbale no. 2022/UN/N/25, available at www.un.org/depts/los/clcs_new/submissions_files/mus2_2022/PICLCSMauritius.pdf

392 United Kingdom's Note Verbale no. 004/23, available at www.un.org/depts/los/clcs_new/submissions_files/mus2_2022/UKNVCSN19012023.pdf

3 The rights and obligations of coastal States in the continental shelf

This chapter analyzes the governance framework concerning the scope of coastal States' sovereign rights in the continental shelf, mainly with respect to the exploration and exploitation of non-living resources. Informal elements, such as the political bargaining process, judicial decisions, and state practice, essentially create a gap between the governance framework and the formal legal regime regulating the continental shelf. The formal legal regime alone cannot explain how in practice coastal States and judicial bodies downplay certain obligations and create new informal norms. Thus, the governance framework is often broader or narrower than the legal regime.

For example, as discussed later, while UNCLOS includes conservation duties regarding the continental shelf and its resources, these rules are hardly implemented in practice. In contrast, with respect to artificial installations in the continental shelf, the governance framework broadens the scope of coastal States' jurisdiction, essentially granting coastal States wider margin of discretion to determine their own competences.

However, obligations concerning state conduct regarding the continental shelf in disputed areas are rarely addressed in international adjudication, despite reflecting significant states interest.[1] The few decisions addressing this issue are inconsistent: In some cases, tribunals effectively conferred wider powers upon the parties to protect their economic interests,[2] downplaying or narrowly interpreting formal legal rules; in other cases, they limited the exercise of sovereign rights in the overlapping area.[3] Thus, state practice and judicial decisions seem to be developing in different directions in this context.

The EEZ regime is an external factor that has influenced the construction and implementation of coastal States' sovereign rights in the continental shelf, even beyond 200 nm. Ostensibly, the EEZ regime incorporates the continental shelf, and since most states have proclaimed an EEZ,[4] it may seem redundant to examine coastal States' rights and duties in the continental shelf. Still, some states have not proclaimed an EEZ, and the EEZ regime does not govern the seabed beyond 200 nm.[5] Thus, it is necessary to examine the scope of rights and duties in the continental shelf independently, apart from the EEZ regime.

DOI: 10.4324/9781003479772-4

1. Coastal States' general rights and obligations

UNCLOS grants coastal States sovereign rights to explore and exploit non-living resources, such as oil and gas, as well as living organisms in their continental shelf.[6] The legal provisions grant coastal States economic jurisdiction over the continental shelf and the EEZ while seeking to balance sovereignty over natural resources with the interests of other states.[7]

1.1 Governance framework for protecting natural resources and the marine environment

Coastal States have sovereign rights concerning natural resources in the continental shelf. However, unlike the EEZ regime, the continental shelf's legal regime does not contain an obligation to "conserve and manage" the resources in this area.[8] Some argue that since the exploitation of non-living resources in the continental shelf causes physical changes in the area, it contradicts the definition of "conservation".[9] However, this distinction does not apply to the EEZ regime, which imposes the same conservation duties for both living and non-living resources.[10]

The continental shelf regime was essentially copied from the CSC and has remained unchanged.[11] The CSC excluded conservation of the marine environment with respect to the continental shelf as it was essentially understood as relating to living resources in the superjacent waters.[12] Thus, coastal States' rights in the continental shelf were limited to exploration and exploitation to preserve freedom of the High Seas and freedom of navigation.[13]

The governance perspective can help to explain the construction of the formal rules through an analysis of the contribution of informal elements, such as the nature of the resources.[14] The governance perspective can also shed light on the significant differences between the legal regime and the practice. As elaborated later, despite coastal States' obligation (derived from "external" legal sources) to protect and preserve the marine environment of the continental shelf and its resources, this obligation is not implemented in practice. This is another example of the gap between the continental shelf's legal regime and the governance framework.

Although the continental shelf's legal regime does not include a legal obligation to conserve and manage natural resources in the continental shelf independent of the EEZ, other UNCLOS chapters include provisions that effectively apply conservation obligations in both the EEZ and the continental shelf. For example, Part XII concerning protection of the marine environment requires coastal States to prevent, reduce, and control pollution also in the continental shelf, similar to "conserve and manage" in the EEZ regime.[15] While Part XII refers to the marine environment and not specifically to natural resources, there is a functional link between the two elements, and both apply to the continental shelf.[16]

In addition, there are other legal framework concerning preservation of the marine environment outside of UNCLOS.[17] For example, the Convention on Biological Diversity (CBD) (which most states are parties to)[18] broadens the scope of coastal States' obligations to preserve the marine environment under UNCLOS, including the shelf's marine environment.[19]

Principles of sustainable development provide an additional external source for conservation rules that apply to coastal States.[20] These principles apply, inter alia, to resources in the continental shelf and thus broaden the scope of coastal States' rights and duties in their shelf.[21] Consequently, while deviating from the formal legal regime, the application of the term "conserve and manage" to non-living resources in the continental shelf is arguably "an implicit element in the evolution of the continental shelf regime under general international law".[22]

Notwithstanding the previous analysis, UNCLOS differentiates between "conservation and management of natural resources" and "marine environmental protection" and subjects them to different rules.[23] UNCLOS's environmental regime contains softer obligations, mostly vague principles, standards, and procedures rather than highly legalized provisions with strict legal obligations.[24] For example, UNCLOS obligates coastal States to "take all measures necessary"[25] and to "adopt laws and regulations"[26] regarding the protection of the marine environment.[27]

Thus, coastal States have mostly procedural duties regarding protection and preservation of the marine environment, including in the continental shelf, such as exchanging information, consultation, cooperation, and acting in good faith.[28] Many of these obligations are due diligence obligations[29] – that is, obligations to prevent harm. This includes the duty to conduct an Environmental Impact Assessment (EIA) on the potential effects of any planned activities on the marine environment and to communicate the results. Failure to take such measures to prevent harm constitutes a breach.[30]

In addition, UNCLOS does not determine the content and extent of states' environmental policies; rather, it establishes general rules of responsibility based on the general obligation to protect the marine environment. This reduces the likelihood of invoking state responsibility in seeking reparations – for example, in cases where there is environmental damage but the responsible state fulfills its procedural obligations.[31]

Thus, in practice, UNCLOS preserves states' sovereignty and discretion to formulate environmental policies on the domestic level, rather than stipulating clear and strict rules in this sphere. In the balance between exploitation and environmental protection, especially with respect to the continental shelf, UNCLOS leans toward the former.[32] In light of this, the jurisprudence has tried to clarify the content and scope of coastal States' due diligence obligations.[33] For example, in the *South China Sea* case, the Arbitral Tribunal determined that the conservation obligation in Article 192 includes a duty to prevent harvest of endangered species.[34]

Judicial interpretation has essentially created new and informal due diligence obligations. As previously discussed, international tribunals are formal actors, whose decisions are informal elements within the broader governance framework. These formal actors have broader competences in practice, establishing informal norms concerning coastal States' sovereign rights in the continental shelf. This process was done through what legal scholars call the "cross-reference of precedents" – that is, by adopting and following the decisions of other tribunals,[35] which is essentially the IR process of institutional deference. However, as analyzed later, state practice deviates from judicial attempt to establish concrete norms in this context.

1.1.1 State practice

State practice, when failing to meet the criteria for establishing such binding rules, can nevertheless be considered an implicit or informal element of the continental shelf's governance framework.[36] Thus, while domestic law is not part of the formal legal regime, it can reflect practices that are part of the governance framework.

Review of domestic laws and state practice concerning the protection of the marine environment and the conservation of natural resources in the continental shelf highlights the differences between the formal legal regime and the governance framework vis-à-vis coastal States' rights and obligations in the continental shelf. State practice essentially downplays the vague legal conservation provisions.[37] Thus, while external instruments, such as judicial decisions, may add informal conservation obligations, state practice further narrows the already weak framework in UNCLOS. Arguably, there may not be a significant gap between the legal regime and the governance framework in this context, but there is still a difference, thus supporting the overall argument of this book. However, there seems to be a conflict between two informal elements of the governance framework: judicial decisions and state practice.

Most domestic laws reflect UNCLOS provisions, which do not include conservation duties in the continental shelf.[38] Some laws concerning the continental shelf still reflect the CSC,[39] while others refer only to the EEZ.[40] This might explain the lack of reference to conservation duties regarding the continental shelf flowing from other chapters of UNCLOS and general international law. Some states have asserted other rights in the continental shelf that are not necessarily in UNCLOS, such as development,[41] although this is probably due to the influence of the EEZ regime.[42] Conversely, some states have determined that their rights are limited to exploring and exploiting resources, even in the EEZ, which narrows the formal legal regime.[43] Some coastal States adopted laws addressing liability and compensation with respect to seabed-based marine pollution, although the liability falls on private actors, such as ship-owners.[44]

Coastal States rarely enforce their conservation jurisdiction in the continental shelf, despite existing domestic and international legal framework.[45] While there has been an increase in environmental litigation under international law,[46] almost no international proceedings have addressed marine environmental protection in the continental shelf.[47] Most of the few proceedings that have been initiated concern fisheries.[48] It is noteworthy that there are regional disputes involving coastal States' rights to natural resources, but no dispute-settlement proceeding has been instituted.[49]

Furthermore, while UNCLOS addresses seabed-based pollution (e.g., continental shelf drilling) and establishes coastal States' responsibility for protection and preservation of the marine environment,[50] most cases concerning environmental harm to the continental shelf are litigated domestically as a civil procedure against drilling companies or ship-owners and masters, which corresponds with domestic liability regimes rather than international proceedings against states for breaching their obligations under UNCLOS.[51] In light of the previous discussion, it seems that state practice goes beyond the legal regime, leaning heavily toward exploitation of marine resources rather than conservation of the marine environment and its resources.

The absence of international proceedings against states may be attributable to the fact that there is no international liability regime that exclusively addresses damages resulting from seabed activities.[52] Other than UNCLOS's vague and general liability regime, there is no international regulation of compensation between states.[53] Some scholars note that states tend to avoid submitting claims against other states for failing to protect and preserve the marine environment. The increasingly accepted solution with respect to pollution damages is to transfer the question from state responsibility under public international law to civil liability under private international law and domestic law.[54]

It seems that states are unwilling to enforce their environmental jurisdiction in the continental shelf under UNCLOS against other states.[55] Thus, in practice, even the vague obligation to conserve resources in the continental shelf has not been implemented. This is another example for how state practice narrows the legal regime, essentially indicating that this subject should not be regulated under UNCLOS, thus "subtracting" these provisions from the Convention. Furthermore, state practice in this context contradicts the informal norm established by judicial bodies.

1.2 Governance framework for artificial installations and safety zones in the continental shelf

UNCLOS assigns coastal States the jurisdiction to construct and regulate artificial islands, installations, and structures.[56] Although artificial installations and structures are generally connected to the seabed and used to extract non-living resources from the seabed,[57] the relevant provisions are part of the EEZ legal regime rather than the continental shelf regime.[58] An attempt to include independent provisions concerning artificial installations in the continental shelf's legal regime was rejected in the early stages of the negotiations.[59] Thus, the EEZ regime influenced coastal States' rights and jurisdictions in the continental shelf, despite UNCLOS's distinction between the legal regimes in terms of jurisdictions over artificial installations.[60]

As elaborated later, while the legal regime concerning artificial installations ostensibly restricts coastal States' jurisdiction over these structures in their continental shelf, in practice, coastal States do not heed these limitations. State practice essentially downplays the formal rules and broadens the governance framework for artificial installations in the continental shelf.

The governance perspective can help to explain the construction of the formal rules by analyzing the contribution of informal elements. In other words, the governance framework may shed light on why states are motivated to establish particular rules. For example, the rules governing artificial installations were influenced by the linkage between the CSC and the EEZ regime.[61] Since this linkage is not a formal part of the legal regime, it can be considered an informal element in the governance framework. This also illustrate the gap between the legal regime and the governance framework concerning the continental shelf.

The EEZ provisions on artificial installations were essentially copied (with some changes) from the CSC.[62] However, there are differences between the two regimes, mainly with respect to the status of the superjacent waters,[63] and these differences create ambiguity regarding the scope of coastal States' rights under UNCLOS. Transferring provisions from the CSC to the EEZ regime ostensibly creates a lacuna where states have not proclaimed an EEZ or in the continental shelf beyond 200 nm. In such cases, the provisions concerning artificial installations, as part of the EEZ legal regime, ostensibly do not apply. However, as elaborated later, state practice essentially fills this lacuna, applying provisions of the EEZ legal regime even in cases where they should not apply, granting coastal States broader jurisdictional zones in the continental shelf.[64]

1.2.1 Safety zones around installations

The jurisdiction of coastal States to establish safety zones around artificial installations exists only in the EEZ, which regulates both the superjacent waters and the seabed.[65] As explained earlier, there is a lacuna regarding the regulation of artificial installations under the continental shelf's legal regime; there is no similar provision in UNCLOS Part VI. The only reference in the continental shelf's legal regime to artificial installations is that the relevant rules in the EEZ legal regime apply *mutatis mutandis*, without addressing the possible differences between the two legal regimes in terms of the status of the superjacent waters, where jurisdiction is exercised.[66]

Regulation of safety zones under the EEZ regime is logical; as it governs the superjacent waters, it is reasonable that it also includes safety zones in the water around structures. In contrast, coastal States ostensibly cannot establish safety zones when there is no EEZ since the superjacent waters are part of the High Seas, where coastal States have no jurisdiction.[67] However, UNCLOS essentially copied the relevant provisions from the CSC to the EEZ regime. The scope of coastal States' rights under the two regimes is not identical. While the CSC allowed establishing safety zones in the High Seas around artificial installations in the continental shelf, UNCLOS limits such rights to areas under coastal States' jurisdiction, i.e., the EEZ.[68] This suggests that states perceived safety zones as encroaching on the freedom of the High Seas.

Not only that UNCLOS transferred the CSC provisions to the EEZ regime but it also applied it to the new continental shelf regime incidentally. UNCLOS applies Article 60 to the continental shelf without any explanation or detailed provisions, only indicating that the scope of rights in the continental shelf is not identical to that in the EEZ and that the application of Article 60 to the continental shelf requires some changes.[69] This created a legal ambiguity regarding jurisdiction in the waters around installations under the continental shelf regime.[70]

This nuance is possibly the result of the structural differences between the 1958 Geneva Conventions and UNCLOS. The 1958 conventions separated the High Seas and the continental shelf into two legal instruments. There was no coherency between the two conventions; thus, the article regarding safety zones in the CSC contradicted provisions concerning the freedom of the High Seas.[71] In contrast, UNCLOS includes both the High Seas and the continental shelf; thus, the High Seas regime addresses coastal States sovereign rights to construct installations on the continental shelf, where the superjacent waters are part of the High Seas.[72]

Arguably, as noted earlier, establishing safety zones on the High Seas breaches its status since no state may claim sovereignty over any part of this area. Thus, the provisions concerning safety zones are not applicable if there is no EEZ. The ILC interpreted the freedom of the High Seas to also mean that "no State may exercise *jurisdiction* over any such stretch of water" (emphasis added).[73] This interpretation might also apply to the High Seas regime under UNCLOS, meaning that there is no competence to establish safety zones around installations outside the EEZ. In such cases, enforcement jurisdiction is transferred to the flag state.[74]

Support for this argument can be found in the fact that safety zones are areas where the coastal State has a greater scope of jurisdiction than in the EEZ. It seems that safety zones are broader jurisdictional zones, somewhere between "sovereign rights" and "sovereignty". Such *sui generis* area cannot exist outside the EEZ since in the High Seas, coastal States have even less jurisdictions.[75] Infringement of the freedom of the High Seas is allowed only to the extent that it strictly necessary to protect coastal States' interests in the continental shelf.[76]

This creates distinctions between the three regimes, certainly between the EEZ and the continental shelf under UNCLOS. Otherwise, the same provisions would also be in Part VI, or at least Article 60 would apply to structures in the continental shelf as is, rather than *mutatis mutandis*. The structure of UNCLOS and the distinctions between all the legal regimes might indicate that, unlike the CSC, coastal States have no jurisdiction to establish safety zones around installations in the continental shelf in cases where the waters superjacent to the seabed are not part of the EEZ and thus not under national jurisdiction.

While most states proclaimed an EEZ,[77] there are states that did not proclaim such zones. In addition, the EEZ regime does not apply to the continental shelf beyond 200 nm. Thus, the scope of coastal States' rights concerning safety zones around installations in the continental shelf, as an independent regime, is still significant. In practice, as explained later, coastal States do not distinguish between the superjacent waters in the EEZ and in the continental shelf regimes with respect to jurisdiction over installations; thus, the governance framework largely broadens their jurisdiction.

Another difference between the legal regime and the governance framework concerning safety zones is that coastal States must explicitly proclaim safety zones, despite no such requirement is stipulated in UNCLOS. This legal requirement was established by international tribunals through interpretation of Article 60(4).[78] However, as detailed later, in practice, coastal States do not always proclaim such zones, even if they have a safety zone or some other type of "enforcement zone" around artificial installations in their continental shelf and EEZ.

1.2.1.1 STATE PRACTICE CONCERNING SAFETY ZONES AROUND INSTALLATIONS

As noted, state practice can be considered an element of the governance framework for the continental shelf. Consequently, domestic law can indicate the development of state practice and thus constitute an element of the governance framework. A review of domestic laws concerning artificial installations and safety zones reveals the gap between the legal regime and the governance framework, with the latter expanding coastal States' jurisdiction.

Most domestic laws concerning artificial installations reflect UNCLOS Article 56, regulating the issue within the EEZ.[79] This suggests that for most coastal States the continental shelf regime is incorporated into the EEZ regime, despite being an independent legal regime. Only a few states regulate artificial installations under the continental shelf regime independently of the EEZ.[80] Some states regulate installations under both regimes.[81]

With respect to *safety zones* around artificial installations, some states do not include specific reference to the issue even when they have laws regulating artificial installations in general.[82] Some states regulate safety zones within the EEZ regime,[83] while others regulate it under the continental shelf regime, which is not in accordance with UNCLOS.[84] Some states regulate safety zones under both legal regimes.[85] Most of the states that regulate safety zones in domestic legislation mention the breadth of 500 meters, but some states do not specify the exact limit of the safety zones.[86]

As noted earlier, it seems that most domestic laws concerning artificial installations reflect the incorporation of the continental shelf's legal regime into the EEZ's legal regime, which may narrow the former. This is also reflected in the laws concerning safety zones. However, domestic laws that regulate artificial installations independently under the continental shelf regime essentially broaden coastal States' jurisdiction in the zone since UNCLOS largely refrains from regulating this issue in the continental shelf. The same can be said with respect to laws regulating safety zones independently under the continental shelf regime, as the safety zone would essentially be on the High Seas.[87] This essentially broadens the legal regime of the continental shelf to include the superjacent waters and affects its status.[88] In addition, legislation that regulates artificial installations and safety zones under both regimes goes beyond UNCLOS by prescribing detailed provisions for both zones, instead of just applying the regulations concerning the EEZ *mutatis mutandis* to the continental shelf.

The practice of some states goes even further than their domestic legislation, broadening their jurisdictions beyond UNCLOS. While the breadth of safety zones has not changed since the adoption of UNCLOS,[89] some states have unilaterally extended the breadth of their "safety zone" beyond 500 meters.[90] Although such practice is uncommon, it seems to have met with little objection from other states.[91] Thus, it can be viewed as the beginning of a new state practice that has yet to become a customary norm.[92] Therefore, it is an element of the governance framework, which is broader than the legal regime in this context.

The only reference I found in the literature to safety zones in the continental shelf where there is no EEZ pertains to enforcement jurisdiction against foreign ships.[93] Most states have proclaimed an EEZ and there is little case law concerning safety zones around artificial installations in the continental shelf, certainly beyond 200 nm.[94] Thus, it is difficult to determine whether state practice in this regard actually indicates a broader governance framework. It seems that the drafters of UNCLOS did not imagine a situation where there is no EEZ. Therefore, in most cases, the continental shelf essentially does not constitute an independent regime in the context of safety zones, even beyond 200 nm.[95] This makes it difficult to present any kind of argument with respect to the continental shelf. Still, there are some indications, as noted earlier, of coastal States' "creeping jurisdiction" in the continental shelf in this context, which can be considered part of the governance framework.

1.2.2 Law enforcement jurisdiction in the continental shelf

The governance perspective can help to explain the formation of the formal rules – that is, the scope of coastal States' law enforcement jurisdiction – by analyzing informal elements. The governance perspective also highlights the gap between the legal regime and actual practice concerning the sovereign rights of coastal States in the continental shelf. As discussed later, subject to certain limitations, the scope of coastal States' jurisdiction in the continental shelf, and specifically law enforcement jurisdiction, is broader than the formal legal regime provides.

UNCLOS confers law enforcement jurisdiction only in the EEZ and specifically with respect to utilization of *living* resources.[96] There is no such legal provision with respect to the continental shelf or *non-living* resources.[97] Strictly speaking, coastal States do not have such jurisdiction with respect to non-living resources (despite the fact that the seabed of the EEZ is the continental shelf).[98] In practice, the term "sovereign rights" seems to grant coastal States powers to legislate and enforce protective measures vis-à-vis the continental shelf and its non-living resources.[99] International tribunals interpreted "sovereign rights" to include "all rights necessary for and connected with the exploration, exploitation, conservation and management of the natural resources, including the right to take the necessary enforcement measures".[100] While this interpretation clearly applies in the EEZ, the usage of the term "sovereign rights" in both regimes implies that this also applies to the continental shelf independently from the EEZ.[101]

In the *Arctic Sunrise* case, the Arbitral Tribunal maintained that coastal States also have law enforcement jurisdiction over *non-living* resources, even if this is not explicitly stipulated in UNCLOS. The Tribunal relied on the ILC's commentary concerning the CSC, interpreting the term "sovereign rights" with respect to the continental shelf to also include jurisdiction for preventing and punishing violations of coastal States' laws.[102] Since UNCLOS Article 77 reflects the CSC regime, the Arbitral Tribunal maintained that law enforcement jurisdiction applies also to non-living resources. In addition, international tribunals have argued that coastal States' sovereign rights also cover non-living resources under the EEZ regime. Thus, Article 73 applies in this context, although the extent of such jurisdiction remains underexplored.[103]

With respect to artificial installations, as discussed earlier, UNCLOS confers coastal States exclusive jurisdiction (including law enforcement jurisdiction) only within the EEZ legal regime.[104] However, UNCLOS provides that other states have exclusive jurisdiction over ships flying their flag in the EEZ.[105] Hence, coastal States may exercise law enforcement jurisdiction over foreign vessels near their artificial installations only with the prior consent of the flag State.[106] Accordingly, the Arbitral Tribunal maintained that coastal States can exercise enforcement jurisdiction in the continental shelf only within the safety zones around installations.[107] Tribunals also indicated that coastal States' enforcement jurisdiction in the safety zone is broader than in the EEZ.[108] This goes beyond the formal text of UNCLOS, broadening the scope of jurisdiction that coastal States can exercise within this area, thus increasing its significance and status.[109]

As previously explained, international tribunals are formal actors, whose decisions are informal elements within the broader governance framework, establishing informal norms concerning the sovereign rights of coastal States in the continental shelf. The jurisprudence has moved beyond the formal legal regime to apply enforcement jurisdiction in the continental shelf, while UNCLOS is silent on this issue. In addition, exercising law enforcement jurisdiction over activities in the continental shelf when no EEZ has been proclaimed or beyond 200 nm means exercising jurisdiction on the High Seas, which also broadens the legal regime. In light of the previous discussion, the governance framework is broader than the legal regime in this context.

1.2.2.1 STATE PRACTICE CONCERNING LAW ENFORCEMENT JURISDICTION IN THE CONTINENTAL SHELF

In practice, few states have enacted legislation to regulate enforcement jurisdiction. Some states have established general rules regarding law enforcement jurisdiction in the continental shelf,[110] and some have included specific enforcement provisions with respect to structures and installations.[111] Other states include law enforcement jurisdiction only with respect to the EEZ.[112] While state practice concerning law enforcement jurisdiction within safety zones around installations is not well developed, the sparse practice that does exist indicates that enforcement measures in the safety zones aim to ensure safe navigation and protect installations. This practice broadens the scope of jurisdiction that coastal States can exercise in this area.[113]

The relatively undeveloped practice concerning law enforcement has elicited little objection from other states. This perhaps indicates the beginning of new state practice as an element of the governance framework, which is broader than the legal regime in this context. The application of criminal or general federal laws in the safety zones goes beyond the competences assigned to coastal States under the formal legal regime since it essentially affects the status of the superjacent waters.[114] The ambiguity of the legal regime concerning the scope of enforcement jurisdiction within safety zones and current, albeit limited, state practice indicate that coastal States have broad competence and discretion to determine what constitutes appropriate measures for ensuring the safety of navigation and installations.[115]

The analysis earlier describes the construction of law enforcement jurisdiction in the continental shelf, which has created a broader governance framework than the formal legal regime – despite limited practice. With respect to military activities and the use of force, UNCLOS does not explicitly contain such enforcement jurisdictions. However, international tribunals have maintained that when all appropriate measures fail, coastal States are allowed to employ force as a last resort, subject to certain limitations.[116] Conversely, when the use of force seems more like a threat of military action than a mere law enforcement activity, it might constitute a threat of use of force under the UN Charter.[117] Therefore, while coastal States have broad jurisdiction to determine the appropriate law enforcement measures in the continental shelf, it is subjected to certain limitations.

2. Coastal States' rights and obligations in the context of delimitation

As discussed in Chapter 2, while coastal States have inherent sovereign rights in their continental shelf, the process of delimitation essentially affects the precise areas in which coastal States can exercise these rights.[118] Thus, in practice, the delimitation of overlapping continental shelves is linked to the exercise of sovereign rights in the overlapping area. This section analyzes the rights and obligations of coastal States during the process of delimitation.

UNCLOS obligates neighboring coastal States to resolve disputes concerning overlapping continental shelves by achieving an equitable solution through either a bilateral agreement or international adjudication.[119] In addition, pending such agreement, the relevant parties should "make every effort" to conclude provisional arrangements and not to hinder reaching a final agreement. The provisional arrangements shall be without prejudice to the final delimitation.[120]

As elaborated later, there is a difference between the legal regime and the governance framework regarding coastal States' rights and obligations during delimitation: The governance framework downplays formal obligations and establishes new informal rules for delimitation. In addition, inconsistent judicial interpretation of the formal rules has essentially narrowed the scope of coastal States' sovereign rights in the process of delimitation.

2.1 Governance framework for coastal States' rights and duties in the context of delimitation

As mentioned, most of the adjudicated maritime disputes have pertained to sovereignty claims and boundary delimitation, while the *scope* of coastal States' sovereign rights has rarely been addressed.[121] A few cases have addressed the rights, obligations, and conduct of coastal States in the continental shelf, such as the right to exploit resources or the obligation not to jeopardize a final delimitation agreement. Most of these cases were arbitral procedures, involving a powerful actor in an asymmetric geo-political context (e.g., Russia and China).[122]

The main IR theoretical streams can highlight different factors and offer various explanations for the types of maritime disputes that reach international adjudication. For example, the realist stream highlights the maximization of material power. Since delimitation affects marine resources' utilizations, it is logical that states are willing to submit their disputes to international adjudication. However, most disputes do not reach judicial dispute-settlement and states prefer to solve them through bilateral agreements. Disputes are submitted to international adjudication when significant interest are involved.[123]

The institutional approach might also support judicial dispute-settlement. Since maritime boundary delimitation affects coastal States' material interests, coastal States will safeguard their interests, with lower costs, by utilizing judicial institutions to coordinate action with other states in disputed maritime zones, ensuring that each party will gain some access to the disputed area and thus to the resources within it. This will promote stable boundaries, allowing better exploitation of natural resources in the continental shelf.[124] Conversely, the constructivists approach might highlight the few disputes that did not address delimitation and still submitted to international adjudication. These cases correspond with the Constructivists approach that emphasizes the social characteristics of international relations and consider the role of accepted social norms such as "distributive justice".[125]

The governance perspective can also help to explain the gap between the legal regime and actual practice with respect to the scope of coastal States' sovereign rights and how this has affected maritime boundary delimitation. For example, coastal States' sovereign rights have influenced international tribunals during delimitation, as well as possible alternatives to boundary delimitation.

2.1.1 State conduct as a relevant circumstance in delimitation

The formal legal regime does not specify how to delimit overlapping continental shelves, only that the solution must be "equitable".[126] However, the jurisprudence has developed new informal rules for delimitation – such as "relevant circumstances", which reflect mostly geographical considerations; these new rules have become part of the governance framework.[127]

In general, coastal States' sovereign rights in their continental shelf have not been addressed independently in international adjudication. In some cases, tribunals have considered this issue while examining the relevant circumstances that might justify the adjustment of the provisional equidistance line.[128] In addition, while tribunals did not formally view delimitation as being influenced by "distributive justice" or "compensatory" considerations, in practice, some of the principles they have developed for maritime delimitation effectively reflect these considerations.[129] Thus, while sovereign rights should not be considered in delimitation under the legal regime, the process of delimitation affects the scope of coastal States' rights in disputed maritime zones, indirectly broadening the governance framework.

As mentioned earlier, resource-related arguments are generally considered relevant circumstances that may affect the provisional boundary. However, in some cases, judicial bodies did not necessarily recognize economic arguments as relevant circumstances for the location of the delimitation line but rather as a means of establishing historical rights, thus indirectly influencing the process of delimitation.[130] In other cases, one party claimed that the other had acquiesced (or tacitly agreed) to its exercise of sovereign rights in the disputed area (e.g., conducting seismic surveys or granting oil concessions). These claims essentially maintained that economic activities (i.e., the exercise of sovereign rights) establish a *de facto* maritime boundary or align with the claimed boundary.[131]

It seems that state conduct (or practice) adds to the scope of coastal States' rights as constructed in the jurisprudence. In this context, acquiescence or tacit agreement cannot be considered part of the formal legal regime since it is hard to recognize "silence" as establishing a treaty or even customary law.[132] As noted, there are two main informal elements of the governance framework: state practice and judicial decisions. Each broadens the scope of coastal States' rights in disputed areas and the process of delimitation, although as discussed later, these elements may not always correspond with each other.

It is noteworthy that arguments concerning the conduct of the parties are usually invoked in cases where the parties were previously subjects of competing colonial powers. The colonial context is considered sufficient justification to consider tacit agreement as establishing a mutually accepted boundary.[133] For example, in the *Tunisia/Libya* case, the ICJ determined that coastal States' oil activities (e.g., petroleum concessions) essentially establish a *de facto* maritime limit due to a tacit long-term *modus vivendi* dating back to the colonial era, concerning offshore exploration and exploitation of the continental shelf. Such *de facto* boundary lines, which were never formally contested by the parties over a long period of time, can constitute "historic rights" and thus be considered a relevant criterion for delimitation of the continental shelf.[134] In contrast, in the *Gulf of Maine* case, the ICJ did consider the economic conduct of the parties but was unable to conclude that it indicated acquiescence to the delimitation line because there was no previous colonial context establishing a *modus vivendi*.[135] Although the ICJ maintained that exercising sovereign rights in disputed areas cannot be relevant in itself for delimitation,[136] the Court did consider the issue indirectly. Therefore, it has at least some significance in the context of delimitation, which broadens the governance framework on this subject.

However, the ICJ disregarded the colonial context in the following cases, despite the existence of such context and despite the parties' arguments that exercising sovereign rights in the disputed area was a decisive factor for delimitation.[137] Thus, despite attempting to develop clearer rules for delimitation, judicial bodies have been inconsistent in weighing the significance of the parties' conduct or sovereign rights in the context of delimitation. For example, while the ICJ has generally rejected oil activities as an independent criterion that justifies the adjustment of the provisional delimitation line,[138] it has been willing to consider such activities as evidence of historic rights.[139] In addition, the Court has recognized that a tacit agreement regarding oil activities can indicate a consensus on the maritime areas to which the disputed parties are entitled. However, the Arbitral Tribunal maintained that the economic conduct of the parties is relevant only if it reflects "an unequivocal pattern" that supports a boundary line.[140]

In contrast, ITLOS rejected the idea that long-term oil practices establish a "customary equidistance line" based on a special agreement between the parties.[141] The Tribunal was not convinced that such practices establish a tacit delimitation agreement, despite observing that activities were essentially confined to each party's side of the "tacit" line and that each party requested the other's permission before crossing the line.[142] The Tribunal also maintained that the "catastrophic repercussions" test only applies to fisheries, not oil activities.[143] This strengthens the argument that judicial bodies treat oil activities inconsistently: sometimes as a relevant circumstance for the location of the boundary line and sometimes as evidence of a tacit bilateral delimitation agreement.

As noted, judicial decisions are part of the governance framework. The question here is whether the governance framework is broader or narrower than the legal regime. It is somewhat difficult to answer this question considering the inconsistent treatment of sovereign rights and state conduct. While in some cases tribunals recognized the significance of states' economic conduct in the process of delimitation, in other cases, they rejected arguments concerning tacit delimitation agreements and ignored state practice, deeming them irrelevant to delimitation.[144] However, despite this inconsistency, it seems that economic activities still have some significance in the context of delimitation, thus broadening the governance framework.

Alternatively, we can argue that the governance framework is narrower than the legal regime in the sense that coastal States' sovereign rights under UNCLOS are not affected by delimitation.[145] Thus, judicial bodies essentially downplay formal legal rules in this context. For example, ITLOS maintained that negotiating a final delimitation agreement should curb the parties' conduct.[146] However, as discussed later, state practice downplays the judicial construction of the significance of sovereign rights (i.e., economic activities) in delimitation and broadens the scope of coastal States' sovereign rights.

The discussion on "acquiescence" also narrows the governance framework. It is noteworthy that judicial bodies do not always distinguish between "tacit agreement" and "acquiescence", despite the difference between the two concepts.[147] Some scholars maintain that these concepts differ in the conduct they require: acquiescence is based on omission (i.e., inaction or lack of protest where action is needed), while tacit agreement is generally understood as positive action.[148] With regard to acquiescence, the jurisprudence recognizes the possibility that silence may be interpreted as consent but only in circumstances where an action is *called for*.[149]

This analysis begs the question of whether there are circumstances that call for a response or objection in the context of maritime boundary delimitation. In the *Somalia/Kenya* case, the Court examined Kenya's conduct – for example, its political proclamations, domestic law, and submission to the CLCS.[150] It is noteworthy that these examples are essentially unilateral acts concerning the *delineation* of the outer limits of its maritime zones and have no bearing on the *delimitation* of overlapping zones. Under UNCLOS, a coastal State's entitlement to a maritime zone does not affect other states' entitlement to the full extent of their maritime zones. Since an overlap in maritime zones does not negate or diminish the rights of other states, there is no requirement to object to others' claims. There are no circumstances that call for a response in the context of maritime boundary disputes. In the *Somalia/Kenya* case, the Court determined that since Kenya's conduct was inconsistent, no response was called for by Somalia. The Court also noted that even if Kenya's conduct was consistent, there was no evidence for Somalia's clear and consistent acceptance of a maritime boundary.[151]

This position essentially conflates delineation and delimitation and is contrary to current international law. While courts and tribunals have rejected claims of acquiescence to a maritime boundary, recognition of such possibility conflicts with UNCLOS Articles 76 and 77 concerning coastal States' entitlement to their continental shelf, thus limiting their rights and broadening their obligations.[152]

2.1.2 The development of Article 83(3) on obligations during delimitation disputes

Article 83(3) concerning coastal States' obligations during dispute-settlement was influenced by informal factors, such as the conflict of interests between broad-margin coastal States and other states[153] and the contribution of the Chairperson of Negotiating Group 7.[154] The interpretation of Article 83(3) also demonstrates the gap between the legal regime and the governance framework concerning coastal States' rights and obligations in the continental shelf.

As analyzed earlier, tribunals have treated issues such as sovereign rights and state conduct inconsistently in the context of delimitation, which can broaden or narrow the legal regime. The judicial interpretation of Article 83(3) concerning obligations pending a delimitation agreement further narrows the governance framework in this context. As elaborated later, this is contrary to state practice, which assigns greater significance to resource utilization than to boundary delimitation, broadening the governance framework.

Pending a delimitation agreement, UNCLOS obligates the parties to make provisional arrangements and not to hamper the conclusion of a final agreement. These provisional arrangements are without prejudice to the final delimitation.[155] The jurisprudence interpreted this legal obligation to include three aspects: a positive obligation to seek a provisional arrangement, a negative obligation not to jeopardize reaching a final agreement, and an understanding that such arrangements are "without prejudice" to the final delimitation agreement.[156]

In accordance with the *positive* obligation, states must make every effort to conclude a provisional arrangement; they are not obligated to be successful, only to negotiate in good faith.[157] This aspect implicitly recognizes that the parties do not have to suspend all their economic activities in the disputed area, provided they do not impair the ability to reach a final agreement. In other words, under the formal legal regime, provisional arrangements should not accord the parties permanent rights in the disputed area.[158] As analyzed later, state practice downplays this interpretation, granting permanent rights even where there is no final agreement.

However, while the parties do not necessarily have to stop their economic activities in the disputed area, the *negative* aspect of Article 83(3) requires them to refrain from unilateral actions that may aggravate the dispute.[159] The third aspect of Article 83(3) reflects the understanding that exercising sovereign rights in disputed areas might change the status quo in a way that prejudices the final agreement.

Article 83(3) does not require complete suspension of seabed activities; rather, it aims to promote economic development of disputed areas while preventing, as much as possible, unilateral action and permanent effects that could aggravate the dispute and threaten international peace and security.[160] Thus, international tribunals have distinguished between activities that cause permanent physical change, such as seabed exploitation, and activities that do not have such permanent effects, such as seismic surveys.[161] This distinction narrows the sovereign rights of coastal States in the continental shelf, limiting the exercise of such rights in disputed areas even if permitted under the formal legal regime.[162] As discussed later, states do not make such distinctions when concluding bilateral agreements.

Scholars have argued that "the Court endorsed the view that delimitation has a constitutive function: it is an act generating sovereign rights for States",[163] thus conflating entitlement and delimitation. Despite this, and contrary to past case law, tribunals have tended to disregard the significance of oil activities in the context of delimitation, mainly due to this conflation and inconsistency concerning the role of oil activities in delimitation.[164] Thus, according to the jurisprudence, the governance framework is narrower than the legal regime in this context. As discussed later, this position conflicts with state practice, which engenders most delimitation agreements.

2.1.2.1 STATE PRACTICE

The governance perspective on delimitation agreements can help to explain the patterns of state practice – for example, by analyzing the contribution of informal actors.[165] In addition, a review of bilateral maritime agreements underlines the gap between the legal regime and the governance framework vis-à-vis the sovereign rights of coastal States in the context of boundary delimitation. As elaborated earlier, the legal regime limits the scope of coastal States' sovereign rights in disputed areas. In contrast, state practice shows that sovereign rights are an important factor in bilateral agreements, including provisional arrangements and final delimitation agreements. In addition, state practice conflicts with another informal element within the governance framework: judicial decisions.

Bilateral maritime agreements vary in the scope of information they include[166] and in the number of parties involved.[167] These agreements regulate a variety of issues, such as a moratorium on all activities in the disputed area, joint development of fisheries, allocation of criminal and civil jurisdiction,[168] and environmental protection.[169] However, it seems that the number of permanent maritime boundary agreements has declined with time.[170]

The relative absence of such agreements might encourage unilateral actions by coastal States, such as granting exploitation and exploration rights or increasing their military presence in disputed areas to strengthen their claims.[171] In light of this, other types of arrangements concerning disputed maritime zones have become more significant – for example, mutual utilization agreements. State practice reveals that joint exploitation of resources, especially those that straddle maritime boundaries, and joint development of offshore reservoirs are critical issues in the context of bilateral maritime agreements.[172]

This practice demonstrates several aspects of the gap between the legal regime and the governance framework concerning coastal States' sovereign rights in the context of delimitation. First, states have regulated the utilization of "straddling" deposits of non-living resources in the seabed,[173] despite UNCLOS's silence on this issue.[174] Second, while the legal regime obligates states to make provisional arrangements and not to jeopardize or hamper the reaching of a final agreement, states have made permanent utilization arrangements concerning disputed areas even prior to or in the absence of final boundary agreements. Third, state practice created new informal obligations for coastal States vis-à-vis other coastal States in disputed areas.

In addition, state practice is contrary to the judicial interpretation of coastal States' sovereign rights in disputed areas.[175] While the jurisprudence generally disregards the role of resource-related considerations in maritime delimitation, state practice (reflected in bilateral agreements) assigns greater significance to the sovereign rights and economic interests of coastal States. For example, bilateral agreements contain resource-related clauses that establish joint development zones (JDZs)[176] or joint "utilization regimes" of hydrocarbon deposits, especially in the case of "straddling reservoirs".[177] In some cases, these agreements divide the reservoirs equally between the parties; in other cases, the reservoirs are allocated to one party.[178]

International oil and gas companies are informal actors in the governance framework and have significantly influenced the conclusion of bilateral agreements. States often rely on the funds, equipment, and expertise of these companies to develop their offshore resources. In addition to geological conditions, political and economic stability also help to promote private investment. Therefore, bilateral agreements encourage international corporations to operate in disputed maritime zones by increasing legal certainty concerning these areas.[179]

This reflects the IR institutional approach concerning coordination and convergence of expectations. As explained in Chapter 1, governance frameworks contain rules, norms, procedures, and institutions that guide actors' behavior vis-à-vis common issues. These frameworks promote cooperation by facilitating transparency and reducing the influence of uncertainty and information deficit.

These bilateral arrangements essentially create new detailed and operable obligations for coastal States vis-à-vis other coastal States in disputed areas that are not explicitly included in the legal regime[180] – for example, the establishment of mechanisms for granting mining rights to potential investors and investor-state cooperation.[181] The legal regime explicitly contains such obligations only with respect to the Area, which is regulated through the International Seabed Authority.[182] Thus, state practice broadens the governance framework in this context.

Some scholars view JDZs and other trans-boundary utilization agreements as alternatives to delimitation agreements that facilitate economic development in disputed areas.[183] Ostensibly, this practice is not in accordance with the legal regime, which only requires a "provisional arrangement of practical nature" (of delimitation, not necessarily of usage).[184] Simultaneously, these scholars maintain that such alternative agreements constitute a type of provisional arrangement under Article 83(3) and that the practice of both coastal States and tribunals indicates that UNCLOS essentially obligates coastal States to make every effort to enter into some type of utilization agreement pending the delimitation of their boundaries.[185]

These utilization agreements may correspond with coastal States' sovereign rights in the continental shelf. However, they may conflict with Article 83 regarding obligations during the delimitation process. While UNCLOS regulates conduct during delimitation negotiations, these agreements regulate the utilization of seabed resources,[186] an issue that is not explicitly mentioned in Article 83. Thus, these agreements may hinder reaching a final delimitation agreement due to permanent changes in the marine environment and the redundancy of boundary agreements due to alternative utilization agreements, contrary to the legal regime.[187]

Joint or unilateral resource utilization prior to a delimitation agreement may alter the environment in a way that affects the possible area that would be allocated to each party. Thus, while "without prejudice" clauses are very common in joint development and trans-boundary utilization agreements,[188] these agreements are likely to prejudice the parties' rights due to possible environmental changes. Thus, these clauses may not have much significance in practice. In addition, states seem to be satisfied with utilization agreements, which safeguard stronger interests (i.e., material power), abandoning reaching final delimitation agreements as required under the legal regime. Hence, the governance framework is broader than the legal regime, giving greater significance to coastal States' sovereign rights in the context of delimitation. In contrast, the governance framework downplays the significance of final delimitation agreements and is thus narrower than the legal regime in this context.

If utilization arrangements are recognized as provisional delimitation agreements or as an alternative to delimitation agreements, this essentially means that exercising sovereign rights affects the breadth of the continental shelf, which is contrary to the legal regime. This may create problems in the future, especially in cases where development and utilization activities precede boundary delimitation agreement.[189] Nevertheless, in practice, development and utilization agreements seem to have become an alternative to boundary agreements and even to provisional arrangements under Article 83(3), despite the lack of reference in the formal legal regime. Thus, to avoid the undesirable results outlined earlier, any boundary agreement must include provisions concerning resource management, especially for existing activities.

This type of informal obligation may run contrary to the legal regime, while broadening the governance framework by adding new informal rules and norms. However, it may also lead to more desirable results by mitigating legal uncertainties concerning resource utilization and the rights of other relevant actors, thus promoting cooperation and a convergence of expectations.

3. Concluding remarks

This chapter analyzes the development and practice of the legal regime concerning the scope of coastal States' sovereign rights in their continental shelf. Each section explains the development of the legal rules and demonstrates the differences between the legal regime and the governance framework. The analysis also shown that the informal elements of the governance framework do not always correlate and may pull the governance framework in different directions.

The first section examines how the governance framework broadens the formal legal regime in some areas, e.g., establishing conservation obligations regarding the continental shelf through external instruments while also downplaying these rules by refraining from applying or enforcing them in practice. The issue of protection and conservation of the continental shelf also reveals a conflict between two informal elements of the governance framework: judicial decisions and state practice. These elements do not always have positive linear relations. Indeed, they sometimes conflict and pull the governance framework in different directions.

In contrast, with respect to coastal States' rights over artificial installations in the continental shelf, the governance framework essentially downplays the formal rules and adds informal principles that broaden the legal regime. These gaps between the legal regime and the governance framework can be explained by informal factors such as previous legal regimes and the EEZ's influence on coastal States' sovereign rights in the continental shelf.

The second section addresses the inconsistent judicial treatment of economic considerations, which can be perceived as both broadening and narrowing the scope of coastal States' sovereign rights in the process of delimitation (although there are more elements that narrow the governance framework in comparison to the legal regime than elements that broaden the governance framework). This inconsistency is influenced by the different roles attributed to sovereign rights in the context of maritime boundary delimitation.

In addition, this section shows how international tribunals interpreted the formal but vague obligations concerning conduct pending final delimitation agreements. However, state practice in this context has essentially downplayed the formal obligations and judicial decisions and interpretation, establishing new informal rules. Thus, the governance framework essentially narrows the legal regime but broadens coastal States' rights vis-à-vis the continental shelf by adding new informal practices.

Annex D

Coastal States sovereign rights legislation[190]

State	*Continental shelf (CS) legislation*	*EEZ?*
	Europe (WEOG)	
1 Norway	*1963* – "the submarine areas . . . sovereignty as regards **exploitation and exploration** of natural resources in the sea-bed or in its subsoil"[191] [No reference to installations and safety zones]. *1981* – "to **exploration for and production and utilization of natural subsea resources on the Norwegian part of the continental shelf**, including decommissioning of facilities".[192] *1996* – Petroleum resources **management** + safety zones under CS regulation.[193]	yes[194]
2 Belgium	*1969* – CS law reflecting the 1958 CSC [including installations and safety zones].[195] *1999* – EEZ law reflecting Article 56 of UNCLOS [including installations and safety zones].[196]	yes
3 Bulgaria	In the CS, "sovereign rights for the purposes of **prospecting, exploration, development, exploitation, protection and management** of its natural resources" [including installations]. (The EEZ provisions might explain the provisions on the CS.) However, in the EEZ, "sovereign rights for the purpose of **exploring, developing, exploiting, protecting and managing** the living".[197]	yes
4 Canada	Law reflects Articles 56 and 77 of UNCLOS.[198] Installations, including safety zones, regulated under CS provisions [all domestic laws apply in these areas]. Apply the criminal code for acts committed in the CS in relation to installations.[199]	yes
5 Croatia	Law reflects Articles 56 and 77 of UNCLOS [safety zones under EEZ provisions].[200]	yes
6 Denmark	CS legislation **reflects the 1958 CSC** [including safety zones and installations].[201] EEZ law reflecting Article 56 of UNCLOS [no reference to safety zones].[202]	yes
7 Estonia	EEZ Act reflecting Article 56 of UNCLOS [including regulation of installations and safety zones].[203] No CS laws.	yes

State	Continental shelf (CS) legislation	EEZ?
8 Finland	*2004* – EEZ law reflects Article 56 of UNCLOS [including installations and safety zones]. Repeals the 1965 CS law that reflects the 1958 CSC (exploring and exploiting, including installations and safety zones).[204]	yes
9 France	*1968* – Law reflecting the 1958 CSC [“**exploring and exploiting**”, including installations and safety zones].[205] *1976* – In the EEZ, “sovereign rights for the purpose of **exploring and exploiting the natural resources**, whether living or non-living, of the seabed and its subsoil and the superjacent waters”.[206]	yes
10 Georgia	“exclusive competence . . . [over] **the status and protection of** territorial waters, airspace, **the continental shelf and the exclusive economic zone**”.[207] No reference to sovereign rights in accordance with UNCLOS.	yes
11 Greece	Law refers to “**prospect, explore and exploit**” resources in the maritime zones.[208]	
12 Germany	Laws on the **exploration and exploitation** of the CS, reflecting the 1958 CSC.[209]	yes[210]
13 Ireland	In the CS, “for the purpose of **exploring** such sea bed and subsoil **and exploiting their natural resources**”.[211] Safety zones under the CS regime.[212]	yes[213]
14 Iceland	Reflecting Articles 56 and 77 of UNCLOS[214] [no reference to installations and safety zones].	yes
15 Italy	Law reflecting the 1958 CSC and Article 77 of UNCLOS.[215]	yes
16 Malta	2014 – CS law reflecting Articles 77 and 81 of UNCLOS [including installations and safety zone].[216] Reflecting Article 246 of UNCLOS.[217]	–[218]
17 Netherlands	EEZ law reflecting Article 56 of UNCLOS.[219] Mining law addressing **exploration and exploitation** of the continental shelf resources.[220]	yes
18 Cyprus	*2004* – EEZ law Reflecting Article 56 of UNCLOS (no reference to safety zones). The law **differentiates between conservation of living resources and exploration and exploitation of non-living resources**.[221] *2014* – Reflecting Article 56 and 77 of UNCLOS.[222] **Conservation only of living resources but exploration and exploitation of both living resources and non-living resources**.[223] Treats installations' construction as in the land territory (installations and safety zones regulated under both regimes).[224]	yes
19 Cyprus/Israel	Delimitation agreement refers to **utilization, joint development, and exploitation** of hydrocarbons reservoirs **in the EEZ**.[225]	
20 Palestine	Reflecting Article 56 (first part) of UNCLOS.[226] No reference to sovereign rights in the CS to installations or to safety zones.	yes

(*Continued*)

(Continued)

State	Continental shelf (CS) legislation	EEZ?
21 Latvia	*1998* – CS and EEZ law. In the CS, "sovereign rights to **explore . . . and utilise** the natural resources". In the EEZ, "exclusive rights to **explore, utilise, protect and regulate** the living and non-living natural resources . . . **utilisation and conservation** of fish and other living natural resources" [installations and safety zones regulated under both regimes].[227] *2010* – Environmental protection law. In the CS, "sovereign rights to **explore . . . and use** the natural resources". In the EEZ, "sovereign rights to **explore, protect, use and manage** the natural resources . . . and manage the use of such resources" [installations regulated under the EEZ regime].[228]	yes
22 Lithuania	Reference to jurisdiction concerning installation and "the **conservation of living marine resources**, the **prospecting, exploration for, and exploitation of resources**, the preservation of the marine environment, the prevention and reduction of pollution, the dumping of wastes and other matter within the exclusive economic zone and on the continental shelf".[229]	yes
23 Poland	Law refers only to EEZ, where Poland has "sovereign rights to **explore, manage and exploit** the natural resources . . . and the **right to conserve** those resources, as well as sovereign rights with respect to other economic undertakings" [installations and safety zones regulated under EEZ provisions].[230]	yes
24 Portugal	*1969* – Reflects the 1958 CSC; "licenses shall be granted for the **prospecting, exploration, evaluation and exploitation** of mineral resources may be extended to the entire continental shelf"[231] [including installations and safety zones]. In the EEZ, "exclusive jurisdiction with regard to **conservation and management of living resources**"[232] [no reference to non-living resources on the seabed or safety zones]. *2006* – Reflects Article 56 of UNCLOS [no reference to safety zones].[233]	yes
25 Romania	The EEZ includes the CS, reflecting Article 56 of UNCLOS [installations and safety zones under EEZ regime].[234]	yes
26 Slovenia	In the CS, "exercises its sovereign rights in compliance with international law". Established *ecological protection zone* where is has "sovereign rights relating to **research and sustainable use, preservation and management** of marine wealth".[235]	–
27 Spain	*1978* – EEZ law reflects Article 77 of UNCLOS concerning the CS within the EEZ + "The authority to enact regulations concerning **the preservation of, exploration for and exploitation of such resources** with a view to the protection of the protection of the marine environment" [no reference to safety zones].[236] *2013* – Decree refers to Article 56 of UNCLOS.[237]	yes

	State	*Continental shelf (CS) legislation*	*EEZ?*
28	Sweden	*1966 CS Act* reflects the 1958 CSC (right to **explore and extract**) [including safety zones in the CS].[238] *1992 EEZ law* – Apply the 1950 Fishing Act to the water column of the EEZ and the 1966 CS Act in the seabed of the EEZ but refers to "rights to **explore** . . . and to **exploit**" instead.[239]	yes
29	UK	*1964* – An act to make provision as to the **exploration and exploitation** of the continental shelf (reference to 1958 High Seas Convention) [including installations and safety zones].[240] *2009* – "This section applies to all rights under Part V of the Convention".[241]	yes
30	Russia	*1968* – "The USSR exercises sovereign rights over the continental shelf . . . for the purpose of **exploring it and exploiting its natural resources**".[242] [Including installations and safety zones]. *1995* – Sovereign rights for the purpose of **exploring the continental shelf and exploiting its mineral and living resources** (sedentary species) + **protection and conservation of the marine environment** in connection with the exploration and exploitation of mineral resources [including installations and safety zones].[243] *1984* – EEZ law, reflecting Article 56 of UNCLOS[244] [including installations and safety zones]. *1998* – Sovereign rights for the purpose of **exploring, exploiting, commercializing, conserving, and managing** living and non-living resources and with regard to other activities for the economic exploration and exploitation of the exclusive economic zone; sovereign rights for the purpose of **exploring the seabed and its subsoil and exploiting mineral and other non-living resources** and with regard to the commercial exploitation of living organisms belonging to sedentary species of the seabed and its subsoil[245] [the EEZ includes the CS].	yes
31	Ukraine	1995 EEZ law Reflecting Article 56 of UNCLOS [including installations and safety zones]. **Conservation and utilization** of **living** resources.[246]	yes
32	US	*1953* – "The Constitution and laws . . . are extended to the . . . Continental Shelf and to all artificial islands and fixed structures . . . for the purpose of **exploring for, developing, removing, and transporting resources** therefrom".[247] *1978* – CS amended law. **Exploration and exploitation** of the CS and "**managing** the resources of the Outer Continental Shelf".[248] Amended in *1982* – " 'area affected by Outer Continental Shelf activities' as a geographic area where **exploration, development, or production** activities have been permitted".[249] *1983* – EEZ proclamation reflects Article 56 of UNCLOS [not affecting US CS policies].[250]	yes

(*Continued*)

(Continued)

State	*Continental shelf (CS) legislation*	*EEZ?*
	Asia/Pacific	
33 Cambodia	*1969* – "Full and **complete sovereignty** over its CS".[251] *1978* – In the CS, sovereign rights "for the purpose of **exploring and exploiting, conserving and managing** all the natural resources of the sea-bed and subsoil" [within the article on the EEZ, using similar terms].[252] *1982* – EEZ provision similar to Article 56 of UNCLOS [including installations]. In the CS, sovereign rights "**exploration, exploitation, preservation and management** of its natural resources" [including installations].[253]	yes
34 China	Reflecting Articles 56 and 77 of UNCLOS [installations and safety zones under both regimes, no reference to safety zones].[254]	yes
35 Viet Nam	*1977* – [EEZ provision reflecting Articles 56 of UNCLOS]. In the CS, sovereign rights "in the **exploration, exploitation, preservation and management** of all natural resources".[255] *2012* – Reflecting Articles 56 and 77 of UNCLOS [installations and safety zones regulated under both regimes].[256]	yes
36 (North) Korea	*1977* – "exercise **sovereignty** over all living and non-living resources within its EEZ".[257] No CS law or other details.	yes
37 (South) Korea	EEZ law reflects Article 56 of UNCLOS.[258] No CS law or other details.	yes
38 Japan	"The laws and regulations of Japan . . . shall apply with respect to the following matters: (1) **Exploring and exploiting, conserving and managing the natural resources**, the establishment, construction, operation and use of artificial islands, **installations and structures**, the protection and preservation of the marine environment and marine scientific **research in the exclusive economic zone or on the continental shelf**"[259] [no reference to safety zones].	yes
39 The Philippines	*1968* – "that all the mineral and other natural resources in the sea bed and subsoil of the continental shelf . . . are subject to its exclusive jurisdiction and control **for purposes of exploration and exploitation**".[260] *1978* – EEZ law reflects Article 56 of UNCLOS, although mentions also "renewable and non-renewable" with respect to the natural resources in the area[261] [installations regulated under EEZ regime, no reference to safety zones]. *2011* – Act reflecting UNCLOS's provisions [no reference to installations or safety zones].[262]	yes
40 Thailand	EEZ proclamation reflecting Article 56 of UNCLOS.[263]	yes

State	Continental shelf (CS) legislation	EEZ?
41 Australia	*1973* – EEZ provisions consistent with Articles 55–57 of UNCLOS. In the CS, "sovereign rights . . . for the purpose of **exploring it and exploiting its natural resources**".[264] Joint exercise of rights with Timor-Leste pursuant to **Article 77** of UNCLOS[265] [no reference to installations and safety zones other than UNCLOS articles in annex]. *2006* – Implementation law refers to **conservation** of resources also in the seabed[266] [also regulates installation, including safety zones].	yes
42 Cook Islands	*1977* – CS law [under New Zealand auspices] reflects Article 77 of UNCLOS [including installations and safety zones].[267] *1977* EEZ law – mostly concerns fishing provisions.[268] *2018* – Consolidated law, reflecting Articles 56 and 77 of UNCLOS [installations regulated under both regimes together].[269]	yes
43 New Zealand	CS law – Sovereign rights for the purpose of **Exploration and exploitation** of continental shelf[270] [including installations and safety zones]. *2005* – Law on EEZ, specifically fisheries [no specific reference to sovereign rights but reference to installations and safety zones].[271] Declarations of safety zone around installation on the continental shelf in specific areas.[272] *2012* – "The purpose of this Act is – (a) to promote the **sustainable management** of the natural resources of the exclusive economic zone and the continental shelf; . . . (2) . . . sustainable management means managing the **use, development, and protection of natural resources**".[273]	yes
44 Marshall Islands	*1984* – EEZ law reflecting Article 56 of UNCLOS.[274] *2016* – Refers to rights in the EEZ and CS, reflecting Article 56 and 77 of UNCLOS [installation regulated under both regimes together].[275]	yes
45 Papua New Guinea	*2015* – Consolidated law, reflecting Article 56 [including installations] and Article 77 [mentions Article 82] of UNCLOS.[276] *However*, regulations concerning non-living resources in the CS "relating to the **exploration, exploitation, conservation, utilization and management** of natural resources **apply to the continental shelf** as they apply to the seabed and subsoil of the territorial sea" [including enforcement authority].[277] Installations are regulated under EEZ regime (reference to EEZ provisions); jurisdiction in accordance with UNCLOS provisions [safety zones regulated in separated article, no details on the relevant regime but reference to "waters of Papua New Guinea"].[278]	yes
46 Niue	Reflecting Articles 56 and 77 of UNCLOS [mentioned together, including installations].[279]	yes
47 Tuvalu	Reflecting Articles 56 and 77 of UNCLOS [mentioned together, including installations].[280]	yes

(*Continued*)

(Continued)

State	Continental shelf (CS) legislation	EEZ?
48 Kiribati	*1983* – The seabed within the EEZ is part of the CS. EEZ provision reflects Article 56 of UNCLOS. Installations and safety zones regulated under EEZ regime.[281] *2011* – Referring to rights in both areas; reflecting Article 56 of UNCLOS (within 200 nm EEZ includes the CS) and **even in CS beyond 200 nm** (exploring, conserving, and managing) [installations under both regimes, mentioned together].[282]	yes
49 Tonga	Reflecting Articles 56 and 77 of UNCLOS [installations under both regimes – refers to Article 80 of UNCLOS but not to safety zones].[283] Mentioned Articles 245–246 of UNCLOS concerning marine research.[284]	yes
50 Samoa	Reflecting Article 56 of UNCLOS [installations and safety zones under EEZ provisions, no separate article on CS sovereign rights].[285]	yes
51 Solomon Islands	EEZ provision reflects the first part of Article 56 of UNCLOS (exploring and exploiting, conserving, and managing) [installations and safety zones under EEZ regime].[286] No reference to sovereign rights in the CS.	yes
52 Fiji	In the CS, "All rights exercisable . . . for the purpose of **exploring that shelf and exploiting those [natural] resources**" [including installations and safety zones – the law reflects the 1958 CSC].[287] EEZ law reflects Article 56 of UNCLOS[288] [including installations and safety zones].	yes
53 Vanuatu	Reflecting Articles 56 and 77 of UNCLOS [installations and safety zones under both EEZ and CS regulation].[289]	yes
54 Nauru	Reflecting Articles 56 and 77 of UNCLOS.[290] No reference to installations or safety zones.	yes
55 Maldives	EEZ law reflects Article 56 of UNCLOS [no reference to safety zones].[291]	yes
56 Palau	EEZ provisions refer to "exclusive **management, conservation, and regulatory authority** over all **living resources** within the exclusive economic zone to the full extent recognized by international law".[292] *2011* – Petroleum law "to govern the prospecting, **exploration, exploitation, development and production** of oil and gas resources . . . within the 200 nm EEZ, or on the continental shelf".[293]	yes
57 Micronesia	Reflecting Articles 56 and reflecting Articles 77, 80–81 from UNCLOS [no reference to safety zones].[294] Mentioned the shelf beyond 200 nm but no reference to this concerning jurisdiction	yes
58 Timor-Leste	Reflecting Articles 56 (**exploring and using, preserving, and managing**) and 77 (**exploring and using**) of UNCLOS[295] [installations under EEZ provision, no reference to safety zones].	yes
59 Bangladesh	*1974* – Installations are regulated under CS provisions (for the exploration and exploitation of its resources).[296] The law differentiates between jurisdiction to **protect (and conserve), use, and exploit** the resources of the **economic zone** and the **exploration and exploitation** of resources within the **continental shelf**.[297]	yes

State	*Continental shelf (CS) legislation*	*EEZ?*
60 India	*1976* – "the Union has in the continental shelf, – (a) sovereign rights for the purposes of **exploration, exploitation, conservation and management of all resources**". However, there are provisions on the EEZ reflecting Article 56 of UNCLOS (which might explain the provisions on the CS)[298] [installations and safety zones regulated by both regimes].	yes
61 Indonesia	Full authority and exclusive rights over the natural resources of the Indonesian continental shelf shall be vested in the State.[299] Declaration concerning the EEZ, reflecting Article 56 of UNCLOS + law enforcement measures in the EEZ.[300] *2014* – "The Unitary State of the Republic of Indonesia has the right to **manage and to utilize** the natural resources and the Sea environment in the Sea area as referred to in section" (i.e., EEZ and CS).[301] "Marine Management means the management of activities, provision, exploitation, and utilization of Marine Resources and the Sea conservation".[302] Installation not under either of the regimes.[303]	yes
62 Malaysia	*1972* – CS law reflects the 1958 CSC [including installations and safety zones].[304] *1984* – EEZ law reflects Articles 56 of UNCLOS [enforcement jurisdiction concerning EEZ + reflects Article 246 but with extra provision for refusal + installations and safety zones under both regimes together].[305]	yes
63 Myanmar	*1977* – "Burma has in the continental shelf . . . sovereign rights for the purposes of **exploration, exploitation, conservation and management of its natural resources**, both living and non-living". However, there are provisions on the EEZ reflecting Article 56 of UNCLOS (which might explain the provisions on the CS)[306] [installation regulated under both regimes, no reference to safety zones]. *2017* – Reflecting Articles 56 of UNCLOS. In the CS, "**exploration, exploitation, conservation and management** of the natural resources" [installation regulated under both regimes, no reference to safety zones].[307]	yes
64 Sri Lanka	*1976* – EEZ provisions reflect Article 56 of UNCLOS. In the CS, sovereign rights for the purpose of **exploration, exploitation, conservation, and management** of the natural resources, both living and non-living [installations regulated by both regimes].[308]	yes
65 Saudi Arabia	*1968* – In the CS . . . individual right **to explore** . . . and **to exploit them**.[309] *2011* – Reflecting Articles 56 (including safety zones) and 77 of UNCLOS.[310]	yes
66 Syria	Reflecting Articles 56 and 77 of UNCLOS [safety zones under both regimes].[311]	yes
67 Iran	Reflecting Article 56 of UNCLOS (including installations and safety zones). The law **applies the same sovereign rights and jurisdiction** also in the CS.[312]	yes

(*Continued*)

(Continued)

	State	*Continental shelf (CS) legislation*	*EEZ?*
68	Iraq	*1957* proclamation mentions the need **to exploit** the natural resources in the CS; therefore, "Iraq has **exclusive general jurisdiction over such resources and over their preservation and exploitation**. It has likewise the exclusive right to take all measures necessary for the **exploration** of such resources and their **exploitation** in such a way as it deems suitable . . . [including] the **protection of all constructions** required by the process of exploration and exploitation".[313]	-
69	Kuwait	*2014* – In the EEZ, "exercise **the same rights** and powers exercised in its **territorial sea** . . . in addition to the rights and powers established **by Article 56** of UNCLOS". In the CS, "exercise the rights and powers it exercises **in its territorial sea** . . . as well as the other rights contained in **Article 77**, of UNCLOS"[314] [no other details].	yes
70	Oman	In the EEZ, "sovereign rights . . . for the purposes of **exploring, developing and exploiting** its natural wealth [in the CS] sovereign rights . . . for the purposes of exploring and exploiting its natural resources"[315] [no reference to installations or safety zones].	yes
71	Pakistan	"exclusive sovereign rights for the purpose of **exploration, development, exploitation, conservation and management** of all resources . . . [in the EEZ] exclusive sovereign rights for the purpose of **exploration, development, exploitation, conservation and management** of all resources"[316] [safety zones regulated under both regimes].	yes
72	Turkey	Reflecting Article 56 of UNCLOS [including installations].[317] No CS law.	yes
73	United Arab Emirates	*1980* – In the EEZ, sovereign rights "for the purpose of the **exploration, exploitation, management, development and conservation** of such resources" (including installations, no reference to safety zones).[318] *1993* – Law reflects Article 56 and 77 of UNCLOS [installations and safety zones regulated under both regimes together].[319]	Yes
74	Yemen	*1977* – Law reflects Article 56 of UNCLOS (reference to renewable and non-renewable resources) [including installations]. In the CS, also "explore, exploit, manage and conserve its natural resources" [including installations].[320]	yes
		Africa	
75	Cabo Verde	Reflecting Articles 56 (including installations) and 77 of UNCLOS.[321]	yes
76	Kenya	Established EEZ, reflects Article 56 of UNCLOS, no reference to CS.[322]	yes
77	Nigeria	*1978* – EEZ law: "sovereign and exclusive rights with respect to the **exploration and exploitation** of the natural resources . . . for the purpose of **exploring and exploiting, conserving and managing the natural resources**".[323] No reference to CS [installations under EEZ regime, no reference to safety zones].	yes

	State	*Continental shelf (CS) legislation*	*EEZ?*
78	Senegal	CS law reflecting Article 77 of UNCLOS.[324]	yes[325]
79	Sao Tome and Principe	EEZ law reflects Article 56 of UNCLOS (including installations, no reference to CS or to safety zones).[326]	yes
80	Comoros	Law reflecting Article 56 of UNCLOS [no reference to artificial installations or safety zones in the EEZ or to the CS].[327]	yes
81	Namibia	EEZ provisions reflecting Article 56 of UNCLOS (+ contiguous zone laws within the EEZ). Sovereign rights in the CS mention only **exploitation**.[328] No reference to installations or safety zones.	yes
82	Mozambique	*1976* – "Patrimonial Sea", reflecting Article 56 of UNCLOS.[329] *1996* – Sovereign rights in the CS for **exploration and exploitation** of non-living resources. No reference to safety zones in the context of CS. Reflecting Article 56 of UNCLOS.[330] *2018* – Reference to regulations concerning the **management and conservation** of the CS and EEZ and the natural resources within.[331]	yes
83	Liberia	2013 law – Reflecting Articles 56 and 77 of UNCLOS.[332]	yes
84	Côte d'Ivoire	Reference only to the EEZ, reflecting Article 56 of UNCLOS.[333]	yes
85	Congo (Kinshasa)	*1974* – Law reflecting the 1958 CSC (**exploring and exploiting**). *2006* constitution – asserts the **permanent sovereignty** . . . over its maritime areas and on the basis of the relevant provisions of UNCLOS.[334]	yes[335]
86	Congo (Brazzaville)	**Exploration and exploitation** of resources in the CS.[336]	
87	South Africa	In the EEZ, "in respect to all natural resources . . . **the same rights and powers as it has in respect of its territorial waters**".[337] In the CS, sovereign rights for the purpose of **exploration and exploitation** of natural resources.[338] Mentions installations and safety zones but not under any specific maritime zone.	yes
88	Sierra Leone	Reflecting Article 56 of UNCLOS (including installations). In the CS, "sovereign rights for the purpose of **exploration, exploitation, conservation and management** of the natural resources" (including installations).[339]	yes
89	Somalia	*1989* – Provisions concerning CS indicate broader sovereign rights (utilization).[340] *2014* – EEZ proclamation: "sovereign rights . . . with regard to the **exploration and conservation of the natural resources**, whether living or non-living" + language of Article 56.[341] No reference to CS.	yes
90	Angola	Law reflects Article 56 of UNCLOS (including installations).[342]	yes
91	Gabon	Established EEZ, reflects Article 56 of UNCLOS.[343] No reference to CS [installations and safety zones under EEZ regime].	yes
92	Gambia	Does not specify its rights but refers to protection of installations.[344]	

(*Continued*)

(Continued)

	State	Continental shelf (CS) legislation	EEZ?
93	Ghana	Established EEZ, reflects Article 56 and 77 of UNCLOS[345] [no reference to safety zones, installations under EEZ provisions].	yes
94	Guinea	Established EEZ, reflects Article 56 of UNCLOS. No reference to CS.[346]	yes
95	Guinea-Bissau	In the CS, within the EEZ, "exclusive right to **explore and exploit** the living and natural resources".[347]	yes
96	Equatorial Guinea	Reference to "full sovereignty" and the right to **explore and exploit exclusively all natural resources, whether living or non-living** in the EEZ; however, it has "sovereign rights for the purpose of **exploiting, exploring, conserving and managing the natural resources**, whether living or non-living" (including installations).[348] No reference to CS or safety zones. However, there is a reference to 500 m safety zones in other regulations.[349]	yes
97	Madagascar	Reflecting Articles 56 of UNCLOS, although no reference to sovereign rights in the CS (mentioned the breadth).[350] No reference to safety zones In the CS, "sovereign rights for the purpose of **exploring it and exploiting its mineral resources**".[351] Safety zones around installations in the High Seas.[352]	yes
98	Cameroon	In the EEZ, rights as provided in UNCLOS, in the CS, rights to **explore and exploit**.[353] No reference to installations or safety zones.	yes
99	Djibouti	Law on the EEZ, reflecting *earlier drafts* (renewable or non-renewable) of Article 56 (including installations) [the CS is within the EEZ].[354]	yes
100	Togo	In the EEZ, "right **to explore and to exploit** living and non-living resources" [no specific mention of the CS].[355]	yes
101	Tanzania	Law on the EEZ, reflecting Article 56.[356] No reference to CS.	yes
102	Mauritania	Law reflecting Articles 56 and 77 of UNCLOS [no reference to installations or safety zones].[357]	yes
103	Mauritius	*1977* – In the CS, "full and exclusive sovereign rights" (no details); however, in the EEZ and CS, "sovereign rights for the purposes of **exploration, exploitation, conservation and management of all resources**"[358] [installations and safety zones regulated under both regimes]. *2005* – Reflecting Articles 56 and 77 of UNCLOS[359] [installations regulated under both regimes].	yes
104	Seychelles	*1977* – In the CS, "full and exclusive sovereign rights" (no details) + no specific reference to sovereign rights in the EEZ. However, the law details the sovereign rights in both areas in accordance with Article 56 of UNCLOS[360] [installations and safety zones regulated under both regimes]. *1999* – Reflecting Articles 56 and 77 of UNCLOS.[361]	yes

	State	*Continental shelf (CS) legislation*	*EEZ?*
105	Mauritius/ Seychelles	**Joint Management of the Continental Shelf beyond 200 nm concerning non-living resources** "shall jointly **control, manage and facilitate the exploration** of the continental shelf . . . **conservation, development and exploitation** of its natural resources".[362] Any reservoir of petroleum or unitary mineral deposit that extends across or straddles the boundary of the JMA into the EEZ of either or both contracting parties shall be treated as a single entity **for exploration, development, and management purposes**.[363]	–
106	Sudan	1970 CS law reflects the 1958 CSC (including installations and safety zones).[364]	–
107	Egypt	1958 Law on CS (United Arab Republic) – reflects the 1958 CSC; however, it has "exclusive right to **explore, prospect and exploit all natural and mineral resources**" [including installations and safety zones].[365]	–[366]
108	Libya	Declaration concerning **preservation and management** of marine living resources.[367] 2009 decision on EEZ reflects the first part of Article 56 of UNCLOS (**exploring and exploiting, conserving and managing the natural resources**) [no reference to installations or safety zones].[368] No specific CS law.	yes
109	Morocco	Law reflects Article 56 of UNCLOS. No reference to CS or safety zones.[369]	yes
110	Tunisia	Law reflects first part of Article 56 of UNCLOS. No reference to CS, installations, or safety zones.[370]	yes
111	Algeria	In the EEZ, "sovereign rights and its jurisdiction **in accordance with UNCLOS, in particular part V** thereof".[371] No CS laws separately.	yes
112	Algeria/ Tunisia	The parties undertake to cooperate and coordinate their activities in the following areas: **conservation of natural resources, in particular, living resources**.[372]	–
		Latin America/Caribbean	
113	Antigua and Barbuda	Law reflects Article 56 of UNCLOS, in the CS, "sovereign rights . . . the **exploration for, the exploitation and managements** of natural resources" [installations regulated under both regimes, no reference to safety zones].[373]	yes
114	Bahamas	1977 law reflects the 1958 CSC with respect to CS and Article 56 with respect to fishery zone.[374] 1993 EEZ law reflects Article 56 of UNCLOS [including installations].[375]	yes
115	Cuba	EEZ law reflects Article 56 of UNCLOS [no safety zones].[376] No specific law on CS.	yes
116	Cuba/Bahamas	"**management and exploitation** of common hydrocarbon reserves".[377]	
117	Barbados	In the EEZ, "**exploration, exploitation, conservation, protection or management**" (including installations and safety zones) [no reference to CS].[378]	yes

(*Continued*)

(Continued)

	State	*Continental shelf (CS) legislation*	*EEZ?*
118	Belize	"*for the purpose of fishing* . . . the **exploration for, and exploitation, conservation and management** of resources" (including non-living resources) [installations and safety zones regulated under EEZ regime, no reference to CS].[379]	yes
119	Dominica	Law reflecting Article 56 of UNCLOS [no reference to CS or safety zones].[380]	Yes
120	Dominican Republic	*1977* – Law reflects Articles 56 and 77 of UNCLOS [installations regulated under EEZ provision, no reference to safety zones].[381] *2007* – In the EEZ, "jurisdiction . . . **as provided for in UNCLOS**" [no reference to CS].[382]	yes
121	Grenada	In the CS, "the **exploration for, and the exploitation and management** of, natural resources". Provision on EEZ reflects Article 56 of UNCLOS [installations regulated under both regimes, no reference to safety zones].[383]	yes
122	Guyana	*1977* – In the CS, "purposes of **exploration, exploitation, conservation and management** of all resources".[384] EEZ provisions reflect Article 56 of UNCLOS [installations and safety zones regulated under both regimes].[385] *2010* – In the CS, "**exploring, exploiting, conserving and managing** of natural resources" + regulation of installation (does not mention safety zones).[386] With respect to the CS and *its superjacent waters,* "the **exploration, exploitation and protection of the resources of the continental shelf** within the designated area" + safety and protection of [artificial installations]. Reflecting article 56 of UNCLOS [including installations]. The law also applies the contiguous zone regime in the CS.[387] Safety zones regulated separately with regards to both regimes.[388]	yes
123	Haiti	EEZ provisions reflect Articles 56 and 77 of UNCLOS [installations under EEZ provision, no reference to safety zones].[389]	yes
124	Jamaica	*1991* – EEZ law reflects Article 56 of UNCLOS [including installations and safety zones].[390] *1996* – Law reflects Article 77 of UNCLOS [including installations, no reference to safety zones].[391]	yes
125	Saint Kitts and Nevis	Law refers to rights in the CS and EEZ together, reflecting Article 56 of UNCLOS (**exploration, exploitation, conservation, and management** in both areas) [including installations; safety zones under both regimes together].[392]	yes
126	Saint Lucia	Law refers to rights in the CS and EEZ together, reflecting Article 56 of UNCLOS (**exploration, exploitation, conservation, and management** in both areas) [including installations; safety zones under both regimes together].[393]	yes
127	Saint Vincent and the Grenadines	Law reflects Articles 56 and 77 of UNCLOS [installations and safety zones regulated under both regimes (safety zones in the same article together)].[394]	yes
128	Suriname	Law reflects Articles 56 (including installations) and 77 (including installations) of UNCLOS [no reference to safety zones].[395]	yes

	State	*Continental shelf (CS) legislation*	*EEZ?*
129	Trinidad and Tobago	*1986* – CS (amended) law refers to rights concerning **exploration and exploitation**, including reference to safety zones without mentioning it explicitly.[396] EEZ law – Reflects Article 56 of UNCLOS but does not affect the Continental Shelf Act [earlier].[397] Includes reference to Article 246 of UNCLOS[398] and to surveillance in the EEZ.[399]	yes
130	Argentina	Law reflecting Article 56 of UNCLOS. No reference to sovereign rights in the CS. Installations regulated under both regimes.[400]	yes
131	Brazil	Law reflecting Articles 56 and 77 of UNCLOS.[401] Reference to military maneuvers in the EEZ[402] [installations regulated under both regimes].	yes
132	Chile	Declaration reflecting Article 77 of UNCLOS.[403] Law reflects Article 56 of UNCLOS. In the CS, "**conserving, exploring and exploiting** its natural resources" [no reference to installations or safety zones but mentioning "other jurisdiction and rights" under relevant international law].[404]	yes
133	Colombia	Law reflecting Articles 56 and 77 of UNCLOS [no reference to installations or safety zones].[405]	yes
134	Costa Rica	In the EEZ (not mentioned explicitly), "special jurisdiction . . . to **protect, conserve, and utilize** . . . all natural resources".[406]	-
135	Ecuador	2012 – Declaration upon ratifying UNCLOS reflects Article 56 of UNCLOS (including installations). In the CS, "sovereign rights for the purposes of **exploring, conserving and exploiting** its natural resources".[407] No reference to safety zones.	yes
136	El Salvador	In the CS sovereign rights, "for the purpose of **conservation, exploration and exploitation**".[408]	
137	Guatemala	*1965* – Constitution refers to exploitation of resources in the CS.[409] *1976* – EEZ provisions reflect Article 56 of UNCLOS (including installations).[410] No reference to safety zones.	yes
138	Honduras	Law reflecting Articles 56 (including installations) and 77(including installations) of UNCLOS.[411] No reference to safety zones.	yes
139	Mexico	Law reflecting Article 56 and 77 of UNCLOS [installations regulated under both regimes].[412]	yes
140	Nicaragua	*1979* – Refers to CS and EEZ (adjacent sea), "The **exploration, exploitation, utilization and administration** of such natural resources are the exclusive right of Nicaragua without prejudice to the rights and obligations contracted through international treaties and agreements".[413]	yes
141	Peru	1947 – "to **reserve, protect, maintain and utilize** natural resources".[414]	
142	Uruguay	Law reflecting Articles 56 (including installations) and 77 of UNCLOS.[415] No reference to safety zones.	yes
143	Venezuela	*1978* – Law reflecting Article 56 of UNCLOS [Including installations and safety zones in the EEZ].[416] *2014* law – reflects also Article 77 of UNCLOS.[417]	yes

It is noteworthy that most states did not include laws concerning the area beyond 200 nm, even broad-shelf states. Russia mentioned the revenue-sharing system.[418] This means that the rights and obligations within the 200 nm EEZ are the same also beyond 200 nm, where there is no EEZ.[419]

Notes

1 Most of the adjudicated maritime cases are delimitation disputes. Few cases deal with question of sovereignty over islands, e.g., Sovereignty over Pedra Branca/Pulau Batu Puteh, Middle Rocks and South Ledge (Malaysia/Singapore), Judgment, ICJ Reports 2008, p. 12. Several cases dealt with enforcement jurisdiction, although they did not directly relate to the continental shelf, e.g., M/V "Saiga" (No. 2) (Saint Vincent and the Grenadines v. Guinea), Judgment, ITLOS Reports 1999, p. 10. Some cases address rights and obligation but with respect to the EEZ, see Alleged Violations of Sovereign Rights and Maritime Spaces in the Caribbean Sea (Nicaragua v. Colombia), Judgment (21 April 2022). Coastal States rights and obligation in their continental shelf, if addressed, were mostly secondary issues. For example, Continental Shelf (Tunisia/Libyan Arab Jamahiriya), Judgment, ICJ Reports 1982, p. 18.

2 For example, Dispute Concerning Delimitation of the Maritime Boundary between Ghana and Côte d'Ivoire in the Atlantic Ocean (Ghana/Côte d'Ivoire), Judgment, ITLOS Reports 2017, p. 4.

3 Bay of Bengal Maritime Boundary Arbitration between Bangladesh and India, Award, case no. 2010–16, 07 July 2014, Permanent Court of Arbitration [PCA], para. 398. See also Leonardo Bernard and Clive Schofield, *Disputes Concerning the Delimitation of the Continental Shelf beyond 200 Nautical Miles, in* New Knowledge and Changing Circumstances in the Law of the Sea 157, 164 (Tomas Heidar (ed.), 2020).

4 See Annex D, 4th column.

5 Although judicial bodies generally treat the continental shelf up to and beyond 200 nm as one unit, see discussion concerning "single continental shelf", Chapter 2, Section 2.1.2.1. See also Dispute concerning delimitation of the maritime boundary between Bangladesh and Myanmar in the Bay of Bengal (Bangladesh/Myanmar), Judgment, ITLOS Reports 2012, p. 4, para. 361; Bangladesh v. India, *supra* note 3, para. 77.

6 1982 UN Convention on the Law of the Sea, 1833 UNTS 397 (UNCLOS), Article 77.

7 For example, preventing interference with military and commercial navigation, see UNCLOS III, 2nd Sess, 22nd Plen Mtg, UN Doc A/CONF.62/SR.22 (28 June 1974), para. 35; H. Gary Knight, *Issues Before the Third United Nations Conference on the Law of the Sea*, 34 LA. L. Rev. 155, 168–169 (1974); Victor Alencar Mayer Feitosa Ventura, Environmental Jurisdiction in the Law of the Sea, The Brazilian Blue Amazon 41, 43, 105 (2020). Other states have rights in coastal States' EEZ and continental shelf, see UNCLOS, *supra* note 6, Articles 58, 79.

8 UNCLOS, *supra* note 6, Articles 56, 77; David M. Ong, *Towards an International Law for the Conservation of Offshore Hydrocarbon Resources within the Continental Shelf?, in* The Law of the Sea: Progress and Prospects 93, 96–97 (David Freestone, Richard Barnes and David Ong (eds.), 2006). During UNCLOS III some states considered adding this obligation, e.g., UNCLOS III, 2nd Sess, 21st Plen Mtg, UN Doc A/CONF.62/SR.21 (28 June 1974), para. 54.

9 Ong, *supra* note 8, p. 95.

10 UNCLOS, *supra* note 6, Article 56(1)(a); Ong, *supra* note 8, p. 95, 98. Even in the early stages of negotiation, it was recognized that coastal States can conserve and manage renewable or non-renewable resources in the EEZ, see UNCLOS III, 2nd Committee, UN Doc A/CONF.62/C.2/L.82 (26 August 1974), Article 2(1).

11 See e.g., UNCLOS III, 2nd Sess, 2nd Committee, 17th Mtg, UN Doc A/CONF.62/C.2/SR.17 (26 July 1974), paras. 10, 12, 14, 16; Tunisia v. Libya, *supra* note 1, Dissenting Opinion of Judge Oda, p. 157, para. 85.

12 1958 Geneva Convention on the Continental Shelf, 499 UNTS 311 (CSC), Article 5.

13 UNCLOS I, Vol. VI, 4th Committee (Continental Shelf): Summary Records, 26th-30th Mtg, UN Doc A/CONF.13/C.4/SR.26–30 (24 February-27 April 1958).

14 The distinction between obligations in the EEZ and in the continental shelf seems to be the result of the distinction between "renewable" and "non-renewable" and "living" and "non-living" resources. See A/CONF.62/C.2/SR.17, *supra* note 11, para. 32. These terms were later changed to "living" and "non-living", UNCLOS III, 4th Sess, UN Doc A/CONF.62/WP.8/REV.1/Part II, Articles 44(1)(a), 65; UNCLOS III, 6th Sess, UN Doc A/CONF.62/WP.10 (15 July 1977), Article 56(1)(a). Conservation does not apply to "non-living" resources and thus is not included in the continental shelf regime, e.g., UNCLOS III, 2nd Sess, 2nd Committee, 18th Mtg, UN Doc A/CONF.62/C.2/SR.18 (29 July 1974), para. 64. However, conservation obligations might apply to living resources on the continental shelf, such as snow crab, which is considered sedentary species under the continental shelf legal regime. See UNCLOS, *supra* note 6, Article 77(4); Andreas Østhagen and Andreas Raspotnik, *Crab! How a Dispute Over Snow Crab Became a Diplomatic Headache Between Norway and the EU*, 98 Marine Policy 58 (2018). However, in the case of snow crabs, Norway proclaimed an EEZ; thus, it is difficult to determine the legal effect on the continental shelf as an independent regime.

15 UNCLOS, *supra* note 6, Articles 192–194, 204, 208, 210, 214, 216. Some of these provisions, such as the duty to prevent environmental harm and environmental impact assessment (EIA), reflect customary international law, see e.g., Legality of the Threat of Use of Nuclear Weapons, Advisory Opinion, ICJ Reports 1996, p. 226, p. 241–242; Responsibilities and obligations of States with respect to activities in the Area, Advisory Opinion, 1 February 2011, ITLOS Reports 2011 (The Area Advisory Opinion), paras. 116, 147–148.

16 Joanna Mossop, *Protecting Marine Biodiversity on the Continental Shelf Beyond 200 Nautical Miles*, 38 Ocean Dev. & Int. Law 283, 289 (2007); Joanna Mossop, *The Relationship Between the Continental Shelf Regime and a New International Instrument for Protecting Marine Biodiversity in Areas Beyond National Jurisdiction*, 75(1) ICES J. Mar. Sci. 444, 446 (2018). For example, damage to the marine environment also affects resources utilization, see The South China Sea Arbitration (The Republic of Philippines v. The People's Republic of China), Award, case no. 2013–19, 12 July 2016, Permanent Court of Arbitration [PCA], paras. 854–855, 857, 860–861, 891–894.

17 See e.g., the 2007 Nairobi International Convention on the removal of wrecks, 3283 UNTS 34. The treaty provides the legal basis for States to remove, or have removed, shipwrecks that may have the potential to affect adversely the safety of lives, goods, and property at sea, as well as the marine environment. International investment law may also add obligations to conserve the marine environment to protect foreign investments. See Nikolaos Giannopoulos, *International Protection of Foreign Investments in Offshore Energy Production and Marine Environmental Protection: Birds of a Feather or Frenemies Forever?*, 68 Neth. Int. Law Rev. 249 (2021).

18 The CBD has more parties than UNCLOS; the CBD has 196 parties, while UNCLOS has 168 parties. See CBD, UN Treaty Collection (UNTC) website, available at https://treaties.un.org/pages/ViewDetails.aspx?src=TREATY&mtdsg_no=XXVII-8&chapter=27; UNCLOS, UNTC website, *supra* note 29. Thus, states parties to UNCLOS have additional obligations under the CBD.

19 Mossop (2007), *supra* note 16, p. 288–289. For more detailed analysis on the obligation to protect the marine environment, see Alexander Proelss, *The Contribution of the ITLOS to Strengthening the Regime for the Protection of the Marine Environment*, *in* Interpretations of the United Nations Convention on the Law of the Sea by International Courts and Tribunals 93 (Angela Del- Vecchio and Roberto- Virzo (eds.), 2019); Alan Boyle, *Protecting the Marine Environment from Climate Change, The LOSC Part XII Regime*, *in* The Law of the Sea and Climate Change 81 (Elise Johansen, Signe Veierud Busch and Ingvild Ulrikke Jakobsen (eds.), 2020).

20 See for example UN Goals, available at https://sdgs.un.org/goals.
21 Ong, *supra* note 8, p. 101–105; Vasco Becker-Weinberg, *Seabed Activities and the Protection and Preservation of the Marine Environment in Disputed Maritime Areas of the Asia-Pacific Region, in* Proceedings From The 2012 Losi-Kiost Conference On Securing The Ocean For The Next Generation 1, 19 (Harry N. Scheiber and Moon Sang Kwon (eds.), 2012).
22 Ong, *supra* note 8, p. 101.
23 Ventura, *supra* note 7, p. 197.
24 Catherine Redgwell, *From Permission to Prohibition: The 1982 Convention on the Law of the Sea and Protection of the Marine Environment, in* The Law of the Sea: Progress and Prospects 180, 182 (David Freestone, Richard Barnes and David Ong (eds.), 2006). For detailed analysis on "legalization", see Kenneth W. Abbott, Robert O. Keohane, Andrew Moravcsik, Anne-Marie Slaughter and Duncan Snidal, *The Concept of Legalization*, 54(3) Int. Org. 401 (2000); Kenneth W. Abbott and Duncan Snidal, *Hard and Soft Law in International Governance*, 54(1) Int. Org. 421 (2000).
25 UNCLOS, *supra* note 6, Article 194(1). See also Becker-Weinberg (2012), *supra* note 21, p. 22.
26 UNCLOS, ibid., Articles 208(1), 210(1).
27 This was the result of a compromise between developed states, which supported strict rules to prevent pollution from seabed activities, and developing states, who argued that restrictions on economic and technological development to protect the marine environment reduce growth opportunities for them. See Knight, *supra* note 7, p. 186–187.
28 Becker-Weinberg (2012), *supra* note 21, p. 14–15.
29 For example, Request for Advisory Opinion submitted by the Sub-Regional Fisheries Commission, Advisory Opinion, 2 April 2015, ITLOS Reports 2015, p. 4 (Fisheries Advisory Opinion), para. 128; The Area Advisory Opinion, *supra* note 15, paras. 110–112. See also the "precautionary approach", Donald K. Anton, *The Principle of Residual Liability in the Seabed Disputes Chamber of the International Tribunal for the Law of the Sea: The Advisory Opinion on Responsibility and Liability for International Seabed Mining (ITLOS Case No. 17)*, 7 Mcgill Int. j. Sust. Dev. l. & Pol'y 241, 248 (2012); Zhang Hua, *The Development of International Law of the Sea by International Courts and Tribunals, A Case Study of Due Diligence Obligation*, 9 Korean J. Int. & Comp. L. 132, 140 (2021).
30 Hua, ibid., p. 140, 144. The South China Sea Arbitration (2016), *supra* note 16, paras. 959–960, 978–979, 983, 987, 991.
31 UNCLOS, *supra* note 6, Article 253; Mehdi D. Piri and Michael Faure, *The Effectiveness of Cross-Border Pipeline Safety and Environmental Regulations (under International Law)*, 40(1) N.C. J. Int. Law & Com. Reg. 55, 118 (2014); Anton, *supra* note 29, p. 244, 251.
32 UNCLOS, *supra* note 6, Articles 194(4), 210(5); Piri and Faure, *supra* note 31, p. 118–119; Ventura, *supra* note 7, p. 197, 208.
33 For example, in the *Area Advisory Opinion*, the Chamber defined the obligation as requiring states to take measures within their domestic legal system. In the *Fisheries Advisory Opinion*, ITLOS established due diligence obligation of the flag State concerning activities of ships flying its flag, despite no specific provision exists on this issue, thus creating a new obligation. Hua, *supra* note 29, p. 140–141, 143, 146.
34 Hua, ibid., p. 144–145, 148. Arguably, this case may not necessarily focus on the continental shelf; however, it does address issues relating to the continental shelf and other rules and principles that affect the governance framework, and thus, the case is significant in the analysis of the book.
35 See Hua, *supra* note 29, p. 146–147.
36 Chapter 1, Section 4.1.3.
37 Some scholars argue the opposite, e.g., Saul Roux and Catherine Horsfield, *Review of National Legislations Applicable to Seabed Mineral Resources Exploitation, in* The

Law of the Seabed 287, 292 (Catherine Banet (ed.), 2020). However, this refers mostly to one type of seabed activity (phosphate mining). In addition, the analysis reviewed legislations of few states, which is insufficient to establish practice. As will be discussed later, in many other cases, the law did not prevent environmental harm or held the responsible parties liable.

38 Annex D, e.g., Canada, no. 4; Russia, no. 30; China, no. 34; Australia, no. 41; Bangladesh, no. 59; Saudi Arabia, no. 65; Ghana, no. 93. Some states specified the type of resources to which their laws apply, see China, no. 34, Article 4; Myanmar, no. 63, law from 2017, Article 24; Croatia, no. 5, Article 44.

39 Annex D, e.g., Belgium, no. 2; France, no. 9; Germany, no. 12; Egypt, no. 107; Bahamas, no. 114.

40 Annex D, e.g., Estonia, no. 7; Finland, no. 8; South Korea, no. 37; Turkey, no. 72; Kenya, no. 76; Nigeria, no. 77; Libya, no. 108; Morocco, no. 109; Argentina, no. 130. However, in some laws the EEZ also includes the continental shelf, See Kiribati, no. 48; Samoa, no. 50; Solomon Islands, no. 51.

41 Annex D, e.g., Bulgaria, no. 3; the United States, no. 32; Japan, no. 38; New Zealand, no. 43; Myanmar, no. 63; Sri Lanka, no. 64; Kuwait, no. 69; Pakistan, no. 71; Mozambique, no. 82; Egypt, no. 107; Grenada, no. 121; Chile, no. 132; Ecuador, no. 135. Some states reserved the option to prescribe other rights, e.g., Myanmar, no. 63, law from 2017, Article 25; Sierra Leone, no. 88, Article 11(2)(d). Some states referred to law enforcement jurisdiction, see e.g., Canada, no. 4; Papua New Guinea, no. 45; Indonesia, no. 61; Malaysia, no. 62; Gambia, no. 92; Guyana, no. 122; Trinidad and Tobago, no. 129; however, in most cases, enforcement jurisdiction was applied in respect to the EEZ.

42 In these cases, the EEZ includes the continental shelf. See Annex D, e.g., Romania, no. 25; Cambodia, no. 33; India, no. 60; Myanmar, no. 63; Iran, no. 67; Guyana, no. 122; Costa Rica, no. 134; Nicaragua, no. 140.

43 These legislations are mostly prior to the adoption of UNCLOS, see Annex D, e.g., France, no. 9.

44 For example, Indonesia's Presidential Regulation on Prevention of Oil Spill in the Sea, No. 109 (2006), available at http://extwprlegs1.fao.org/docs/pdf/ins72643.pdf, Article 2(3); Papua New Guinea's Marine Pollution (Ships and Installations) Act, No. 34 (2013), available at http://extwprlegs1.fao.org/docs/pdf/png148580.pdf, see Part VII, Article 40(3), Part VIII, Article 43(4); Egypt's Law on Environment, No. 4 (1994), available at http://extwprlegs1.fao.org/docs/pdf/egy4984E.pdf, Article 96. For laws on liability and compensation concerning marine pollution in general, see e.g., Shane Bosma, *The Regulation of Marine Pollution Arising from Offshore Oil and Gas Facilities – An Evaluation of the Adequacy of Current Regulatory Regimes and the Responsibility of States to Implement a New Liability Regime*, 26 Austl. & N.Z. Mar. L. J. 89 (2012).

45 See United States nonenforcement with respect to vessels fishing for sedentary species on the continental shelf, see Ventura, *supra* note 7, p. 239.

46 See Maiko Meguro, *Litigating Climate Change Through International Law: Obligations Strategy* and *Rights Strategy*, 33 Leiden J. Int. Law 933 (2020).

47 One case did concern environmental protection, although not necessarily relating to the continental shelf. See MOX Plant (Ireland v. United Kingdom), Provisional Measures, Order of 3 December 2001, ITLOS Reports 2001, p. 95. The only case dealing directly with non-living resources was the *Area Advisory Opinion*, see The Area Advisory Opinion, *supra* note 15, p. 10. However, there are cases where environmental protection was raised indirectly, see Delimitation of the maritime boundary in the Atlantic Ocean (Ghana/Côte d'Ivoire), Provisional Measures, Order of 25 April 2015, ITLOS Reports 2015, p. 146, para. 67; Constantinos Yiallourides and Natalia Ermolina, *States' Environmental Obligations in Disputed Maritime Areas and the Limits of International Law*, in Comparative Law Yearbook of International Business 125, 133–134, 145 (Christian Campbell (ed), 2021), available at https://ssrn.com/abstract=3184800.

48 For example, Review Panel established under the Convention on the Conservation and Management of High Seas Fishery Resources in the South Pacific Ocean, Findings and Recommendations of the Review Panel, case no. 2018–13, 5 June 2018; The Fisheries Advisory Opinion, *supra* note 29; Southern Bluefin Tuna (New Zealand-Japan, Australia-Japan), 4 August 2000, Reports of International Arbitral Awards, Vol. XXIII, p. 1.

49 See discussion on the EU-Norway snow crab fisheries dispute, *supra* note 14. Furthermore, the regional mechanism has yet to be invoked in disputes between contracting parties regarding marine pollution from offshore resources, including in relation to the continental shelf. Yoshifumi Tanaka, *State Responsibility for Marine Pollution from Seabed Activities within National Jurisdiction in the Marine Arctic*, *in* Responsibility and Liability for Commercial Activity in the Arctic, The Example of Greenland 93, 105 (Vibe Ulfbeck, Anders Møllmann and Bent Ole Gram Mortensen (eds.), 2016). For the regional mechanism, see 1992 Convention for the Protection of the Marine Environment of the North-East Atlantic, 2354 UNTS 67 (OSPAR); OSPAR website, available at www.ospar.org/convention.

50 UNCLOS, *supra* note 6, Articles 208, 214, 235; Law of the Sea, A Policy Primer, Presented by The Fletcher School's LL.M. Program in International Law & Maritime Studies Program, Tufts University (2017), available at https://sites.tufts.edu/lawofthesea/chapter-seven/, at Chapter 7.

51 For example, the *Deepwater Horizon* oil spill in the Gulf of Mexico, see John C. Cruden, Steve O'Rourke and Sarah D. Himmelhoch, *The Deepwater Horizon Oil Spill Litigation: Proof of Concept for the Manual for Complex Litigation and the 2015 Amendments to the Federal Rules of Civil Procedure*, 6 Mich. J. Envtl. & Admin. L. 65 (2016). See also the 2009 *Montara* platform oil spill incident. Indonesia filed a lawsuit against Australia, which was later withdrawn and submitted as a class action against the operator of the platform in an Australian federal court. See e.g., Australian Government, Department of Agriculture, Water and the Environment website, available at www.environment.gov.au/marine/marine-pollution/montara-oil-spill; Maurice Blackburn Lawyers website, available at www.mauriceblackburn.com.au/class-actions/current-class-actions/montara-oil-spill-class-action/. See also liability lawsuit filed against Shell Company in The Netherlands for oil spill in Nigeria, Business and Human Rights Resource Center website, available at www.business-humanrights.org/en/latest-news/shell-lawsuit-re-oil-pollution-in-nigeria/. For more offshore incidents, see Bureau of Safety and Environmental Enforcement website, available at www.bsee.gov/newsroom/library/offshore-incident-archive.

52 There are customary environmental principles, such as "due diligence" discussed earlier. See also Riccardo Pisillo-Mazzeschi, *The Due Diligence Rule and the Nature of the International Responsibility of States*, *in* State Responsibility in International Law 97, 126 (René Provost (ed.), 2016). However, these principles are not specifically with respect to maritime activities. There are also general rules on state responsibility for wrongful acts, which considered as costmary law. See International Law Commission, Responsibility of States for Internationally Wrongful Acts, 2001, Supplement No. 10 (A/56/10), chp. IV.E.1. See also James Crawford, *Articles on Responsibility of States for Internationally Wrongful Acts, 2001* (2012), Audiovisual Library of International Law, UN website, available at https://legal.un.org/avl/ha/rsiwa/rsiwa.html. However, these principles do not establish substantial rights and obligations in respect to conservation of the marine environment.

53 See María Carolina Romero Lares, *International Regime or Regional Solution? An Overview of the Current State of Affairs of Pollution Liabilities Resulting from Offshore Oil Exploration and Exploitation Activities in Seabed Areas of National Jurisdiction*, IMSC 1, 2, 5 (2013). There is an international civil liability regime but only for vessel-based pollution. José Juste-Ruíz, *Compensation for Pollution Damage Caused by Oil Tanker Accidents: From "Erika" to "Prestige"*, 1 Aegean Rev. Law Sea 37, 41–42 (2010); The International Oil Pollution Compensation Funds

website, available at https://iopcfunds.org/about-us/legal-framework/. There is the 1994 Protocol for the Protection of the Mediterranean Sea against Pollution Resulting from Exploration and Exploitation of the Continental Shelf and the Seabed and its Subsoil, available at https://wedocs.unep.org/bitstream/handle/20.500.11822/2961/94ig4_4_protocol_eng.pdf. However, only few states have signed the protocol, see UNEP website, available at www.unep.org/unepmap/who-we-are/contracting-parties/offshore-protocol.

54 Juste-Ruíz, *supra* note 53, p. 40; Tullio Scovazzi, *Maritime Accidents with Particular Emphasis on Liability and Compensation for Damage from the Exploitation of Mineral Resources of the Seabed*, *in* International Disaster Response Law 287, 301 (Andrea de Guttry, Marco Gestri and Gabriella Venturini (eds.), 2012).

55 The only legal proceedings that were initiated between states relate to violations of coastal States' sovereign rights in the EEZ, mostly for bunkering and "ship-to-ship" (STS) operations. "Bunkering" is a general term for refueling or selling fuel to other vessels while at sea. "Ship-to-ship" (STS) operations is a term that normally understood as transferring cargo between two seagoing vessels. It could be oil or fuel or any other type of cargo. See David Testa, *Comments on Coastal and Flag State Jurisdiction in the M/T "San Padre Pio" Dispute*, EjilTalk! (September 3, 2019), availableatwww.ejiltalk.org/comments-on-coastal-and-flag-state-jurisdiction-in-the-m-t-san-padre-pio-dispute/. For such proceedings, see for example M/V "Virginia G" (Panama/Guinea-Bissau), Judgment, ITLOS Reports 2014, p. 4; The "Enrica Lexie" Incident (Italy v. India), Award, case no. 2015–28, 21 May 2020, Permanent Court of Arbitration [PCA].

56 It seems that the only differences between "jurisdiction" and "sovereign rights" are different dispute-settlement rules and that "sovereign rights" concern resources, while "jurisdiction" reflects discretionary powers with respect to other activities in the maritime zones. Barbara Kwiatkowska, *Creeping Jurisdiction beyond 200 Miles in the Light of the 1982 Law of the Sea Convention and State Practice*, 22 Ocean Dev. & Int. Law 153, 160 (1991); Tuillio Treves, *Coastal States' Rights in the Maritime Areas under UNCLOS*, 12 Braz. J. Int. L. 40, 41 (2015).

57 There are different types of offshore rigs, platforms, and installations, which have different uses. Some are fixed to the seabed with metal legs, and some are floating platforms anchored to the seabed. See for example http://maritime-connector.com/wiki/platforms/and American Petroleum Institute website, available at www.api.org/oil-and-natural-gas/wells-to-consumer/exploration-and-production/offshore/offshore-production-facilities

58 The continental shelf regime defers to the EEZ regime, see UNCLOS, *supra* note 6, Articles 60, 80; UNCLOS III, 7th Sess, 2nd Committee, 53rd Mtg, UN Doc A/CONF.62/C.2/SR.53 (17 April 1978), para. 4. This is perhaps since some of the structures are floating platforms, for example, UNCLOS III, 2nd Sess, 3rd Committee, 10th Mtg, UN Doc A/CONF.62/C.3/SR.10 (26 July 1974), para. 48; IMO, Resolution A.671(16) concerning Safety Zones and Safety of Navigation Around offshore Installations and Structures (1989), p. 3.

59 See UNCLOS III, UN Doc A/CONF.62/C.2/L.47 (8 August 1974), Article 28; UNCLOS III, UN Doc A/CONF.62/L.8/REV.1 (17 October 1974), p. 118. There was also an attempt to construct an independent regime, i.e., separated chapter, for artificial installations, which was also rejected in an early stage, see ibid., p. 139; UNCLOS III, 3rd Sess, UN Doc A/CONF.62/WP.8/PART II, p. 163, Article 66.

60 UNCLOS confers enforcement jurisdiction over artificial structures only through the EEZ regime. UNCLOS, *supra* note 4, Article 73.

61 As mentioned, although most artificial installations are physically connected to the seabed and their purpose is directly related to the seabed (exploitation of non-living resources), coastal States' jurisdiction over such installations was constructed under the EEZ regime, which is based on the 1958 CSC. UNCLOS III, 2nd Sess, 2nd Committee, 41st Mtg, UN Doc A/CONF.62/C.2/SR.41 (16 August 1974), paras. 21, 23.

62 UNCLOS, *supra* note 6, Article 60; CSC, *supra* note 11, Article 5. See also *supra* note 61.

63 In the 1958 CSC, the waters superjacent to the continental shelf were part of the High Seas, while under UNCLOS, the waters superjacent to the continental shelf are under coastal States jurisdiction (i.e., EEZ).

64 This practice ostensibly infringes on the freedom of the High Seas, as coastal State's rights in the continental shelf are not supposed to affect the legal status of the superjacent waters. UNCLOS, *supra* note 6, Article 78(1); CSC, *supra* note 11, Article 3(1); Yearbook of the International Law Commission (YILC), 8th Sess, UN Doc. A/CN.4/102/Add.1, II. (United Nations, New York, 1956), p. 298, commentary to Article 69. However, the freedom of the High Sea in the CSC referred only to navigation and fishing. Thus, coastal States had jurisdiction over artificial installations despite the waters above being part of the High Sea. YILC, ibid., p. 299, commentary to Article 71. Nevertheless, coastal States have the duty to ensure that such structures will not unjustifiably interfere with navigation and other uses of the sea. CSC, *supra* note 11, Article 5; John R. Stevenson and Bernard H. Oxman, *The Third United Nations Conference on the Law of the Sea: The 1974 Caracas Session*, 69 Am. J. Int L. 1, 23 (1975).

65 UNCLOS, *supra* note 6, Articles 56(1)(a), 60(4).

66 UNCLOS, *supra* note 6, Article 80; A/CONF.62/C.2/SR.53, *supra* note 58, para. 4. The phrase "mutatis mutandis" indicates that the scope of rights in the continental shelf is not identical to those in the EEZ; applying Article 60 to the continental shelf requires some changes, see A. X. Fellmeth and M. Horwitz, Guide to Latin in International Law 189 (2009); Gemma Andreone, *The Exclusive Economic Zone*, *in* The Oxford Handbook of the Law of the Sea 159, 171 (Donald R. Rothwell, Alex G. Oude Elferink, Karen N. Scott and Tim Stephens (eds.), 2015). There was an attempt to include an independent provision concerning safety zones around installations in the continental shelf regime, which was rejected at the beginning of the negotiations. See *supra* note 59 and text next to it. There is almost no discussion on Article 80, which created a legal ambiguity regarding jurisdiction in the waters around installations, especially considering the drafters' original intention to include identical provisions for both the EEZ and continental shelf regimes, see UNCLOS III, 10th Sess, UN Doc A/CONF.62/L.76 (18 August 1981), p. 160, Articles 6(d), 8(a).

67 UNCLOS, *supra* note 6, Articles 78, 87. Some states did not proclaim an EEZ or proclaimed different types of zones, such as "fishery zones". See Annex D; Andreone, *supra* note 66, p. 163–164; Shani Friedman, *The Concept of Entitlement to an Exclusive Economic Zone as Reflected in International Judicial Decisions*, 53(1) ISR. Law Rev. 101, 107 (2020). As mentioned earlier, the relevant provisions do not apply in the continental shelf beyond 200 nm.

68 CSC, *supra* note 11, Article 5; UNCLOS, *supra* note 6, Article 60. States can establish safety zones around installations in the international seabed, where the superjacent waters are part of the High Seas; however, this is regulated by the ISA, rather than under national jurisdiction. See UNCLOS, *supra* note 6, Article 147.

69 *Supra* note 66.

70 See A/CONF.62/L.76, *supra* note 66, p. 160, Articles 6(d), 8(a); IMO document, LEG/MISC.8 (30 January 2014), available at https://wwwcdn.imo.org/localresources/en/OurWork/Legal/Documents/LEG%20MISC%208.pdf, p. 39.

71 CSC, *supra* note 11, Article 5; 1958 Geneva Convention on the High Seas, 450 UNTS 11, Article 2. See also ILC, Law of the sea – régime of the high seas, Summary record of the 69th Mtg, UN Doc A/CN.4/SR.69, YILC vol. I (1950), p. 235, paras. 82–84. The only concession to the special status of the High Seas is the clarification that safety zones should be defined narrowly in terms of breadth. ILC, Law of the sea – régime of the high seas, Summary record of the 131st Mtg, UN Doc A/CN.4/L.27, YILC vol. I (1951), p. 410, para. 82.

72 UNCLOS, *supra* note 6, Article 87(1)(d).

73 Articles concerning the Law of the Sea with commentaries, YILC, Vol. II, 8th Sess, ILC Doc A/CN.4/SER.A/1956/Add.l (1956), Article 27, comment 1.

74 UNCLOS, *supra* note 6, Articles 92, 94.

75 See detailed analysis on law enforcement jurisdiction in Section 1.2.2 later.

76 Mossop (2018), *supra* note 16, p. 445.

77 See *supra* note 4.

78 The Arbitral Tribunal determined that a coastal State must take steps, in accordance with the applicable procedures under its domestic law, to establish the safety zone and give due notice of its establishment, see The Arctic Sunrise Arbitration (Netherlands v. Russia), Award on the Merits, case no. 2014–02, 14 August 2015, Permanent Court of Arbitration [PCA], paras. 211–212, 215, 248. See also Maria Gavouneli, *The Environmental Parameters of Maritime Security: The Case of Energy Installations*, *in* Droit De La Mer Et Droits De L'homme: Enjeux Et Perspectives, Liber Amicorum Haritini Dipla (Laurence Boisson de Chazournes, Emmanuela Doussis, Gemma Andreone and Antonia Zervaki (eds.), 2020) [Forthcoming], available at https://ssrn.com/abstract=3519806.

79 See Annex D, e.g., Croatia, no. 5; Romania, no. 25; Russia, no. 30; Ukraine, no. 31; Cambodia, no. 33; The Philippines, no. 39; Samoa, no. 50; Iran, no. 67; Bahamas, no. 114.

80 Annex D, e.g., Canada, no. 4; Ireland, no. 13; Malta, no. 16; Australia, no. 41; Bangladesh, no. 59. Most of these laws reflect the CSC, although UNCLOS was supposed to prevail over it, see UNCLOS, *supra* note 6, Article 311(1). See e.g., Belgium, no. 2; Denmark, no. 6; Finland, no. 8; France, no. 9; Portugal, no. 24; Sweden, no. 28; Fiji, no. 52; Iraq, no. 68; Sudan, no. 106; Egypt, no. 107. See also UK, no. 29, which refers to the 1958 High Seas Convention.

81 Annex D, e.g., Cyprus, no. 18; Lithuania, no. 22; Russia, no. 30; China, no. 34; Japan, no. 38; New Zealand, no. 43; Tonga, no. 49; Sierra-Leone, no. 88; Mauritius, no. 103; Guyana, no. 122; Brazil, no. 131; Honduras, no. 138.

82 Annex D, e.g., Bulgaria, no. 3; Denmark, no. 6; Cambodia, no. 33; China, no. 34; The Philippines, no. 39; Tonga, no. 49; Nigeria, no. 77; Grenada, no. 121.

83 Annex D, e.g., Belgium, no. 2; Croatia, no. 5; Finland, no. 8; Fiji, no. 52; Saudi Arabia, no. 65; Jamaica, no. 124; Venezuela, no. 143. In some cases, this is due to lack of legislation concerning the continental shelf, e.g., Estonia, no. 7; Samoa, no. 50; Solomon Islands, no. 51; Iran, no. 67; Gabon, no. 91; Barbados, no. 117; Belize, no. 118.

84 Annex D, e.g., Norway, no. 1; Canada, no. 4; Malta, no. 16; Portugal, no. 24; New Zealand, no. 43; Fiji, no. 52; Sudan, no. 106; Egypt, no. 107; Trinidad and Tobago, no. 129. In some cases, it is because the legislation reflects the CSC, e.g., Belgium, no. 2; Portugal, no. 24; Fiji, no. 52; Malaysia, no. 62; Iraq, no. 68; Egypt, no. 107.

85 Annex D, e.g., Cyprus, no. 18; Russia, no. 30; Viet Nam, no. 35; Cook Islands, no. 42; New Zealand, no. 43; Marshall Islands, no. 44; India, no. 60; Pakistan, no. 71; Guyana, no. 122.

86 Mikhail Kashubsky and Anthony Morrison, *Security of offshore Oil and Gas Facilities: Exclusion Zones and Ships' Routeing*, 5(1) Aust. J. Marit. & Ocean Aff. 1, 4 (2013).

87 For example, Canada, Norway, Portugal, UK, Ireland, Fiji, and New Zealand made submissions to the CLCS with respect to the continental shelf beyond 200 nm, see list of submissions, Division for Ocean Affairs and the Law of the Sea (DOALOS) website, submissions to the Commission on the Limits of the Continental Shelf, pursuant to article 76, paragraph 8, available at www.un.org/Depts/los/clcs_new/commission_submissions.htm. Malta on the other hand did not proclaim an EEZ, see Annex D, Malta, no. 16. In such cases, the safety zone would be on the High Sea.

88 Contrary to UNCLOS's continental shelf regime, UNCLOS, *supra* note 6, Article 78.

89 Although UNCLOS confers competence to the IMO to recommend extending the breadth of safety zones, it has yet to do so. See UNCLOS, *supra* note 6, Article 60(5); LEG/MISC.8, *supra* note 70, p. 38–39, 111.

90 For example, Nigeria did not establish safety zones but has a three-mile "restricted area" around its offshore installations, see Annex D, Nigeria, no. 77; Kashubsky and

Morrison, *supra* note 86, p. 4. Iraq did not proclaim an EEZ and addressed security of offshore installations without mentioning the term "safety zones". In practice, it established a 2 nm "security zone", a 3,000 meter "warning zone", and a 2,000 meter "exclusion zone" around two installations in the Persian Gulf. Annex D, Iraq, no. 68; *Offshore and Out of Sight: The Ran in the North Arabian Gulf*, 6 Semaphore (2008), available at www.navy.gov.au/sites/default/files/documents/Semaphore_2008_6.pdf [publication of the Australian Navy, Department of Defence, Australia]. Lastly, while Equatorial Guinea's law refers to 500 meters safety zones, it established an approximately 4 nm "restricted area" around its offshore installation. Annex D, Equatorial Guinea, no. 96; Kashubsky and Morrison, ibid.

91 Although the Arbitral Tribunal in the *Arctic Sunrise* case rejected this practice as establishing a "safety zone" within the meaning of UNCLOS, see The Arctic Sunrise Arbitration, *supra* note 78, paras. 207–209. The existence of a dispute-settlement procedure indicates that at least one state objected.

92 It might become customary norm in the future if the lack of objection would indicate an acceptance of a new norm, see ILC, Draft conclusions on identification of customary international law, with commentaries, A/73/10 (2018), p. 117, at p. 139, para. 5; Prosecutor v. Sam Hinga Norman – Decision on Preliminary Motion Based on Lack of Jurisdiction (Child Recruitment), Case No. SCSL-2004–14-AR72(E), Special Court for Sierra Leone, 31 May 2004, para. 20.

93 For example, Kashubsky and Morrison, *supra* note 86, p. 3.

94 The prominent case is the Arctic Sunrise arbitration, *supra* note 91. There are domestic cases concerning artificial installations, mostly between oil companies and private vessels concerning collision and damages. For example, Conocophillips (UK) LTD v. Partnereederei Ms Jork [2010] EWHC 1214 (Comm). However, these cases do not necessarily relate to safety zones where there is no EEZ (in the earlier case, the oil rig was within UK's EEZ).

95 Most states did not include laws concerning the area beyond 200 nm, even broad-shelf states. This indicates to the contrary that the rights and obligations within the 200 nm are the same also beyond 200 nm, where there is no EEZ. See Annex D, notes in the end. The notion of "single continental shelf" supports this argument, see Chapter 2, Section 2.1.2.10.

96 UNCLOS, *supra* note 6, Article 73(1); The Arctic Sunrise Arbitration, *supra* note 78, para. 280.

97 At UNCLOS III, proposals to extend enforcement powers also to non-living resources were not accepted. The Arctic Sunrise Arbitration, *supra* note 78, para. 281.

98 In the "Louisa" case, ITLOS rejected the argument that Article 73 can be the basis for law enforcement activities concerning the protection of underwater cultural heritage found on the EEZ's seabed. M/V "Louisa" (Saint Vincent and the Grenadines v. Kingdom of Spain), Judgment, ITLOS Reports 2013, p. 4, paras. 104–105.

99 Some scholars maintain that UNCLOS Article 77 also includes enforcement jurisdiction regarding exploration and exploitation of the continental shelf and its resources and management of these resources, i.e., conservation and protection duties, see e.g., Ventura, *supra* note 7, p. 208. See also *infra* note 103.

100 For example, M/V "Virginia G" case, *supra* note 55, paras. 211, 255.

101 UNCLOS, *supra* note 6, Articles 56, 77(1); Tunisia v. Libya, *supra* note 1, Dissenting Opinion of Judge Oda, p. 157, p. 231, Section III.

102 The ILC interpreted the term "sovereign rights" to cover all rights necessary for and connected with the exploration and exploitation of the natural resources in the continental shelf, including law enforcement jurisdiction. A/CN.4/SER.A/1956/Add.l, *supra* note 73, Article 68, comment 2; The Arctic Sunrise Arbitration, *supra* note 78, para. 283; Joanna Mossop, *Protests against Oil Exploration at Sea: Lessons from the Arctic Sunrise Arbitration*, 31 Int. J. Marine & Coastal L. 60, 71 (2016).

103 M/V "Virginia G" case, *supra* note 55, Dissenting Opinion of Judge Ndiaye, para. 174; The Arctic Sunrise Arbitration, *supra* note 78, paras. 282–284.

104 Since coastal States operate in the superjacent waters. See UNCLOS, *supra* note 6, Article 60, 73; The Arctic Sunrise Arbitration, *supra* note 78, para. 229.

105 UNCLOS, *supra* note 6, Article 58(2).

106 The Arctic Sunrise Arbitration, *supra* note 78, para. 231.

107 The Arbitral Tribunal maintained that no consent required if the conditions for "hot pursuit" are satisfied, which requires that the pursuit commenced within one of the maritime zones under the coastal State's jurisdiction. Therefore, to protect structures on the continental shelf, coastal States can commence pursuit only when a foreign ship is within the safety zone. The Arctic Sunrise Arbitration, *supra* note 78, paras. 244–245, 253. See also Alex G. Oude Elferink, *The Arctic Sunrise Incident: A Multi-faceted Law of the Sea Case with a Human Rights Dimension*, 29 Int. J. Marine & Coastal L. 244, 274 (2014); Sebastian tho Pesch, *Coastal State Jurisdiction around Installations: Safety Zones in the Law of the Sea*, 30 Int. J. Marine & Coastal L. 512, 527–528 (2015).

108 See discussion on law enforcement measures against possible terrorist offences in the safety zone, which is not possible in the EEZ under UNCLOS. The Arctic Sunrise Arbitration, *supra* note 78, para. 278. See also M/V "Virginia G" case, *supra* note 55, Separate Opinion of Judge Paik, paras. 4–5.

109 However, even in the safety zones, enforcement jurisdiction is limited; enforcement measures have to be in connection to the goal of ensuring the safety of the installations and navigation, see Oude Elferink (2014), *supra* note 107, p. 270; Pesch, *supra* note 107, p. 528.

110 Annex D, e.g., Bulgaria, no. 3, law from 2000, Article 44; Canada, no. 4, Article 22; Croatia, no. 5, Article 1035; Papua New Guinea, no. 45.

111 Annex D, e.g., Cyprus, no. 18, part IV; Article 20; Japan, no. 38; Myanmar, no. 63, law from 2017, Chapter X; Iran, no. 67. For example, Canada's legislation applies the criminal code for acts committed in the continental shelf, on installations, and in the safety zones around them. See ibid., Canada, no. 4; Wylie Spicer, *Canada, the Law of the Sea Treaty and International Payments: Where Will the Money Come from?*, 31(8) University of Calgary, The School of Public Policy, Spp Research Papers 8 (2015).

112 Annex D, Indonesia, no. 61; Malaysia, no. 62, law from 1984.

113 See *supra* note 109 and connected text. See also Annex D, Russia, no. 30, law from 1995; Australia, no. 41, law from 2006; United States Code of Federal Regulations, Title 33, Chapter I, Subchapter N, Part 147, available at www.ecfr.gov/cgi-bin/text-idx?SID=2961df533a6e9c56e8a73fcb5c1c7e91&mc=true&node=pt33.2.147&rgn=div5.

114 Oude Elferink (2014), *supra* note 107, p. 257–258; Pesch, *supra* note 107, p. 526.

115 Oude Elferink (2014), ibid., p. 257.

116 Such as appropriate warning and the duty not to endanger life and the principles are necessity and reasonableness. M/V "Saiga" case, *supra* note 1, paras. 155–156; Guyana v. Suriname, Award, case no. 2004–04, 17 September 2007, Permanent Court of Arbitration [PCA], para. 445. See also the right of "hot pursuit", which must be carried out by military forces, UNCLOS, *supra* note 6, Article 111(5).

117 Guyana v. Suriname, ibid., para. 445.

118 For example, Maritime Delimitation in the Area between Greenland and Jan Mayen, Judgment, ICJ Reports 1993, p. 38 (The Jan Mayen case), Separate Opinion of Judge Shahabuddeen, p. 161, 169–170, 173. See also detailed discussion in Chapter 2, Section 2.

119 UNCLOS, *supra* note 6, Article 83(1); Sean D. Murphy, *Obligations of States in Disputed Areas of the Continental Shelf*, *in* New Knowledge and Changing Circumstances in the Law of the Sea 183, 183–184 (Tomas Heidar (ed.), 2020).

120 UNCLOS, *supra* note 6, Article 83(3).

121 *Supra* note 1.

122 See The *Arctic Sunrise* case was the only case to concern other rights and activities in the EEZ and continental shelf, see The Arctic Sunrise Arbitration, *supra* note 78; The South China Sea Arbitration (2016), *supra* note 16. Some cases address other activities, but they are not necessarily relating to the continental shelf, see discussion

on "bunkering" and STS operations, *supra* note 55. However, see the Ghana/Côte d'Ivoire case, which deviates from the other cases. See *supra* note 2.

123 Which may explain why environmental issues do not reach judicial dispute-settlement, see Section 1.1 earlier.

124 See discussion on the institutional approach in Chapter 1 and on judicial bodies' goals in Chapter 5.

125 See discussion in Chapter 1, Chapter 2, Section 2.1.2, and Chapter 5.

126 UNCLOS, *supra* note 6, Article 83(1).

127 See Chapter 2, Section 2.

128 The ICJ, for example, stated that exercising rights in the continental shelf can indicate the location of a boundary line, see Tunisia v. Libya, *supra* note 1, paras. 81, 102, 107. See Norway's similar argument, The Jan Mayen case, *supra* note 118, paras. 22, 33.

129 See analysis in Chapter 2 and Chapter 5. See also Continental Shelf (Libyan Arab Jamahiriya/Malta), Judgment, ICJ reports 1985, p. 13, Separate Opinion of Judge Valticos, p. 104, para. 26; The Jan Mayen case, *supra* note 118, Separate Opinion of Judge Schwebel, p. 120.

130 See Chapter 2, Section 2.1.2.2.

131 For example, Land and Maritime Boundary between Cameroon and Nigeria (Cameroon v. Nigeria: Equatorial Guinea intervening), Judgment, ICJ Reports 2002, p. 303; Guyana v. Suriname, *supra* note 116, paras. 184, 195–196; Ghana v. Côte d'Ivoire (2017), *supra* note 2, paras. 109, 115, 124, 146, 215, 604.

132 See *infra* note 141. With regards to customary law, "silence" negates one of the critical conditions, "opinio juris" which should be explicitly expressed. See Chapter 1, Section 4.1.3. With respect to treaties, formally, they must be in written forms. See 1969 Vienna Convention on the Law of Treaties, 1155 UNTS 331 (VCLT), Article 2(1)(a). Arguably, non-written agreements are not subject to international law. See ibid., Article 3. Thus, they may be part of state practice as an informal element of the governance framework.

133 Tunisia v. Libya, *supra* note 1, para. 118; Delimitation of the Maritime Boundary in the Gulf of Maine Area, Judgment, ICJ reports 1984, p. 246, para. 150; Barbados v. Trinidad and Tobago, Award, case no. 2004–02, 11 April 2006, Permanent Court of Arbitration [PCA]; Guyana v. Suriname, *supra* note 116, paras. 234, 381, 383; Ghana v. Côte d'Ivoire (2017), *supra* note 2, paras. 113, 458, 472.

134 Tunisia v. Libya, *supra* note 1, paras. 82, 86, 93–96, 117, 133B, and Separate Opinion of Judge Jiménez De Aréchaga, p. 100, para. 85; Ghana v. Côte d'Ivoire (2017), *supra* note 2, paras. 472–475. In the *Libya/Malta case*, the Court applied the same test, and although both cases involved the same party (Libya), it concluded that there was no sufficient evidence to determine an acquiescence on the location of the boundary line. See Libya v. Malta, *supra* note 129, p. 29, paras. 25, 50; Guyana v. Suriname, *supra* note 116, para. 384.

135 Gulf of Maine Area case, *supra* note 133, paras. 62, 126, 137, 145, 148, 150, 152.

136 Ibid., para. 237. Some judges argued that the Court should have explained the reasons why using the subsoil and water column does not influence the determination of the boundary line. See ibid., Dissenting Opinion of Judge Gros, p. 360, at paras. 15, 30, 48.

137 For example, Nigeria argued that exploitation practices such as oil concessions established a *de facto* boundary line and that the Court cannot redistribute these concessions. The ICJ essentially ignored the colonial context since the maritime boundary was not the subject of negotiations until relatively recently. See Cameroon v. Nigeria, *supra* note 131, paras. 38, 282–283, 303. See also the *Qatar/Bahrain* case, where the ICJ disregarded the colonial context, despite its potential relevance to the delimitation process. The Court explained that the colonial context cannot be relevant since the British decisions referred only to the seabed, while the parties sought to delimit also the EEZ. Maritime Delimitation and Territorial Questions between Qatar and Bahrain, Merits, Judgment, ICJ Reports 2001, p. 40, paras. 239–240. See also Maritime Delimitation in the Indian Ocean (Somalia v. Kenya), Judgment, ICJ Reports 2021, p. 206.

138 Cameroon v. Nigeria, *supra* note 131, para. 304; Barbados v. Trinidad and Tobago, *supra* note 133, Chapter III and para. 364; Guyana v. Suriname, *supra* note 116, para. 386; Territorial and Maritime Dispute (Nicaragua v. Colombia), Judgment, ICJ Reports 2012, p. 624, paras. 220, 223.

139 See *supra* note 130. In the *Nicaragua/Honduras* case, the Court acknowledged that in certain circumstances, the *uti possidetis juris* principle may be relevant for delimitation, e.g., historic bays, as an indication for previous colonial context. However, short-term practices are not sufficient to conclude that there was a legally established *de facto* boundary line between the parties. Territorial and Maritime Dispute between Nicaragua and Honduras in the Caribbean Sea (Nicaragua v. Honduras), Judgment, ICJ Reports 2007, p. 659, paras. 232–233, 253, 256.

140 Arbitration between Newfoundland and Labrador and Nova Scotia concerning portions of the limits of their offshore areas as defined in the Canada-Nova Scotia Offshore Petroleum Resources Accord Implementation Act and the Canada-Newfoundland Atlantic Accord Implementation Act, Award of the Tribunal in the second phase, 26 March 2002, available at www.cnsopb.ns.ca/sites/default/files/resource/phaseii_award_english.pdf, para. 3.5; Guyana v. Suriname, *supra* note 116, para. 390.

141 Ghana v. Côte d'Ivoire (2017), *supra* note 2, paras. 100–101, 107, 149, 226. However, ITLOS acknowledged a tacit boundary agreement regarding the territorial sea, see Edwin E. Egede and Lawrence Apaalse, *Dispute concerning Delimitation of the Maritime Boundary between Ghana and Cote D'Ivoire in the Atlantic Ocean – Lessons from Another Maritime Delimitation Case arising from the African Region*, 29 Ind. Int. & Comp. L. Rev. 55, 71–72 (2019).

142 Ghana v. Côte d'Ivoire (2017), *supra* note 2, paras. 146–147, 164. ITLOS also rejected the possible effects of oil activities on delimitation beyond 200 nm; Ghana argued that the parties' submissions to the CLCS also indicate a tacit boundary agreement since each submission was confined to the relevant party's side of the "line".

143 Ibid., para. 441.

144 For example, ibid., para. 163.

145 See UNCLOS, *supra* note 6, Article 77.

146 Ghana v. Côte d'Ivoire (2017), *supra* note 2, para. 225. It rejected the idea of "tacit delimitation agreements" since it conflicts with Article 83(3) and influence delimitation process rather than the opposite. Although as analyzed earlier, judicial decisions did recognize the influence of conduct or sovereign rights on delimitation.

147 See for example an implicit indication in Somalia v. Kenya (2021), *supra* note 137, para. 44.

148 See for example Malcolm N. Shaw, International Law 75 (9th ed., 2021); Christoph Saake, *A Straight Line Towards the Sea, A Comment on the Judgment in the case of Maritime Delimitation in the Indian Ocean (Somalia v Kenya)*, voelkerrechtsblog (18 October 2021), available at https://voelkerrechtsblog.org/a-straight-line-towards-the-sea/. See support also in Somalia v. Kenya (2021), *supra* note 137, Partly Concurring and Partly Dissenting, of Judge Robinson, para. 48.

149 Somalia v. Kenya (2021), ibid., para. 51; A/73/10, *supra* note 92, p. 79, 142.

150 Somalia v. Kenya (2021), ibid., paras. 73–78.

151 Ibid., paras. 71, 80.

152 This strengthens the analysis in Chapter 2, Section 1.2.3.

153 See UNCLOS III, 8th Sess, 2nd Committee, 57th Mtg, UN Doc A/CONF.62/C.2/SR.57 (24 April 1979), paras. 32, 34, 48, 51; UNCLOS III, 9th Sess, 128th Plen Mtg, UN Doc A/CONF.62/SR.128 (3 April 1980), para. 29.

154 The group dealt with questions concerning delimitation, UNCLOS III, 8th Sess, 2nd Committee, 58th Mtg, UN Doc A/CONF.62/C.2/SR.58 (24 April 1979), para. 6.

155 UNCLOS, *supra* note 6, Article 83(3). See also Murphy, *supra* note 119, p. 195.

156 Guyana v. Suriname, *supra* note 116, paras. 272, 459; Ghana v. Côte d'Ivoire (2017), *supra* note 2, para. 626; Robert Beckman and Leonardo Bernard, *Framework for the Joint Development of Hydrocarbon Resources*, 22 Asian Y.B. Int. Law 86, 91 (2018);

Youri Van Logchem, The Rights and Obligations of States in Disputed Maritime Areas 183 (2021).

157 For example, Guyana v. Suriname, *supra* note 116, paras. 460–461, 476; Ghana v. Côte d'Ivoire (2017), *supra* note 2, paras. 627, 629; Nicholas A. Ioannides, *Rights and Obligations of States in Undelimited Maritime Areas: The Case of the Eastern Mediterranean Sea, in* Stress Testing The Law of the Sea 311, 313 (Stephen Minas and Jordan Diamond (eds.), 2018). See also general obligation to act in good faith, UNCLOS, *supra* note 6, Article 300.

158 For example, Murphy, *supra* note 119, p. 195–197; Ioannides, *supra* note 157, p. 313. In the *Ghana/Cote d'Ivoire* case, ITLOS acknowledged that a provisional order for suspension of ongoing exploration or exploitation activities would have caused huge financial loss for Ghana, which would prejudice its rights. Ghana v. Côte d'Ivoire (2017), *supra* note 2, paras. 651–652; Egede and Apaalse, *supra* note 141, p. 66.

159 This also includes the obligation not to cause harm to the marine environment in the disputed area by conducting exploration or exploitation activities, see e.g., The South China Sea Arbitration (2016), *supra* note 16, para. 1178. However, this is also an obligation of conduct rather than result, see Murphy, *supra* note 119, p. 198; Ioannides, *supra* note 157, p. 315, 317.

160 For example, Guyana v. Suriname, *supra* note 116, paras. 470, 484; Bangladesh v. India, *supra* note 3, para. 218. See also Ioannides, *supra* note 157, p. 316; Murphy, *supra* note 119, p. 198. However, in the *Ghana/Côte d'Ivoire* case, ITLOS determined that activities in an area of the continental shelf which has been attributed to another state would not violate the latter's sovereign rights if the activities were carried out before the judgment was delivered and both states made claims in that area in good faith. In contrast, in *the South China Sea* case, the Arbitral Tribunal considered China to breach its obligations not to aggravate the dispute. It seems that the identity of the parties is significant. This seems opposite to the IR realist approach, which gives greater significance to strong actors. See Ghana v. Côte d'Ivoire (2017), *supra* note 2, para. 592; The South China Sea Arbitration (2016), *supra* note 16, para. 1177. See also Somalia v. Kenya (2021), *supra* note 137, para. 203.

161 Guyana v. Suriname, *supra* note 116, para. 272; Beckman and Bernard, *supra* note 156, p. 92. Although it might be permissible by a bilateral agreement, see Guyana v. Suriname, ibid., paras. 466–467, 479–480; Ghana v. Côte d'Ivoire (2017), *supra* note 2, para. 630; Ioannides, *supra* note 157, p. 319; Van Logchem, *supra* note 156, p. 183.

162 Guyana v. Suriname, *supra* note 116, paras. 466–469, 479–481; Ghana v. Côte d'Ivoire (2017), *supra* note 2, para. 630; Ioannides, *supra* note 157, p. 316–317, 319. This conflict with Article 77 allows coastal States to utilize the resources in the continental shelf in any circumstances, see UNCLOS, *supra* note 6, Article 77.

163 Nicholas A. Ioannides and Constantinos Yiallourides, A Commentary on the Dispute Concerning the Maritime Delimitation in the Indian Ocean (Somalia v Kenya), EJIL:Talk! Blog (22 October 2021), available at www.ejiltalk.org/a-commentary-on-the-dispute-concerning-the-maritime-delimitation-in-the-indian-ocean-somalia-v-kenya/.

164 See also Ioannides, *supra* note 157, p. 318.

165 As discussed later, international oil and gas companies influenced delimitation and utilization agreements.

166 Some agreements include only the coordinates of the boundary line. See Delimitation Agreement between the Government of the French Republic and the Government of the Republic of Madagascar (2005), 71 Law of the Sea Bulletin 23 (2009). Others include scientific information or specification of the method of delimitation. For example, Delimitation Treaty between the Islamic Republic of Mauritania and the Republic of Cape Verde (2003), 55 Law of the Sea Bulletin 32 (2004); Delimitation Agreement between the Gabonese Republic and the Democratic Republic of Sao Tome and Principe (2001), DOALOS website, available at www.un.org/Depts/

los/LEGISLATIONANDTREATIES/PDFFILES/TREATIES/GAB-STP2001MB.PDF. Equidistance is a common delimitation method, but states also employed other criteria for the delimitation, see Tunisia v. Libya, *supra* note 1, para. 109. See also Thomas Cottier, Equitable Principles of Maritime Boundary Delimitation: The Quest for Distributive Justice in International Law 243 (2015).

167 There are bilateral agreements, see examples in *supra* note 166. There are also trilateral agreements, which are separate forms of maritime boundary delimitation. See e.g., Delimitation Agreement between the Government of the Kingdom of Thailand, the Government of the Republic of India and the Government of the Republic of Indonesia in the Andaman Sea (1978), DOALOS website, available at www.un.org/Depts/los/LEGISLATIONANDTREATIES/PDFFILES/TREATIES/THA-IND-IDN1978TP.PDF; Agreement between the Government of the Republic of Finland, the Government of the Republic of Estonia and the Government of the Kingdom of Sweden on the common maritime boundary point in the Baltic Sea (2001), DOALOS website, available at www.un.org/Depts/los/LEGISLATIONANDTREATIES/PDFFILES/TREATIES/FIN-EST-SWE2001BS.PDF.

168 Beckman and Bernard, *supra* note 156, p. 93–94.

169 For example, Agreement between Albania and Italy for the determination of the continental shelf (1992), DOALOS website, available at www.un.org/Depts/los/LEGISLATIONANDTREATIES/PDFFILES/TREATIES/ALB-ITA1992CS.pdf, Article 4; Treaty between the Federated States of Micronesia and the Republic of Palau concerning Maritime Boundaries and Cooperation on Related Matters (2006), DOALOS website, available at www.un.org/Depts/los/LEGISLATIONANDTREATIES/PDFFILES/FSM-PALAU.pdf, Article 5. See also Vasco Becker-Weinberg, Joint Development of Hydrocarbon Deposits in the Law of the Sea 133–134 (2014).

170 John W. Donaldson, *Oil and Water: Assessing the Link Between Maritime Boundary Delimitation and Hydrocarbon Resources*, *in* The Limits of Maritime Jurisdiction 127, 134 (Clive H. Schofield, Seokwoo Lee, and Moon-Sang Kwon (eds.), 2014). See also Snjólaug Árnadóttir, *Provisional Boundaries and Alternative Solutions to Maritime Delimitation*, 35(2) Leiden J. Int. Law 397, 402 (2022).

171 Becker-Weinberg (2012), *supra* note 21, p. 5.

172 Dispute between the Government of the State of Eritrea and the Government of the Republic of Yemen, Award of the Arbitral Tribunal in the Second Stage of the Proceedings (Maritime Delimitation), case no. 1996–04, 17 December 1999, Permanent Court of Arbitration [PCA], para. 84; Julia Lisztwan, *Stability of Maritime Boundary Agreements*, 37 Yale J. Int. L. 153, 180–181 (2012); Constantinos Yiallourides, *Joint Development of Seabed Resources in Areas of Overlapping Maritime Claims: An Analysis of Precedents in State Practice*, 31 U.S.F. Mar. L.J. 129 (2018); Van Logchem, *supra* note 156, p. 249. It seems that such cooperation is critical to promote stability.

173 See for example the Treaty Between the Republic of Vanuatu and the Solomon Islands (2016), DOALOS website, available at www.un.org/Depts/los/LEGISLATIONANDTREATIES/PDFFILES/TREATIES/vut_slb_wsm_2016.pdf, Article 7; Agreement between Tuvalu and Kiribati concerning their maritime boundary, FAOLEX database, available at http://extwprlegs1.fao.org/docs/pdf/bi-158701.pdf, Article 3.

174 UNCLOS regulates straddling fishing stocks within the EEZ regime but does not address "straddling" deposits of non-living resources in the seabed, see UNCLOS, *supra* note 6, Articles 63–64. There are no similar provisions in Part VI concerning the continental shelf.

175 See also Van Logchem, *supra* note 156, p. 285–288.

176 A "joint development zone" is an area where the parties agree to conduct joint operations, usually based on equal share of the benefits. See Yiallourides, *supra* note 172, p. 132. For example, Agreement on Provisional Arrangements for the Delimitation of the Maritime Boundaries between the Republic of Tunisia and the People's Democratic Republic of Algeria (2002), 2238 UNTS 208; Delimitation Agreement between the Government of the Cook Islands and the Government of Niue (2012), DOALOS

website, available at www.un.org/Depts/los/LEGISLATIONANDTREATIES/PDFFILES/DEPOSIT/cok_mzn96_2013.pdf.

177 For example, Timor Sea Treaty (2002), DOALOS website, available at www.un.org/Depts/los/LEGISLATIONANDTREATIES/PDFFILES/TREATIES/AUS-TLS2002TST.PDF; Treaty between the Kingdom of Norway and the Russian Federation concerning Maritime Delimitation and Cooperation in the Barents Sea and the Arctic Ocean (2010), DOALOS website, available at www.un.org/Depts/los/LEGISLATIONANDTREATIES/PDFFILES/TREATIES/NOR-RUS2010.PDF. See also Becker-Weinberg (2014), *supra* note 169, p. 49–50, 53; Massimo Lando, Maritime Delimitation as a Judicial Process 196–197 (2019).

178 For example, Agreement between Qatar and Abu Dhabi (1969), DOALOS website, available at www.un.org/Depts/los/LEGISLATIONANDTREATIES/PDFFILES/TREATIES/QAT-ARE1969MB.PDF; Delimitation Agreement between the Kingdom of Saudi Arabia and the United Arab Emirates (1974), 1733 UNTS 30, Article 3.

179 Yiallourides, *supra* note 172, p. 138–140. Some agreements obligate the parties to adopted measures to safeguard operators' rights in the disputed areas. For example, Maritime Delimitation Agreement between the Russian Federation and the Kingdom of Norway (2007), 67 Law of the Sea Bulletin 42 (2008), Article 3. See also Becker-Weinberg (2014), *supra* note 169, p. 128.

180 See examples in Cottier, *supra* note 166, Chapter 5.

181 Another example are joint utilization plans based on good oilfield practices, cooperation, and regulation of "excessive drilling", see Yiallourides, *supra* note 172, p. 134, 136, 141.

182 UNCLOS, *supra* note 6, Part XI.

183 For example, Becker-Weinberg (2014), *supra* note 169, p. 100; Yiallourides, *supra* note 172, p. 129, 133, 138; Beckman and Bernard, *supra* note 156, p. 95; Yiallourides and Ermolina, *supra* note 47, p. 139; Árnadóttir, *supra* note 170, p. 404.

184 UNCLOS, *supra* note 6, Article 83(3).

185 Yiallourides, *supra* note 172, p. 148, 150; Beckman and Bernard, *supra* note 156, p. 94–95.

186 Especially in cases where the agreements contain clauses explicitly indicating that they are "without prejudice" to future delimitation agreements, see Yiallourides, *supra* note 172, p. 144–145. Such agreements contain an inherent contradiction; a link between resources utilization and delimitation by reference to Article 83(3) while also containing "without prejudice" clauses. See Timor Sea Conciliation (Timor-Leste v. Australia), Report and Recommendations of the Compulsory Conciliation Commission between Timor-Leste and Australia on the Timor Sea, case no. 2016–10, 09 May 2018, Permanent Court of Arbitration [PCA], para. 241.

187 However, it might correspond with a narrow interpretation of Article 83(3). Activities that cause permanent physical changes in the marine environment are permissible under an agreement between the parties. See *supra* note 161.

188 Beckman and Bernard, *supra* note 156, p. 100.

189 Yiallourides, *supra* note 172, p. 152.

190 This list is not exhaustive; rather, it is a list of available legislation in English.

191 Royal Decree (1963), DOALOS website, available at www.un.org/Depts/los/LEGISLATIONANDTREATIES/PDFFILES/NOR_1963_Decree.pdf; Act of 21 June 1963 Relating to Exploration and Exploitation of Submarine Natural Resources, DOALOS website, available at www.un.org/Depts/los/LEGISLATIONANDTREATIES/PDFFILES/NOR_1963_Act.pdf

192 Pollution Act (No. 6, 1981) (translate), FAOLEX database, available at www.fao.org/faolex/results/en/#querystring=JmVuZHN0cmluZz0x, Article 4

193 Act No. 72 (1996) relating to petroleum activities, available at www.npd.no/en/regulations/acts/act-29-november-1996-no2.-72-relating-to-petroleum-activities/, Sections 1–2 and 9–4.

194 Act No. 91 (1976), DOALOS website, available at www.un.org/Depts/los/LEGISLATIONANDTREATIES/PDFFILES/NOR_1976_Act.pdf. Does not reflect UNCLOS.

195 Act on the exploration and exploitation of non-living resources in the territorial sea and the continental shelf (1969), DOALOS website, available at www.un.org/Depts/los/LEGISLATIONANDTREATIES/PDFFILES/BEL_1969_Act.pdf, Articles 1, 5–6. See also Royal Decree on Measures to Protect Navigation, Sea Fishing, the Environment and Other Essential Interests in the Exploration and Exploitation of the Mineral and Other Non-living Resources of the Sea-Bed and Subsoil in the Territorial Sea and on the Continental Shelf, 1974 as amended by the Royal Decree (1983), DOALOS website, available at www.un.org/Depts/los/LEGISLATIONANDTREATIES/PDFFILES/bel_1983_protection_decree.pdf

196 Act concerning the exclusive economic zone of Belgium in the North Sea (1999), DOALOS website, available at www.un.org/Depts/los/LEGISLATIONANDTREATIES/PDFFILES/BEL_1999_Act.pdf, Article 4 and Chapter V. This law amends the 1969 Act, see in Chapter IV, which also refers to the exploration and exploitation of non-living resources and to regulation of artificial installations.

197 Act governing the ocean space of the People's Republic of Bulgaria (1987), DOALOS website, available at www.un.org/Depts/los/LEGISLATIONANDTREATIES/PDFFILES/bgr_1987_ct.pdf, Articles 42, 48; Maritime Space, Inland Waterways and Ports Act (2000), DOALOS website, available at www.un.org/Depts/los/LEGISLATIONANDTREATIES/PDFFILES/BGR_2000_Act-.PDF, Articles 42, 47. The language of the 1987 law is somewhat different; it does not mention sovereign right of "prospecting" with respect to the CS and uses the term "conserving" instead of "protecting".

198 Oceans Act of 18 December 1996, DOALOS website, available at www.un.org/Depts/los/LEGISLATIONANDTREATIES/PDFFILES/CAN_1996_Act.pdf, Articles 14, 18

199 *Ibid.*, Article 20

200 The Maritime Code (1994), DOALOS website, available at www.un.org/Depts/los/LEGISLATIONANDTREATIES/PDFFILES/HRV_1994_Code.pdf, Articles 34–36, 38, 44, 46; Decision on the Extension of the Jurisdiction of the Republic of Croatia in the Adriatic Sea (2003), DOALOS website, available at www.un.org/Depts/los/LEGISLATIONANDTREATIES/PDFFILES/HRV_2003_Decision.pdf

201 Royal Decree of 7 June 1963 concerning the exercise of Danish sovereignty over the Continental Shelf, DOALOS website, available at www.un.org/Depts/los/LEGISLATIONANDTREATIES/PDFFILES/DNK_1963_Decree.pdf, Article 2; Act No. 259 concerning the Continental Shelf (1971) as amended by Act No. 278 (1972) and Act No. 654 (1977), DOALOS website, available at www.un.org/Depts/los/LEGISLATIONANDTREATIES/PDFFILES/DNK_1971_Act.pdf, para. 7

202 Exclusive Economic Zones Act No. 411 (1996), DOALOS website, available at www.un.org/Depts/los/LEGISLATIONANDTREATIES/PDFFILES/DNK_1996_Act.pdf

203 Exclusive Economic Zone Act (1993), Estonia legislation database, available at www.riigiteataja.ee/en/eli/ee/520012015003/consolide, Article 2

204 Continental Shelf Law No. 149 (1965), DOALOS website, available at www.un.org/Depts/los/LEGISLATIONANDTREATIES/PDFFILES/FIN_1965_Law.pdf, Articles 1, 5; Exclusive Economic Zone Act (2004), 57 Law of the Sea Bulletin 106 (2005), Sections 2, 7, 24

205 Act No. 68–1181 of 30 December 1968 relating to the exploration of the Continental Shelf and to the exploitation of its natural resources, DOALOS website, available at www.un.org/Depts/los/LEGISLATIONANDTREATIES/PDFFILES/FRA_1968_Act.pdf, Articles 1, 3–4. This Act was amended by Act No. 77–485 (1977), DOALOS website, available at www.un.org/Depts/los/LEGISLATIONANDTREATIES/PDFFILES/FRA_1977_Act.pdf; however, it did not change France's rights and jurisdiction in the continental shelf, as determined in the 1968 Act.

206 Law No. 76–655 of 16 July 1976 relating to the Economic Zone off the coasts of the territory of the Republic, DOALOS website, available at www.un.org/Depts/los/LEGISLATIONANDTREATIES/PDFFILES/FRA_1976_Law.pdf, Article 1
207 Constitution of Georgia, FAOLEX database, available at http://extwprlegs1.fao.org/docs/pdf/geo127811ENG.pdf, Article 7(f)
208 Law No. 2289/1995, as amended by Law No. 4001/2011, DOALOS website, available at www.un.org/Depts/los/LEGISLATIONANDTREATIES/PDFFILES/GRC_2011_Law.pdf
209 Declaration by the Federal Government (1964), DOALOS website, available at www.un.org/Depts/los/LEGISLATIONANDTREATIES/PDFFILES/DEU_1964_Declaration.pdf; Continental Shelf Act (1964), as Amended in 1974, DOALOS website, available at www.un.org/Depts/los/LEGISLATIONANDTREATIES/PDFFILES/DEU_1974_Act.pdf
210 Exclusive Economic Zone Proclamation (1994), DOALOS website, available at www.un.org/Depts/los/LEGISLATIONANDTREATIES/PDFFILES/deu_1994_eez_proclamation.pdf. No reference to rights and obligations
211 Continental Shelf Act No. 14 (1968), DOALOS website, available at www.un.org/Depts/los/LEGISLATIONANDTREATIES/PDFFILES/IRL_1968_Act.pdf, Article 2; Continental Shelf (Designated Areas) Order, S.I. No. 87 (2014), DOALOS website, available at www.un.org/Depts/los/LEGISLATIONANDTREATIES/PDFFILES/IRL_2014_Order87.pdf, p. 5
212 Continental Shelf (Protection of Installations) (Kinsale Head Field) Order, S.I. No. 285 (1977), DOALOS website, available at www.un.org/Depts/los/LEGISLATIONANDTREATIES/PDFFILES/IRL_1977_Order285.pdf; Continental Shelf (Protection of Installations) (Ballycotton Field) Order, S.I. No. 226 (1991), DOALOS website, available at www.un.org/Depts/los/LEGISLATIONANDTREATIES/PDFFILES/IRL_1991_Order226.pdf; Continental Shelf (Protection of Installations) (Connemara Field) Order, S.I. No. 267 (1997), DOALOS website, available at www.un.org/Depts/los/LEGISLATIONANDTREATIES/PDFFILES/IRL_1997_Order267.pdf
213 Maritime Jurisdiction (Boundaries of Exclusive Economic Zone) Order 2014, DOALOS website, available at www.un.org/Depts/los/LEGISLATIONANDTREATIES/PDFFILES/IRL_2014_Order86.pdf, although there is no reference to rights and obligations in this area
214 Law No. 41 of 1 June 1979 concerning the Territorial Sea, the Economic Zone and the Continental Shel, DOALOS website, available at www.un.org/Depts/los/LEGISLATIONANDTREATIES/PDFFILES/ISL_1979_Law.pdf, Articles 4, 6
215 Act No. 613 and Amendments to Act No. 6 (1967), DOALOS website, available at www.un.org/Depts/los/LEGISLATIONANDTREATIES/PDFFILES/ITA_1967_Act.pdf, Article 2
216 Continental Shelf Act, No. XXVIII (2014), FAOLEX database, available at http://extwprlegs1.fao.org/docs/pdf/mlt139078.pdf, Articles 3–4; See also Regulation of safety zones in the CS in Malta, Continental Shelf Regulations, L.N. 235 (2015), FAOLEX database, available at http://extwprlegs1.fao.org/docs/pdf/mlt147865.pdf, Articles 1(3), 3(1), 7
217 Malta, Continental Shelf Regulations, ibid., Article 6
218 See "Legislation Malta" website, available at https://legislation.mt. There is no law concerning the EEZ.
219 Exclusive Economic Zone (Establishment) Act (1999), DOALOS website, available at www.un.org/Depts/los/LEGISLATIONANDTREATIES/PDFFILES/NLD_1999_Act.pdf, Section 3; See also Outer Limits Decree (2010), DOALOS website, available at www.un.org/Depts/los/LEGISLATIONANDTREATIES/PDFFILES/NLD_EEZ_decree2010.pdf, p. 4
220 Mining Act 2003 (translation), available at www.nlog.nl/sites/default/files/2018-11/2018-11-04%20%20Translation%20MBW%20English%20%20MINING%20ACT%20OF%20THE%20NETHERLANDS%20PDF.pdf

221 Exclusive Economic Zone Law (2004), DOALOS website, available at www.un.org/Depts/los/LEGISLATIONANDTREATIES/PDFFILES/cyp_2004_eez_proclamation.pdf, Articles 4, 6, 8
222 Exclusive Economic Zone and the Continental Shelf Laws (2004 and 2014), FAOLEX database, available at http://extwprlegs1.fao.org/docs/pdf/cyp159196.pdf, Articles 4, 5B. Repeals the 1974 Continental Shelf Law, which reflects the 1958 CSC (including installations and safety zones), see Continental Shelf Law, No. 8 (1974), DOALOS website, available at www.un.org/Depts/los/LEGISLATIONANDTREATIES/PDFFILES/CYP_1974_Law.pdf
223 Exclusive Economic Zone and the Continental Shelf Laws, 2004 and 2014, ibid., Articles 6, 7–8, 11(2)
224 Ibid., Article 8B
225 Agreement between the Government of the State of Israel and the Government of the Republic of Cyprus on the delimitation of the exclusive economic zone, FAOLEX database, available at http://extwprlegs1.fao.org/docs/pdf/bi-158714.pdf, Article 2
226 Declaration regarding the maritime boundaries of the State of Palestine (2015), DOALOS website, available at www.un.org/Depts/los/LEGISLATIONANDTREATIES/PDFFILES/PSE_2015_Declaration.pdf, Article 8; Declaration regarding the maritime boundaries of the State of Palestine (2019), DOALOS website, available at www.un.org/Depts/los/LEGISLATIONANDTREATIES/PDFFILES/PSE_Deposit_09-2019.pdf, p. 3, Article 2
227 Law On the Continental Shelf and the Exclusive Economic Zone (1998), Sections 4, 6, 8
228 Marine Environment Protection and Management Law (2010), FAOLEX database, available at http://extwprlegs1.fao.org/docs/pdf/lat172860.pdf, Section 3, Articles 4–6 (repeals the 1993 EEZ and continental shelf law)
229 Resolution No. 1597 concerning limits of the maritime zones (2004), 61 Law of the Sea Bulletin 17 (2006), Article 2.1
230 Maritime Areas Act (1991), DOALOS website, available at www.un.org/Depts/los/LEGISLATIONANDTREATIES/PDFFILES/POL_1991_Act.pdf, Articles 2, 17, 22 and Section 4
231 Decree-Law No. 49–369 (1969), *supra* note 255, Article 1(1)
232 Act No. 33/77 (1977), DOALOS website, available at www.un.org/Depts/los/LEGISLATIONANDTREATIES/PDFFILES/PRT_1977_Act.pdf, Article 4
233 Lei no. 34/2006, available at https://dre.pt/application/file/a/539336 [Portuguese], Article 16(1)(c) (unofficial translation)
234 Exclusive Economic Zone Decree No. 142 (1986), DOALOS website, available at www.un.org/Depts/los/LEGISLATIONANDTREATIES/PDFFILES/ROM_1986_Decree.pdf, Articles 1, 3, 8–9
235 Ecological Protection Zone and Continental Shelf Act (2005), 60 Law of the Sea Bulletin 56 (2006), Articles 2(2), 3
236 Economic Zone Act No. 15/1978 (1978), DOALOS website, available at www.un.org/Depts/los/LEGISLATIONANDTREATIES/PDFFILES/ESP_1978_Act.pdf, Article 1
237 Exclusive Economic Zone Royal Decree No. 236/2013 (2013), DOALOS website, available at www.un.org/Depts/los/LEGISLATIONANDTREATIES/PDFFILES/ESP_2013_Decree_eng.pdf, p. 1
238 Continental Shelf Act No. 314 (1966), DOALOS website, available at www.un.org/Depts/los/LEGISLATIONANDTREATIES/PDFFILES/SWE_1966_Act.pdf, Articles 2, 6
239 Economic Zone Act (1992), DOALOS website, available at www.un.org/Depts/los/LEGISLATIONANDTREATIES/PDFFILES/SWE_1992_Act.pdf, Article 4
240 Continental Shelf Act (1964), DOALOS website, available at www.un.org/Depts/los/LEGISLATIONANDTREATIES/PDFFILES/GBR_1964_Act.pdf, preamble and Articles 2–3
241 Marine and Coastal Access Act (2009), DOALOS website, available at www.legislation.gov.uk/ukpga/2009/23/pdfs/ukpga_20090023_en.pdf, Chapter 4, part 2, p. 25 [Article 41(2)]

242 Continental Shelf Decree of the Presidium (1968), DOALOS website, available at www.un.org/Depts/los/LEGISLATIONANDTREATIES/PDFFILES/RUS_1968_Decree.pdf, Article 1
243 Federal Law on the Continental Shelf of the Russian Federation, adopted by the State Duma on 25 October 1995, DOALOS website, available at www.un.org/Depts/los/LEGISLATIONANDTREATIES/PDFFILES/RUS_1995_Law.pdf, Articles 5, 16
244 Economic Zone Decree of the Presidium (1984), DOALOS website, available at www.un.org/Depts/los/LEGISLATIONANDTREATIES/PDFFILES/RUS_1984_Decree.pdf, Article 2
245 Federal Act on the exclusive economic zone (1998), DOALOS website, available at www.un.org/Depts/los/LEGISLATIONANDTREATIES/PDFFILES/RUS_1998_Act_EZ.pdf, Article 5
246 Exclusive (Marine) Economic Zone Law (1995), DOALOS website, available at www.un.org/Depts/los/LEGISLATIONANDTREATIES/PDFFILES/UKR_1995_Law.pdf, Articles 4, 7, 9–11
247 Outer Continental Shelf Lands Act (1953), DOALOS website, available at www.un.org/Depts/los/LEGISLATIONANDTREATIES/PDFFILES/USA_1953_Act.pdf, Paragraph 1333.
248 Outer Continental Shelf Lands Act Amendments (1978), Congress website, available at www.congress.gov/bill/95th-congress/senate-bill/9?q=%7B%22search%22%3A%5B%22continental+shelf%22%5D%7D&r=11&s=4
249 A bill to improve the operation of the Fishermen's Contingency Fund established to compensate commercial fishermen for damages resulting from oil and gas exploration, development, and production in areas of the Outer Continental Shelf, 1982, Congress website, available at www.congress.gov/bill/97th-congress/house-bill/3816?q=%7B%22search%22%3A%5B%22continental+shelf%22%5D%7D&r=23&s=4
250 Exclusive Economic Zone Presidential Proclamation 5030 (1983), DOALOS website, available at www.un.org/Depts/los/LEGISLATIONANDTREATIES/PDFFILES/USA_1983_Proclamation.pdf, p. 1
251 Report of the US embassy in Phnom Penh concerning the 1969 declaration on territorial sea and continental shelf, available at www.cia.gov/library/readingroom/docs/CIA-RDP08C01297R000100230010-7.pdf
252 Statement Issued by the Spokesman of the Ministry of Foreign Affairs (1978), DOALOS website, available at www.un.org/Depts/los/LEGISLATIONANDTREATIES/PDFFILES/KHM_1978_Statement.pdf, Article 3
253 Decree of the Council of State (1982), DOALOS website, available at www.un.org/Depts/los/LEGISLATIONANDTREATIES/PDFFILES/KHM_1982_Decree.pdf, Articles 5–6
254 Exclusive Economic Zone and Continental Shelf Act, *supra* note 274, Articles 3–4, 8
255 Statement on the Territorial Sea, the Contiguous Zone, the Exclusive Economic Zone and the Continental Shelf (1977), DOALOS website, available at www.un.org/Depts/los/LEGISLATIONANDTREATIES/PDFFILES/VNM_1977_Statement.pdf, Articles 3–4
256 Order No. 16/2012/L-CTN on the promulgation of the Law of the Sea of Vietnam No. 18/2012/QH13, FAOLEX database, available at http://extwprlegs1.fao.org/docs/pdf/vie124619.pdf, Articles 16, 18, 34
257 Economic Zone Decree (1977), DOALOS website, available at www.un.org/Depts/los/LEGISLATIONANDTREATIES/PDFFILES/PRK_1977_Decree.pdf
258 Exclusive Economic Zone Act No. 5151 (1996), DOALOS website, available at www.un.org/Depts/los/LEGISLATIONANDTREATIES/PDFFILES/KOR_1996_EEZAct.pdf, Article 3
259 Law on the Exclusive Economic Zone and the Continental Shelf (Law No. 74 of 1996), 35 Law of the Sea Bulletin 94 (1997), Article 3
260 Continental Shelf Presidential Proclamation No. 370 (1968), DOALOS website, available at www.un.org/Depts/los/LEGISLATIONANDTREATIES/PDFFILES/PHL_1968_Proclamation.pdf

261 Presidential Decree No. 1599 of 11 June 1978 establishing an Exclusive Economic Zone and for other purposes, DOALOS website, available at www.un.org/Depts/los/LEGISLATIONANDTREATIES/PDFFILES/PHL_1978_Decree.pdf, Section 2(A)
262 Act to Define the Maritime Zones of the Republic of the Philippines (2011), available at www.congress.gov.ph/legisdocs/third_15/hbt4185.pdf. See also Act to Define the Maritime Zones of the Republic of the Philippines (2019), available at www.congress.gov.ph/legisdocs/third_16/hbt4889.pdf
263 Exclusive Economic Zone Royal Proclamation (1981), DOALOS website, available at www.un.org/Depts/los/LEGISLATIONANDTREATIES/PDFFILES/THA_1981_Proclamation.pdf
264 Seas and Submerged Lands Act 1973 (including amendments up to 2019), FAOLEX database, available at http://extwprlegs1.fao.org/docs/pdf/aus5017.pdf, Articles 10B, 11
265 Ibid., Article 13AA
266 Offshore Petroleum and Greenhouse Gas Storage Act 2006, Vol. 1, FAOLEX database, available at http://extwprlegs1.fao.org/docs/pdf/aus64464volume1.pdf, for example, Article 280(2)(c); Offshore Petroleum and Greenhouse Gas Storage Act 2006, Vol. 2, available at www.legislation.gov.au/Details/C2015C00159/Html/Volume_2#_Toc416691713, Chapter 6.6
267 Continental Shelf Act, No. 28 (1964) as Amended by the Continental Shelf Amendment Act, No. 17 (1977), DOALOS website, available at www.un.org/Depts/los/LEGISLATIONANDTREATIES/PDFFILES/COK_1977_Act17.pdf, Article 3 [repealed by 2018 law]
268 Territorial Sea and Exclusive Economic Zone Act, No. 16 (1977), DOALOS website, available at www.un.org/Depts/los/LEGISLATIONANDTREATIES/PDFFILES/COK_1977_Act16.pdf [repealed by 2018 law]
269 Maritime Zones Act No. 1 (2018), FAOLEX database, available at http://extwprlegs1.fao.org/docs/pdf/cok183766.pdf, Article 18
270 Continental Shelf Act (No. 28, 1964), FAOLEX database, available at http://extwprlegs1.fao.org/docs/pdf/nze5174.pdf, Article 3. This law applied also to Cook Islands until it was replaced, see Continental Shelf Act, No. 28 (1964) as Amended by the Continental Shelf Amendment Act, No. 17 (1977), *supra* note 267. The law was amended several times, see New Zealand legislation website, available at www.legislation.govt.nz/act/public/1964/0028/latest/LMS304788.html?search=qs_act%40bill%40regulation%40deemedreg_continental+shelf+1964_resel_25_h&p=1. However, these amendments did not change the provisions concerning sovereign rights.
271 Territorial Sea, Contiguous Zone, and Exclusive Economic Zone Act (1977), as amended in 2005, available at www.legislation.govt.nz/act/public/1977/0028/latest/whole.html, Articles 9–10, 27
272 New Zealand legislation website, for example at www.legislation.govt.nz/all/results.aspx?search=qs_act%40bill%40regulation%40deemedreg_continental+shelf_resel_25_h&p=2
273 Exclusive Economic Zone and Continental Shelf (Environmental Effects) Act (No. 72, 2012), FAOLEX database, available at http://extwprlegs1.fao.org/docs/pdf/nze115256.pdf, Article 10; Exclusive Economic Zone and Continental Shelf (Environmental Effects) Amendment Act 2013, FAOLEX database, available at http://extwprlegs1.fao.org/docs/pdf/nze151614.pdf, Article 7
274 Marine Zones (Declaration) Act 1984, DOALOS website, available at www.un.org/Depts/los/LEGISLATIONANDTREATIES/PDFFILES/MHL_1984_Act.pdf, Section 10 [repealed by 2016 law]
275 Maritime Zones Declaration Act (P.L. 2016–5) (2016), FAOLEX database, available at http://extwprlegs1.fao.org/docs/pdf/mas158412.pdf, Article 116
276 Maritime Zones Act No. 47 (2015), FAOLEX database, available at http://extwprlegs1.fao.org/docs/pdf/png188723.pdf, Articles 28, 31
277 Ibid., Article 32

278 Ibid., Articles 35–36, 37
279 Maritime Zones Act 2013 (No. 323 of 2013), FAOLEX database, available at http://extwprlegs1.fao.org/docs/pdf/niu136342.pdf, Article 15
280 Maritime Zones Act 2012, FAOLEX database, available at http://extwprlegs1.fao.org/docs/pdf/tuv126505.pdf, Article 15
281 Marine Zones (Declaration) Act, 1983, DOALOS website, available at www.un.org/Depts/los/LEGISLATIONANDTREATIES/PDFFILES/KIR_1983_Act.pdf, Articles 7(6), 8(2), 10(c) [repealed by 2011 law]
282 Marine Zones (Declaration) Act, 2011, DOALOS website, available at www.un.org/Depts/los/LEGISLATIONANDTREATIES/PDFFILES/KIR_2011_Act.pdf, Article 11
283 Maritime Zones Act No. 10 (2009), Pacific Agricultural Policy Programme website, available at https://pafpnet.spc.int/attachments/article/648/Tonga%20Maritime%20Zones%20Act%202009.pdf, Articles 13, 16
284 *Ibid.*, Article 18
285 Maritime Zones Act 1999, FAOLEX database, available at http://extwprlegs1.fao.org/docs/pdf/sam35516.pdf, Articles 20, 27 and PART VII
286 The Delimitation of Marine Waters Act, No. 32 (1978), DOALOS website, available at www.un.org/Depts/los/LEGISLATIONANDTREATIES/PDFFILES/SLB_1978_Act.pdf, Articles 9, 11
287 Continental Shelf Act, No. 9 (1970), DOALOS website, available at www.un.org/Depts/los/LEGISLATIONANDTREATIES/PDFFILES/FJI_1970_Act.pdf, Articles 2–3
288 Marine spaces Act, No. 18 (1977), as amended by the Marine Spaces (Amendment) Act, No. 15 (1978), Pacific Islands Legal Information Institute, available at www.paclii.org/fj/legis/consol_act_OK/msa132/, Article 9
289 Maritime Zones Act (No. 6, 2010), FAOLEX database, available at http://extwprlegs1.fao.org/docs/pdf/van99597.pdf, Articles 10, 12–13
290 Sea Boundaries Act (No. 16, 1997), FAOLEX database, available at http://extwprlegs1.fao.org/docs/pdf/nau28262.pdf, Article 6(4), 7
291 Law No. 30/76 relating to the Exclusive Economic Zone (1976), DOALOS website, available at www.un.org/Depts/los/LEGISLATIONANDTREATIES/PDFFILES/MDV_1976_Law30.pdf, Article 2 [repealed]; Maritime Zones of Maldives Act No. 6/96, *supra* note 275, Article 9
292 Act to amend Chapter 1 of Title 27 of the Palau National Code (2003), DOALOS website, available at www.un.org/Depts/los/LEGISLATIONANDTREATIES/PDFFILES/PLW_2003_PNC.pdf, Article 144(b)
293 The Petroleum Act, RPPL 8–37 (2011), Pacific Islands Legal Information Institute, available at www.paclii.org/cgi-bin/sinodisp/pw/legis/num_act/tpaotropr8372011417/tpaotropr8372011417.html?stem=&synonyms=&query=continental%20shelf, preamble
294 Chapter 1 of Title 18 of the Code of the Federated States of Micronesia (Annotated), as amended by Public Law No. 19–172 (2017), DOALOS website, available at www.un.org/Depts/los/LEGISLATIONANDTREATIES/PDFFILES/Title18FSMCode.pdf, Section 105, 105D
295 National Parliament, Law No. 7/2002, Maritime Borders of the Territory of the Democratic Republic of Timor-Leste, FAOLEX database, available at http://extwprlegs1.fao.org/docs/pdf/tim39858.pdf, Article 10
296 Territorial Waters and Maritime Zones Act 1974, Act No. XXVI of 1974, DOALOS website, available at www.un.org/Depts/los/LEGISLATIONANDTREATIES/PDFFILES/BGD_1974_Act.pdf, Article 7, Section 7(4)
297 Ibid., Section 9
298 The Territorial Waters, Continental Shelf, Exclusive Economic Zone and other Maritime Zones Act, No. 80 (1976), *supra* note 264, Articles 6(3), 7(4); see also India's legislation database, available at www.indiacode.nic.in/handle/123456789/1484?view_type=search&sam_handle=123456789/1362

299 See legislation as detailed in Etty R. Agoes, *Indonesia and the LOS Convention: Recent Developments in Ocean Law, Policy and Management*, 15(2) Marine Policy 122, 125–126 (1991)
300 Declaration by the Government concerning the Exclusive Economic Zone of Indonesia 21 March 1980, DOALOS website, available at www.un.org/Depts/los/LEGISLATIONANDTREATIES/PDFFILES/IDN_1980_DeclarationEEZ.pdf; Act No. 5 of 1983 on the Indonesian exclusive economic zone, 18 October 1983, DOALOS website, available at www.un.org/Depts/los/LEGISLATIONANDTREATIES/PDFFILES/IDN_1983_Act.pdf, Article 4 and Chapter VI
301 Law of the Republic of Indonesia about the Sea, no. 32 (2014), available at http://extwprlegs1.fao.org/docs/pdf/ins161826.pdf, Articles 6–7, 20
302 Ibid., Article 1(8)
303 Ibid., Article 32
304 Continental Shelf Act 1966, as Amended by Act No. 83 (1972), DOALOS website, available at www.un.org/Depts/los/LEGISLATIONANDTREATIES/PDFFILES/MYS_1966_Act.pdf, Articles 3, 5–6
305 Exclusive Economic Zone Act, 1984, Act No. 311, DOALOS website, available at www.un.org/Depts/los/LEGISLATIONANDTREATIES/PDFFILES/MYS_1984_Act.pdf, Articles 4, 17, 21, and Part VIII
306 Territorial Sea and Maritime Zones Law, Pyithu Hluttaw Law No. 3 of 9 April 1977, DOALOS website, available at www.un.org/Depts/los/LEGISLATIONANDTREATIES/PDFFILES/MMR_1977_Law.pdf, Articles 14, 18 [repealed]
307 Myanmar Territorial Sea and Maritime Zones Law (No.14, 2017), *supra* note 269, Articles 20, 25(a)
308 Maritime Zones Law No. 22 of 1 September 1976, DOALOS website, available at www.un.org/Depts/los/LEGISLATIONANDTREATIES/PDFFILES/LKA_1976_Law.pdf, Sections 5(3), 6(3)
309 Royal Decree, No. M-27 (1968), DOALOS website, available at www.un.org/Depts/los/LEGISLATIONANDTREATIES/PDFFILES/SAU_1968_Decree.pdf, Section 3
310 Statute of Maritime Delimitation of the Kingdom of Saudi Arabia (Royal Decree No. 6, 2011), FAOLEX database, available at http://extwprlegs1.fao.org/docs/pdf/sau158713.pdf, Articles 13–14, 18
311 Territorial Sea, Continental Shelf, and the Exclusive Economic Zone Law No. 28 (2003), FAOLEX database, http://extwprlegs1.fao.org/docs/pdf/syr53778E.pdf, Articles 22, 25, 27, 29
312 Marine Areas Act (1993), DOALOS website, available at www.un.org/Depts/los/LEGISLATIONANDTREATIES/PDFFILES/IRN_1993_Act.pdf, Articles 14–15
313 Official Proclamation (1957), DOALOS website, available at www.un.org/Depts/los/LEGISLATIONANDTREATIES/PDFFILES/IRQ_1957_Proclamation.pdf
314 Decree No. 317 (2014), DOALOS website, available at www.un.org/Depts/los/LEGISLATIONANDTREATIES/PDFFILES/Kuwait_Decree_317-2014-E.pdf, Articles 6–7
315 Royal Decree concerning the territorial sea, continental shelf, and exclusive economic zone, 1981, DOALOS website, available at www.un.org/Depts/los/LEGISLATIONANDTREATIES/PDFFILES/OMN_1981_Decree.pdf, Articles 4, 6
316 Territorial Waters and Maritime Zones Act, 1976 (of 22 December 1976), DOALOS website, available at www.un.org/Depts/los/LEGISLATIONANDTREATIES/PDFFILES/PAK_1976_Act.pdf, Articles 5(2), 6(2)
317 Decree No. 86/11264 (1986), DOALOS website, available at www.un.org/Depts/los/LEGISLATIONANDTREATIES/PDFFILES/TUR_1986_Decree.pdf, Articles 1–2
318 Declaration concerning the Exclusive Economic Zone and its delimitation (1980), DOALOS website, available at www.un.org/Depts/los/LEGISLATIONANDTREATIES/PDFFILES/ARE_1980_Declaration.pdf, Article 4
319 Federal Law No. 19 (1993), DOALOS website, available at www.un.org/Depts/los/LEGISLATIONANDTREATIES/PDFFILES/ARE_1993_Law.pdf, Articles 13–14, 18, 20–21

320 Act No. 45 (1977), DOALOS website, available at www.un.org/Depts/los/LEGISLATIONANDTREATIES/PDFFILES/YEM_1977_Act.pdf, Articles 14, 16
321 Law No. 60/IV/92 (1992), DOALOS website, available at www.un.org/Depts/los/LEGISLATIONANDTREATIES/PDFFILES/CPV_1992_Law.pdf, Articles 13, 18
322 Chapter 371, The Maritime Zones Act 1989, DOALOS website, available at www.un.org/Depts/los/LEGISLATIONANDTREATIES/PDFFILES/KEN_1989_Maritime.pdf, Articles 4–5. This Act repealed the previous law concerning the continental shelf, see FAOLEX database, available at www.fao.org/faolex/results/details/en/c/LEX-FAOC003534
323 Exclusive Economic Zone Decree No. 28 of 5 October 1978, DOALOS website, available at www.un.org/Depts/los/LEGISLATIONANDTREATIES/PDFFILES/NGA_1978_Decree.pdf, Articles 2, 3
324 Act No. 85–14 (1985), DOALOS website, available at www.un.org/Depts/los/LEGISLATIONANDTREATIES/PDFFILES/SEN_1985_Act.pdf, Article 7
325 Fishing Zone, Act 87–27 (1987), DOALOS website, available at www.un.org/Depts/los/LEGISLATIONANDTREATIES/PDFFILES/SEN_1987_Act.pdf
326 Law No. 1/98 (1998), DOALOS website, available at www.un.org/Depts/los/LEGISLATIONANDTREATIES/PDFFILES/STP_1998_Law.pdf, Article 6
327 Law No. 82–005 (1982), DOALOS website, available at www.un.org/Depts/los/LEGISLATIONANDTREATIES/PDFFILES/COM_1982_Law.pdf, Article 7
328 Territorial Sea and Exclusive Economic Zone of Namibia, Act No. 3 of 1990, 30 June 1990, DOALOS website, available at www.un.org/Depts/los/LEGISLATIONANDTREATIES/PDFFILES/NAM_1990_Act.pdf, Articles 4(3), 6(2)
329 Decree Law No. 31/76 (1976), DOALOS website, available at www.un.org/Depts/los/LEGISLATIONANDTREATIES/PDFFILES/MOZ_1976_Law.pdf, Article 2
330 Sea Law 4/96 (1996), FAOLEX database, available at http://extwprlegs1.fao.org/docs/pdf/moz22054.pdf, Articles 11, 15, 17 (unofficial translation from Portuguese)
331 Constitution of the Republic of Mozambique (Revised 2018), FAOLEX database, available at http://extwprlegs1.fao.org/docs/pdf/moz117331ENG_original.pdf, Article 98
332 Executive Order No. 48 (10 January 2013), Extension of Executive Order No. 39 Delimiting the Maritime Zones of the Republic of Liberia, DOALOS website, available at www.un.org/Depts/los/LEGISLATIONANDTREATIES/PDFFILES/LBR_10Jan2013_Act_EO48.pdf, Sections 5(2), 6(2)
333 Law No. 77–926 delimiting the Maritime Zones placed under the National Jurisdiction of the Republic of Ivory Coast of 17 November 1977, DOALOS website, available at www.un.org/Depts/los/LEGISLATIONANDTREATIES/PDFFILES/CIV_1977_Law.pdf, Article 3
334 Maritime Areas Law (2009), FAOLEX database, available at http://extwprlegs1.fao.org/docs/pdf/con96746E.pdf, at p. 2
335 Exclusive Economic Zone Act (1992), DOALOS website, available at www.un.org/Depts/los/LEGISLATIONANDTREATIES/PDFFILES/ZAR_1992_Act.pdf
336 See details in www.internationallawoffice.com/Newsletters/Energy-Natural-Resources/Africa/Herbert-Smith/Congo-Brazzaville-New-Legislation-Concerning-the-Dismantling-of-Oil-Installations#
337 Maritime Zones Act, No. 15 of 1994, DOALOS website, available at www.un.org/Depts/los/LEGISLATIONANDTREATIES/PDFFILES/ZAF_1994_Act.pdf, Article 7
338 Ibid., Article 8(3)
339 The Maritime Zones (Establishment) Decree, 1996, DOALOS website, available at www.un.org/Depts/los/LEGISLATIONANDTREATIES/PDFFILES/SLE_1996_Decree.pdf, Articles 9, 11(2)
340 Law No. 5 dated 26 January 1989, available at https://wwwex.ilo.org/dyn/natlex2/natlex2/files/download/108745/SOM108745.pdf, Article 8 (text in Somali, unofficially translated)
341 Proclamation by the President of the Federal Republic of Somalia (2014), FAOLEX database, available at http://extwprlegs1.fao.org/docs/pdf/som158857.pdf, p. 1, Preamble and Article 2

342 Law No. 21/92 (1992), DOALOS website, available at www.un.org/Depts/los/LEGISLATIONANDTREATIES/PDFFILES/AGO_1992_Law21.pdf, Article 8

343 Exclusive Economic Zone Act No. 9/84, DOALOS website, available at www.un.org/Depts/los/LEGISLATIONANDTREATIES/PDFFILES/GAB_1984_Act.pdf, Article 3

344 Continental Shelf Act (No. 1 of 1965), FAOLEX database, available at http://extwprlegs1.fao.org/docs/pdf/gam41165.pdf, Articles 3–4

345 Maritime Zones (Delimitation) Law, 1986, DOALOS website, available at www.un.org/Depts/los/LEGISLATIONANDTREATIES/PDFFILES/GHA_1986_Law.pdf, Articles 5–6

346 Decree No. 336/PRG (1980), DOALOS website, available at www.un.org/Depts/los/LEGISLATIONANDTREATIES/PDFFILES/GIN_1980_Decree.pdf, Article 3. There is a reference to the CS in a Decree concerning maritime zones under the sovereignty or jurisdiction of the Republic of Guinea, 89 Law of the Sea Bulletin 15 (2016), Article 3

347 Act No. 3/85 (1985), DOALOS website, available at www.un.org/Depts/los/LEGISLATIONANDTREATIES/PDFFILES/GNB_1985_Act3.pdf, Article 3

348 Act No. 15/1984 (1984), DOALOS website, available at www.un.org/Depts/los/LEGISLATIONANDTREATIES/PDFFILES/GNQ_1984_Act.pdf, p. 1 and Articles 12–13

349 Petroleum Regulations of the Republic of Equatorial Guinea (2013), available at https://egronda.com/oilandgas/docs/petroleum_regulations_egronda_eng.pdf, Article 138

350 Ordinance No. 85–013 determining the limits of the maritime zones (territorial sea, continental shelf and exclusive economic zone) of the Democratic Republic of Madagascar, 16 September 1985, as amended and ratified by Law No. 85–013 of 11 December 1985), DOALOS website, available at www.un.org/Depts/los/LEGISLATIONANDTREATIES/PDFFILES/MDG_1985_Ordinance.pdf, Articles 5, 7

351 Maritime Code, 2004, 56 Law of the Sea Bulletin 60 (2004), p. 68, Article 1.3.03

352 Ibid., Article 1.3.04

353 Law No. 2000–2 (2000), available at http://oceansbeyondpiracy.org/sites/default/files/Cameroon_Delimitation_of_Waters_Law_2000.pdf, sections 12, 14

354 Law No. 52/AN/78 (1979), DOALOS website, available at www.un.org/Depts/los/LEGISLATIONANDTREATIES/PDFFILES/DJI_1979_Law.pdf, Article 13

355 Ordinance No. 24 (1977), DOALOS website, available at www.un.org/Depts/los/LEGISLATIONANDTREATIES/PDFFILES/TGO_1977_Ordinance.pdf, Article 3; Act No. 2016–007 (2016), DOALOS website, available at www.un.org/Depts/los/LEGISLATIONANDTREATIES/PDFFILES/TogoESPACESMARITIMES.pdf, Article 6

356 Territorial Sea and Exclusive Economic Zone Act, 1989, DOALOS website, available at www.un.org/Depts/los/LEGISLATIONANDTREATIES/PDFFILES/TZA_1989_Act.pdf, Article 9

357 Ordinance 88–120 (1988), DOALOS website, available at www.un.org/Depts/los/LEGISLATIONANDTREATIES/PDFFILES/MRT_1988_Ordinance.pdf, Articles 7–8

358 Maritime Zones Act 1977 (Act No. 13 of 3 June 1977), DOALOS website, available at www.un.org/Depts/los/LEGISLATIONANDTREATIES/PDFFILES/MUS_1977_Act.pdf, Articles 5(2), 7, 9, 15

359 Maritime Zone Act 2005 (Act No. 2 of 2005), 62 Law of the Sea Bulletin 52 (2006), Articles 15, 19

360 Maritime Zones Act No. 15 (1977), DOALOS website, available at www.un.org/Depts/los/LEGISLATIONANDTREATIES/PDFFILES/SYC_1977_Act.pdf, Article 5(2), 6–7

361 Maritime Zones Act, 1999 (Act No. 2 of 1999), DOALOS website, available at www.un.org/Depts/los/LEGISLATIONANDTREATIES/PDFFILES/SYC_1999_Act2.pdf, part III

362 Maritime Zones (Amendment) Act (No. 6, 2012), FAOLEX database, available at http://extwprlegs1.fao.org/docs/pdf/mat116801.pdf, 4th schedule, p. 123, at Article 3(b)

363 Ibid., 4th schedule, p. 123, at Article 10; See also Treaties between Republic of Mauritius and the Republic of Seychelles regarding the Mascarene Plateau signed by the Government of the Republic of Mauritius and the Government of the Republic of

Seychelles at Clarisse House, Vacoas in Mauritius on 13 March 2012, 79 Law of the Sea Bulletin 25 (2012), p. 46

364 Territorial Waters and Continental Shelf Act, 1970, DOALOS website, available at www.un.org/Depts/los/LEGISLATIONANDTREATIES/PDFFILES/SDN_1970_Act.pdf, Articles 10–11

365 Presidential Decision No. 1051 (1958), DOALOS website, available at www.un.org/Depts/los/LEGISLATIONANDTREATIES/PDFFILES/EGY_1958_Decision.pdf

366 No law on EEZ, only delimitation agreement with Cyprus, Agreement between the Republic of Cyprus and the Arab Republic of Egypt on the Delimitation of the Exclusive Economic Zone 17 February 2003, DOALOS website, available at www.un.org/Depts/los/LEGISLATIONANDTREATIES/PDFFILES/TREATIES/EGY-CYP2003EZ.pdf

367 Fisheries Protection Zone Declaration (2005), A/60/68, available at https://documents-dds-ny.un.org/doc/UNDOC/GEN/N05/293/85/PDF/N0529385.pdf?OpenElement

368 Decision No. 260 of A.J. 1377 (A.D. 2009), DOALOS website, available at www.un.org/Depts/los/LEGISLATIONANDTREATIES/PDFFILES/lby_2009_declaration_e.pdf, Article 2

369 Act No. 1–81 (1980), Promulgated by Dahir No. 1–81–1 9 (1981), DOALOS website, available at www.un.org/Depts/los/LEGISLATIONANDTREATIES/PDFFILES/MAR_1981_Act.pdf, Articles 2, 4

370 Act No. 50/2005 (2005), 58 Law of the Sea Bulletin 19 (2005), Article 2

371 Presidential Decree No. 18–96 (2018), DOALOS website, available at www.un.org/Depts/los/LEGISLATIONANDTREATIES/PDFFILES/DZA_2018_Decree_1896_en.pdf, Article 3

372 Agreement on Provisional Arrangements for the Delimitation of the Maritime Boundaries between the Republic of Tunisia and the People's Democratic Republic of Algeria, *supra* note 176, Article 6

373 Maritime Areas Act No. 18 (1982), DOALOS website, available at www.un.org/Depts/los/LEGISLATIONANDTREATIES/PDFFILES/ATG_1982_18.pdf, Articles 10, 11A

374 Fisheries Resources (Jurisdiction and Conservation) Act, 1977, No. 13 of 16 June 1977, DOALOS website, available at www.un.org/Depts/los/LEGISLATIONANDTREATIES/PDFFILES/BHS_1977_13.pdf, Articles 2, 11(3)

375 Act No. 37 (1993), DOALOS website, available at www.un.org/Depts/los/LEGISLATIONANDTREATIES/PDFFILES/BHS_1993_37.pdf, Article 9(2)

376 Legislative Decree No. 2 (1977), DOALOS website, available at www.un.org/Depts/los/LEGISLATIONANDTREATIES/PDFFILES/CUB_1977_Decree2.pdf, Article 2

377 Agreement between the Commonwealth of the Bahamas and the Republic of Cuba for the Delimiting Line between their Maritime Zones, FAOLEX database, available at http://extwprlegs1.fao.org/docs/pdf/bi-119575.pdf, Article IV(g)

378 Marine Boundaries and Jurisdiction Act (1978), DOALOS website, available at www.un.org/Depts/los/LEGISLATIONANDTREATIES/PDFFILES/BRB_1978_3.pdf, Articles 5, 20

379 Maritime Areas Act 1992, as amended by the Maritime Areas (Amendment) Act 2019, DOALOS website, available at www.un.org/Depts/los/LEGISLATIONANDTREATIES/PDFFILES/MAA1992_2019.pdf, Articles 9, 24(2)(c)

380 Territorial Sea, Contiguous Zone, Exclusive Economic and Fishery Zones Act, No. 26 (1981), DOALOS website, available at www.un.org/Depts/los/LEGISLATIONANDTREATIES/PDFFILES/DMA_1981_Act.pdf, Article 8

381 Act No. 573 (1977), DOALOS website, available at www.un.org/Depts/los/LEGISLATIONANDTREATIES/PDFFILES/DOM_1977_Act.pdf, Articles 5, 7. The law uses the terms "exploration and exploitation, conservation and **administration**" rather than the exact words of Article 56.

382 Law 66–07 (2007), 65 Law of the Sea Bulletin 18 (2007), Article 15
383 Territorial Sea and Maritime Boundaries Act No. 25 (1989), DOALOS website, available at www.un.org/Depts/los/LEGISLATIONANDTREATIES/PDFFILES/grd_act_25_1989.pdf, Article 11(a), 13(a)
384 Maritime Boundaries Act, 1977, Act No. 10 of 30 June 1977, DOALOS website, available at www.un.org/Depts/los/LEGISLATIONANDTREATIES/PDFFILES/GUY_1977_Act.pdf, Article 10
385 Ibid., Articles 12, 16, 18 (although part [i] is somewhat different)
386 Maritime Zones Act No. 18 (2010), FAOLEX database, available at http://extwprlegs1.fao.org/docs/pdf/guy141190.pdf, Article 21(1)
387 Ibid., Articles 23, 27
388 Ibid., Article 50
389 Decree No. 38 (1977), DOALOS website, available at www.un.org/Depts/los/LEGISLATIONANDTREATIES/PDFFILES/HTI_1977_Decree.pdf, Articles 5, 9
390 Exclusive Economic Zone Act No. 33 (1991), DOALOS website, available at www.un.org/Depts/los/LEGISLATIONANDTREATIES/PDFFILES/JAM_1991_Act.pdf, Articles 4, 21(d). Articles 6–8 refer to the right to "**explore and exploit**" both living and non-living resources, while Article 21(n) refers to "**conservation and management**" and the "**optimum utilization**" of living and non-living resources.
391 Maritime Areas Act (1996), FAOLEX database, available at http://extwprlegs1.fao.org/docs/pdf/jam7862.pdf, Article 22
392 The Maritime Areas Act (No. 3, 1984), DOALOS website, available at www.un.org/Depts/los/LEGISLATIONANDTREATIES/PDFFILES/KNA_1984_Act.pdf, Articles 12, 29(3)(c)
393 Maritime Areas Act No. 6 (1984), DOALOS website, available at www.un.org/Depts/los/LEGISLATIONANDTREATIES/PDFFILES/LCA_1984_Act.pdf, Articles 12, 29(3)(c)
394 Maritime Areas Act (No. 15, 1983), DOALOS website, available at www.un.org/Depts/los/LEGISLATIONANDTREATIES/PDFFILES/VCT_1983_Act.pdf, Articles 20–21, 22
395 Law concerning the extension of the Territorial Sea and the establishment of a Contiguous Economic Zone (1978), DOALOS website, available at www.un.org/Depts/los/LEGISLATIONANDTREATIES/PDFFILES/SUR_1978_Law.pdf, Article 4; Maritime Zones Act (2017), DOALOS website, available at www.un.org/Depts/los/LEGISLATIONANDTREATIES/PDFFILES/DEPOSIT/sur_mzn131_2018.pdf, Articles 10, 15
396 Continental Shelf Act, 1969 (Cap. 1:52) (amended in 1986), FAOLEX database, available at http://extwprlegs1.fao.org/docs/pdf/tri105075.pdf, Articles 3(1), 4(1)
397 Archipelagic Waters and Exclusive Economic Zone Act, 1986 (Cap. 51:06), FAOLEX database, available at http://extwprlegs1.fao.org/docs/pdf/tri105030.pdf, Articles 18–19, 21
398 Ibid., Article 24
399 Ibid., Article 28
400 Act No. 23.968 of 14 August 1991, DOALOS website, available at www.un.org/Depts/los/LEGISLATIONANDTREATIES/PDFFILES/ARG_1991_23968.pdf, Articles 5–6, 9
401 Law No. 8.617 of 4 January 1993, on the territorial sea, the contiguous zone, the exclusive economic zone, and the continental shelf(1), DOALOS website, available at www.un.org/Depts/los/LEGISLATIONANDTREATIES/PDFFILES/BRA_1993_8617.pdf, Articles 7–8, 12; Constitution of the Federative Republic of Brazil (with amendment n. 64, 2010), OAS website, available at https://web.oas.org/mla/en/Countries_Intro/bra_pt_const.pdf, Article 20, part XI(1) (unofficially translated from Portuguese)
402 Law No. 8.617 (1993), ibid., Article 9

403 Declaration by the Ministry of Foreign Affairs, 14 September 1985, DOALOS website, available at www.un.org/Depts/los/LEGISLATIONANDTREATIES/PDFFILES/CHL_1985_Declaration.pdf

404 Law No. 18.565 (1986), DOALOS website, available at www.un.org/Depts/los/LEGISLATIONANDTREATIES/PDFFILES/CHL_1986_18565.pdf, Article 2

405 Act No. 10 (1978), DOALOS website, available at www.un.org/Depts/los/LEGISLATIONANDTREATIES/PDFFILES/COL_1978_Act.pdf, Articles 8, 10

406 Constitution as amended by Decree No. 5699 of 5 June 1975, DOALOS website, available at www.un.org/Depts/los/LEGISLATIONANDTREATIES/PDFFILES/CRI_1975_Decree5699.pdf, Article 6

407 Declaration of Ecuador, declarations and reservations, United Nations Convention on the Law of the Sea, Chapter XXI, UN treaty collection (UNTC) website, available at https://treaties.un.org/Pages/ViewDetailsIII.aspx?src=TREATY&mtdsg_no=XXI-6&chapter=21&Temp=mtdsg3&clang=_en, Articles IV, V

408 See 2004 Civil Code, as cited in Maritime Claims Reference Manual, United States Department of Defence (JAG website), available at www.jag.navy.mil/organization/documents/mcrm/el_salvador_2014.pdf

409 Constitution of the Republic of Guatemala of 5 September 1965, DOALOS website, available at www.un.org/Depts/los/LEGISLATIONANDTREATIES/PDFFILES/GTM_1965_Constitution.pdf

410 Legislative Decree No. 20–76 (1976), DOALOS website, available at www.un.org/Depts/los/LEGISLATIONANDTREATIES/PDFFILES/GTM_1976_Decree.pdf, Article 3 (uses terms from earlier drafts, i.e., "renewable and non-renewable").

411 Decree No. 921 (1980), DOALOS website, available at www.un.org/Depts/los/LEGISLATIONANDTREATIES/PDFFILES/HND_1980_Decree.pdf, Article 1 (no reference to installations or safety zones); Act on Honduras Maritime Areas, 49 Law of the Bulletin 15 (2002), Articles 7, 11

412 Federal Act relating to the Sea, 8 January 1986, DOALOS website, available at www.un.org/Depts/los/LEGISLATIONANDTREATIES/PDFFILES/MEX_1986_Act.pdf, Chapter II, Articles 46 (although there is reference to renewable and non-renewable resources together with living or non-living), 57

413 Act No. 205 of 19 December 1979 on the Continental Shelf and Adjacent Sea, DOALOS website, available at www.un.org/Depts/los/LEGISLATIONANDTREATIES/PDFFILES/NIC_1979_Act.pdf, Article 5

414 Presidential Decree No. 781, 1947, DOALOS website, available at www.un.org/Depts/los/LEGISLATIONANDTREATIES/PDFFILES/PER_1947_Decree.pdf, Article 2

415 Act No, 17,033 (1998), FAOLEX database, available at http://extwprlegs1.fao.org/docs/pdf/uru21321.pdf, Articles 5–6, 11

416 Exclusive Economic Zone Act (1978), DOALOS website, available at www.un.org/Depts/los/LEGISLATIONANDTREATIES/PDFFILES/VEN_1978_Act.pdf, Articles 3, 8; Aquatic Areas Organic Act, Decree No. 1,446 (2014), DOALOS website, available at www.un.org/Depts/los/LEGISLATIONANDTREATIES/PDFFILES/Venezuela_ENG.pdf, Articles 46, 49 [see other rights in Article 50] (p. 16–17)

417 Ibid., Article 57 (p. 20)

418 Federal Law on the Continental Shelf of the Russian Federation, *supra* note 243, Article 40. See also explanations in Suriname's Maritime Zones Act (2017), *supra* note 395, p. 13. New Zealand also addressed exploration and exploitation of its continental shelf beyond 200 nm, see Continental Shelf Act 1964 (Reprint as at 13 January 2020), available at www.legislation.govt.nz/act/public/1964/0028/latest/whole.html#DLM351675

419 See for example Annex D earlier, Kiribati, no. 48. See also joint management agreement between Mauritius and Seychelles, no. 105. On the other hand, see Micronesia, no. 57

4 Procedural issues concerning the continental shelf

The procedural aspects in international law, as in domestic law, refer to principles, standards, and rules concerning remedies, procedures, and enforcement of substantive legal principles and rules, i.e., those specifying rights and obligations. Procedural rules and principles are usually employed in the context of international institutions.[1]

The jurisprudence on the continental shelf is fragmented – that is, it is governed by multiple legal regimes: by overlapping institutions that have jurisdiction under UNCLOS and by those that operate outside UNCLOS but may have jurisdiction over disputes pertaining to it.[2] This legal and regulatory overlap may lead to a conflict of rules or inconsistency concerning similar issues.[3] From governance perspective, this regulatory overlap is not necessarily a problem but rather a common part of the governance framework, enhancing its effectiveness and promoting cooperation.[4] The analysis later demonstrates how the regulatory overlap affects the governance framework concerning procedural questions vis-à-vis the continental shelf, which in turn affects the legal regime – highlighting the role of informal actors, processes, and institutions.

1. The governance framework concerning the Meeting of States Parties (SPLOS)

The governance perspective sheds light on the evolution and practical function of SPLOS. Within this forum, states act both individually and as a collective body, in accordance with self-established rules and practices.[5] As analyzed later, SPLOS is an informal actor with informal law-making capabilities. The scope of SPLOS's competence has developed through state practice, which is also an informal element of the governance framework.[6] The function of SPLOS also demonstrates the gap between the legal regime and the practice relating to the continental shelf. As discussed later, while UNCLOS assigns SPLOS limited financial and administrative functions,[7] in practice, it exerts significant influence on the development and interpretation of substantive issues.

DOI: 10.4324/9781003479772-5

1.1 SPLOS as an informal actor

UNCLOS implicitly established a specialized forum – the Meeting of States Parties (SPLOS) that can be considered a "treaty body". The Convention does not explicitly mention the establishment of SPLOS. However, it states that one of the UN Secretary-General (UNSG)'s functions as "depositary" is to convene a meeting of States Parties as necessary.[8] While UNCLOS's provisions do not specify the scope, function, composition, or decision-making procedures of this body, it grants SPLOS limited powers to elect ITLOS's judges and members of the CLCS and to receive reports from the Preparatory Commission for the International Seabed Authority.[9] In practice, SPLOS has determined its own scope and functions, broadening its competence beyond what UNCLOS conferred upon it. The analysis of SPLOS's development and function again demonstrates that the governance framework is often broader than the formal legal regime.

In November 1994, after UNCLOS entered into force, the UNSG convened an *ad hoc* meeting of SPLOS to discuss the formation of ITLOS.[10] UN specialized agencies and a non-governmental organization also participated in the meeting.[11] Thus, informal elements were involved in constructing SPLOS. In the *ad hoc* meeting, the UNSG also specified actions that would be required in the future. This essentially established SPLOS as a *permanent* institution, assigning SPLOS a purview that extended beyond its formal powers under the Convention.[12]

SPLOS elected a president and four vice-presidents,[13] established its own rules of procedure,[14] and decided to reconvene on a regular basis[15] and to receive reports from the UNSG.[16] These functions support the premise that SPLOS is not an *ad hoc* forum but rather a permanent institution with broader competences beyond those provided in UNCLOS. Here again, the governance framework concerning the continental shelf is broader than the legal regime.

In addition, SPLOS adopted decisions that went beyond the formal competences explicitly conferred to it in UNCLOS. For example, while SPLOS is competent to elect ITLOS's judges and the CLCS's members, it also determines the geographic distribution of these institutions. UNCLOS provides that ITLOS and the CLCS should include at least three representatives from each of the geographical groups established by the UN General Assembly,[17] but SPLOS decided to allocate more members to the African group.[18] While this decision does not conflict with the legal regime, it expands the mandate explicitly assigned to SPLOS. This example also demonstrates the informal powers SPLOS adopted for itself and the gap between the legal regime and governance framework.

Another example of SPLOS exceeding the mandate UNCLOS conferred upon it is its role in reviewing "ocean and law of the sea issues".[19] For example, some delegations suggested that SPLOS should receive information on the responsibilities of relevant specialized agencies under UNCLOS and how they are applied.[20] In addition, SPLOS has discussed issues regarding the liability of ship-owners for oil pollution damage, which is outside UNCLOS's competences, as this is an issue of private international law.[21] SPLOS also addressed issues of maritime security and weapons smuggling, which are beyond its formal competence.[22]

The examples earlier concerning the extended mandate of SPLOS are supported by the delegations' prevalent view that SPLOS is the "supreme organ for the implementation of the Convention"[23] and "custodian" of UNCLOS,[24] despite no such indication in the Convention itself. In response to some critique regarding the lack of legal basis for such expansion,[25] some delegations argued that it is the "logical forum" to discuss all issues relevant to UNCLOS's implementation and that SPLOS's expanded role would increase its effectiveness.[26] In addition, these advocates maintained that SPLOS already exercises broader functions.[27] In other words, there is no legal basis for the extended role of SPLOS other than the fact that it decided so and acted accordingly, contrary to the legal regime but with the support of at least some states.

1.2 ITLOS's annual reports to SPLOS

SPLOS is an informal institution of UNCLOS and the main forum to which ITLOS is accountable with respect to three issues: the election of judges, the Tribunal's budget, and judicial accountability.[28] While ITLOS is an independent tribunal and UNCLOS assigned only administrative-financial competences to SPLOS concerning ITLOS, in practice, SPLOS exerts significant influence on the Tribunal's functions.[29] The interactions between SPLOS and ITLOS also influenced SPLOS's own functions, significantly broadening the legal regime.

ITLOS reports annually to SPLOS on its judicial work, although SPLOS does not "approve" the report. This obligation to report is not explicitly mentioned in the Convention but was stipulated by SPLOS in its Rules of Procedures (ROP).[30] As noted, SPLOS established its own ROP in the absence of explicit provisions in UNCLOS. SPLOS acknowledged that under the Convention, ITLOS's reports were covered in the UNSG's annual report to the UN General Assembly, but it "encouraged" the Tribunal to report directly to SPLOS.[31] SPLOS has essentially become the Tribunal's governing body. This is an example of an informal body establishing an informal procedure that significantly broadened the governance framework.

While acknowledging its independence,[32] ITLOS did not object to reporting to SPLOS. The Tribunal submitted its first report to SPLOS in April 1998.[33] ITLOS included updates on its administrative and procedural issues, as well as updates relating to its judicial work (such as the status of cases submitted, decision-making procedures, and judgments reached).[34] Although it seems that SPLOS only receive information rather than examine it in depth, such reporting may encourage greater state intervention in judicial matters. For example, in the SPLOS meeting after receiving the first report on ITLOS's judicial work, SPLOS emphasized the need for expeditious proceedings.[35] In the subsequent SPLOS meeting, its president indicated that the Tribunal had made a *special effort* to deliver judgments within a short period.[36] It seems that SPLOS tried to influence the proceedings, at least in terms of timeframe, which is outside its mandate. However, ITLOS accepted and internalized SPLOS's comments, instead of objecting or arguing that it has no such mandate, which reinforces SPLOS's broader informal powers.

Individual states have also expressed their opinions on ITLOS's judicial work.[37] For example, some delegations noted that the judgment in the *Myanmar/Bangladesh* case was consistent with existing jurisprudence on maritime boundary delimitation.[38] Furthermore, some delegations affirmed ITLOS's jurisdiction to deliver advisory opinions, although others maintained that UNCLOS does not explicitly grant such jurisdiction and that other legal instruments provide for a more limited jurisdiction.[39]

ITLOS's reporting process also influences SPLOS's role concerning the parties that appear before the Tribunal. For example, ITLOS reported receiving communications from Saint Vincent and the Grenadines concerning compliance with the M/V "Saiga" (No. 2) judgment.[40] In response, SPLOS's president reminded the member states that they are obligated to comply promptly with the Tribunal's decisions.[41] A number of delegations have also raised concerns that some states had refused to participate in arbitral proceedings.[42] This again may indicate further involvement of SPLOS in ITLOS's proceedings, which is beyond its mandate under UNCLOS.

The reporting process has also strengthened ITLOS's position vis-à-vis member states. For example, during discussions on ITLOS's reports, the president of the Tribunal has used the opportunity to urge states to utilize the Tribunal when settling their disputes.[43] This can be viewed as an attempt to strengthen the status of ITLOS over other means of dispute-settlement.[44] In addition, parties that have appeared before the Tribunal have encouraged other states to choose ITLOS as the appropriate forum for dispute-settlement. For example, during SPLOS's discussion on the proceedings in the *Myanmar/Bangladesh* case, both parties tried to convince other states to choose the Tribunal in future proceedings, arguing that it is less costly.[45] Lastly, SPLOS's delegations have expressed agreement with ITLOS's decisions,[46] strengthening its legitimacy.

The interaction between the two institutions broadens the mandate of SPLOS with each new question it addresses. It seems that SPLOS has established itself as an informal "plenary body" of UNCLOS, where representatives of the member states meet at regular intervals, with supervisory and guiding powers with respect to other UNCLOS institutions.[47]

2. The governance framework for procedural issues concerning the CLCS

Chapter 2 analyzes substantial informal aspects concerning the role and operation of the CLCS, demonstrating the contribution of governance theory to understanding the development of the legal regime. This section focuses on the CLCS's procedures, demonstrating the contribution of the governance perspective in elucidating the procedural aspect of the Commission's role. As discussed later, the development of certain CLCS procedures underlines the difference between the legal regime and the governance framework concerning the continental shelf.

2.1 The CLCS's reports to SPLOS

As analyzed, the CLCS has greater significance than UNCLOS confers upon it, essentially functioning as a semi-judicial body. The significance of the CLCS was also influenced by the somewhat subordinate relationship with SPLOS, which also affected the latter. The interaction between SPLOS and the CLCS, like that of SPLOS and ITLOS, goes beyond what is prescribed in UNCLOS provisions and broadens the mandate and functions of both institutions, which in turn broadens the legal regime in this context.

As with ITLOS, SPLOS decided on its own, without any formal mandate, to request reports from the CLCS on its workload and proceedings (although minding confidentiality issues).[48] The Chairman of the CLCS indicated that the Commission should be accountable to SPLOS despite being "an autonomous body established by the Convention with no formal accountability to the Meeting of States Parties".[49] Establishing such procedures for accountability essentially makes SPLOS the governing body not only of ITLOS but also of the CLCS, despite the independent and confidential work of both institutions. This broadens SPLOS's mandate beyond the legal regime's provisions.

Reporting to SPLOS also allows other states to publicly express their views on the Commission's proceedings, even though they are unilateral, supposedly having no effect on other states.[50] Reporting to SPLOS essentially established an informal process similar to the one described in Chapter 2 regarding other states' reactions to submissions communicated to the CLCS or to the UNSG. Both processes strengthen the role of the CLCS as a semi-judicial and semi-adversarial institution. This process also influenced the CLCS to change its ROP and internal work methods.[51] The interaction between these institutions broadens the governance framework in this context, conferring greater significance to both bodies than UNCLOS prescribes.

The interaction between the CLCS and SPLOS also influenced the CLCS's proceedings concerning disputed areas. Reporting to SPLOS strengthened the semi-adversarial character of the CLCS also in the context of disputed areas by promoting peaceful dispute-settlement and influencing states to make changes in their submissions.[52] For example, SPLOS noted in response to the CLCS's report on the UK's submission that there is a dispute between Argentina and the UK concerning sovereignty over the Falkland (Malvinas) Islands.[53] Arguably, SPLOS influenced the CLCS's evaluation of the existence of disputes and thus affected its ability to exercise its functions.[54]

In addition, the CLCS reported to SPLOS that it had deferred consideration of a submission because there was no indication that all relevant states had consented to its involvement.[55] Not only individual states can "block" other states' submissions to CLCS, but SPLOS, as a collective body, can influence the CLCS's work by reflecting states' views concerning its proceedings. This is an example of how informal actors develop informal practices within the governance framework, broadening its purview relative to the legal regime.

In some cases, reporting to SPLOS and explaining its actions may have influenced the role of the CLCS as a mediator. For example, the Commission decided in 2012 to actively solicit Bangladesh's view on Myanmar's submission and to communicate it to Myanmar. After receiving communications from both states, the CLCS decided to postpone the proceedings to consider any further developments that might occur in the intervening period.[56]

Some delegations expressed concern about what seems to be an indefinite postponement of some of the submissions.[57] While such postponement is in accordance with the CLCS's ROP,[58] it may violate coastal States' rights to extend the outer limit of the continental shelf.[59] If the governing institution essentially denies certain broad-margin states the opportunity to extend the outer limit of their continental shelf, in practice, it circumvents UNCLOS Article 76. In this sense, the governance framework may be narrower than the legal regime. Thus, the interaction between SPLOS and the CLCS pulls the governance framework of the continental shelf in different directions: broadening the powers of the CLCS and SPLOS but also downplaying coastal States' rights.

The interaction between SPLOS and the CLCS also conferred upon SPLOS certain legal functions. As discussed in Chapter 2, the CLCS in practice exercises semilegal functions such as interpretation of the legal rules. Some delegations have argued that the CLCS has no mandate to interpret UNCLOS and should seek legal guidance from SPLOS, which has the *exclusive power* to provide such guidance.[60] This view goes beyond the limited competences conferred to SPLOS. Similarly, SPLOS has maintained that the Tribunal can solve legal questions relating to the work of the CLCS, such as interpretation of UNCLOS.[61] In this sense, SPLOS functions as an intermediate body operating in the space between ITLOS and the CLCS with respect to scientific questions.

2.2 *The time limit for making submissions to the CLCS*

SPLOS also influenced changing the timeframe for making submissions to the CLCS. This issue again demonstrates the difference between the legal regime and the practice. SPLOS essentially changed the timeframe established in UNCLOS, thus effectively amending the Convention. This, in turn, increased the significance of SPLOS as an informal actor and broadened the continental shelf's governance framework in this context.

In accordance with Article 76, a coastal State must make a submission to the CLCS no later than ten years after UNCLOS entered into force for that state. For many coastal States, this meant the deadline was in 2004.[62] Many states, especially developing states, opposed this provision, arguing that it is difficult to comply with the timeline.[63] Thus, SPLOS and the Commission developed informal procedures to circumvent and extend the formal ten-year time limit.[64] In this sense, the informal actors narrowed the governance framework.

The extension of the timeframe was established within SPLOS in stages: first, selecting a date from which the ten-year limit is calculated and then formulating legal justifications for extending the time limit.[65] SPLOS set May 13, 1999 (the adoption date of the CLCS's Scientific and Technical Guidelines), as the commencement date for the ten-year countdown. States where UNCLOS had entered into force prior to that date basically received an extension to make submissions.[66] Furthermore, recognizing that some states, especially developing states, face challenges in submitting information to the Commission due to financial and technical difficulties, SPLOS allowed for the "suspension" of the ten-year time limit for states that submitted only "preliminary information".[67]

The Commission also contributed to extending the time limit for submissions. The CLCS's ROP allow states to make partial submissions to avoid prejudicing disputed areas. In such cases, submissions regarding other portions of the continental shelf are not subjected to the ten-year time limit, thus suspending the time limit, contrary to the legal regime.[68] This correlates with the analysis in Chapter 2 of the CLCS's role regarding disputed continental shelves and the suspension of proceedings in such cases. However, such practice may circumvent UNCLOS provisions that prevent the Commission from getting involved in maritime disputes.[69]

This can be viewed as part of the governance framework's operation rather than conflict or "fragmentation".[70] Unlike the examples in Section 1 earlier, which relate to temporal changes in the legal regime, this issue reflects a permanent change in the Convention. SPLOS and the CLCS essentially amended UNCLOS without going through the formal amendment proceedings stipulated in the Convention. According to SPLOS, this was a substantive issue that did not require formal amendment.[71] Thus, the governance framework can be considered narrower than the legal regime because formal rules are essentially ignored. However, the governance framework can also be considered broader because informal actors developed new informal norms and practices that provide coastal States with flexibility in proceedings before the CLCS.

3. The governance framework for settling disputes involving the continental shelf

As discussed in Chapter 3, most of the disputes concerning the continental shelf are essentially delimitation disputes. Coastal States' primary obligation is to settle delimitation disputes by bilateral agreements based on international law. If disputing parties cannot conclude an agreement within a reasonable period, UNCLOS refers them to one of the dispute-settlement procedures in Part XV.[72] This section briefly analyzes UNCLOS's dispute-settlement mechanism from the perspective of governance theory to demonstrate the contribution of IR theories to the construction and interpretation of the legal regime. This section focuses mostly on state practice, while Section 4 addresses judicial dispute-settlement.

3.1 Construction of the legal rules

The governance perspective can help explain the construction of the formal rules concerning delimitation by analyzing the contribution of informal actors, such as the chairs of UNCLOS III's committees.[73] In addition, as previously discussed,

UNCLOS's negotiation is essentially a political process and is thus considered an informal element of the governance framework. This element can explain the construction of the legal regime and the gap between it and the practice.

As in the case of Article 76, Part XV was drafted as a political compromise between various conflicting interest-groups, rather than a result of consensus.[74] Part XV reflects a conflict between states that wanted a limited or non-compulsory mechanism to preserve state sovereignty and states that supported a more comprehensive and compulsory mechanism, with fewer exceptions.[75] Thus, it seems that political considerations affected the construction of the legal regime, which in turn influenced the practice in this context.

It is noteworthy that there is a correlation between states that supported a compulsory and binding dispute-settlement mechanism, states that supported the 200 nm distance criterion for the outer limit of the continental shelf, and states that the role of the CLCS, between states that wanted a "boundary commission". All these positions reflect the interests of developing and geographically disadvantaged states.[76]

A detailed and binding mechanism with limited exceptions would benefit developing states, especially against developed and more powerful states since all parties would be equal before judicial organs. This would also ensure convergence of the parties' expectations because the process would be more predictable, based on clear and agreed rules.[77] This is especially critical in light of the vagueness of the legal rules for delimitation.[78] Judicial dispute-settlement essentially mitigates asymmetric power relations, thus weaker parties are more likely to protect their interests and gain more by choosing one of the dispute-settlement platforms in Part XV, especially when facing more powerful parties. This position reflects the IR institutional approach, which emphasizes the role of international institutions in promoting cooperation for the benefit of all actors.

In contrast, broad-margin coastal States promoted the opposite positions: supporting the limit of the edge of the continental margin, supporting the CLCS as having only recommendatory powers, and promoting the preservation of sovereignty and advocated for a non-compulsory dispute-settlement mechanism in which they could leverage their geo-political position in a diplomatic-like process.[79] These positions reflects the IR realist approach, which emphasizes power relations between actors and the protection of material interests.

Some states have contended that *domestic* organs should have the competence to settle disputes concerning the continental shelf.[80] From this perspective, compulsory international dispute-settlement should be the exception, a recourse reserved for cases in which a coastal State deliberately infringes another state's rights and freedoms.[81] However, the final text established the duty to submit disputes to an international judicial dispute-settlement. Nevertheless, this obligation is subject to certain limitations and exceptions, such as delimitation disputes.[82] Thus, the final legal formula contains some aspects that favor broad-margin states' interests.

As in other aspects, the interests reflected in the final text affected the implementation of the legal regime. The difference is that the substantive practices are influenced mainly by the interests of landlocked and disadvantaged coastal States, while the procedural practices may be influenced by the interests of broad-margin states. While UNCLOS Part XV reflects some of the latter's interests, arguably, it mainly favors landlocked and disadvantaged states' interests because it includes a binding dispute-settlement mechanism. As discussed later, this may explain why, in practice, coastal States do not employ Part XV to resolve their maritime disputes and tend to prefer other instruments that may better protect their interests. In this sense, the patterns arising from the governance framework analysis are narrower than the legal regime, effectively weakening the role of the formal rules.

3.2 State practice

In recent decades, judicial dispute-settlement concerning the continental shelf has increased, both in the number of cases and in the diversity of judicial forums.[83] In the first two decades following the adoption of UNCLOS, most of the delimitation disputes were submitted to the ICJ. Since then, the role of ITLOS and Annex VII Arbitral Tribunal has increased.[84] It seems that states engage in "forum shopping" and choose the forum that best suits their interests. Transferring disputes from one tribunal to another reflects a core element of UNCLOS Part XV: a multiplicity of judicial forums, which allows the parties flexibility and choice.[85]

As of December 2023, approximately 45 states had expressed a preference to settle disputes in ITLOS, and 13 of them chose ITLOS exclusively. Thirty states chose the ICJ as a dispute-settlement forum; five of them chose it exclusively. Eleven states accepted Annex VII arbitration, and two of them chose it as their only dispute-settlement forum.[86] Some states did not choose any dispute-settlement forum. If states do not select a dispute-settlement forum, Annex VII Arbitral Tribunal is the default forum.[87]

Despite many states' support and acceptance of ITLOS as the main dispute-settlement forum, in practice, only three delimitation disputes involving the continental shelf have been submitted to it.[88] A larger number of delimitation disputes have been submitted to Annex VII Arbitration, mostly since the parties did not made an Article 287 declaration or chose different forums – and not because they directly opted for this forum.[89] However, most delimitation disputes were submitted to the ICJ outside of the UNCLOS mechanism.

While there is an increase in adjudicated maritime disputes, to date, nearly 32 disputes have been submitted to international tribunals.[90] Most maritime disputes are still resolved by bilateral diplomatic means.[91] Governance framework analysis may explain the gap between the legal regime and the practice. As mentioned earlier, Part XV constituted a compromise between conflicting interests of different groups of states. While some provisions reflect the interests of broad-margin states, it generally reflects the interests of developing and geographically disadvantaged states. Since broad-margin states mostly supported diplomatic dispute-settlement, it might explain the scarce employment of UNCLOS's mechanisms and recourse to other means that might better protect the interests of individual states. In some cases, states have tried to pressure the other party not to submit the dispute to international adjudication, although such efforts have not always been successful.[92] This demonstrates that the governance framework is narrower than the legal regime in this context, downplaying parts of the Convention.

Even those disputes that were submitted to international tribunals were not submitted under UNCLOS Part XV but rather in accordance with other agreements, mostly the compulsory jurisdiction of the ICJ.[93] Governance theory analysis may also offer an explanation in this context. During UNCLOS III negotiations, many developing and geographically disadvantaged states preferred ITLOS as the primary dispute-settlement forum since they expected the Tribunal to ensure a larger role for them and viewed it as a technical and scientific expert.[94]

In contrast, many developed and broad-margin states saw no need to establish a new Tribunal, preferring diplomatic dispute-settlement.[95] Thus, it seems logical that those states that did not support UNCLOS Part XV chose not to employ it and turned to other judicial bodies outside the Convention. In practice, it seems that coastal States downplay UNCLOS's dispute-settlement procedures and prefer to employ diplomatic means while broadening the governance framework by invoking other legal instruments to settle maritime boundary disputes.[96]

Considering the previous discussion, it seems that political considerations affect the choice of dispute-settlement forum, which in turn affects the governance framework in this context. Broad-margin states anxious to protect their sovereignty and material interests tend to prefer diplomatic dispute-settlement while developing or geographically disadvantaged states preferred recourse to UNCLOS Part XV. The practice reflects the interests of broad-margin states.

4. Procedural issues in the context of judicial dispute-settlement

International tribunals are formal actors within the governance framework but play an informal law-making role, creating new informal rules and norms concerning maritime boundary delimitation and downplaying existing formal legal rules. Thus, the jurisprudence has a significant contribution to the continental shelf's governance framework. These institutions have considerable influence not only on the substantive law but also on procedural rules, especially in specific fields characterized by the absence of formal procedural law.[97]

4.1 Third-party impact on maritime delimitation disputes

The general procedural provisions of international law and UNCLOS prohibit encroachment on third-party's rights by international adjudicatory proceedings. For example, contentious judicial proceedings affect only the parties to the proceedings, and international tribunals do not have jurisdiction over the claims of third parties.[98] While this issue is not unique to maritime disputes, it has special significance in this context, especially with respect to closed and semi-closed seas. In such cases, the need to respect third parties' rights is especially prominent due to the close inter-relations between all states bordering the area to be delimited, as well as the need for cooperation and coordination. Thus, other states may have an interest in the outcome of the proceedings. These actors' rights have significant influence on maritime boundary delimitation disputes, essentially broadening the formal legal regime.[99]

Non-disputing third parties have sought to protect their interests – for example, by requesting to intervene under Article 62 of the ICJ's Statute. This provision does not grant other states the right to intervene; rather, it gives the Court the discretion to allow such intervention.[100] ITLOS has also established procedures for intervention by third states in its proceedings.[101] In contrast, Annex VII Arbitral Tribunal is silent on this issue, and to date, there has been no case where the parties established rules on this matter. However, as indicated in the *South China Sea* case, it is theoretically possible to request permission to intervene in Annex VII arbitration.[102]

In some cases, tribunals have rejected the requests of third parties to intervene, claiming that the third parties had not shown that the relevant proceedings would cause direct harm to their interest but had only pointed toward potential implications.[103] This is a somewhat peculiar interpretation because the delimitation of a continental shelf that appertains to several coastal States is likely to affect the maritime zones of third parties due to geographical proximity. It seems that judicial bodies tend to conflate third-party intervention and the fact that the tribunal's decision obligates only the parties to the dispute.[104]

The ICJ has allowed third parties to intervene in only two maritime delimitation disputes.[105] In the *El Salvador/Honduras* case, the Court accepted Nicaragua's claim that its interests in the Gulf of Fonseca would be affected by the proceedings. However, since Nicaragua did not show that a decision on delimitation would affect its interests, it was allowed to intervene but not on the issue of delimitation.[106] In the *Cameroon/Nigeria* case, the ICJ recognized that Equatorial Guinea's legal interests would be affected by its decision.[107] However, tribunals have generally not allowed third parties to intervene in maritime delimitation disputes.[108]

Since the adoption of UNCLOS, judicial bodies have developed an informal practice of rejecting requests to intervene while considering third parties' interests as part of the merits (i.e., determination of the boundary line). Thus, tribunals have essentially allowed implicit intervention.[109] Judicial bodies sometimes left the precise endpoints of the boundary undefined to avoid prejudicing the rights of third states. Indeed, this became a new informal principle for delimitation where third parties might be affected by the decision. For example, in the *Tunisia/Libya* case, the ICJ suggested an open-ended boundary line in cases where several states share a maritime zone, believing that this approach would avoid infringement of other states' rights in the area.[110]

In some cases, the rights of third parties were classified as "relevant circumstances"[111] that could affect the boundary line or as an element in determining the "relevant area" for delimitation.[112] In some cases, the rights of third parties were considered part of the proportionality test.[113] Governance analysis reveals that in practice the rights and interests of third parties influence the final delimitation line.[114]

Thus, international judicial bodies have implicitly considered the rights of other states. On the one hand, this downplays the formal rules that protect third parties from potential detrimental effects of international adjudication. On the other hand, tribunals have implicitly asserted jurisdiction over third-party's claims and rights contrary to the procedural rules, thus expanding the legal regime. Although this issue is not only relevant to boundary delimitation disputes, one can argue that it is especially salient in this context, broadening the governance framework of the continental shelf and even general international law.

4.2 The role of scientific evidence in maritime boundary delimitation

Since the continental shelf is a natural-physical component, scientific evidence is crucial for delineation and delimitation of the continental shelf. For example, delineation of the outer limit beyond 200 nm requires geological proof in accordance with the formulas stipulated in Article 76 (such as geo-morphological continuity).[115] Scientific evidence is also pertinent to judicial dispute-settlement concerning delimitation.[116]

As discussed in Chapter 2, the continental shelf has evolved from a physical-scientific notion to a legal concept. Many informal elements have contributed to this trend. One of the contributing factors is the interaction between the CLCS and international tribunals; the latter have conferred greater significance to the Commission. The other side of the coin is the procedural judicial practice in the context of boundary delimitation disputes; tribunals have essentially circumvented scientific questions and turned them into legal questions. As analyzed later, the governance framework concerning the continental shelf is narrower in this sense.

There are no evidentiary rules in UNCLOS or in tribunals' statutes and Rules of Procedures, certainly with respect to scientific evidence. UNCLOS only states that international tribunals may be assisted by technical experts in disputes involving scientific or technical issues. Ostensibly, there are no restrictions on how international judges evaluate evidence, and it is up to the tribunals, or the disputing parties in the case of arbitration, to determine evidentiary rules.[117] International tribunals have developed general evidentiary principles that are not necessarily directly related to scientific evidence or the law of the sea.[118]

The evaluation of scientific evidence also depends on the mandate of each tribunal.[119] Maritime delimitation disputes require evaluation of scientific facts and evidence. This calls for methodological examination of science rather than legal analysis.[120] Some scholars argue that international judges intentionally avoid conducting scientific fact-finding evaluations even when required, by resorting to procedural or evidentiary rules.[121] This practice can be explained by the fact that tribunals do not possess scientific expertise.[122] Thus, it seems that tribunals are often reluctant to examine scientific questions concerning delimitation disputes.[123]

For example, the creation of the distance criterion replaced the need to examine geological factors within 200 nm to determine the parties' entitlements.[124] The *North Sea Continental Shelf* cases developed the concept of "natural prolongation" as the basis for entitlement to the continental shelf, which requires geological evidence.[125] However, as discussed in Chapter 2, since the adoption of UNCLOS, judicial and state practice have emphasized the distance criterion as the main principle in defining and delimiting the continental shelf.

The change in the concept of the continental shelf also affected the role of scientific evidence in maritime delimitation cases: Since the concept of the continental shelf was no longer based on geology, the need for scientific evidence to prove entitlement for the purpose of delimitation was considerably reduced. As discussed later, this in turn contributed to the practice of circumventing formal physical elements in the legal regime, thus making the governance framework narrower. Alternatively, the practice of international tribunals broadened the governance framework by increasing the informal significance of the CLCS.

The procedural judicial practice can be classified into two main approaches: First, tribunals do not address scientific questions when there is conflicting evidence; scientific evidence is considered only when the parties agree on the evidence. Second, scientific evidence has relevance only regarding the continental shelf beyond 200 nm, and even in such cases, judicial bodies have generally relied on the CLCS's information as evidence. The latter practice developed because judges generally do not possess the required scientific knowledge and are unable to choose between conflicting but equally plausible evidence.[126] Consequently, adjudicators are willing to consider scientific evidence beyond 200 nm because they mostly rely on the proceedings of the CLCS and the information in the parties' submissions.

In some cases, tribunals regarded conflicting scientific evidence as irrelevant or insufficient to establish the claimed facts due to their inability to determine which party's evidence prevails. Thus, contested evidence essentially makes it impossible to establish facts or render a decision on scientific-technical issues.[127] The ICJ even indicated that conflicting evidence should be settled by bilateral negotiations rather than in judicial proceedings.[128]

Judicial bodies even seem to prefer to rely on outdated but confirmed evidence rather than having to decide between the parties' conflicting scientific arguments,[129] despite considering contemporaneous sources as being more probative and credible.[130] In some cases, the judicial body did not examine one party's scientific evidence on the grounds that similar evidence was not submitted by the other party. Instead, it chose to rely on older evidence without any clear reasoning.[131] In other cases, the ICJ did not even consider any scientific evidence or data relating to the continental shelf.[132] Instead, tribunals tried to circumvent the need to consider scientific questions,[133] which reflects the general practice of replacing geological examination (i.e., natural prolongation) with what they have perceived to be a clearer legal-geographical consideration (i.e., the distance criterion).[134]

Generally, judicial bodies have indicated that geological evidence is relevant only for the delimitation of the continental shelf beyond 200 nm.[135] Even in these cases, tribunals rely on the parties' submissions to the CLCS.[136] This correlates with the approach of the CLCS's exclusive jurisdiction concerning delimitation beyond 200 nm.[137] In cases where there is no significant "scientific uncertainty", mainly where the parties do not contest the scientific facts, judicial bodies do consider the parties' scientific evidence. However, since the evidence is uncontested, it is usually accepted together with the parties' submissions to the CLCS without being evaluated.[138] This correlates with the "primary" approach to jurisdiction regarding the continental shelf beyond 200 nm since it still confers greater weight to the Commission (which is composed of scientific experts).[139]

Thus, governance analysis reveals that in practice tribunals disregard relevant geological evidence even with respect to the continental shelf beyond 200 nm. Judicial bodies do not conduct an independent examination of Article 76; rather, they are satisfied with the legal and factual claims in the CLCS's submissions. This exposes the deficiency in the evaluation of scientific evidence, relying on another institution and the parties' unilateral demarcation of the continental shelf even in cases where the CLCS did not make any recommendations.[140] Thus, judicial practice reflects its weakness in addressing complex and contested scientific data.

A governance analysis of the practice of international judicial bodies with respect to the procedural question of evaluating scientific evidence demonstrates the gap between the legal regime and the governance framework. As discussed, the legal regime recognizes the continental shelf as a physical-geological element, while coastal States and judicial practice have transformed it into a legal concept based on the 200 nm distance criterion.[141] This transformation affects and is affected by informal rules, principles, and methods. The practice of international tribunals can be interpreted as broadening the legal regime in the sense that procedural issues have influenced and conferred greater significance to the CLCS or as narrowing the legal regime in the sense that it downplays formal rules and principles.

5. Concluding remarks

This chapter analyzes procedural issues concerning the continental shelf regime from the perspective of governance theory. Each section demonstrates the differences between the legal regime and the governance framework concerning the continental shelf. The discussion in Section 1 focuses on how governance analysis reveals that the governance framework is broader than the legal regime, essentially creating a new informal actor (SPLOS) that has established informal procedures and influenced other actors. SPLOS, although mentioned in the Convention, is largely an informal actor with significantly expanded informal powers.

The analysis in Section 2 also demonstrates how the governance perspective adds informal roles, norms, and practices. As discussed in Chapter 2, the CLCS has greater significance within the governance framework of the continental shelf than within the formal purview defined by UNCLOS. The discussion on the procedural aspects of the Commission also demonstrates the differences between the legal regime and the practice. The interaction between SPLOS and the CLCS has broadened both bodies' significance and mandate beyond the legal regime prescribes, strengthened the CLCS as a semi-judicial body, and contributed to the broader mandate of SPLOS as a permanent "plenary body", contrary to the legal regime.

Conversely, the interaction between these informal actors has also downplayed formal legal rules. SPLOS essentially amended UNCLOS outside the formal procedures and changed the significant requirement regarding the timeframe for making submissions to the CLCS. In this sense, the governance framework is narrower, circumventing formal rules that are not applicable in practice. Thus, informal elements of the governance framework pull it in different directions.

The discussion in Section 3 also demonstrates that the governance framework concerning the UNCLOS dispute-settlement mechanism is narrower, downplaying formal rules regarding judicial jurisdiction and employing external dispute-settlement mechanisms. Section 3 also demonstrates the influence of informal elements, such as political considerations, on the construction of the legal rules and the governance framework. This analysis also reveals how the different IR approaches contribute to the analysis of the legal regime.

The discussion in Section 4 concerning judicial dispute-settlement again illustrates the difference between the legal regime and the governance framework and how the latter operates in different directions. For example, implicitly considering the rights of third parties in the context of delimitation demonstrates how the governance framework adds informal procedures on the one hand while downplaying formal legal rules on the other hand. The procedural aspects also strengthen substantive developments – for example, the inception of the continental shelf as a legal concept rather than a physical element. The practices of judicial bodies with respect to scientific evidence have contributed to the primacy of the distance criterion, which is perceived to be clearer.

Annex E

Jurisdiction of international judicial bodies in maritime disputes[142]

	Year	Body	The parties	Basis for jurisdiction
1	1982	ICJ	Tunisia/Libya	UNCLOS hasn't entered into force. Submitted to the Court by special agreement.[143] Not within UNCLOS dispute-settlement mechanism.
2	1984	ICJ	Gulf of Maine (USA/Canada)	UNCLOS hasn't entered into force. Submitted to the Court by special agreement.[144] Not within UNCLOS dispute-settlement mechanism.
3	1985	ICJ	Libya/Malta	UNCLOS hasn't entered into force. Submitted to the Court by special agreement.[145] Malta made an Article 36(2) declaration but excluded delimitation disputes.[146] Not within UNCLOS dispute-settlement mechanism. Not within UNCLOS dispute-settlement mechanism.
4	1991	ICJ	Guinea-Bissau/ Senegal	UNCLOS hasn't entered into force. Not within UNCLOS dispute-settlement mechanism, submitted based on an Article 36(2) declaration of both states.[147] Senegal made reservations to Article 36(2) regarding disputes that the parties agreed to recourse to other methods of settlement. Guinea-Bissau made a declaration on condition of reciprocity.[148]
5	1992	ICJ	El Salvador/ Honduras	UNCLOS hasn't entered into force. Submitted to the Court by special agreement.[149] Not within UNCLOS dispute-settlement mechanism.
6	1993	ICJ	Jan Mayen (Denmark/ Norway)	UNCLOS hasn't entered into force. Not within UNCLOS dispute-settlement mechanism. Both parties chose the ICJ under Article 287 and did not accept the Annex VII Arbitral Tribunal for any of the categories of disputes mentioned in article 298.[150] However, these declarations were made after the dispute.[151] Thus, both parties based the jurisdiction of the Court on Article 36(2) declarations.[152] Denmark conditioned the declaration on reciprocity, while Norway made no reservations.[153]
7	1995	ICJ	Guinea-Bissau/ Senegal	Not within UNCLOS dispute-settlement mechanism, submitted based on an Article 36(2) declaration of both states [see declarations and reservations earlier].[154]

	Year	*Body*	*The parties*	*Basis for jurisdiction*
8	1998	PCA	Eritrea/Yemen	Eritrea is not a party to UNCLOS, while Yemen did not make an Article 287 declaration.[155] However, an agreement between the parties requested an Arbitral Tribunal to give an award on maritime boundaries based on UNCLOS and other relevant laws.[156] Both states did not accept ICJ jurisdiction under Article 36(2).[157] Not within UNCLOS dispute-settlement mechanism.
9	2001	ICJ	Qatar/Bahrain	Neither state made an Article 287 declaration.[158] Neither state made an Article 36(2) declaration.[159] The parties agreed to submit the dispute to the ICJ, in accordance with Article 36(1) of the ICJ Statute.[160] At the time of the dispute, Bahrain has ratified UNCLOS, but Qatar was only a signatory to it.[161] Not within UNCLOS dispute-settlement mechanism. See dissenting opinion concerning lack of jurisdiction.[162]
10	2002	ICJ	Cameroon/ Nigeria	Cameroon did not make an Article 287 declaration. Nigeria declared that it accepts the jurisdiction of ITLOS but for a specific dispute.[163] Therefore, the dispute should have gone to Annex VII arbitration.[164] However, the dispute submitted to the ICJ based on Article 36(2) of the Court Statute.[165] Cameroon did not make any reservations, but Nigeria made an Article 36(2) declaration on condition of reciprocity and excluded delimitation disputes and disputes where the parties agreed to recourse to other methods of settlement.[166] In the preliminary objections stage, the Court addressed Nigeria's Article 36(2) declaration from 1965, which did not contain any reservation,[167] rather than the declaration from April 1998, which contain the earlier declarations. Thus, the Court did not address Nigeria's reservation to Article 36(2) excluding delimitation disputes, although the new declaration was in force at the time.[168] Nigeria did not raise such argument. The Court did refer to UNCLOS Part XV and that one of the procedures for dispute-settlement is the Court,[169] but it did not address that fact that under UNCLOS, the dispute should have been submitted to Annex VII arbitration. Not within UNCLOS dispute-settlement mechanism.
11	2006	PCA	Barbados/ Trinidad and Tobago	Barbados did not make an Article 287 declaration. Trinidad and Tobago chose ITLOS and the ICJ as dispute-settlement forums.[170] However, at the time of the dispute, neither party made an Article 287 declaration. Therefore, the dispute went to Annex VII arbitration.[171] Barbados accepted ICJ jurisdiction under Article 36(2) with some reservations. Trinidad and Tobago did not make an Article 36(2) declaration.[172] The Arbitral Tribunal also recognized the hierarchy in Article 282 – first bilateral or multilateral dispute-settlement agreement, and if there is no such agreement then Part XV procedures apply.[173]

(*Continued*)

(Continued)

	Year	*Body*	*The parties*	*Basis for jurisdiction*
12	2007	ICJ	Nicaragua/ Honduras	Nicaragua accepted the jurisdiction of the ICJ in accordance with Article 287. Honduras chose the ICJ, as the dispute-settlement forum, and ITLOS on a case-by-case basis.[174] However, the jurisdiction on the Court in this case was based on Article 36 of the Court statute.[175] Not within UNCLOS dispute-settlement mechanism, this might be since the proceedings were initiated before Nicaragua ratified UNCLOS and before Honduras made the declaration.[176] Nicaragua accepted the ICJ jurisdiction except for disputes based on treaties or awards before 1901. Honduras accepted the Court jurisdiction with some reservations, excluding disputes where the parties agreed to recourse to other methods of settlement and disputes concerning sovereignty and jurisdiction over maritime zones.[177] Despite this, neither the parties nor the Court address these possible objections to its jurisdiction.
13	2007	PCA	Guyana/ Suriname	Neither state made an Article 287 declaration.[178] Thus, Annex VII Arbitral Tribunal has jurisdiction.[179] Guyana did not make an Article 36(2) declaration. Suriname did make such declaration, with reservation that gives priority to other agreements that set a different dispute-settlement means.[180]
14	2009	ICJ	Romania/ Ukraine	Romania made no Article 287 declaration. Ukraine chose Annex VII Arbitral Tribunal pursuant to Article 287 but excluded delimitation disputes from compulsory dispute-settlement under Article 298.[181] Thus, the dispute should have been submitted to compulsory conciliation.[182] However, the dispute was submitted to the ICJ based on an agreement between the parties and in pursuant of Article 36(1) of the Court statute, ignoring Part XV of UNCLOS.[183] Not within UNCLOS dispute-settlement mechanism.
15	2012	ITLOS	Myanmar/ Bangladesh	The proceedings were initiated pursuant to Annex VII of UNCLOS, but the parties also agreed to accept ITLOS jurisdiction.[184] Myanmar and Bangladesh accepted the jurisdiction of ITLOS under Article 287(1) of UNCLOS. Although in 2010, Myanmar withdrew its declaration.[185] Despite this, the parties agreed to proceed before ITLOS, and the Tribunal noted that the declarations were in force at the time of the institution of the proceedings.[186] Neither state made an Article 36(2) declaration.[187]

	Year	*Body*	*The parties*	*Basis for jurisdiction*
16	2012	ICJ	Nicaragua/ Colombia	Nicaragua accepted the jurisdiction of the ICJ in accordance with Article 287. Colombia has not ratified UNCLOS and has not made an Article 287 declaration.[188] Not within UNCLOS dispute-settlement mechanism. The jurisdiction of the Court in this case is based on Article 36.[189] Nicaragua accepted the ICJ jurisdiction except for disputes based on treaties or awards before 1901. In 2001, Colombia withdrew its consent under Article 36(2).[190] The Court determined that it had jurisdiction under the Pact of Bogotá.[191] While the Court addressed the reservation and the withdrawal since it had jurisdiction under the Pact of Bogotá, it did not examine the question of Article 36(2) declarations.[192]
17	2014	ICJ	Peru/Chile	Peru is not a party to UNCLOS. Chile chose ITLOS and Annex VIII Arbitral Tribunal as dispute-settlement forums. Chile also excluded delimitation disputes from the procedures in Article 287.[193] The parties submitted the dispute to the ICJ based on an agreement and pursuant to Article 36(1) of the Court Statute.[194] Not within UNCLOS dispute-settlement mechanism.
18	2014	PCA	India/ Bangladesh	Bangladesh accepted the jurisdiction of ITLOS, while India did not choose a specific forum in advance.[195] Thus, the dispute was initiated pursuant to UNCLOS Annex VII.[196] Bangladesh made no Article 36(2) declaration, while India made such declaration, with some reservations including exclusion of delimitation disputes.[197]
19	2014	PCA	Arctic Sunrise (Netherlands/ Russia)	Russia chose the annex VII Arbitral Tribunal as the dispute-settlement forum, while the Netherlands chose the ICJ. Russia also made Article 298 declaration, excluding all types of permitted disputes from compulsory dispute-settlement.[198] Thus, the proceedings initiated in accordance with UNCLOS Annex VII.[199] Russia opposed to the proceedings based on its Article 298 declaration.[200] The Tribunal interpreted Russia's declaration and determined that a "Declaration cannot and does not exclude from the jurisdiction of the procedures in Section 2 of Part XV of the Convention any dispute that concerns 'law-enforcement activities in regard to the exercise of sovereign rights or jurisdiction' unless the dispute is also excluded from the jurisdiction of a court or tribunal under paragraph 2 or 3 of article 297".[201] Thus, the dispute is not excluded from the Tribunals jurisdiction.[202] In addition, Article 297(1) does not apply when it is alleged that the coastal state has acted in contravention of the provisions of the Convention in regard to the freedom of navigation, which could apply in this case.[203] The Netherland accepted the ICJ jurisdiction under Article 36(2), while Russia did not make such declaration.[204]

(*Continued*)

(Continued)

	Year	*Body*	*The parties*	*Basis for jurisdiction*
20	2015	PCA	Chagos Marine Protected Area	In 2010, Mauritius submitted a claim against the United Kingdom in accordance with UNCLOS's Annex VII.[205] UK chose the ICJ as the primary dispute-settlement forum and ITLOS on a case-by-case basis. Mauritius did not make any declarations under Article 287. UK also made an Article 298 declaration.[206] Thus, the proceedings were initiated pursuant to UNCLOS Annex VII.[207] The Tribunal maintained that neither Party made any relevant declaration pursuant to Article 298, distinguishing between sovereignty questions and boundary delimitation.[208] In 2017, the UK made an Article 36(2) declaration with some reservations. Mauritius also made such declaration with reservations.[209]
21	2016	ICJ	Nicaragua/ Colombia II [under deliberations] [judgment on the merits in 2022]	Nicaragua accepted the jurisdiction of the ICJ in accordance with Article 287. Colombia has not ratified UNCLOS and has not made an Article 287 declaration.[210] The dispute initiated in accordance with Article 36 of the ICJ Statute.[211] Not within UNCLOS dispute-settlement mechanism. Nicaragua accepted the ICJ jurisdiction except for disputes based on treaties or awards before 1901. In 2001, Colombia withdrew its consent under Article 36(2).[212] Unlike the 2012 case, Colombia denounced the Pact of Bogotá before Nicaragua initiated the proceedings.[213] The Court noted that it has jurisdiction even if a treaty ceases to be in force between the parties or either party's declaration under Article 36(2) of the Statute of the Court expires or is withdrawn after the application has been filed. Thus, it still has jurisdiction in this case.[214]
22	2016	ICJ	Nicaragua/ Colombia III [pending]	Nicaragua accepted the jurisdiction of the ICJ in accordance with Article 287. Colombia has not ratified UNCLOS and has not made an Article 287 declaration.[215] The dispute initiated in accordance with Article 36 of the ICJ Statute.[216] Not within UNCLOS dispute-settlement mechanism. Nicaragua accepted the ICJ jurisdiction except for disputes based on treaties or awards before 1901. In 2001, Colombia withdrew its consent under Article 36(2).[217]
23	2016	PCA	Timor Sea Conciliation (Timor-Leste v. Australia)	Timor-Leste agreed to choose any of the four means for dispute-settlement. Australia chose ITLOS and the ICJ as the dispute-settlement forums under Article 287(1). Australia also excluded delimitation disputes under Article 298.[218] Thus, the case went to conciliation.[219] In 2015, Timor-Leste also initiated arbitral proceedings pursuant to the 2002 Timor Sea Treaty (bilateral boundary treaty).[220] Both states made an Article 36(2) declaration, although Australia excluded delimitation dispute from the declaration.[221]

	Year	*Body*	*The parties*	*Basis for jurisdiction*
24	2016	PCA	South China Sea dispute	Both China and the Philippines made no declaration under Article 287. China made an Article 298 declaration.[222] The Philippines initiated proceedings pursuant to UNCLOS Annex VII.[223] While not drafted so, the Philippines essentially sought the Tribunal's declaration on questions of delimitation and sovereignty, which is outside the Tribunal jurisdiction.[224] Thus, the proceedings should have been submitted to conciliation.[225] However, the Tribunal rejected this claim and asserted jurisdiction, despite the obvious merits of the argument.[226] In addition, the Tribunal also recognized the hierarchy between Article 282 and Section 2 of Part XV of UNCLOS.[227] However, it interpreted Article 282 strictly and narrowly, requiring clear preference for express language, excluding Part XV mechanisms. In addition, the agreement should involve an alternative compulsory and binding procedure to automatically opt out from Part XV, Section 2.[228] It seems that the Tribunal conflates between questions requiring a merit determination and questions excluding the Tribunal's jurisdiction.[229] The Philippines made an Article 36(2) declaration with some reservation, while China did not make such declaration.[230]
25	2017	PCA	Croatia/ Slovenia	Croatia chose ITLOS and the ICJ as dispute-settlement forums. Slovenia chose Annex VIII arbitration and made an Article 298 declaration.[231] Both states did not accept the jurisdiction of the ICJ pursuant to Article 36(2).[232] The dispute was submitted to the PCA based on an arbitration agreement outside of UNCLOS.[233]
26	2017	ITLOS	Ghana/Côte d'Ivoire	Ghana made no declaration under Article 287[234] but made declaration under Article 298(1)(a) [including delimitation],[235] which was withdrawn in 2014.[236] Côte d'Ivoire also made no declaration under Article 287.[237] Thus, this dispute should have gone to annex VII Arbitral Tribunal.[238] However, the parties participated in consultations with the president under UNCLOS Annex VII. Thus, a special agreement between the parties suspended the proceedings in the Arbitral Tribunal and submitted the dispute to a special chamber of ITLOS pursuant to article 15(2), of the Statute of the Tribunal.[239] Côte d'Ivoire also made an Article 36(2) declaration, conferring compulsory jurisdiction to the ICJ, but conditioned it on reciprocity. Ghana did not make such declaration.[240]

(*Continued*)

(Continued)

	Year	Body	The parties	Basis for jurisdiction
27	2018	ICJ	Costa Rica/ Nicaragua	Nicaragua accepted the jurisdiction of the ICJ in accordance with Article 287. Costa Rica did not make an Article 298(1) declaration.[241] Therefore, the dispute should have gone to Annex VII arbitration.[242] Not within UNCLOS dispute-settlement mechanism. The dispute initiated in accordance with Article 36 of the ICJ Statute.[243] This might be since the proceedings also included a decision on land boundary, although there is no reference at all to UNCLOS Part XV. In its memorial, Costa Rica refers also to UNCLOS Article 282, which is consistent with Article 36(2) of the Court Statute.[244]
28	2020	ICJ	Guatemala/ Belize [pending]	Neither state made an Article 298(1) declaration.[245] Therefore, the dispute should have gone to Annex VII arbitration.[246] The dispute was submitted to the ICJ based on a special agreement between the parties in accordance with Article 36(1) of the ICJ Statute,[247] and based on the recommendation by the OAS Secretary-General.[248]
29	2020	PCA	Russia/Ukraine	Both chose the Annex VII Arbitral Tribunal as the dispute-settlement forum.[249] Russia invoked Article 298(1), which excludes delimitation disputes concerning the continental shelf from UNCLOS Part XV procedures.[250] It is noteworthy that the Russia/Ukraine dispute does not really concern delimitation since it requires that both parties have land territory that generates entitlement to continental shelf; thus, the dispute actually concerns sovereignty over Crimea, which is outside UNCLOS competence and the Tribunal's jurisdiction.[251] However, the Tribunal decided to decide on some objections in the proceedings on the merits.[252] In 2003, the parties signed a treaty that provide for dispute-settlement by agreement between the parties.[253] This agreement should have precedence over Part XV.[254]
30	2021	ICJ	Gabon/ Equatorial Guinea [pending]	Both states did not make an Article 287 declaration but did so under Article 298, excluding delimitation disputes.[255] Therefore, the dispute should have gone to compulsory conciliation.[256] The dispute was submitted to the ICJ based on a special agreement between the parties.[257]

	Year	*Body*	*The parties*	*Basis for jurisdiction*
31	2021	ICJ	Somalia/Kenya	Somalia and Kenya made no declaration under Article 287. Kenya did make a declaration under Article 298 to exclude delimitation disputes from the procedures in Part XV Section 2.[258] Under UNCLOS, the dispute should go to Annex VII arbitration.[259] However, Somalia initiated the proceedings against Kenya in the ICJ, based on both parties' acceptance of compulsory jurisdiction under Art. 36(2) of the Court's Statute.[260] Kenya had reservations to the jurisdiction of the Court; Article 36(2) would not apply to "disputes in regard to which the parties to the dispute have agreed or shall agree to have recourse to some other method or methods of settlement".[261] The ICJ invoked the hierarchy in Article 282, claiming that the parties' Article 36(2) declarations provide an alternative dispute-settlement procedure that exclude Part XV procedures.[262] Kenya argued that Section 2 of Part XV falls under the reservation; thus, the dispute must be submitted to Annex VII arbitration in accordance with Article 287(3).[263] The ICJ essentially ignores Kenya's reservation, giving priority to Article 36(2) over UNCLOS Part XV, Section 2, even if there are reservations.[264]
32	2021	ITLOS	Mauritius/ Maldives	Neither state made an Article 287(1) or an Article 298(1) declaration.[265] Therefore, the dispute should have gone to Annex VII arbitration.[266] The proceedings were initiated pursuant to Annex VII of UNCLOS.[267] However, a special agreement between the parties submitted the dispute to a special chamber of ITLOS pursuant to article 15(2) of the Statute of the Tribunal.[268] The Maldives raises five preliminary objections to the jurisdiction of the special chamber and the admissibility of Mauritius's claims.[269] One of the objections is that there is a sovereignty dispute over Chagos Archipelago between UK and Mauritius, which is outside of UNCLOS's scope.[270] ITLOS rejected this argument based on an advisory opinion of the ICJ, determining that the Chagos Archipelago was an integral part of Mauritius in 1965.[271]

Notes

1 Katrin Fenrich, The Evolving International Procedural Capacity of Individuals 2 (2019). See also International Law Commission, *Report of the Study Group on Fragmentation of International law: Difficulties arising from the Diversification and Expansion of International Law*, A/CN.4/L.644 (18 July 2003), para. 6.

2 Roberto Virzo, *The 'General Rule of Interpretation' in the International Jurisprudence Relating to the United Nations Convention on the Law of the Sea, in* Interpretations of the United Nations Convention on the Law of the Sea by International Courts and Tribunals 15, 15–16 (Angela Del Vecchio and Roberto Virzo (eds.), 2019); Niels M. Blokker, *Governance of the International Tribunal of the Law of the Sea: The Role of the Meeting of States Parties to the Law of the Sea Convention, in* Interpretations of the United Nations Convention on the Law of the Sea by International Courts and Tribunals 81, 82 (Angela- Del- Vecchio and Roberto- Virzo (eds.), 2019).

3 ILC, *Fragmentation of International Law: Difficulties Arising from The Diversification and Expansion of International Law*, Report of the Study Group of the International Law Commission, Finalized by Martti Koskenniemi, A/CN.4/L.682 (2006); Malcolm N. Shaw, International Law 54–55 (9th ed., 2021). See also Chapter 1, Section 3.

4 See Chapter 1, Section 3.

5 Blokker, *supra* note 2, p. 86.

6 See also Francesca Romanin Jacur, *Formalism and Law-making in Treaty-based Ocean Governance: Limits and Challenges, in* Regime Interaction in Ocean Governance 156, 167 (Seline Trevisanut, Nikolaos Giannopoulos and Rozemarijn Roland Holst (eds.), 2020)

7 See e.g., Sandrine W. De Herdt and Tafsir Malick Ndiaye, *The International Tribunal for the Law of the Sea and the Protection and Preservation of the Marine Environment: Taking Stock and Prospects*, 57 The Canadian Yearbook of International Law 353, ft 117 (2019).

8 1982 UN Convention on the Law of the Sea, 1833 UNTS 397 (UNCLOS), Article 319(2)(e).

9 UNCLOS, *supra* note 8, Annex I, Article 10, Annex II, Article 2, Annex VI, Article 4(4); James Harrison, Making the Law of the Sea, A Study in the Development of International Law 70, 75 (2011); Blokker, *supra* note 2, p. 85–86; Jacur, *supra* note 6, p. 167.

10 UNGAOR, 49th Sess, UN Doc A/49/631 (16 November 1994), para. 16; SPLOS, 1st Mtg, UN Doc SPLOS/3 (28 February 1995), paras. 1–2.

11 SPLOS/3, ibid., para. 6.

12 A/49/631, *supra* note 10, p. 9.

13 SPLOS/3, *supra* note 10, paras. 9–10. The elected officials continued in following meetings, see e.g., SPLOS, 2nd Mtg, UN Doc SPLOS/4 (26 July 1995), para. 3.

14 SPLOS/4, ibid., para. 21.

15 Ibid., para. 37; SPLOS, 3rd Mtg, UN Doc SPLOS/5 (22 February 1996), para. 24. For the "regular basis" see Rules of Procedure for Meetings of States Parties, UN Doc SPLOS/2/Rev.5 (7 May 2020), Rule 4; Harrison, *supra* note 9, p. 70–71. This conflicts with Article 319 which refers to an ad-hoc basis. See UNCLOS, *supra* note 8, Article 319(2)(e); SPLOS/2/Rev.5, ibid., Rule 3(1); Harrison, ibid., p. 71.

16 SPLOS, 11th Mtg, UN Doc SPLOS/73 (14 June 2001), para. 85; Harrison, *supra* note 9, p. 72. It should be noted that while UNCLOS requires the Secretary-General to report to all States Parties, it does not require the Secretary-General to report to SPLOS. UNCLOS, *supra* note 8, Article 319(2)(a) and (e); SPLOS/73, ibid., paras. 86, 89.

17 UNCLOS, *supra* note 8, Annex II, Article 2(3) and Annex VI, Article 3(2).

18 Ibid., Annex VI, Article 2(1); Harrison, *supra* note 9, p. 77–78. See e.g., SPLOS, 5th Mtg, UN Doc SPLOS/14 (20 September 1996), para. 15; SPLOS, 6th Mtg, UN Doc SPLOS/20 (20 March 1997), para. 13.

19 Some delegations wanted to expand the role of SPLOS and its competences. SPLOS, 7th Mtg, UN Doc SPLOS/24 (12 June 1997), paras. 35–36, 38. For example, on sustainable development, SPLOS/3, *supra* note 10, para. 69. Many delegations maintained that SPLOS's powers should be beyond budgetary and administrative issues, SPLOS, 10th Mtg, UN Doc SPLOS/60 (22 June 2000), para. 74; SPLOS/73, *supra* note 16, para. 88. See additional issues in SPLOS, 15th Mtg, UN Doc SPLOS/135 (25 July 2005), paras. 78–79.
20 SPLOS/24, *supra* note 19, para. 37.
21 SPLOS, 9th Mtg, UN Doc SPLOS/48 (15 June 1999), para. 54.
22 SPLOS, 16th Mtg, UN Doc SPLOS/148 (28 July 2006), para. 85. SPLOS also regarded political issues, for example with respect to Russian occupation of the Crimean Peninsula and its legal status, SPLOS, 25th Mtg, UN Doc SPLOS/287 (13 July 2015), para. 94; SPLOS, 26th Mtg, UN Doc SPLOS/303 (2 August 2016), paras. 108–110.
23 SPLOS/73, *supra* note 16, para. 90.
24 Ibid., para. 80.
25 SPLOS, 12th Mtg, UN Doc SPLOS/91 (13 June 2002), para. 113; SPLOS, 14th Mtg, UN Doc SPLOS/119 (23 July 2004), para. 80.
26 SPLOS/119, *supra* note 25, para. 81; SPLOS/135, *supra* note 19, para. 81.
27 For example, decisions concerning the time limit for submissions to the CLCS. SPLOS/91, *supra* note 25, para. 114; SPLOS, 13th Mtg, UN Doc SPLOS/103 (25 June 2003), para. 97. See also Section 2.20 later.
28 SPLOS/3, *supra* note 10, para. 2; SPLOS, 7th Mtg, UN Doc SPLOS/21 (9 May 1997); Blokker, *supra* note 2, p. 87–89.
29 Blokker, ibid., p. 88–89.
30 SPLOS/2/Rev.5, *supra* note 15, Rule 6(3)(d); Blokker, ibid., p. 89.
31 SPLOS/14, *supra* note 18, para. 36. This function can be viewed as similar to the ICJ's report to the UN General Assembly, see Charter of the United Nations, 24 October 1945, 1 UNTS XVI (UN Charter), Article 15(2).
32 SPLOS, 8th Mtg, UN Doc SPLOS/27 (23 April 1998).
33 Ibid., para. 2.
34 SPLOS, 8th Mtg, UN Doc SPLOS/31 (4 June 1998), para. 12; SPLOS/27, *supra* note 32, para. 49, 60.
35 SPLOS/48, *supra* note 21, para. 15; SPLOS, 23rd Mtg, UN Doc SPLOS/263 (8 July 2013), paras. 18–19.
36 SPLOS/73, *supra* note 16, para. 23.
37 Blokker, *supra* note 2, p. 89.
38 SPLOS/263, *supra* note 35, para. 19.
39 SPLOS, 21st Mtg, UN Doc SPLOS/231 (29 June 2011), para. 25; SPLOS/263, *supra* note 35, para. 21; SPLOS/287, *supra* note 22, para. 23; Blokker, *supra* note 2, p. 89–90.
40 SPLOS, 11th Mtg, UN Doc SPLOS/63 (6 April 2001), para. 61(a).
41 SPLOS/73, *supra* note 16, para. 27.
42 SPLOS/287, *supra* note 22, para. 21.
43 SPLOS/103, *supra* note 27, para. 26; SPLOS/119, *supra* note 25, para. 16.
44 See for example SPLOS/148, *supra* note 22, paras. 20–21; SPLOS, 17th Mtg, UN Doc SPLOS/164 (16 July 2007), para. 16; SPLOS/263, *supra* note 35, para. 18.
45 SPLOS, 20th Mtg, UN Doc SPLOS/218 (13 July 2010), para. 31.
46 SPLOS/287, *supra* note 22, para. 22.
47 On plenary bodies see e.g., Jochen von Bernstorff, *Procedures of Decision-Making and the Role of Law in International Organizations*, 9(11) German Law J. 1939, 1942 (2008); Jan Klabbers, An Introduction to International Institutional Law 155 (2nd ed. 2009).
48 SPLOS/48, *supra* note 21, paras. 49–50; SPLOS/60, *supra* note 19, para. 73–74. See also CLCS, 21st Sess, UN Doc CLCS/40/Rev.1 (17 April 2008), Annex II, Article 5.
49 SPLOS/73, *supra* note 16, para. 61.

50 See e.g., letter from the Chairman of the CLCS, SPLOS, 16th Mtg, UN Doc SPLOS/140 (19 May 2006), para. 9; SPLOS, 19th Mtg, UN Doc SPLOS/203 (24 July 2009), para. 78. See also Chapter 2, Section 1.2.2.

51 See SPLOS, 18th Mtg, UN Doc SPLOS/184 (21 July 2008), para. 81; SPLOS, 28th Mtg, UN Doc SPLOS/324 (9 July 2018), paras. 55–56.

52 For example, SPLOS/203, *supra* note 50, paras. 76, 78; SPLOS/287, *supra* note 22, para. 59.

53 SPLOS, 19th Mtg, UN Doc SPLOS/INF/22/Corr.1 (1 July 2009); SPLOS, 19th Mtg, UN Doc SPLOS/199 (6 July 2009)

54 This might contradict the perception of the CLCS its own role as an independent evaluator of disputes, see discussion in Chapter 2, Section 1.2.2.2.

55 SPLOS, 21st Mtg, UN Doc SPLOS/225 (5 May 2011), para. 19; SPLOS, 22nd Mtg, UN Doc SPLOS/245 (1 May 2012), para. 8; SPLOS, 23rd Mtg, UN Doc SPLOS/259 (1 April 2013), para. 15. See also the postponement of Myanmar's submission due to Bangladesh's lack of consent and similar decision regarding Kenya's submission, SPLOS/259, ibid., paras. 14, 22; SPLOS, 24th Mtg, UN Doc SPLOS/270 (14 April 2014), para. 6.

56 See Bangladesh's Note Verbale no. PMBNY/67/UNCLOS/2012, available at www.un.org/depts/los/clcs_new/submissions_files/mmr08/2012_09_30_BGD_NV_UN.pdf. See also SPLOS/259, *supra* note 55, paras. 14, 22. See also SPLOS, 27th Mtg, UN Doc SPLOS/316 (10 July 2017), para. 62; SPLOS, 28th Mtg, UN Doc SPLOS/319 (2 April 2018), para. 29.

57 SPLOS, 24th Mtg, UN Doc SPLOS/277 (14 July 2014), para. 81; SPLOS/316, *supra* note 56, para. 57; SPLOS/319, *supra* note 56, para. 29.

58 For example, SPLOS/303, *supra* note 22, para. 61; SPLOS/319, *supra* note 56, para. 29.

59 See UNCLOS, *supra* note 8, Article 76.

60 SPLOS/148, *supra* note 22, para. 81; SPLOS/203, *supra* note 50, paras. 71–73; Signe Veierud Busch, Establishing Continental Shelf Limits Beyond 200 Nautical Miles By The Coastal State 201 (2016). See also individual international judges' position, Ioannis Konstantinidis, *Between Villa Schröder (ITLOS) and the Peace Palace (ICJ): Diverging Approaches to Continental Shelf Delimitation Beyond 200 Nautical Miles*, 3(2) J. Territorial Marit. Stud. 28, 48 (2016).

61 SPLOS/231, *supra* note 39, para. 88.

62 UNCLOS, *supra* note 8, Annex II, Article 4; Alex G. Oude Elferink, *Meeting of States Parties to the UN Law of the Sea Convention*, 23 Int. J. Marine & Coastal L. 769, 770 (2008); Øystein Jensen, The Commission On The Limits of the Continental Shelf, Law and Legitimacy 51 (2014).

63 Harrison, *supra* note 9, p. 80; SPLOS/60, *supra* note 19, para. 61; SPLOS/73, *supra* note 16, para. 68.

64 Jensen (2014), *supra* note 62, p. 51.

65 SPLOS/73, *supra* note 16, para. 73; Oude Elferink (2008), *supra* note 62, p. 771; Jensen (2014), *supra* note 62, p. 53–55.

66 States indicated that they had knowledge on preparing a submission only after the adoption of the Scientific and Technical Guidelines, SPLOS/73, *supra* note 16, paras. 71, 74, 81; CLCS/40/Rev.1, *supra* note 48, Rule 45. See also Harrison, *supra* note 9, p. 80; Jensen (2014), *supra* note 62, p. 54.

67 SPLOS/73, *supra* note 16, para. 77; SPLOS, 18th Mtg, UN Doc SPLOS/183 (20 June 2008); Oude Elferink (2008), *supra* note 62, p. 776; Jensen (2014), *supra* note 62, p. 55–56.

68 CLCS/40/Rev.1, *supra* note 48, Annex I, Rule 3; Jensen (2014), *supra* note 62, p. 58, 146. See also SPLOS/148, *supra* note 22, para. 73.

69 UNCLOS, *supra* note 8, Article 76(10) and Annex II, Article 9; Jensen (2014), *supra* note 62, p. 58.

70 See Chapter 1, Section 3. Although some scholars view this issue as "treaty conflict" in which UNCLOS prevails. For example, Jensen (2014), *supra* note 62, p. 59.
71 Oude Elferink (2008), *supra* note 62, p. 771; Harrison, *supra* note 9, p. 82; Jensen (2014), *supra* note 62, p. 57. For the formal rule concerning amendments of UNCLOS, see UNCLOS, *supra* note 8, Article 312.
72 UNCLOS, *supra* note 8, Articles 83, 279–281; Bernard H. Oxman, *A Tribute to Louis Sohn – Is the Dispute Settlement System under the Law of the Sea Convention Working*, 39 Geo. Wash. Int. L. Rev. 655, 656 (2007).
73 See UNCLOS III, 4th Sess, 57th Plen Mtg, UN Doc A/CONF.62/SR.57 (15 March 1976), para. 28; UNCLOS III, 8th Sess, 2nd Committee, 57th Mtg, UN Doc A/CONF.62/C.2/SR.57 (24 April 1979), para. 49. See the contribution of the Chairman of negotiating group 7 concerning UNCLOS's dispute-settlement mechanism, UNCLOS III, 7th Sess, 105th Plen Mtg, UN Doc A/CONF.62/SR.105 (19 May 1978), paras. 41–42; UNCLOS III, 8th Sess, 112th Plen Mtg, UN Doc A/CONF.62/SR.112 (25 April 1979); UNCLOS III, 9th Sess, 128th Plen Mtg, UN Doc A/CONF.62/SR.128 (3 April 1980), para. 27.
74 A/CONF.62/SR.105, *supra* note 73, para. 87; A/CONF.62/SR.112, *supra* note 73, paras. 3, 18, 38; UNCLOS III, 9th Sess, UN Doc A/CONF.62/L.47 (24 March 1980), para. 2. See discussion on the "packaged-deal" in Chapter 2, Section 1.1.
75 Douglas Guilfoyle, *The South China Sea Award: How Should We Read the UN Convention on the Law of the Sea?* 8 Asian J. Int. Law 51, 53–55 (2018).
76 See e.g., UNCLOS III, 4th Sess, 58th Plen Mtg, UN Doc A/CONF.62/SR.58 (5 April 1976), paras. 3–4, 5, 7, 20, 22; UNCLOS III, 4th Sess, 59th Plen Mtg, UN Doc A/CONF.62/SR.59 (5 April 1976), para. 39. On the role of the CLCS see discussion in Chapter 2, Section 1.2.1.
77 A/CONF.62/SR.58, *supra* note 76, paras. 20, 23–24, 30–31; UNCLOS III, 4th Sess, 60th Plen Mtg, UN Doc A/CONF.62/SR.60 (6 April 1976), paras. 15, 54; A/CONF.62/SR.128, *supra* note 73, para. 105. For positions on the need for limited exceptions to jurisdiction, see A/CONF.62/SR.58, ibid., paras. 35, 37; A/CONF.62/SR.59, *supra* note 76, para. 59; UNCLOS III, 4th Sess, 61st Plen Mtg, UN Doc A/CONF.62/SR.61 (6 April 1976), para. 60.
78 A/CONF.62/SR.60, *supra* note 77, para. 49; UNCLOS III, 9th Sess, 126th Plen Mtg, UN Doc A/CONF.62/SR.126 (2 April 1980), paras. 30, 161. For the vague criteria for delimitation, see Chapter 2, Section 2.
79 For example, A/CONF.62/SR.58, *supra* note 76, paras. 13, 27; A/CONF.62/SR.59, *supra* note 76, paras. 42, 46, 48, 63; UNCLOS III, 7th Sess, 106th Plen Mtg, UN Doc A/CONF.62/SR.106 (19 May 1978), para. 26; UNCLOS III, 4th Sess, 62nd Plen Mtg, UN Doc A/CONF.62/SR.62 (7 April 1976), paras. 43–44. See also Chapter 2, Section 1.1.1 and Section 1.2.1.
80 See e.g., A/CONF.62/SR.59, *supra* note 76, para. 44; A/CONF.62/SR.61, *supra* note 77, paras. 37, 43, 48–50, 63; UNCLOS III, 4th Sess, 63rd Plen Mtg, UN Doc A/CONF.62/SR.63 (8 April 1976), paras. 14, 21; A/CONF.62/SR.62, *supra* note 79, paras. 9–10; A/CONF.62/SR.112, *supra* note 73, para. 3.
81 For example, UNCLOS III, 4th Sess, 65th Plen Mtg, UN Doc A/CONF.62/SR.65 (12 April 1976), paras. 10, 20; A/CONF.62/SR.112, *supra* note 73, para. 10.
82 UNCLOS, *supra* note 8, Article 298(1)(a)(i).
83 Øystein Jensen and Nigel Bankes, *Compulsory and Binding Dispute Resolution under the United Nations Convention on the Law of the Sea: Introduction*, 48(3–4) Ocean Dev. & Int. Law 209, 209 (2017); Alex G. Oude Elferink, Tore Henriksen and Signe Veierud Busch, *The Judiciary and the Law of Maritime Delimitation: Setting the Stage*, *in* Maritime Boundary Delimitation: The Case Law: Is It Consistent and Predictable? 1, 20 (Alex G. Oude Elferink, Tore Henriksen and Signe Veierud Busch (eds.), 2018).
84 Annex E; Jensen and Bankes, *supra* note 83, p. 209. Some disputes initially submitted to ITLOS for provisional measures before addressing the merits in other

dispute-settlement procedures. For example, the *Arctic Sunrise* case was submitted to Annex VII Arbitration, see list of cases, ITLOS website, available at www.itlos.org/en/main/cases/list-of-cases/.

85 Randa Salama, *Fragmentation of International Law: Procedural Issues Arising in Law of the Sea Disputes*, 19 Austl. & N.Z. Mar. L. J. 24, 27 (2005); John E. Noyes, *Judicial and Arbitral Proceedings and the Outer Limits of the Continental Shelf*, 42 Vand. J. Transnat'l L. 1211 (2009). See also Chapter 1, Section 3.

86 See declarations and reservations, United Nations Convention on the Law of the Sea, Chapter XXI, UN treaty collection (UNTC) website, available at https://treaties.un.org/Pages/ViewDetailsIII.aspx?src=TREATY&mtdsg_no=XXI-6&chapter=21&Temp=mtdsg3&clang=_en.

87 Ibid.; UNCLOS, *supra* note 8, Article 287(3). See also Judith Levine and Garth L. Schofield, *Navigating Uncharted Procedural Waters in a Rising Sea of Cases at the Permanent Court of Arbitration, in* Stress Testing The Law of the Sea 95, 100 (2018); Edwin E. Egede and Lawrence Apaalse, *Dispute concerning Delimitation of the Maritime Boundary between Ghana and Cote D'Ivoire in the Atlantic Ocean – Lessons from Another Maritime Delimitation Case arising from the African Region*, 29 Ind. Int. & Comp. L. Rev. 55, 63–64 (2019).

88 Dispute concerning delimitation of the maritime boundary between Bangladesh and Myanmar in the Bay of Bengal (Bangladesh/Myanmar), Judgment, ITLOS Reports 2012, p. 4; Dispute Concerning Delimitation of the Maritime Boundary between Ghana and Côte d'Ivoire in the Atlantic Ocean (Ghana/Côte d'Ivoire), Judgment, ITLOS Reports 2017, p. 4; Dispute concerning delimitation of the maritime boundary between Mauritius and Maldives in the Indian Ocean (Mauritius/Maldives), Judgment, case no. 28, ITLOS (28 April 2023).

89 See Annex E. For example, in the *Barbados/Trinidad and Tobago* case, Trinidad and Tobago chose ITLOS or the ICJ, while Barbados did not choose a forum. Guyana and Suriname did not make an Article 287 declaration. In the *India/Bangladesh* case, India did not choose a forum. In the *Chagos Marine Protected Area* case, the UK chose the ICJ, while Mauritius did not make any Article 287 declaration. In the *South China Sea* dispute, both China and the Philippines made no declaration under Article 287. See UNTC website, *supra* note 86.

90 See Annex E.

91 For example negotiations, see discussion in Chapter 3, Section 2.1.2.1; Jensen and Bankes, *supra* note 83, p. 210–211; Oude Elferink et al., *supra* note 83, p. 19–20.

92 For example, see China's position on the Philippines's initiation of arbitration, UNGAOR, 69th Sess, UN Doc A/69/429 (8 October 2014), para. 7; Position Paper of the Government of the People's Republic of China on the Matter of Jurisdiction in the South China Sea Arbitration Initiated by the Republic of the Philippines, 7 December 2014, available at www.fmprc.gov.cn/mfa_eng/wjdt_665385/2649_665393/201412/t20141207_679387.html, paras. 74, 86. See also Russia's position on other means of dispute-settlement, Dispute Concerning Coastal State Rights in the Black Sea, Sea of Azov, and Kerch Strait (Ukraine v. the Russian Federation), Award Concerning the Preliminary Objections of the Russian Federation, case No. 2017–06, 21 February 2020, Permanent Court of Arbitration [PCA] (Sea of Azov case), paras. 451–463. However, the arbitration proceedings between Australia and Timor-Leste were terminated, and the parties signed a delimitation agreement. See Arbitration under the Timor Sea Treaty (Timor-Leste v. Australia), Termination Order, case no. 2013–16, 20 March 2017, Permanent Court of Arbitration [PCA]; Australian Government, Department of Foreign Affairs and Trade, available at www.dfat.gov.au/geo/timor-leste/Pages/joint-communique.

93 See Annex E; Oude Elferink et al., *supra* note 83, p. 18. See also Declarations recognizing as compulsory the jurisdiction of the International Court of Justice under Article 36, paragraph 2, of the Statute of the Court, UN Treaty Collection website,

available at https://treaties.un.org/pages/ViewDetails.aspx?src=TREATY&mtdsg_no=I-4&chapter=1&clang=_en.

94 See for example A/CONF.62/SR.63, *supra* note 80, paras. 4, 14; A/CONF.62/SR.65, *supra* note 81, para. 21.

95 For example, A/CONF.62/SR.58, *supra* note 76, at para. 13; A/CONF.62/SR.60, *supra* note 77, para. 58; A/CONF.62/SR.61, *supra* note 77, para. 10; A/CONF.62/SR.65, *supra* note 81, para. 7.

96 See also Kai-chieh Chan, *The ICJ's Judgement in Somalia v. Kenya and Its Implications for the Law of the Sea*, 34 Utrecht J. Int. & Eur. L. 195, 199 (2018).

97 Sergey M. Punzhin, *Procedural Normative System of the International Court of Justice*, 30 Leiden J. Int. Law 661, 672 (2017).

98 Statute of the International Court of Justice, San Francisco, 24 October 1945, Article 59; UNCLOS, *supra* note 8, Annex VI, Article 33(2); Thomas Cottier, Equitable Principles of Maritime Boundary Delimitation: The Quest for Distributive Justice in International Law 491–492 (2015).

99 See also Cottier, ibid., p. 491, 494; Levine and Schofield, *supra* note 87, p. 113.

100 ICJ Statute, *supra* note 98, Article 62; Cottier, *supra* note 98, p. 495, 497.

101 UNCLOS, *supra* note 8, Annex VI, Article 31; International Tribunal for the Law of the Sea, Rules of the Tribunal, ITLOS/8, 25 March 2021, Section 5.

102 The South China Sea Arbitration (The Republic of Philippines v. The People's Republic of China), Award on Jurisdiction and Admissibility, case no. 2013–19, 29 October 2015, Permanent Court of Arbitration [PCA]; The South China Sea Arbitration (The Republic of Philippines v. The People's Republic of China), Award, case no. 2013–19, 12 July 2016, Permanent Court of Arbitration [PCA]; Levine and Schofield, *supra* note 87, p. 113–114, 116.

103 See e.g., Continental Shelf (Tunisia/Libyan Arab Jamahiriya), Application to Intervene, Judgment, ICJ Reports 1981, p. 3, paras. 19, 33–34, 37; Territorial and Maritime Dispute (Nicaragua v. Colombia), Application by Honduras for Permission to Intervene, Judgment, ICJ Reports 2011, p. 420, para. 37; Territorial and Maritime Dispute (Nicaragua v. Colombia), Application by Costa Rica for Permission to Intervene, Judgment, ICJ Reports 2011, p. 348, para. 67.

104 See for example Nicaragua v. Colombia, Costa Rica's Application to Intervene, *supra* note 103, Dissenting opinion of Judge Al- Khasawneh, paras. 11, 14 and Joint Dissenting opinion of Judges Cançado Trindade and Yusuf, para. 21 and Section V. See also Territorial and Maritime Dispute (Nicaragua v. Colombia), Judgment, ICJ Reports 2012, p. 624, Declaration of Judge *Ad Hoc* Mensah, p. 762, para. 13.

105 Cottier, *supra* note 98, p. 498.

106 Land, Island and Maritime Frontier Dispute (El Salvador/Honduras), Application to Intervene, Judgment, ICJ Reports 1990, p. 92, para. 72, 79, 105.

107 Land and Maritime Boundary between Cameroon and Nigeria, Application to Intervene, Order of 21 October 1999, ICJ Reports 1999, p. 1029, paras. 14, 18.

108 In some cases, tribunals rejected requests to intervene due to conflation with the "monetary gold" principle; a customary principle constructed by the ICJ that provides that "a court or tribunal cannot exercise its jurisdiction in the absence of an indispensable party". Case of the monetary gold removed from Rome in 1943 (Preliminary Question), Judgment, ICJ Reports 1954, p. 19, at p. 32; Dispute concerning delimitation of the maritime boundary between Mauritius and Maldives in the Indian Ocean (Mauritius/Maldives), Preliminary Objections, Judgment, case no. 28, ITLOS (28 January 2021), para. 101, para. 82. It seems that tribunals thought that intervention means being a party to the dispute without the disputing parties' consent. See e.g., Continental Shelf (Libyan Arab Jamahiriya/Malta), Application to Intervene, Judgment, ICJ Reports 1984, p. 3, paras. 40–41; Bangladesh v. Myanmar, *supra* note 88, paras. 362–363, 367.

109 For example, Libya v. Malta, Application to Intervene, *supra* note 108, paras. 38, 41, and Dissenting Opinion of Judge Schwebel, p. 173; Dispute between the Government

of the State of Eritrea and the Government of the Republic of Yemen, Award of the Arbitral Tribunal in the Second Stage of the Proceedings (Maritime Delimitation), case no. 1996–04, 17 December 1999, Permanent Court of Arbitration [PCA], paras. 45, 164; Land and Maritime Boundary between Cameroon and Nigeria (Cameroon v. Nigeria: Equatorial Guinea intervening), Judgment, ICJ Reports 2002, p. 303, paras. 238, 269; Nicaragua v. Colombia, Honduras's Application to Intervene, *supra* note 103, Declaration of Judge Keith, para. 11; Bay of Bengal Maritime Boundary Arbitration between Bangladesh and India, Award, case no. 2010–16, 07 July 2014, Permanent Court of Arbitration [PCA], Concurring and Dissenting Opinion of Dr. P.S. Rao, para. 13.

110 Similar reasoning in the *Libya/Malta* case led to consideration of a limited area of the overlapping zone and delimiting only part of the boundary. In following cases, tribunals avoided extending the maritime boundary in areas where other states have potential rights. See Cottier, *supra* note 98, p. 492–494; Territorial and Maritime Dispute between Nicaragua and Honduras in the Caribbean Sea (Nicaragua v. Honduras), Judgment, ICJ Reports 2007, p. 659; Bangladesh v. Myanmar, *supra* note 88, para. 366.

111 Bangladesh v. India, *supra* note 109, paras. 417, 477, and Concurring and Dissenting Opinion of Dr. P.S. Rao, para. 18; Barbados v. Trinidad and Tobago, Award, case no. 2004–02, 11 April 2006, Permanent Court of Arbitration [PCA], paras. 86, 117, 164–165, 371–372, 382. For discussion on "relevant circumstances", see Chapter 2, Section 2.

112 For example, Cameroon v. Nigeria, *supra* note 109, paras. 291–292; Barbados v. Trinidad and Tobago, *supra* note 111, paras. 347–349; Maritime Delimitation in the Black Sea (Romania v. Ukraine), Judgment, ICJ Reports 2009, p. 61, paras. 112, 114; Bangladesh v. Myanmar, *supra* note 88, paras. 332, 480; Maritime Delimitation in the Caribbean Sea and the Pacific Ocean (Costa Rica v. Nicaragua) and Land Boundary in the Northern Part of Isla Portillos (Costa Rica v. Nicaragua), Judgment, ICJ Reports 2018, p. 139, paras. 117, 121, 144, 164. See also Cottier, *supra* note 98, p. 492–493; Andreas Zimmermann, *Business as Usual? The International Court of Justice's 2012 Judicial Practice: Facing New Procedural and Jurisdictional Questions*, 4(3) J. Int. Dispute Settlement 521, 531 (2013). See discussion on "relevant area" in Chapter 2, Section 2.1.2.1.

113 Bangladesh v. Myanmar, *supra* note 88, para. 494. For the "proportionality test", see Chapter 2, Section 2.1.2.1.2.

114 See e.g., Nicaragua v. Honduras, *supra* note 110, paras. 260, 262, 286, 313, 315, 317, 319–320; Romania v. Ukraine, *supra* note 112, paras. 177–178, 209, 219; Maritime Delimitation in the Indian Ocean (Somalia v. Kenya), Judgment, ICJ Reports 2021, p. 206, paras. 164, 183, 196. Although some cases rejected this practice, see Ghana v. Côte d'Ivoire (2017), *supra* note 88, paras. 323–324.

115 Tullio Treves, *Law and Science in the Jurisprudence of the International Tribunal for the Law of the Sea*, *in* Science, Technology, And New Challenges to Ocean Law 13, 15 (Harry N. Scheiber, James Kraska and Moon-Sang Kwon (eds.), 2015); Xuexia Liao, *Evaluation of Scientific Evidence by International Courts and Tribunals in the Continental Shelf Delimitation Cases*, 48(2) Ocean Dev. & Int. Law 136, 136, 138 (2017).

116 For other issues that require technical expertise, see Clive Schofield and Chris Carleton, *Technical Considerations in Law of the Sea Dispute Resolution*, *in* Oceans Management in the 21st Century: Institutional Frameworks and Responses 231 (A.G. Oude Elferink and D.R. Rothwell (eds.), 2004).

117 For example, UNCLOS, *supra* note 8, Article 289, Annex VI, Article 27, Annex VII, Article 6; ICJ Statute, *supra note* 98, Article 48; ICJ, Rules of Court (1978), Article 58; ITLOS/8, *supra* note 101, Article 73. See also Lucas Carlos Lima, *The Evidential Weight of Experts before the ICJ: Reflections on the Whaling in the Antarctic Case*, 6 J. Int. Dispute Settlement 621, 623–624 (2015).

118 For example, the Court determined that it would treat with caution evidence from secondary sources, Alleged Violations of Sovereign Rights and Maritime Spaces in the Caribbean Sea (Nicaragua v. Colombia), Judgment (21 April 2022), para. 64. See also Brendan Plant, *Expert Evidence and the Challenge of Procedural Reform in International Dispute Settlement*, 9 J. Int. Dispute Settlement 464 (2018).
119 Joan E. Donoghue, *Expert Scientific Evidence in a Broader Context*, 9 J. Int. Dispute Settlement 379, 381 (2018).
120 Makane Moise Mbengue, *International Courts and Tribunals as Fact-Finders: The Case of Scientific Fact-Finding in International Adjudication*, 34 Loy. L.A. Int. & Comp. L. Rev. 53, 56 (2011); Donoghue, *supra* note 119, p. 381–382.
121 Mbengue, *supra* note 120, p. 69; Jose E. Alvarez, *Are International Judges Afraid of Science?: A Comment on Mbengue*, 34 Loy. L.A. Int. & Comp. L. Rev. 81, 81, 85 (2011).
122 Alvarez, *supra* note 121, p. 91, 94; Giorgio Gaja, *Assessing Expert Evidence in the ICJ*, 15 Law Pract. Int. Courts Trib. 409, 409–410 (2015); Lima, *supra* note 117, p. 621; Schofield and Carleton, *supra* note 116.
123 Lima, *supra* note 117, p. 622; Torsten Stirner, The Procedural Law Governing Facts and Evidence in International Human Rights Proceedings 425 (2021); Donoghue, *supra* note 119, p. 382.
124 See Chapter 2, Sections 1.1 and 2. See also Treves, *supra* note 115, p. 18.
125 Liao, *supra* note 115, p. 141.
126 See further discussion in Chapter 5.
127 For example, Continental Shelf (Tunisia/Libyan Arab Jamahiriya), Judgment, ICJ Reports 1982, p. 18, paras. 60–61, 66; Liao, *supra* note 115, p. 141–142. See also Continental Shelf (Libyan Arab Jamahiriya/Malta), Judgment, ICJ reports 1985, p. 13, para. 41; Maritime Delimitation and Territorial Questions between Qatar and Bahrain, Merits, Judgment, ICJ Reports 2001, p. 40, para. 190. See also ITLOS position with respect to *uncontested* scientific materials, Bangladesh v. Myanmar, *supra* note 88, para. 411.
128 Libya v. Malta, *supra* note 127, para. 38.
129 For example, Qatar v. Bahrain (2001), *supra* note 127, paras. 192, 195. The Court was willing to consider the British Government's view from 1947. In the Peru/Chile case, the Court relied on a point the parties previously agreed upon rather than determine the starting point of the maritime boundary, see Maritime Dispute (Peru v. Chile), Judgment, ICJ Reports 2014, p. 3, paras. 174–176. However, in the Romania/Ukraine case, the Court referred to more contemporaneous maps than those Romania based its argument on. See Romania v. Ukraine, *supra* note 112, para. 64.
130 Nicaragua v. Colombia (2022), *supra* note 118, para. 64.
131 See for example topographical surveys in the *Ghana/Cote d'Ivoire* case, Egede and Apaalse, *supra* note 87, p. 70. See also Bangladesh v. India, *supra* note 109, paras. 169, 171.
132 For example, Maritime Delimitation in the Area between Greenland and Jan Mayen, Judgment, ICJ Reports 1993, p. 38 (The Jan Mayen case); Cameroon v. Nigeria, *supra* note 109; Nicaragua v. Honduras, *supra* note 110; Costa Rica v. Nicaragua (2018), *supra* note 112; Bangladesh v. India, *supra* note 109, p. 98–100 and para. 399. See also the latest ICJ decision in the Nicaragua and Colombia cases, Question of the Delimitation of the Continental Shelf between Nicaragua and Colombia beyond 200 Nautical Miles from the Nicaraguan Coast (Nicaragua v. Colombia), Judgement (13 July 2023). This was criticized in dissenting and separate opinions, see e.g., Separate Opinion of Judge Xue.
133 For example, by determining a fixed reference point in the coast for the purpose of delimitation, Tunisia v. Libya, *supra* note 127, paras. 123–124.
134 *Supra* note 124. See also Liao, *supra* note 115, p. 143.
135 Libya v. Malta, *supra* note 127, para. 39; Bangladesh v. Myanmar, *supra* note 88, para. 404; Bangladesh v. India, *supra* note 109, para. 407. See also Liao, *supra* note 115,

p. 142. However, in the *South China Sea* Arbitration, the Tribunal addressed scientific evidence with respect to environmental protection and to determine the status of certain islands and maritime features. The South China Sea Arbitration (2016), *supra* note 102, paras. 137, 306, 318, 320, 327, 373, 428, 577, 821, 917.

136 For example, in the 2012 *Nicaragua/Colombia* Case, the Court maintained it cannot consider delimitation beyond 200 nm since Nicaragua did not make a submission to the CLCS, Nicaragua v. Colombia (2012), *supra* note 104, paras. 127–130. See also Bangladesh v. India, *supra* note 109, at p. A-6-A-7; Liao, *supra* note 115, p. 137, 147–148.

137 See Chapter 2, Section 1.2.3.

138 Bangladesh v. Myanmar, *supra* note 88, paras. 412, 420, 425, 446. See also Treves, *supra* note 115, p. 24–25; Liao, *supra* note 115, p. 137, 144–146. In the *Somalia/Kenya* Case, both parties made a submission to the CLCS, which was not contested by the other party, see Somalia v. Kenya (2021), *supra* note 114, paras. 190, 194. In contrast, when the parties are conflicted on the evidence, tribunals seem to disregard the CLCS altogether. For example, the difference between the 2012 and the 2023 Nicaragua v. Colombia cases seems to be the parties' conflicting positions in the 2023 decision, where in 2012, they agreed. Nicaragua v. Colombia (2023), *supra* note 132, part V(B).

139 Chapter 2, Section 1.2.3.

140 Liao, *supra* note 115, p. 137, 145–146, 147–148.

141 See also Cottier, *supra* note 98, p. 201. In many cases, the parties themselves did not submit scientific evidence; rather, the claims for the boundary line were based on practice, historic rights, acquiescence, and other non-geological arguments. See e.g., Eritrea v. Yemen, *supra* note 109; Barbados v. Trinidad and Tobago, *supra* note 111; Guyana v. Suriname, Award, case no. 2004–04, 17 September 2007, Permanent Court of Arbitration [PCA]; Ghana v. Côte d'Ivoire (2017), *supra* note 88.

142 The annex addresses only maritime disputes relating to the continental shelf, mostly boundary delimitation disputes but also other disputes concerning the continental shelf. Other types of maritime disputes are not included, as they are outside the scope of the book.

143 Tunisia v. Libya, *supra* note 127, para. 2

144 Delimitation of the Maritime Boundary in the Gulf of Maine Area, Judgment, ICJ reports 1984, p. 246, para. 1

145 Libya v. Malta, *supra* note 127, para. 1

146 Declarations recognizing as compulsory the jurisdiction of the International Court of Justice under Article 36, paragraph 2, *supra* note 93.

147 Arbitral Award of 31 July 1989, Judgment, ICJ Reports 1991, p. 53, paras. 1, 22

148 Art. 36(2) declarations, *supra* note 146

149 Land, Island and Maritime Frontier Dispute (El Salvador/Honduras: Nicaragua intervening), Judgment, ICJ Reports 1992, para. 1

150 Declarations upon signing or ratifying UNCLOS, UNTC website, *supra* note 86.

151 Ibid.; Declarations made upon signature, ratification, accession, succession, or anytime thereafter, DOALOS website, available at www.un.org/depts/los/convention_agreements/convention_declarations.htm

152 Maritime Delimitation in the Area between Greenland and Jan Mayen (Denmark v. Norway), Application Instituting Proceedings, ICJ 1988. See also Jonathan I. Charney, *Progress in International Maritime Boundary Delimitation Law*, 88(2) Am. J. Int. Law 227, 254 (1994)

153 Art. 36(2) declarations, *supra* note 146

154 Maritime Delimitation between Guinea-Bissau and Senegal (Guinea-Bissau v. Senegal), Application instituting proceedings, ICJ 1991

155 Declarations upon signing or ratifying UNCLOS, *supra* note 150

156 Eritrea v. Yemen, *supra* note 109

157 Art. 36(2) declarations, *supra* note 146

158 Declarations upon signing or ratifying UNCLOS, *supra* note 150
159 Art. 36(2) declarations, *supra* note 146
160 Maritime Delimitation and Territorial Questions between Qatar and Bahrain, Application instituting proceedings, ICJ 1991, para. 40; Maritime Delimitation and Territorial Questions between Qatar and Bahrain, Jurisdiction and Admissibility, Judgment, ICJ Reports 1994, p. 112, para. 44
161 Qatar v. Bahrain (2001), *supra* note 127, para. 167. Qatar ratified UNCLOS in 2002, see Declarations upon signing or ratifying UNCLOS, *supra* note 150
162 Qatar v. Bahrain, Jurisdiction and Admissibility, *supra* note 160, Dissenting Opinion of Judge Oda, para. 36; Maritime Delimitation and Territorial Questions between Qatar and Bahrain, Jurisdiction and Admissibility, Judgment, ICJ Reports 1995, p. 6, Dissenting Opinion of Judge Valticos, p. 74
163 Declarations upon signing or ratifying UNCLOS, *supra* note 150
164 UNCLOS, *supra* note 8, Article 287(3)
165 Cameroon v. Nigeria, *supra* note 109, paras. 1, 239
166 Art. 36(2) declarations, *supra* note 146
167 Nigeria's 1965 declaration recognizing as compulsory the jurisdiction of the International Court of Justice, in conformity with Article 36, paragraph 2, of the Statute of the International Court of Justice, 544 UNTS 113, available at https://treaties.un.org/doc/Publication/UNTS/Volume%20544/v544.pdf
168 Land and Maritime Boundary between Cameroon and Nigeria, Preliminary Objections, Judgment, ICJ Reports 1998, p. 275
169 Ibid., para. 108
170 Declarations upon signing or ratifying UNCLOS, *supra* note 150
171 Barbados v. Trinidad and Tobago, case no. 2004–02, Statement of Claim (Barbados), 16 February 2004, Permanent Court of Arbitration [PCA]; Barbados v. Trinidad and Tobago, *supra* note 111, paras. 1–3; UNCLOS, *supra* note 8, Article 287(3)
172 Art. 36(2) declarations, *supra* note 146
173 Barbados v. Trinidad and Tobago, *supra* note 111, para. 200
174 Declarations upon signing or ratifying UNCLOS, *supra* note 150
175 Territorial and Maritime Dispute between Nicaragua and Honduras in the Caribbean Sea (Nicaragua v. Honduras), Application instituting proceedings, ICJ 1999, para. 1
176 Declarations upon signing or ratifying UNCLOS, *supra* note 150
177 Art. 36(2) declarations, *supra* note 146
178 Declarations upon signing or ratifying UNCLOS, *supra* note 150
179 Guyana v. Suriname, *supra* note 141, paras. 1–4
180 Art. 36(2) declarations, *supra* note 146
181 Declarations upon signing or ratifying UNCLOS, *supra* note 150
182 UNCLOS, *supra* note 8, Article 298(1)(a)(i)
183 Maritime Delimitation in the Black Sea (Romania v. Ukraine), Application instituting proceedings, ICJ 2004, para. 4; Romania v. Ukraine, *supra* note 112, paras. 20–22
184 Dispute concerning delimitation of the maritime boundary between Bangladesh and Myanmar in the Bay of Bengal (Bangladesh/Myanmar), Notification submitted by Bangladesh, ITLOS, 13 December 2009
185 Declarations upon signing or ratifying UNCLOS, *supra* note 150; Bangladesh v. Myanmar, *supra* note 108, para. 8; Kamrul Hasan Arif, *Bangladesh-Myanmar Maritime Boundary Delimitation in the Bay of Bengal: An Analysis on the Development of International Law*, 6 Kathmandu Sch. L. Rev. 53, 56 (2018)
186 Bangladesh v. Myanmar, *supra* note 88, paras. 10, 44, 47
187 Art. 36(2) declarations, *supra* note 146
188 Declarations upon signing or ratifying UNCLOS, *supra* note 150
189 Territorial and Maritime Dispute (Nicaragua v. Colombia), Application instituting proceedings, ICJ 2001, para. 1; Nicaragua v. Colombia (2012), *supra* note 104, para. 1
190 Art. 36(2) declarations, *supra* note 146

191 Territorial and Maritime Dispute (Nicaragua v. Colombia), Preliminary Objections, Judgment, ICJ Reports 2007, p. 832, para. 120
192 Ibid., paras. 122, 132
193 Declarations upon signing or ratifying UNCLOS, *supra* note 150
194 Maritime Dispute (Peru v. Chile), Application instituting proceedings, ICJ 2008
195 Declarations upon signing or ratifying UNCLOS, *supra* note 150
196 Bangladesh v. India, *supra* note 109, paras. 1–3, 66
197 Art. 36(2) declarations, *supra* note 146
198 Declarations upon signing or ratifying UNCLOS, *supra* note 150
199 The Arctic Sunrise Arbitration (Netherlands v. Russia), case no. 2014–02, Award on Jurisdiction, 26 November 2014, Permanent Court of Arbitration [PCA], para. 7; UNCLOS, *supra* note 8, Article 287(3); Alex G. Oude Elferink, *The Arctic Sunrise Incident: A Multi-faceted Law of the Sea Case with a Human Rights Dimension*, 29 Int. J. Marine & Coastal L. 244, 276 (2014)
200 Oude Elferink (2014), ibid., p. 276; Otto Spijkers, *Non-participation in Arbitral Proceedings Under Annex VII United Nations Convention on the Law of the Sea: Arctic Sunrise and South China Sea Compared*, *in* Interpretations of the United Nations Convention on the Law of the Sea by International Courts and Tribunals 171, 173 (Angela- Del- Vecchio and Roberto- Virzo (eds.), Springer, 2019). See also Russia's declarations, UNTC website, *supra* note 86
201 Netherlands v. Russia (2014), *supra* note 199, para. 69. See also Oude Elferink (2014), *supra* note 199, p. 276–277
202 Netherlands v. Russia (2014), ibid., para. 78.
203 Oude Elferink (2014), *supra* note 199, p. 276–277
204 Art. 36(2) declarations, *supra* note 146
205 Mario Gervasi, *The Interpretation of the United Nations Convention on the Law of the Sea in the Chagos Marine Protected Area Arbitration: The Influence of the Land Sovereignty Dispute*, *in* Interpretations of the United Nations Convention on the Law of the Sea by International Courts and Tribunals 191, 194 (Angela Del Vecchio and Roberto Virzo (eds.), 2019)
206 Declarations upon signing or ratifying UNCLOS, *supra* note 150
207 UNCLOS, *supra* note 8, Article 287(3); Chagos Marine Protected Area Arbitration (Mauritius v. United Kingdom), Award, case no. 2011–03, 18 March 2015, Permanent Court of Arbitration [PCA] (Chagos MPA Arbitration), para. 14
208 Chagos MPA Arbitration, ibid., paras. 206, 216
209 Art. 36(2) declarations, *supra* note 146
210 Declarations upon signing or ratifying UNCLOS, *supra* note 150
211 Alleged Violations of Sovereign Rights and Maritime Spaces in the Caribbean Sea (Nicaragua v. Colombia), Application instituting proceedings, ICJ 2013, p. 4, para. 1; Alleged Violations of Sovereign Rights and Maritime Spaces in the Caribbean Sea (Nicaragua v. Colombia), Preliminary Objections, Judgment, ICJ Reports 2016, p. 3, para. 1
212 Art. 36(2) declarations, *supra* note 146
213 Nicaragua v. Colombia (2016), *supra* note 211, para. 20
214 *Ibid.*, paras. 33, 111
215 Declarations upon signing or ratifying UNCLOS, *supra* note 150
216 Question of the Delimitation of the Continental Shelf between Nicaragua and Colombia beyond 200 nautical miles from the Nicaraguan Coast (Nicaragua v. Colombia), Application instituting proceedings, ICJ 2013, para. 1; Question of the Delimitation of the Continental Shelf between Nicaragua and Colombia beyond 200 Nautical Miles from the Nicaraguan Coast (Nicaragua v. Colombia), Preliminary Objections, Judgment, ICJ Reports 2016, p. 100, para. 1
217 Art. 36(2) declarations, *supra* note 146
218 Declarations upon signing or ratifying UNCLOS, *supra* note 150

219 See also Timor Sea Conciliation (Timor-Leste v. Australia), case no. 2016–10, conciliation, decision on competence, 19 September 2016, Permanent Court of Arbitration [PCA], para. 2
220 See Permanent Court of Arbitration website, available at https://pca-cpa.org/en/cases/141/
221 Art. 36(2) declarations, *supra* note 146
222 Declarations upon signing or ratifying UNCLOS, *supra* note 150
223 The South China Sea Arbitration (The Republic of Philippines v. The People's Republic of China), The Philippines' Memorial – Volume I, case no. 2013–19, 30 March 2014, Permanent Court of Arbitration [PCA], para. 1.1. Although China argued that its agreement with ASEAN constitution an agreement on dispute-settlement that prevent recourse to UNCLOS dispute-settlement procedures, see Guilfoyle, *supra* note 75, p. 57
224 The South China Sea Arbitration (2015), *supra* note 102, paras. 4–6, 14, 133–139. See also 15 specific submissions at the end of the Philippines' Memorial of 30 March 2014, *supra* note 223, p. 271–272. See also Chinese Society of International Law, The South China Sea Arbitration Awards: A Critical Study 217 (2018).
225 UNCLOS, *supra* note 8, Article 298(1)(a)(i)
226 The South China Sea Arbitration (2015), *supra* note 102, at paras. 153, 155. See the Tribunal's discussion on "maritime entitlements" and its relation to sovereignty, ibid., para. 164–167
227 Ibid., paras. 192, 224
228 Guilfoyle, *supra* note 75, p. 58–59
229 See analysis on "overlapping entitlements" and interpretation of "military activities", The South China Sea Arbitration (2015), *supra* note 102, paras. 393, 396.
230 Art. 36(2) declarations, *supra* note 146
231 Declarations upon signing or ratifying UNCLOS, *supra* note 150
232 Art. 36(2) declarations, *supra* note 146
233 Arbitration Between the Republic of Croatia and the Republic of Slovenia, PCA website, available at https://pca-cpa.org/en/cases/3/
234 Declarations upon signing or ratifying UNCLOS, *supra* note 150
235 Declarations upon signing or ratifying UNCLOS, available at https://treaties.un.org/doc/Publication/CN/2009/CN.890.2009-Eng.pdf
236 Declarations upon signing or ratifying UNCLOS, available at https://treaties.un.org/doc/Publication/CN/2014/CN.568.2014-Eng.pdf; Ghana v. Côte d'Ivoire (2017), *supra* note 88, para. 80
237 Declarations upon signing or ratifying UNCLOS, *supra* note 150. See also Egede and Apaalse, *supra* note 87, p. 62
238 UNCLOS, *supra* note 8, Article 287(3)
239 Consultations by the President of the Tribunal with representatives of Ghana and Cote d'Ivoire, under article 3 of annex VII to the United Nations Convention on the Law of the Sea, available at www.itlos.org/fileadmin/itlos/documents/cases/case_no.23_merits/pleadings/C23_Special_Agreement.pdf, at p. 7, para. 1; UNCLOS, *supra* note 8, Annex VI, Section 1, Article 15(2); Ghana v. Côte d'Ivoire (2017), *supra* note 88, para. 3
240 Art. 36(2) declarations, *supra* note 146
241 Declarations upon signing or ratifying UNCLOS, *supra* note 150
242 UNCLOS, *supra* note 8, Article 287(3)
243 Maritime Delimitation in the Caribbean Sea and the Pacific Ocean (Costa Rica v. Nicaragua (2014), *supra* note 113, paras. 4–5; Costa Rica v. Nicaragua (2018), *supra* note 112, para. 2
244 Maritime Delimitation in the Caribbean Sea and the Pacific Ocean (Costa Rica v. Nicaragua), Memorial of Costa Rica, ICJ 2015, para. 1.7
245 Declarations upon signing or ratifying UNCLOS, *supra* note 150
246 UNCLOS, *supra* note 8, Article 287(3)

247 Guatemala's Territorial, Insular and Maritime Claim (Guatemala/Belize), Special Agreement, ICJ 2008
248 Guatemala's Territorial, Insular and Maritime Claim (Guatemala/Belize), Protocol to the Special Agreement, ICJ 2015
249 Declarations upon signing or ratifying UNCLOS, *supra* note 150
250 UNCLOS, *supra* note 8, Article 298(1)(a)(i); Sea of Azov case, *supra* note 92, para. 109
251 UNCLOS, *supra* note 8, Article 288(1); Sea of Azov case, ibid., paras. 43, 156–157, 166, 178, 197, 377, 379–383
252 Sea of Azov case, ibid., paras. 382–383, 388–389
253 Valentin J. Schatz and Dmytro Koval, *Russia's Annexation of Crimea and the Passage of Ships Through Kerch Strait: A Law of the Sea Perspective*, 50 Ocean Dev. & Int. Law 275, 278–279 (2019)
254 UNCLOS, *supra* note 8, Article 282
255 Declarations upon signing or ratifying UNCLOS, *supra* note 150
256 UNCLOS, *supra* note 8, Article 298(1)(a)(i)
257 Land and Maritime Delimitation and Sovereignty over Islands (Gabon/Equatorial Guinea), Special Agreement, ICJ 2016
258 Declarations upon signing or ratifying UNCLOS, *supra* note 150
259 UNCLOS, *supra* note 8, Articles 287(3) and 287(5); Natalie Klein, Dispute Settlement in the UN Convention on the Law of the Sea 52–53, 57 (2005); Ted L. McDorman, *Global Ocean Governance and International Adjudicative Dispute Resolution*, 43 Ocean Coast. Manag. 255, 259 (2000); Alexander Proelss, *The Contribution of the ITLOS to Strengthening the Regime for the Protection of the Marine Environment*, *in* Interpretations of the United Nations Convention on the Law of the Sea by International Courts and Tribunals 93, 94 (Angela Del Vecchio and Roberto Virzo (eds.), 2019). See also Kenya's argument, Chan, *supra* note 96, p. 198
260 Chan, ibid., p. 195
261 Maritime Delimitation in the Indian Ocean (Somalia v. Kenya), Preliminary Objections, Judgment, ICJ Reports 2017, p. 3, para. 119; Art. 36(2) declarations, *supra* note 146
262 Somalia v. Kenya (2017), ibid., para. 126; Chan, *supra* note 96, p. 198
263 Somalia v. Kenya (2017), ibid., para. 123
264 Ibid., paras. 129–133; Chan, *supra* note 96, p. 198
265 Declarations upon signing or ratifying UNCLOS, *supra* note 150
266 UNCLOS, *supra* note 8, Article 287(3)
267 Mauritius v. Maldives, *supra* note 108, para. 1
268 Special Agreement and Notification of 24 September 2019, ITLOS website, available at www.itlos.org/fileadmin/itlos/documents/cases/28/C28_Special_Agreement.pdf; UNCLOS, *supra* note 8, Annex VI, Section 1, Article 15(2); Mauritius v. Maldives, *supra* note 108, para. 2
269 Mauritius v. Maldives, *supra* note 108, para. 79
270 Ibid., paras. 101–102, 105
271 Ibid., paras. 171, 174, 190, 202

5 Conclusion

The book analyzes the international legal rules applying to the continental shelf from the perspective of IR theories, primarily global governance theory. Governance theory and IL interact and overlap. Essentially, governance systems include and employ IL rules and institutions to regulate global society. Consequently, each field of IL can be analyzed as a particular governance framework with its own set of explicit and implicit rules, norms, roles, actors, and institutions.

For many legal scholars, the prominent question is whether IL matters. From the perspective of governance theory, it does matter, and the real question is *how* it matters – that is, how it influences rules and actors. The book offers an innovative and broader IR approach that sheds new light on this well-researched legal field. This perspective highlights and explains largely hidden legal-social trends and developments concerning the continental shelf. The book demonstrates how IL matters and, particularly, the mechanisms underlying its operation. This understanding of the legal-social reality may generate proposals for better legal mechanisms to cope with new challenges arising in this significant sphere.

Governance frameworks are networks of formal and informal bundles of rules, norms, actors, institutions, and practices that facilitate management of common affairs and problems requiring collective action. This study posits that analysis of international legal regimes should focus not only on formal legal elements but also on informal elements such as political considerations and processes and non-state actors. The governance framework of the continental shelf includes formal legal rules and informal elements, such as soft norms, political interest-groups, technology, individuals, commercial companies, and exogenous institutions and treaties.

Each chapter examined the influence of informal elements on both the construction of the formal rules and the development of the legal regime in practice. In addition, each chapter demonstrated the differences between the formal legal regime and the governance framework. As discussed throughout the book, governance perspective can be broader or narrower than the formal legal regime. In each case study, the book uncovers the ways in which the governance framework broadens the legal regime by adding informal norms, rules, and institutions or by adding roles to formal actors beyond what is prescribed in UNCLOS. This process is done by considering actors, norms, interests, roles, and institutions outside the narrow legal regime of the continental shelf. In some cases, the governance framework

DOI: 10.4324/9781003479772-6

narrows the legal regime by downplaying or circumventing formal rules that are not implemented in practice.

The governance perspective not only addresses how the governance framework is broader or narrower than the formal legal regime but also exposes the impact of informal elements within the governance framework – that is, how these elements affected actors' behavior. For example, political considerations and material interests have not only shaped the legal regime but have also affected the implementation of formal rules.

1. Patterns of the continental shelf's governance framework

The analysis in the previous chapters leads to several broader conclusions and possible explanations with respect to the development of the continental shelf's governance framework and its dynamics.

1.1 Contribution of IR theories to the continental shelf's governance framework

The analysis does not single out a particular IR approach as the salient influence in shaping the continental shelf's governance framework. Instead, different elements of the governance framework reflect different IR approaches. Nonetheless, one can argue that the governance framework of the continental shelf reflects mostly realism and institutionalism.

For example, the final text of UNCLOS Article 76 (and specifically, the parts that address the continental shelf beyond 200 nm) reflects the realist approach, which regards actors' power relations and maximization of interests as key factors. The same can be argued for the final formula of UNCLOS Part XV, which allows limitations and exceptions to compulsory dispute-settlement. The exclusion of boundary delimitation disputes from compulsory dispute-settlement and the employment of diplomatic dispute-settlement generally favor powerful broad-margin coastal States, allowing them to maximize their material interests rather than submitting to judicial mechanisms that tend to mitigate power asymmetries.

In contrast, the fact that there are compulsory procedures reflects the institutional approach, which recognizes the benefits of international institutions. International judicial dispute-settlement allows coastal States – and especially developing and geographically disadvantaged states – to safeguard their interests at lower costs. In addition, the decisions of international tribunals on the "relevant circumstances" in maritime delimitation reflect mostly the institutional approach and some elements of the constructivist stream, such as the principle of distributive justice.[1] It seems that international judicial bodies tend to safeguard the interests of developing or geographically disadvantaged states more than those of strong developed states, thus rejecting the realist approach.

However, the *practice* concerning dispute-settlement reflects mostly the realist approach. As discussed, most maritime disputes are not submitted to international adjudication, and states prefer to resolve disputes through diplomatic means. The scarce employment of the UNCLOS Part XV mechanism may be explained by the fact that broad-margin states generally opt for diplomatic, bilateral dispute-settlement, in addition to the fact that UNCLOS dispute-settlement mechanisms seem to favor developing and geographically disadvantaged states.

On the one hand, bilateral agreements concerning resource utilization reflect the institutional approach since they prevent unilateral action, increase transparency and stability, and provide clear rules around which the parties' expectations converge, thus promoting cooperation. On the other hand, these agreements highlight resource-related considerations that tend to reflect realism and emphasize the significance of raw material interests.

1.2 Interaction of judicial decisions and state practice

As discussed extensively, the continental shelf's governance framework pulls the legal regime in different directions by adding informal elements while also downplaying or practically erasing certain formal rules. The main informal elements of the continental shelf's governance framework are judicial decisions and state practice. These elements sometimes exhibit similar patterns and sometimes exhibit conflicting or inconsistent patterns. This affects the operation of the governance framework, pulling the legal regime in different directions.

For example, judicial decisions and state practice have both downplayed the formal definition of the continental shelf as a scientific-physical component and together contributed to the primacy of the distance criterion. In addition, both elements have helped to boost the significance of the CLCS as a semi-judicial body, whose importance goes much beyond its defined role in the formal legal regime. Similarly, both informal elements contributed to the formation and broad competences of SPLOS, beyond what UNCLOS prescribes.

However, state conduct and judicial decisions sometimes conflict, establishing different trends and practices within the governance framework of the continental shelf. For example, judicial decisions and state practice diverge with respect to safety zones around installations in the continental shelf. While the formal legal regime does not explicitly require coastal States to proclaim safety zones, international tribunals developed an informal requirement to proclaim such zones. Thus, they broadened the governance framework by adding informal norms that are not included in the legal regime. In contrast, state practice seems to downplay this requirement; coastal States do not always proclaim safety zones, or they establish some other type of "enforcement zones" around installations. It is noteworthy that the latter practice seems to broaden the governance framework even beyond what judicial decisions have established.

Judicial decisions and state practice also diverge on the scope of coastal States' sovereign rights in the context of delimitation. For example, tribunals have interpreted Article 83(3) in a way that narrows coastal States' sovereign rights, requiring them to limit unilateral seabed activities during the process of delimitation. In contrast, state practice not only indicates that such activities are permitted but has also created additional types of arrangements and informal obligations vis-à-vis other coastal States that go beyond both the jurisprudence and the formal legal regime. In addition, while tribunals generally disregard the role of resource-related considerations in maritime delimitation, state practice indicates that coastal States' sovereign rights and economic interests have greater significance.

In some cases, these informal elements do not necessarily conflict but also not necessarily coincide. The absence of one element essentially opens space for the other to gain significance beyond the legal regime. For example, tribunals are expected to apply *existing* rules, rather than create new legal rules. Nonetheless, the structure of delimitation, the absence of state practice (i.e., delimitation agreements), and the conflation of evolving delimitation methodology and new legal rules increased the significance of tribunals, which essentially exercised law-making functions regarding maritime delimitation. As discussed, this is contrary to the formal rules that provide that judicial decisions are only a subsidiary mean of interpretation of the formal legal rules. Arguably, there is a role reversal between states and tribunals; the latter essentially established the customary law on maritime delimitation, which formally is the role of states.[2]

1.3 Interaction of law and science, and tribunals' lack of scientific expertise

An analysis of the continental shelf's governance framework can help explain the conduct of judicial bodies. For example, their lack of scientific expertise and their need to promote the predictability, legitimacy, and stability of judicial maritime boundaries can shed light on the development of the governance framework.

The interaction of law and science is critical for the development of the broader governance framework of the continental shelf, which regulates physical and technical issues. As discussed, the concept of the continental shelf is physical-scientific in origin: Article 76 includes scientific terms and formulas in its definition of the continental shelf. In addition, the CLCS is composed of scientific experts. In contrast, international adjudicators often do not possess scientific expertise in this field. Thus, international tribunals developed an informal delimitation method that is more convenient to evaluate and relies less on scientific evidence.

Generally, international tribunals have transformed scientific questions into legal questions, often practically ignoring scientific data, or they have relied on other institutions (deference). For example, in its latest decision, the ICJ deliberately change a question of delimitation with question of entitlement: Instead of determining whether the parties have entitlement to a continental shelf, and whether they overlap, the Court considered a different question – whether a state's entitlement to a continental shelf beyond 200 nm may extend within 200 nm from the baselines of another state.[3] Instead of considering a scientific question (the parties' entitlement to a continental shelf and an overlap), the Court circumvented the question by turning the issue into a legal question (existence of rules allowing overlap).[4]

Adjudicators lack of scientific expertise can also explain the primacy of geographical circumstances in delimitation. For example, analyzing data to establish "natural prolongation" would be difficult. Furthermore, adjudicators are also at a disadvantage in choosing between conflicting but equally plausible scientific evidence. Thus, tribunals developed a method that relied on elements such as the coast for delimitation, which are more convenient and easier to measure. This process influenced the decline in the role of scientific evidence in maritime delimitation; judicial bodies do not address scientific questions when there is conflicting evidence.

This lack of expertise also explains tribunals' relations with the CLCS concerning delimitation beyond 200 nm. Although judicial bodies have asserted parallel jurisdiction, the CLCS has primary jurisdiction in cases of scientific uncertainty or information deficit concerning the existence of an extended continental shelf, and judicial bodies exercise their functions beyond 200 nm only in appropriate circumstances (for example, when the CLCS has not exercised its functions, leaving the situation in deadlock). Thus, beyond 200 nm, judicial bodies can rely on the CLCS to mitigate their lack of scientific expertise.[5]

In contrast, tribunals ostensibly have no such expert institution to rely on when adjudicating cases pertaining to the zone within 200 nm. In such cases, they often employ geographic principles that are easier to operationalize and are perceived as objective. For example, equidistance and coast length are easily measured or calculated to avoid the inherent disadvantage that stems from a lack of scientific expertise.

Despite the analysis earlier, science is crucial for the delimitation of the continental shelf. Geological and environmental changes affect the shape of coastlines and boundary lines, which may have implications for the stability of maritime boundary delimitation agreements. For example, climate changes can alter the coasts and baselines (e.g., following sea level rise). Shifting coastlines would also make it difficult to determine the "relevant area" for delimitation. However, UNCLOS did not envision an environmental effect on maritime boundaries and is silent on the issue.[6]

Since the legal regime, states, and tribunals do not (or rather cannot) address this issue, arguably, this is where the governance framework offers an alternative course of action. This might explain the creation of informal norms and procedures concerning maritime delimitation while also downplaying formal principles relating to the continental shelf. For example, employing the distance criterion and measuring straight lines from the coast circumvents the problems posed by environmental changes.[7]

1.4 Predictability and stability in judicial maritime dispute-settlement

Another possible explanation for tribunals' contribution to the gap between the legal regime and the continental shelf's governance framework is their desire to promote consistency, predictability, and stability of judicial boundaries. Despite the physical particularity of each dispute, tribunals have applied general principles and criteria, such as geographical factors, to boost the legitimacy of the method and to ensure the stability of judicially established boundaries.[8]

The goal of promoting consistency, predictability, and stability correlates with the interaction of science and law. As discussed earlier, the tribunals' lack of scientific expertise has influenced the creation of informal rules and norms that circumvent formal scientific principles, transforming the continental shelf from a physical concept to a legal concept. Similarly, the goals of predictability and stability influenced the development of delimitation methods that emphasize geography, which are perceived as more objective, convenient, and practical.

Geographical factors are objective also in the sense that they circumvent "geological uncertainties" not addressed in UNCLOS, for example, environmental changes due to man-made or natural factors, such as coastline shifts, disappearance of islands, and the melting of glaciers. Such uncertainties could lead to unstable boundaries and the demand to renegotiate the bargains achieved during UNCLOS III, thus affecting international law and international politics in general. Therefore, tribunals employ fixed factors to create permanent boundaries, which mitigate environmental changes and promote stability and predictability.[9]

However, despite the preference of international tribunals for objective principles, the desire to enhance the stability and legitimacy in maritime delimitation has also engendered flexible methods, although in a more implicit manner. For example, while tribunals have explicitly rejected flexible elements such as distributive justice, in practice, the "non-cut-off" principle essentially reflects such considerations.[10] These considerations reflect the tribunals' implicit perception that claiming the full extent of the maritime zones allocated to coastal States in UNCLOS may be legal but undesirable. Thus, tribunals tend to delimit maritime boundaries in a way that allocates all parties at least some access to the disputed area, regardless of the actual physical situation.[11] Tribunals employ these principles to avoid unjust outcomes, thus promoting the stability and legitimacy of the boundaries and judicial decisions. This contributed to the gap between the formal legal regime and the broader governance framework concerning the definition of the breadth of the continental shelf.

1.5 The concept of maritime delimitation

The conduct of international tribunals and states can also be explained, in part, by their perception of what is maritime delimitation. The definition and operation of maritime boundary delimitation have also shaped the governance framework in this subject-field. As discussed earlier, the attempt by international tribunals to achieve stability, predictability, and legitimacy for judicially established maritime boundaries promoted the primacy of geographical principles, contrary to the legal regime, which grants primacy to geological principles.

This process also led to the conflation of entitlement to the continental shelf and its breadth and the delimitation of overlapping continental shelves.[12] The concept of delimitation essentially shaped the definition of the continental shelf, both in terms of entitlement and breadth. International tribunals essentially ignored the question of entitlement to the continental shelf in the process of delimitation; this affected the rules of delimitation and contributed to the gap between the continental shelf's legal regime and its governance framework.

The jurisprudence has essentially linked three distinct (though related) questions: entitlement to the continental shelf, the extent of entitlement, and delimitation of overlapping areas.[13] Entitlement to the continental shelf is *ipso facto* and *ab initio* based on geology and does not depend on any further procedural action by the coastal state. In contrast, determining the outer limit does require procedural (albeit a unilateral) action by coastal States. In addition, while entitlement to the continental shelf does not require knowledge of its precise outer limit, delimitation does require such knowledge to determine whether (and to what extent) the shelf overlaps with another state's shelf.

However, judicial bodies tend to conflate these three distinct issues. For example, the distance criterion became both a measure for the breadth of the continental shelf and a legal basis for entitlement to it. In addition, the process of delimitation defined the breadth of the continental shelf. This conflation may stem from uncertainty concerning what the delimitation process entails; it seems that judicial bodies differ on whether delimitation means allocation of entitlements or division of geographical areas between equally entitled parties.

The legal regime does not require a judicial decision on entitlement, as it is an inherent right of coastal States. There is no rule that confers tribunals the competence to identify, let alone grant, entitlement. However, the structure of maritime dispute-settlement influenced the conflation in the role of international tribunals in maritime delimitation. Judicial bodies had to define and justify their competences in this context, especially since the legal rule gives primacy to bilateral agreements in settling disputes. For example, the ICJ maintained that any delimitation dispute entails some determination of entitlement to the areas to be delimited.[14]

This conflation of the three concepts affected the rules concerning both entitlement to the continental shelf and boundary delimitation. For example, as discussed earlier, the concept of "single continental shelf" circumvents the question of entitlement to the continental shelf beyond 200 nm.[15] This conflation also affected the conflict between geology and geography and contributed to the primacy of the distance criterion – not only regarding the breadth of the continental shelf but eventually also for entitlement to it. Since in practice, delimitation is perceived to determine the parties' entitlements, "distance" also became the main element in defining the continental shelf and thus the basis for entitlement.[16]

Employing the distance principle in delimitation also emphasizes the role of the coastline as the starting point for delimitation and promotes the idea that the delimitation process should balance the effects of the parties' coasts in terms of maritime entitlements.[17] This correlates with the employment of the distance principle to define the continental shelf and its breadth and the detachment of the continental shelf from its geological origins. In contrast, through judicial delimitation, natural prolongation has shifted from the basis for entitlement to one of the relevant circumstances in delimitation, which pertains to the breadth of the continental shelf.[18] This demonstrates that judicial bodies do not distinct clearly between "entitlement" and "delimitation", which influenced the gap between the legal regime of the continental shelf and the governance framework.

1.6 Effectiveness of the continental shelf's governance framework

An analysis of governance frameworks can provide a better understanding of the legal-social reality concerning the law of the sea and can help to predict developments in this field based on broader considerations than those of the legal regime. A governance analysis not only examines formal and informal elements within the framework but also the effectiveness of the framework – that is, how these elements influence and change actors' behavior. An effective governance framework facilitates cooperation despite contradictory short-term interests and obstacles imposed by the anarchic nature of the international system.[19]

The analysis in this book shows that the governance framework of the continental shelf is an effective since it facilitates cooperation despite the disparate interests of individual States. For example, there is a high level of cooperation and dialogue with the CLCS and with other states in the context of the Commission, despite the outer limit of the continental shelf is a matter for states to determine individually in accordance with UNCLOS Article 76.

In addition, arguably, the governance framework has managed to promote bilateral agreements and judicial dispute-settlement concerning delimitation and resource utilization, where the mechanism of the Convention alone may have led to opposite behavior. It seems that at least some states do not view UNCLOS Part XV as promoting their interests. Consequently, they employ their geo-political resources to settle their disputes outside UNCLOS. In this way, many judicial disputes circumvent the mechanism provided in the Convention. However, this very conduct eventually encourages cooperation between states and with international tribunals.

Governance frameworks also facilitate effective multilateral cooperation by creating unified rules, standards of behavior, and harmonization through institutional deference, which promotes compliance and lowers transaction costs. As discussed throughout the book, many provisions in UNCLOS are vague. In interpreting these provisions, international tribunals sometimes create informal rules and principles that promote clear and more coherent standards that establish mutual expectations about others' behavior and promote actors' credibility. These concrete criteria also promote the predictability and legitimacy of international tribunals.

In addition, the governance framework of the continental shelf, by employing broader considerations and elements than the legal regime, influences actors' behavior without enforcement or coercion. For example, the transformation of the continental shelf from a scientific-physical element to a legal concept was changed through practice and without any coercive action. Similarly, as discussed in the book, the governance framework circumvented or downplayed formal obligations without coercion but rather from uncoordinated and spontaneous state practice, for example, by transferring enforcement to the domestic level or to private international law.

Governance frameworks also produce unintended or unforeseen effects. These side effects can take the form of unforeseen distributive consequences. For example, in the governance framework of the continental shelf, international tribunals implicitly accepted distributive justice considerations in maritime delimitation. Another side effect is a change of the nature and operation of the institutional arrangement itself. For example, the interaction between SPLOS and the CLCS changed the legal regime and its institutions. These side effects have significant impact and often prompt other changes that might affect future institutional design and performance assessments.

It is noteworthy that most of the changes and effects described throughout the book are changes *within* the governance system, i.e., changes of the rules and decision-making procedures that comprise the system's operational or implementation mechanisms. However, the change in the concept of the continental shelf itself (from a physical component to a legal concept) is a change *of* the governance system – that is, a change in the system's defining characteristics.[20] This indicates that the continental shelf's governance framework is mostly resilient in the face of challenges and external pressures.

Considering the previous discussion, one can argue that the governance framework of the continental shelf is effective in the sense that it influences actors' behavior, mainly informal actors, and promotes changes in the nature and operation of the legal regime. This process has transformed the legal regime into a broader framework that might better manage common resources, problems, and conflicts based on shared values. Essentially, the governance framework of the continental shelf can be viewed as a public good that enhances the welfare of all members.

2. UNCLOS – a "constitution for the oceans"?

The governance analysis of the continental shelf's legal regime not only provides unique perspective in this specific issue but also may provide broader understanding of the law of the sea in general. Governance perspective provides new insights into the significance and operation of UNCLOS itself.

UNCLOS is considered "the constitution for the oceans",[21] serving as the main legal framework for establishing the rights and jurisdictions of coastal States in their maritime zones. Although UNCLOS has yet to gain the universal participation of all states, it has a significant effect on international law, and specifically the law of the sea, creating a universal legal framework for the regulation of the oceans and marine resources.[22]

While application of domestic constitutional law may pose some problems, some comparisons can be drawn in this context, such as the comprehensiveness and legitimacy of UNCLOS and the wide participation within its frameworks.[23] Other relevant features are the inclusion of rules governing law-making, judicial and executive functions, and dispute-settlement.[24] Some scholars argue that one of the prominent features borrowed from constitutional law is the Convention's ability to provide channels for change within the framework; thus, it can be considered a "living treaty" while still safeguarding itself from being easily changed.[25] For example, UNCLOS includes a complicated process of amendments, which have not been implemented thus far but have no provisions for termination. This makes UNCLOS more entrenched, which fits within the framework of constitutional law.[26] Thus, although not free from criticism and with some key features missing, UNCLOS is generally accepted as the "constitution for the oceans".[27]

Looking from a purely legalistic perspective, the perception concerning UNCLOS's (almost) constitutional status is correct. However, from a governance perspective, this analysis misses underlined interaction, practice, roles, and principles, which may change the perception concerning the status of the Convention. Governance framework analysis reveals that in practice, the main elements that ostensibly grant UNCLOS its status as a "superior" legal source are sometimes downplayed, circumvented, or ignored altogether and that the governing practices, rules, and principles were established outside the formal legal regime.

With respect to governance of law-making, while UNCLOS contains some rules that govern law-making, many rules were established informally and outside the formal legal regime. For example, international tribunals exercise informal law-making powers in the process of delimitation. This is not only outside the competence of international tribunals, but many of these informal norms conflicted with the formal legal regime. In addition, state practice downplays formal rules in UNCLOS while also creating new informal rules and practices that broaden their rights and are inconsistent with the Convention. In this sense, UNCLOS does not govern rulemaking within its frameworks.

Constitutions also govern judicial and executive functions and division of labor of the system's institutions. However, governance analysis shows that while UNCLOS establish new bodies, it does not define or govern their mandate and function. For example, the CLCS has broader mandate than conceived in the formal legal regime. In addition, SPLOS's powers have been significantly expanded through its own practices and its interaction with ITLOS, CLCS, and member states.

Another example as to why UNCLOS arguably does not enjoy constitutional status is the feature of dispute-settlement. Ostensibly, the Convention includes a very elaborated dispute-settlement mechanism. However, its implementation poses some challenges to the perception of UNCLOS. The governance framework downplays UNCLOS's dispute-settlement mechanism and practically enhances the role of external mechanisms. First, most maritime disputes are still resolved diplomatically, rather than through international adjudication. Second, even those disputes that were submitted to international tribunals were not submitted under UNCLOS but rather under other frameworks. This aspect seems to weaken UNCLOS's "constitutional" status.

Lastly, a key feature of constitutions is their entrenchment, so they cannot be changed easily. Formally, UNCLOS has a complex procedure for amendments, which has not been employed yet, thus supporting its perception as a constitution. However, governance analysis reveals that UNCLOS has been changed in practice without going through the formal legal procedures. For example, the change of Article 76(1) and the definition of the continental shelf or the timeframe for making submissions to the CLCS, without going through the formal amendment procedures.

While UNCLOS may not be close to a constitutional status as commonly perceived, it, of course, has great significance in the development of the law of the sea and, specifically, the regime governing the continental shelf. It may not have established "the rules of the game" as such, but it created common ground for understandings and convergence of expectations that allow different actors to preserve their interests and develop new rules and principles while still "speaking the same language".

3. The governance framework of the continental shelf and the international system

Governance theory is embedded in IR discipline and, specifically, the institutional approach. Thus, it is important to analyze how the findings of the book with respect to the continental shelf correspond with other trends and elements of IR, mainly, the actors and structure of the international system, to provide an updated account of the “back end of international law”, meaning how the system develops and operates.

While this section mostly addresses substantive issues in current IR studies, it is worth mention at least one methodological aspect in which this research seems to correlate with current trends. In recent years, the scholarship moved from employing one theory to explain the international system to the understanding that IR theories overlap in some respects and thus able to coexist and correspond with one another (“theoretical dialogue”).[28] This book seems to correspond with this methodological trend, as while the governance theory is the main analytical tool, the book addresses and employs other corresponding IR theories. Thus, the book truly reflects an interdisciplinary theoretical dialogue.

Regarding substantive elements, arguably, the governance framework of the continental shelf reflects and corresponds with general theories concerning the structure and operation of the international system. For example, actors’ power relations as a key factor that influences behavior. As discussed throughout the book, the power relations between broad-margin coastal States and geographically disadvantaged states contributed to the formation of the continental shelf’s governance framework. For example, regarding the definition of the continental shelf and maritime judicial dispute-settlement.

However, the influence of power relations within the governance framework does not always yield the expected results: in some cases, it influenced behavior contrary to IR assumptions. For example, the final text of Article 76 reflects broad-margin states’ interests, both with respect to the outer limit of the continental shelf and the role of the CLCS. However, in practice, informal rules and practices essentially reflect the interests of geographically disadvantaged states. These states influenced the governance framework in a way that changed the outcome of UNCLOS’s negotiations. In these cases, the assumption that power enhances the value of certain actors does not correspond with the practice in this context.

The continental shelf’s governance framework also corresponds with the current analysis on the structure of the international system. While most of IR approaches view the state as the main actor, there are other non-state actors that influence behavior and shape outcomes.[29] The analysis in this book reflects this multi-actor structure; it does not only include states but also institutions, IGOs, NGOs, private people, companies, and so on. However, arguably, coastal States are still the main bearers of rights and obligations and influence both the formal legal regime and the governance framework of the continental shelf. As demonstrated, states are one of the two most influential actors in forming and maintaining the continental shelf’s governance framework.

Furthermore, the governance framework of the continental shelf reflects the shift from a unipolar world (where the United States were the sole superpower) or bipolar world (where the United States and Russia are the superpowers) to a multipolar world (where there are many powerful states).[30] Within the continental shelf’s governance framework, the United States is not a superpower (let alone the sole superpower) that influences behavior. As mentioned earlier, other groups are significant in shaping the continental shelf’s governance framework. However, the IR assumption concerning the dominance of western developed states[31] may not be true for the governance framework of the continental shelf. As discussed, geographically and economically disadvantaged states had significantly influenced and developed the governance framework of the continental shelf.[32]

Notes

1 In addition, tribunals' desire to increase their legitimacy reflects the constructivist approach. See discussion in Section 1.4 later.

2 See also Michael Byers and Andreas Østhagen, *Settling Maritime Boundaries: Why Some Countries Find It Easy, and Others Do Not, in* The Future of Ocean Governance and Capacity Development 162, 164 (The International Ocean Institute-Canada (ed.), 2018); Massimo Lando, Maritime Delimitation as a Judicial Process 290–291 (2019).

3 Question of the Delimitation of the Continental Shelf between Nicaragua and Colombia beyond 200 Nautical Miles from the Nicaraguan Coast (Nicaragua v. Colombia), Judgement (13 July 2023), para. 53

4 See also Question of the Delimitation of the Continental Shelf between Nicaragua and Colombia beyond 200 Nautical Miles from the Nicaraguan Coast (Nicaragua v. Colombia), Order of 4 October 2022. On the fact that the Court formulated the questions examined in the decision and not the parties see also Malcolm D. Evans and Nicholas A. Ioannides, A Commentary on the 2023 Nicaragua v Colombia case, EJIL:Talk! (4 August 2023)

5 The "single continental shelf" approach can be seen as mitigating this problem, circumventing questions of entitlement and the role of the CLCS in the delimitation process, by promoting geographical factors. See Jianjun Gao, *The Delimitation Method for the Continental Shelf Beyond 200 Nautical Miles: A Reflection on the Judicial and Arbitral Decisions*, 51(2) Ocean Dev. & Int. Law 116, 127 (2020). Article 83 does not distinct between the area up to and beyond 200 nm. Therefore, tribunals consistently decided that they have jurisdiction to delimit the whole continental shelf, essentially ignoring the difference between the areas. For example, Bay of Bengal Maritime Boundary Arbitration between Bangladesh and India, Award, case no. 2010–16, 07 July 2014, Permanent Court of Arbitration [PCA], para. 437; Dispute Concerning Delimitation of the Maritime Boundary between Ghana and Côte d'Ivoire in the Atlantic Ocean (Ghana/Côte d'Ivoire), Judgment, ITLOS Reports 2017, p. 4, paras. 490–491; Gao, ibid., p. 126–127; Edwin E. Egede and Lawrence Apaalse, *Dispute concerning Delimitation of the Maritime Boundary between Ghana and Cote D'Ivoire in the Atlantic Ocean – Lessons from Another Maritime Delimitation Case arising from the African Region*, 29 Ind. Int. & Comp. L. Rev. 55, 85 (2019). In practice, tribunals alternate between maintaining jurisdiction to delimit the continental shelf in its entirety and hesitancy to proceed with delimitation beyond 200 nm due to scientific uncertainty. See Signe Veierud Busch, *The Delimitation of the Continental Shelf beyond 200 nm: Procedural Issues, in* Maritime Boundary Delimitation: The Case Law: Is It Consistent and Predictable? 319, 342 (Alex G. Oude Elferink, Tore Henriksen and Signe Veierud Busch (eds.), 2018); Giovanny Vega-Barbosa, *The Admissibility of Outer Continental Shelf Delimitation Claims Before the ICJ Absent a Recommendation by the CLCS*, 49(2) Ocean Dev. & Int. Law 103, 107 (2018).

6 Massimo Lando, *Stability of Maritime Boundaries and the Challenge of Geographical Change: A Reply to Snj´olaug Árnad´ottir*, 35(2) Leiden J. Int. Law 379, 379–381, 388 (2022).

7 See also Ibid., p. 388.

8 Continental Shelf (Tunisia/Libyan Arab Jamahiriya), Judgment, ICJ Reports 1982, p. 18, paras. 70–71; Malcolm D. Evans, *Maritime Boundary Delimitation, in* The Oxford Handbook of the Law of the Sea 254, 276 (Donald R. Rothwell, Alex G. Oude Elferink,

Karen N. Scott and Tim Stephens (eds.), 2015); Alex G. Oude Elferink, Tore Henriksen and Signe Veierud Busch, *The Judiciary and the Law of Maritime Delimitation: Setting the Stage*, *in* Maritime Boundary Delimitation: The Case Law: Is It Consistent and Predictable? 1, 5 (Alex G. Oude Elferink, Tore Henriksen and Signe Veierud Busch (eds.), 2018). Although others argued that this practice achieved exactly the opposite of predictability. For example, Julia Lisztwan, *Stability of Maritime Boundary Agreements*, 37 Yale J. Int. L. 153, 165 (2012); Nuno Marques Antunes and Vasco Becker-Weinberg, *Entitlement to Maritime Zones and Their Delimitation: In the Doldrums of Uncertainty and Unpredictability*, *in* Maritime Boundary Delimitation: The Case Law: Is It Consistent and Predictable? 62, 77 (Alex G. Oude Elferink, Tore Henriksen and Signe Veierud Busch (eds.), 2018).

9 See e.g., Lisztwan, *supra* note 8, p. 154–155, 160, 170; Signe Veierud Busch, *Law of the Sea Responses to Sea-level Rise and Threatened Maritime Entitlements, Applying an Exception Rule to Manage an Exceptional Situation*, *in* The Law of the Sea and Climate Change 309 (Elise Johansen, Signe Veierud Busch and Ingvild Ulrikke Jakobsen (eds.), 2020).

10 See also the critique regarding the "relevant coasts" principle, which might not be entirely objective, Yurika Ishii, *Relevant Coasts and Relevant Area in the Maritime Delimitation of the EEZ and Continental Shelf*, 51(4) Ocean Dev. & Int. Law 307, 308 (2020).

11 It seems that tribunals take a "corrective" approach to reach an equitable solution, essentially trying to prevent excessive claims and curb states' behavior, rather than establishing a coherent criterion for delimitation. For example, in the *Jan Mayen* case, the Court argued that allowing one party its full claim while attributing the other the residual area left would not be equitable, although it maintained that delimitation does not have to involve an equal partition of the disputed area. Maritime Delimitation in the Area between Greenland and Jan Mayen, Judgment, ICJ Reports 1993, p. 38 (The Jan Mayen case), Dissenting Opinion of Judge Fischer, paras. 9–10, Separate Opinion of Judge Ajibola, p. 290–291, Separate Opinion of Judge Schwebel, p. 127, and Separate Opinion of Judge Oda, para. 46; Yunus Emre Acikgonul, *Reflections on the Principle of Non-Cut off: A Growing Concept in Maritime Boundary Delimitation Law*, 47(1) Ocean Dev. & Int. Law 52, 52–53, 65–66 (2016).

12 Some argued that the linkage between entitlement and delimitation is one way of achieving greater predictability in the applicable law. See Oude Elferink et al., *supra* note 8, p. 22.

13 This linkage perpetuates through "schematas" produced by judicial decisions, see Chapter 2, Section 1.1.5.

14 The Jan Mayen case, *supra* note 11, Separate Opinion of Judge Oda, para. 80 and Separate Opinion of Judge Shahabuddeen, p. 161.

15 *Supra* note 5.

16 See also the Jan Mayen case, *supra* note 11, Separate Opinion of Judge Oda, p. 99.

17 Some judges maintained that the previous delimitation method of "equidistance/special-circumstances" determines the extent of continental shelf *title* in a given situation, similar to "natural prolongation/outer edge of the continental margin" in UNCLOS. Others argued that delimitation is equal to the renouncement the full extent of the entitlement. See Continental Shelf (Libyan Arab Jamahiriya/Malta), Judgment, ICJ reports 1985, p. 13, Separate Opinion of Judge Mbaye, p. 95–96; The Jan Mayen case, *supra* note 11, Dissenting Opinion of Judge Fischer, at para. 9, and Separated Opinion of Judge Ajibola, at p. 291.

18 The Court maintained that where the continental margin does not extend up to 200 nm, ostensibly, "natural prolongation" is defined by distance from the shore; thus, "distance" became essential as a legal basis of the continental shelf, i.e., entitlement. In contrast, "natural prolongation" became one of several circumstances to determine an "equitable

solution", rather than the basis for entitlement. Libya v. Malta, *supra* note 17, para. 34 and Separate Opinion of Judge Mbaye, p. 94, 98, and Dissenting Opinion of Judge Oda, para. 61; Oude Elferink et al., *supra* note 8, p. 11.

19 See Chapter 1, Section 2.3.

20 See Chapter 1, Section 2.4.

21 For example, Natalie Klein, *Meaning, Scope, and Significance of Informal Lawmaking in the Law of the Sea, in* Unconventional Lawmaking in the Law of the Sea 3, 3 (Natalie Klein (ed.), 2022); Rozemarijn Roland Holst, Change in the Law of the Sea: Context, Mechanisms and Practice 4 (2022).

22 See e.g., James Harrison, Making the Law of the Sea, A Study in the Development of International Law 48, 51 (2011); Yoshifumi Tanaka, The International Law of the Sea 38 (3rd ed., 2019); Tanaka, *supra* note 11, p. 38; Robin R. Churchill, *The 1982 United Nation Convention on the Law of the Sea, in* The Oxford Handbook of the Law of the Sea 24, 27, 34–35 (Donald R. Rothwell, Alex G. Oude Elferink, Karen N. Scott and Tim Stephens (eds.), 2015).

23 Churchill, ibid., p. 45; Holst, *supra* note 21, p. 4–5.

24 Shirley V. Scott, *The LOS Convention as a Constitutional Regime for the Oceans, in* Stability and Change in the Law of the Sea 9, 15 (Alex G. Oude Elferink (ed.), 2005).

25 Holst, *supra* note 21, p. 5–6.

26 Scott, *supra* note 24, p. 19.

27 Ibid., p. 20. See also criticism in the comments on Scott's chapter within the book.

28 For example, Bhaso Ndzendze and Tshilidzi Marwala, Artificial Intelligence and International Relations Theories 26 (2023).

29 See also Patricia Owens, John Baylis, and Steve Smith, *Introduction: From International Politics to World Politics, in* Globalization of World Politics, An Introduction to International Relations 5, 6 (John Baylis, Steve Smith and Patricia Owens (eds.), 8th ed., 2020); Georg Sørensen, Jørgen Møller and Robert H. Jackson, Introduction to International Relations: Theories and Approaches 11–12 (2022).

30 Anthony McGrew, *Globalization and Global Politics, in* Globalization of World Politics, An Introduction to International Relations 19, 28 (John Baylis, Steve Smith and Patricia Owens (eds.), 8th ed., 2020).

31 See Sørensen et al., *supra* note 29, p. 20, 29.

32 This corresponds with the scholarship concerning "post-western" global order, see e.g., McGrew, *supra* note 30, p. 31.

Bibliography

International Treaties

1945 Charter of the United Nations, 24 October 1945, 1 UNTS XVI

1945 Statute of the International Court of Justice, San Francisco, 24 October 1945

1958 Geneva Convention on the Continental Shelf, 499 UNTS 311

1958 Geneva Convention on the High Seas, 450 UNTS 11

1969 Vienna Convention on the Law of Treaties, 1155 UNTS 331

1982 UN Convention on the Law of the Sea, 1833 UNTS 397

1992 Convention for the Protection of the Marine Environment of the North-East Atlantic, 2354 UNTS 67

2007 Nairobi International Convention on the removal of wrecks, 3283 UNTS 34

1994 Protocol for the Protection of the Mediterranean Sea against Pollution Resulting from Exploration and Exploitation of the Continental Shelf and the Seabed and its Subsoil, available at https://wedocs.unep.org/bitstream/handle/20.500.11822/2961/94ig4_4_protocol_eng.pdf

Bilateral Treaties

Agreement between Albania and Italy for the determination of the continental shelf (1992), DOALOS website, available at www.un.org/Depts/los/LEGISLATIONANDTREATIES/PDFFILES/TREATIES/ALB-ITA1992CS.pdf

Agreement between Qatar and Abu Dhabi (1969), DOALOS website, available at www.un.org/Depts/los/LEGISLATIONANDTREATIES/PDFFILES/TREATIES/QAT-ARE1969MB.PDF

Agreement between Sri Lanka and India (1974), DOALOS website, available at www.un.org/Depts/los/LEGISLATIONANDTREATIES/PDFFILES/TREATIES/LKA-IND1974BW.PDF

Agreement between the Government of the State of Israel and the Government of the Republic of Cyprus on the delimitation of the Exclusive Economic Zone, FAOLEX database, available at http://extwprlegs1.fao.org/docs/pdf/bi-158714.pdf

Agreement between the Republic of Cyprus and the Arab Republic of Egypt on the Delimitation of the Exclusive Economic Zone 17 February 2003, DOALOS website, available at www.un.org/Depts/los/LEGISLATIONANDTREATIES/PDFFILES/TREATIES/EGY-CYP2003EZ.pdf

Agreement between the Government of the Republic of Finland, the Government of the Republic of Estonia and the Government of the Kingdom of Sweden on the common maritime boundary point in the Baltic Sea (2001), DOALOS website, available at www.un.org/Depts/los/LEGISLATIONANDTREATIES/PDFFILES/TREATIES/FIN-EST-SWE2001BS.PDF

Agreement between the Solomon Islands and Papua New Guinea (2004), available at www.fao.org/faolex/results/details/fr/c/LEX-FAOC067017/
Agreement between Tuvalu and Kiribati concerning their maritime boundary, FAOLEX database, available at http://extwprlegs1.fao.org/docs/pdf/bi-158701.pdf
Agreement on Provisional Arrangements for the Delimitation of the Maritime Boundaries between the Republic of Tunisia and the People's Democratic Republic of Algeria (2002), 2238 UNTS 208
Agreement between the Commonwealth of the Bahamas and the Republic of Cuba for the Delimiting Line between their Maritime Zones, FAOLEX database, available at http://extwprlegs1.fao.org/docs/pdf/bi-119575.pdf
Delimitation Agreement between the Gabonese Republic and the Democratic Republic of Sao Tome and Principe (2001), DOALOS website, available at www.un.org/Depts/los/LEGISLATIONANDTREATIES/PDFFILES/TREATIES/GAB-STP2001MB.PDF
Delimitation Agreement between the Government of the Cook Islands and the Government of Niue (2012), DOALOS website, available at www.un.org/Depts/los/LEGISLATIONANDTREATIES/PDFFILES/DEPOSIT/cok_mzn96_2013.pdf
Delimitation Agreement between the Government of the French Republic and the Government of the Republic of Madagascar (2005), 71 Law of the Sea Bulletin 23 (2009)
Delimitation Agreement between the Government of the Kingdom of Thailand, the Government of the Republic of India and the Government of the Republic of Indonesia in the Andaman Sea (1978), DOALOS website, available at www.un.org/Depts/los/LEGISLATIONANDTREATIES/PDFFILES/TREATIES/THA-IND-IDN1978TP.PDF
Delimitation Agreement between the Kingdom of Saudi Arabia and the United Arab Emirates (1974), 1733 UNTS 30
Delimitation Treaty between the Islamic Republic of Mauritania and the Republic of Cape Verde (2003), 55 Law of the Sea Bulletin 32 (2004)
Maritime Delimitation Agreement between the Russian Federation and the Kingdom of Norway (2007), 67 Law of the Sea Bulletin 42 (2008)
Memorandum of Understanding between the Government of the Republic of Kenya and the Transitional Federal Government of the Somali Republic to Grant to Each Other No-Objection in Respect of Submissions on the Outer Limits of the Continental Shelf beyond 200 Nautical Miles to the Commission on the Limits of the Continental Shelf 7 April 2009, 70 Law of the Sea Bulletin 52 (2009)
Timor Sea Treaty (2002), DOALOS website, available at www.un.org/Depts/los/LEGISLATIONANDTREATIES/PDFFILES/TREATIES/AUS-TLS2002TST.PDF
Treaties between Republic of Mauritius and the Republic of Seychelles regarding the Mascarene Plateau signed by the Government of the Republic of Mauritius and the Government of the Republic of Seychelles at Clarisse House, Vacoas in Mauritius on 13 March 2012, 79 Law of the Sea Bulletin 25 (2012)
Treaty between the Federated States of Micronesia and the Republic of Palau concerning Maritime Boundaries and Cooperation on Related Matters (2006), DOALOS website, available at www.un.org/Depts/los/LEGISLATIONANDTREATIES/PDFFILES/FSM-PALAU.pdf
Treaty between the Kingdom of Norway and the Russian Federation concerning Maritime Delimitation and Cooperation in the Barents Sea and the Arctic Ocean (2010), DOALOS website, available at www.un.org/Depts/los/LEGISLATIONANDTREATIES/PDFFILES/TREATIES/NOR-RUS2010.PDF
Treaty between the Republic of Lithuania and the Russian Federation (1997), DOALOS website, available at www.un.org/Depts/los/LEGISLATIONANDTREATIES/PDFFILES/TREATIES/LTU-RUS1997CS.PDF
Treaty between the Republic of Vanuatu and the Solomon Islands (2016), DOALOS website, available at www.un.org/Depts/los/LEGISLATIONANDTREATIES/PDFFILES/TREATIES/vut_slb_wsm_2016.pdf

Treaty between the Republic of Venezuela and the Kingdom of the Netherlands (1978), DOALOS website, available at www.un.org/Depts/los/LEGISLATIONANDTREATIES/PDFFILES/TREATIES/VEN-NLD1978BD.PDF

Treaty between the State of Barbados and the Republic of Guyana (2003), 55 Law of the Sea Bulletin 36 (2004)

International Courts and Tribunals' decisions

Alleged Violations of Sovereign Rights and Maritime Spaces in the Caribbean Sea (Nicaragua v. Colombia), Application instituting proceedings, ICJ 2013

Alleged Violations of Sovereign Rights and Maritime Spaces in the Caribbean Sea (Nicaragua v. Colombia), Preliminary Objections, Judgment, ICJ Reports 2016, p. 3

Alleged Violations of Sovereign Rights and Maritime Spaces in the Caribbean Sea (Nicaragua v. Colombia), Judgment (21 April 2022)

Arbitral Award of 31 July 1989, Judgment, ICJ Reports 1991, p. 53

Arbitration between Newfoundland and Labrador and Nova Scotia concerning portions of the limits of their offshore areas as defined in the Canada-Nova Scotia Offshore Petroleum Resources Accord Implementation Act and the Canada-Newfoundland Atlantic Accord Implementation Act, Award of the Tribunal in the second phase, 26 March 2002, available at *www.cnsopb.ns.ca/sites/default/files/resource/phaseii_award_english.pdf*

Arbitration under the Timor Sea Treaty (Timor-Leste v. Australia), Termination Order, case no. 2013–16, 20 March 2017, Permanent Court of Arbitration [PCA]

Barbados v. Trinidad and Tobago, case no. 2004–02, Statement of Claim (Barbados), 16 February 2004, Permanent Court of Arbitration [PCA]

Barbados v. Trinidad and Tobago, Award, case no. 2004–02, 11 April 2006, Permanent Court of Arbitration [PCA]

Bay of Bengal Maritime Boundary Arbitration between Bangladesh and India, Award, case no. 2010–16, 07 July 2014, Permanent Court of Arbitration [PCA]

Case of the monetary gold removed from Rome in 1943 (Preliminary Question), Judgment, ICJ Reports 1954, p. 19

Chagos Marine Protected Area Arbitration (Mauritius v. United Kingdom), Award, case no. 2011–03, 18 March 2015, Permanent Court of Arbitration [PCA]

Continental Shelf (Tunisia/Libyan Arab Jamahiriya), Application to Intervene, Judgment, ICJ Reports 1981, p. 3

Continental Shelf (Tunisia/Libyan Arab Jamahiriya), Judgment, ICJ Reports 1982, p. 18

Continental Shelf (Libyan Arab Jamahiriya/Malta), Application to Intervene, Judgment, ICJ Reports 1984, p. 3

Continental shelf (Libyan Arab Jamahiriya/Malta), Judgment, ICJ Reports 1985, p. 13

Delimitation of the Maritime Boundary in the Gulf of Maine Area, Judgment, ICJ Reports 1984, p. 246

Dispute between the Government of the State of Eritrea and the Government of the Republic of Yemen, Award of the Arbitral Tribunal in the Second Stage of the Proceedings (Maritime Delimitation), case no. 1996–04, 17 December 1999, Permanent Court of Arbitration [PCA]

Dispute concerning delimitation of the maritime boundary between Bangladesh and Myanmar in the Bay of Bengal (Bangladesh/Myanmar), Notification submitted by Bangladesh, ITLOS, 13 December 2009

Dispute concerning delimitation of the maritime boundary between Bangladesh and Myanmar in the Bay of Bengal (Bangladesh/Myanmar), Judgment, ITLOS Reports 2012, p. 4

Delimitation of the maritime boundary in the Atlantic Ocean (Ghana/Côte d'Ivoire), Provisional Measures, Order of 25 April 2015, ITLOS Reports 2015, p. 146

Dispute Concerning Delimitation of the Maritime Boundary between Ghana and Côte d'Ivoire in the Atlantic Ocean (Ghana/Côte d'Ivoire), Judgment, ITLOS Reports 2017, p. 4

Dispute Concerning Coastal State Rights in the Black Sea, Sea of Azov, and Kerch Strait (Ukraine v. the Russian Federation), Award Concerning the Preliminary Objections of the Russian Federation, case No. 2017–06, 21 February 2020, UNCLOS, Annex VII Arbitral Tribunal, Permanent Court of Arbitration [PCA]
Dispute concerning delimitation of the maritime boundary between Mauritius and Maldives in the Indian Ocean (Mauritius/Maldives), Preliminary Objections, Judgment, case no. 28, ITLOS (28 January 2021)
Dispute concerning delimitation of the maritime boundary between Mauritius and Maldives in the Indian Ocean (Mauritius/Maldives), Judgment, case no. 28, ITLOS (28 April 2023)
Fisheries case, Judgment, ICJ Reports 1951, p. 116
Guatemala's Territorial, Insular and Maritime Claim (Guatemala/Belize), Special Agreement, ICJ 2008
Guatemala's Territorial, Insular and Maritime Claim (Guatemala/Belize), Protocol to the Special Agreement, ICJ 2015
Guyana v. Suriname, Award, case no. 2004–04, 17 September 2007, Permanent Court of Arbitration [PCA]
Land and Maritime Boundary between Cameroon and Nigeria, Preliminary Objections, Judgment, ICJ Reports 1998, p. 275
Land and Maritime Boundary between Cameroon and Nigeria, Application to Intervene, Order of 21 October 1999, ICJ Reports 1999, p. 1029
Land and Maritime Boundary between Cameroon and Nigeria (Cameroon v. Nigeria: Equatorial Guinea intervening), Judgment, ICJ Reports 2002, p. 303
Land and Maritime Delimitation and Sovereignty over Islands (Gabon/Equatorial Guinea), Special Agreement, ICJ 2016
Land, Island and Maritime Frontier Dispute (El Salvador/Honduras), Application to Intervene, Judgment, ICJ Reports 1990, p. 92
Land, Island and Maritime Frontier Dispute (El Salvador/Honduras: Nicaragua intervening), Judgment, ICJ Reports 1992
Legality of the Threat of Use of Nuclear Weapons, Advisory Opinion, ICJ Reports 1996, p. 226
M/V "Louisa" (Saint Vincent and the Grenadines v. Kingdom of Spain), Judgment, ITLOS Reports 2013, p. 4
M/V "Saiga" (No. 2) (Saint Vincent and the Grenadines v. Guinea), Judgment, ITLOS Reports 1999, p. 10
M/V "Virginia G" (Panama/Guinea-Bissau), Judgment, ITLOS Reports 2014, p. 4
Maritime Delimitation and Territorial Questions between Qatar and Bahrain, Application instituting proceedings, ICJ 1991
Maritime Delimitation and Territorial Questions between Qatar and Bahrain, Jurisdiction and Admissibility, Judgment, ICJ Reports 1994, p. 112
Maritime Delimitation and Territorial Questions between Qatar and Bahrain, Jurisdiction and Admissibility, Judgment, ICJ Reports 1995, p. 6
Maritime Delimitation and Territorial Questions between Qatar and Bahrain, Merits, Judgment, ICJ Reports 2001, p. 40
Maritime Delimitation between Guinea-Bissau and Senegal (Guinea-Bissau v. Senegal), Application instituting proceedings, ICJ 1991
Maritime Delimitation in the Area between Greenland and Jan Mayen (Denmark v. Norway), Application Instituting Proceedings, ICJ 1988
Maritime Delimitation in the Area between Greenland and Jan Mayen, Judgment, ICJ Reports 1993, p. 38
Maritime Delimitation in the Black Sea (Romania v. Ukraine), Application instituting proceedings, ICJ 2004
Maritime Delimitation in the Black Sea (Romania v. Ukraine), Judgment, ICJ Reports 2009, p. 61
Maritime Delimitation in the Caribbean Sea and the Pacific Ocean (Costa Rica v. Nicaragua), Application instituting proceedings, ICJ 2014

Maritime Delimitation in the Caribbean Sea and the Pacific Ocean (Costa Rica v. Nicaragua), Memorial of Costa Rica, ICJ 2015
Maritime Delimitation in the Caribbean Sea and the Pacific Ocean (Costa Rica v. Nicaragua) and Land Boundary in the Northern Part of Isla Portillos (Costa Rica v. Nicaragua), Judgment, ICJ Reports 2018, p. 139
Maritime Delimitation in the Indian Ocean (Somalia V. Kenya), Application, Instituting Proceedings, ICJ (28 August 2014)
Maritime Delimitation in the Indian Ocean (Somalia v. Kenya), Judgment, ICJ Reports 2021, p. 206
Maritime Delimitation in the Indian Ocean (Somalia v. Kenya), Preliminary Objections, Judgment, ICJ Reports 2017, p. 3
Maritime Dispute (Peru v. Chile), Application instituting proceedings, ICJ 2008
Maritime Dispute (Peru v. Chile), Judgment, ICJ Reports 2014, p. 3
MOX Plant (Ireland v. United Kingdom), Provisional Measures, Order of 3 December 2001, ITLOS Reports 2001, p. 95
North Sea Continental Shelf, Judgment, ICJ reports 1969, p. 3
Prosecutor v. Sam Hinga Norman – Decision on Preliminary Motion Based on Lack of Jurisdiction (Child Recruitment), Case No. SCSL-2004–14-AR72(E), Special Court for Sierra Leone, 31 May 2004
Question of the Delimitation of the Continental Shelf between Nicaragua and Colombia beyond 200 nautical miles from the Nicaraguan Coast (Nicaragua v. Colombia), Application instituting proceedings, ICJ 2013
Question of the Delimitation of the Continental Shelf between Nicaragua and Colombia beyond 200 Nautical Miles from the Nicaraguan Coast (Nicaragua v. Colombia), Preliminary Objections, Judgment, ICJ Reports 2016, p. 100
Question of the Delimitation of the Continental Shelf between Nicaragua and Colombia beyond 200 Nautical Miles from the Nicaraguan Coast (Nicaragua v. Colombia), Order of 4 October 2022
Question of the Delimitation of the Continental Shelf between Nicaragua and Colombia beyond 200 Nautical Miles from the Nicaraguan Coast (Nicaragua v. Colombia), Judgement (13 July 2023)
Responsibilities and obligations of States with respect to activities in the Area, Advisory Opinion, 1 February 2011, ITLOS Reports 2011
Request for Advisory Opinion submitted by the Sub-Regional Fisheries Commission, Advisory Opinion, 2 April 2015, ITLOS Reports 2015, p. 4
Review Panel established under the Convention on the Conservation and Management of High Seas Fishery Resources in the South Pacific Ocean, Findings and Recommendations of the Review Panel, case no. 2018–13, 5 June 2018
Southern Bluefin Tuna (New Zealand-Japan, Australia-Japan), 4 August 2000, Reports of International Arbitral Awards, Vol. XXIII, p. 1
Sovereignty over Pedra Branca/Pulau Batu Puteh, Middle Rocks and South Ledge (Malaysia/Singapore), Judgment, ICJ Reports 2008, p. 12
Territorial and Maritime Dispute (Nicaragua v. Colombia), Application instituting proceedings, ICJ 2001
Territorial and Maritime Dispute (Nicaragua v. Colombia), Preliminary Objections, Judgment, ICJ Reports 2007, p. 832
Territorial and Maritime Dispute between Nicaragua and Honduras in the Caribbean Sea (Nicaragua v. Honduras), Application instituting proceedings, ICJ 1999
Territorial and Maritime Dispute between Nicaragua and Honduras in the Caribbean Sea (Nicaragua v. Honduras), Judgment, ICJ Reports 2007, p. 659
Territorial and Maritime Dispute (Nicaragua v. Colombia), Application by Honduras for Permission to Intervene, Judgment, ICJ Reports 2011, p. 420
Territorial and Maritime Dispute (Nicaragua v. Colombia), Application by Costa Rica for Permission to Intervene, Judgment, ICJ Reports 2011, p. 348

Territorial and Maritime Dispute (Nicaragua v. Colombia), Judgment, ICJ Reports 2012, p. 624
The Arctic Sunrise Arbitration (Netherlands v. Russia), case no. 2014–02, Award on Jurisdiction, 26 November 2014, Permanent Court of Arbitration [PCA]
The Arctic Sunrise Arbitration (Netherlands v. Russia), Award on the Merits, case no. 2014–02, 14 August 2015, Permanent Court of Arbitration [PCA]
The South China Sea Arbitration (The Republic of Philippines v. The People's Republic of China), The Philippines' Memorial – Volume I, case no. 2013–19, 30 March 2014, Permanent Court of Arbitration [PCA]
The South China Sea Arbitration (The Republic of Philippines v. The People's Republic of China), Award on Jurisdiction and Admissibility, case no. 2013–19, 29 October 2015, Permanent Court of Arbitration [PCA]
The South China Sea Arbitration (The Republic of Philippines v. The People's Republic of China), Award, case no. 2013–19, 12 July 2016, Permanent Court of Arbitration [PCA]
Timor Sea Conciliation (Timor-Leste v. Australia), case no. 2016–10, conciliation, decision on competence, 19 September 2016, Permanent Court of Arbitration [PCA]
Timor Sea Conciliation (Timor-Leste v. Australia), Report and Recommendations of the Compulsory Conciliation Commission between Timor-Leste and Australia on the Timor Sea, case no. 2016–10, 09 May 2018, Permanent Court of Arbitration [PCA]
The "Enrica Lexie" Incident (Italy v. India), Award, case no. 2015–28, 21 May 2020, Permanent Court of Arbitration [PCA]

Domestic Courts and Tribunal's decisions

Conocophillips (UK) LTD v. Partnereederei Ms Jork [2010] EWHC 1214 (Comm)

Domestic legislation

2004 Civil Code, as cited in Maritime Claims Reference Manual, United States Department of Defence (JAG website), available at www.jag.navy.mil/organization/documents/mcrm/el_salvador_2014.pdf
A bill to improve the operation of the Fishermen's Contingency Fund established to compensate commercial fishermen for damages resulting from oil and gas exploration, development, and production in areas of the Outer Continental Shelf, 1982, Congress website, available at www.congress.gov/bill/97th-congress/house-bill/3816?q=%7B%22search%22%3A%5B%22continental+shelf%22%5D%7D&r=23&s=4
Act concerning the exclusive economic zone of Belgium in the North Sea (1999), DOALOS website, available at www.un.org/Depts/los/LEGISLATIONANDTREATIES/PDFFILES/BEL_1999_Act.pdf
Act governing the ocean space of the People's Republic of Bulgaria (1987), DOALOS website, available at www.un.org/Depts/los/LEGISLATIONANDTREATIES/PDFFILES/bgr_1987_ct.pdf
Act No, 17,033 (1998), FAOLEX database, available at http://extwprlegs1.fao.org/docs/pdf/uru21321.pdf
Act No. 10 (1978), DOALOS website, available at www.un.org/Depts/los/LEGISLATIONANDTREATIES/PDFFILES/COL_1978_Act.pdf
Act No. 15/1984 (1984), DOALOS website, available at www.un.org/Depts/los/LEGISLATIONANDTREATIES/PDFFILES/GNQ_1984_Act.pdf
Act No. 1–81 (1980), Promulgated by Dahir No. 1–81–1 9 (1981), DOALOS website, available at www.un.org/Depts/los/LEGISLATIONANDTREATIES/PDFFILES/MAR_1981_Act.pdf
Act No. 2016–007 (2016), DOALOS website, available at www.un.org/Depts/los/LEGISLATIONANDTREATIES/PDFFILES/TogoESPACESMARITIMES.pdf

Act No. 205 of 19 December 1979 on the Continental Shelf and Adjacent Sea, DOALOS website, available at www.un.org/Depts/los/LEGISLATIONANDTREATIES/PDFFILES/NIC_1979_Act.pdf
Act No. 23.968 of 14 August 1991, DOALOS website, available at www.un.org/Depts/los/LEGISLATIONANDTREATIES/PDFFILES/ARG_1991_23968.pdf
Act No. 259 concerning the Continental Shelf (1971) as amended by Act No. 278 (1972) and Act No. 654 (1977), DOALOS website, available at www.un.org/Depts/los/LEGISLATIONANDTREATIES/PDFFILES/DNK_1971_Act.pdf
Act No. 3/85 (1985), DOALOS website, available at www.un.org/Depts/los/LEGISLATIONANDTREATIES/PDFFILES/GNB_1985_Act3.pdf
Act No. 33/77 (1977), DOALOS website, available at www.un.org/Depts/los/LEGISLATIONANDTREATIES/PDFFILES/PRT_1977_Act.pdf
Act No. 37 (1993), DOALOS website, available at www.un.org/Depts/los/LEGISLATIONANDTREATIES/PDFFILES/BHS_1993_37.pdf
Act No. 45 (1977), DOALOS website, available at www.un.org/Depts/los/LEGISLATIONANDTREATIES/PDFFILES/YEM_1977_Act.pdf
Act No. 5 of 1983 on the Indonesian exclusive economic zone, 18 October 1983, DOALOS website, available at www.un.org/Depts/los/LEGISLATIONANDTREATIES/PDFFILES/IDN_1983_Act.pdf
Act No. 50/2005 (2005), 58 Law of the Sea Bulletin 19 (2005)
Act No. 573 (1977), DOALOS website, available at www.un.org/Depts/los/LEGISLATIONANDTREATIES/PDFFILES/DOM_1977_Act.pdf
Act No. 68–1181 of 30 December 1968 relating to the exploration of the Continental Shelf and to the exploitation of its natural resources, DOALOS website, available at www.un.org/Depts/los/LEGISLATIONANDTREATIES/PDFFILES/FRA_1968_Act.pdf
Act No. 613 and Amendments to Act No. 6 (1967), DOALOS website, available at www.un.org/Depts/los/LEGISLATIONANDTREATIES/PDFFILES/ITA_1967_Act.pdf
Act No. 72 (1996) relating to petroleum activities, available at www.npd.no/en/regulations/acts/act-29-november-1996-no2.-72-relating-to-petroleum-activities/
Act No. 77–485 (1977), DOALOS website, available at www.un.org/Depts/los/LEGISLATIONANDTREATIES/PDFFILES/FRA_1977_Act.pdf
Act No. 85–14 (1985), DOALOS website, available at www.un.org/Depts/los/LEGISLATIONANDTREATIES/PDFFILES/SEN_1985_Act.pdf
Act No. 91 (1976), DOALOS website, available at www.un.org/Depts/los/LEGISLATIONANDTREATIES/PDFFILES/NOR_1976_Act.pdf
Act of 21 June 1963 Relating to Exploration and Exploitation of Submarine Natural Resources, DOALOS website, available at www.un.org/Depts/los/LEGISLATIONANDTREATIES/PDFFILES/NOR_1963_Act.pdf
Act of 22 March 1985 No. 11 Pertaining to Petroleum Activities, DOALOS website, available at www.un.org/Depts/los/LEGISLATIONANDTREATIES/PDFFILES/NOR_1985_Act.pdf
Act on Honduras Maritime Areas, 49 Law of the Bulletin 15 (2002)
Act on the exploration and exploitation of non-living resources in the territorial sea and the continental shelf (1969), DOALOS website, available at www.un.org/Depts/los/LEGISLATIONANDTREATIES/PDFFILES/BEL_1969_Act.pdf
Act to amend Chapter 1 of Title 27 of the Palau National Code (2003), DOALOS website, available at www.un.org/Depts/los/LEGISLATIONANDTREATIES/PDFFILES/PLW_2003_PNC.pdf
Act to Define the Maritime Zones of the Republic of the Philippines (2011), available at www.congress.gov.ph/legisdocs/third_15/hbt4185.pdf
Act to Define the Maritime Zones of the Republic of the Philippines (2019), available at www.congress.gov.ph/legisdocs/third_16/hbt4889.pdf
An Act to amend title 18 of the Code of the Federated States of Micronesia by amending sections 101, 102, 103, 104, 105 and 107 and by adding a new section 108 to establish

an Exclusive Economic Zone in the oceans surrounding the Federated States of Micronesia, to expand the size of the Territorial Sea, to make the chapter consistent with the current political status of the Federated States of Micronesia, and for other purposes (16 December 1988), DOALOS website, available at www.un.org/Depts/los/LEGISLATIONANDTREATIES/PDFFILES/FSM_1988_Act.pdf

Aquatic Areas Organic Act, Decree No. 1,446 (2014), DOALOS website, available at www.un.org/Depts/los/LEGISLATIONANDTREATIES/PDFFILES/Venezuela_ENG.pdf

Archipelagic Waters and Exclusive Economic Zone Act, 1986 (Cap. 51:06), FAOLEX database, available at http://extwprlegs1.fao.org/docs/pdf/tri105030.pdf

Chapter 1 of Title 18 of the Code of the Federated States of Micronesia (Annotated), as amended by Public Law No. 19–172 (2017), DOALOS website, available at www.un.org/Depts/los/LEGISLATIONANDTREATIES/PDFFILES/Title18FSMCode.pdf

Chapter 371, The Maritime Zones Act 1989, DOALOS website, available at www.un.org/Depts/los/LEGISLATIONANDTREATIES/PDFFILES/KEN_1989_Maritime.pdf

Constitution as amended by Decree No. 5699 of 5 June 1975, DOALOS website, available at www.un.org/Depts/los/LEGISLATIONANDTREATIES/PDFFILES/CRI_1975_Decree5699.pdf

Constitution of Georgia, FAOLEX database, available at http://extwprlegs1.fao.org/docs/pdf/geo127811ENG.pdf

Constitution of the Federative Republic of Brazil (with amendment n. 64, 2010), OAS website, available at https://web.oas.org/mla/en/Countries_Intro/bra_pt_const.pdf (unofficially translated from Portuguese)

Constitution of the Republic of Guatemala of 5 September 1965, DOALOS website, available at www.un.org/Depts/los/LEGISLATIONANDTREATIES/PDFFILES/GTM_1965_Constitution.pdf

Constitution of the Republic of Mozambique (Revised 2018), FAOLEX database, available at http://extwprlegs1.fao.org/docs/pdf/moz117331ENG_original.pdf

Continental Shelf (Amendment) Act, 1986 (Act No. 23 of 1986), DOALOS website, available at www.un.org/Depts/los/LEGISLATIONANDTREATIES/STATEFILES/TTO.htm

Continental Shelf (Designated Areas) Order 2014, S.I. No. 87 of 2014, DOALOS website, available at www.un.org/Depts/los/LEGISLATIONANDTREATIES/PDFFILES/IRL_2014_Order87.pdf

Continental Shelf (Protection of Installations) (Ballycotton Field) Order, S.I. No. 226 (1991), DOALOS website, available at www.un.org/Depts/los/LEGISLATIONANDTREATIES/PDFFILES/IRL_1991_Order226.pdf

Continental Shelf (Protection of Installations) (Connemara Field) Order, S.I. No. 267 (1997), DOALOS website, available at www.un.org/Depts/los/LEGISLATIONANDTREATIES/PDFFILES/IRL_1997_Order267.pdf

Continental Shelf (Protection of Installations) (Kinsale Head Field) Order, S.I. No. 285 (1977), DOALOS website, available at www.un.org/Depts/los/LEGISLATIONANDTREATIES/PDFFILES/IRL_1977_Order285.pdf

Continental Shelf Act (1964), as Amended in 1974, DOALOS website, available at www.un.org/Depts/los/LEGISLATIONANDTREATIES/PDFFILES/DEU_1974_Act.pdf

Continental Shelf Act (1964), DOALOS website, available at www.un.org/Depts/los/LEGISLATIONANDTREATIES/PDFFILES/GBR_1964_Act.pdf

Continental Shelf Act (No. 1 of 1965), FAOLEX database, available at http://extwprlegs1.fao.org/docs/pdf/gam41165.pdf

Continental Shelf Act (No. 28, 1964), FAOLEX database, available at http://extwprlegs1.fao.org/docs/pdf/nze5174.pdf

Continental Shelf Act 1964 (Reprint as at 13 January 2020), available at www.legislation.govt.nz/act/public/1964/0028/latest/whole.html#DLM351675

Continental Shelf Act 1966, as Amended by Act No. 83 (1972), DOALOS website, available at www.un.org/Depts/los/LEGISLATIONANDTREATIES/PDFFILES/MYS_1966_Act.pdf

Continental Shelf Act No. 314 (1966), DOALOS website, available at www.un.org/Depts/los/LEGISLATIONANDTREATIES/PDFFILES/SWE_1966_Act.pdf
Continental Shelf Act No. 14 (1968), DOALOS website, available at www.un.org/Depts/los/LEGISLATIONANDTREATIES/PDFFILES/IRL_1968_Act.pdf
Continental Shelf Act, 1969 (Cap. 1:52) (amended in 1986), FAOLEX database, available at http://extwprlegs1.fao.org/docs/pdf/tri105075.pdf
Continental Shelf Act, 1970, available at http://laws.bahamas.gov.bs/cms/images/LEGISLATION/PRINCIPAL/1970/1970-0017/ContinentalShelfAct_1.pdf
Continental Shelf Act, No. 28 (1964) as Amended by the Continental Shelf Amendment Act, No. 17 (1977), DOALOS website, available at www.un.org/Depts/los/LEGISLATIONANDTREATIES/PDFFILES/COK_1977_Act17.pdf [repealed by 2018 law]
Continental Shelf Act, No. 9 (1970), DOALOS website, available at www.un.org/Depts/los/LEGISLATIONANDTREATIES/PDFFILES/FJI_1970_Act.pdf
Continental Shelf Act, No. XXVIII (2014), FAOLEX database, available at http://extwprlegs1.fao.org/docs/pdf/mlt139078.pdf
Continental Shelf Decree of the Presidium (1968), DOALOS website, available at www.un.org/Depts/los/LEGISLATIONANDTREATIES/PDFFILES/RUS_1968_Decree.pdf
Continental Shelf Law No. 149 (1965), DOALOS website, available at www.un.org/Depts/los/LEGISLATIONANDTREATIES/PDFFILES/FIN_1965_Law.pdf
Continental Shelf Law, No. 8 (1974), DOALOS website, available at www.un.org/Depts/los/LEGISLATIONANDTREATIES/PDFFILES/CYP_1974_Law.pdf
Continental Shelf Order 2018, DOALOS website, available at www.un.org/Depts/los/LEGISLATIONANDTREATIES/PDFFILES/NZL_2018_Order.pdf
Continental Shelf Presidential Proclamation No. 370 (1968), DOALOS website, available at www.un.org/Depts/los/LEGISLATIONANDTREATIES/PDFFILES/PHL_1968_Proclamation.pdf
Decision No. 260 of A.J. 1377 (A.D. 2009), DOALOS website, available at www.un.org/Depts/los/LEGISLATIONANDTREATIES/PDFFILES/lby_2009_declaration_e.pdf
Decision on the Extension of the Jurisdiction of the Republic of Croatia in the Adriatic Sea (2003), DOALOS website, available at www.un.org/Depts/los/LEGISLATIONANDTREATIES/PDFFILES/HRV_2003_Decision.pdf
Declaration by the Federal Government (1964), DOALOS website, available at www.un.org/Depts/los/LEGISLATIONANDTREATIES/PDFFILES/DEU_1964_Declaration.pdf
Declaration by the Government concerning the Exclusive Economic Zone of Indonesia 21 March 1980, DOALOS website, available at www.un.org/Depts/los/LEGISLATIONANDTREATIES/PDFFILES/IDN_1980_DeclarationEEZ.pdf
Declaration by the Ministry of Foreign Affairs, 14 September 1985, DOALOS website, available at www.un.org/Depts/los/LEGISLATIONANDTREATIES/PDFFILES/CHL_1985_Declaration.pdf
Declaration concerning the Exclusive Economic Zone and its delimitation (1980), DOALOS website, available at www.un.org/Depts/los/LEGISLATIONANDTREATIES/PDFFILES/ARE_1980_Declaration.pdf
Declaration on the continental shelf, 19 September 1985, DOALOS website, available at www.un.org/Depts/los/LEGISLATIONANDTREATIES/PDFFILES/ECU_1985_Declaration.pdf
Declaration regarding the maritime boundaries of the State of Palestine (2015), DOALOS website, available at www.un.org/Depts/los/LEGISLATIONANDTREATIES/PDFFILES/PSE_2015_Declaration.pdf
Declaration regarding the maritime boundaries of the State of Palestine (2019), DOALOS website, available at www.un.org/Depts/los/LEGISLATIONANDTREATIES/PDFFILES/PSE_Deposit_09-2019.pdf
Decree concerning maritime zones under the sovereignty or jurisdiction of the Republic of Guinea, 89 Law of the Sea Bulletin 15 (2016)
Decree Law No. 31/76 (1976), DOALOS website, available at www.un.org/Depts/los/LEGISLATIONANDTREATIES/PDFFILES/MOZ_1976_Law.pdf

Decree No. 317 (2014), DOALOS website, available at www.un.org/Depts/los/LEGISLATIONANDTREATIES/PDFFILES/Kuwait_Decree_317-2014-E.pdf
Decree No. 336/PRG (1980), DOALOS website, available at www.un.org/Depts/los/LEGISLATIONANDTREATIES/PDFFILES/GIN_1980_Decree.pdf
Decree No. 38 (1977), DOALOS website, available at www.un.org/Depts/los/LEGISLATIONANDTREATIES/PDFFILES/HTI_1977_Decree.pdf
Decree No. 86/11264 (1986), DOALOS website, available at www.un.org/Depts/los/LEGISLATIONANDTREATIES/PDFFILES/TUR_1986_Decree.pdf
Decree No. 921 (1980), DOALOS website, available at www.un.org/Depts/los/LEGISLATIONANDTREATIES/PDFFILES/HND_1980_Decree.pdf
Decree no. 95 Determining the Maritime Zones from Punta Puga to Diego Ramírez Islands, 23 August 2021, DOALOS website, available at www.un.org/Depts/los/LEGISLATIONANDTREATIES/PDFFILES/2113525E.pdf
Decree of the Council of State (1982), DOALOS website, available at www.un.org/Depts/los/LEGISLATIONANDTREATIES/PDFFILES/KHM_1982_Decree.pdf
Decree-Law No. 49–369 of 11 November 1969, DOALOS website, available at www.un.org/Depts/los/LEGISLATIONANDTREATIES/PDFFILES/PRT_1969_Decree.pdf
Ecological Protection Zone and Continental Shelf Act (2005), 60 Law of the Sea Bulletin 56 (2006)
Economic Zone Act (1992), DOALOS website, available at www.un.org/Depts/los/LEGISLATIONANDTREATIES/PDFFILES/SWE_1992_Act.pdf
Economic Zone Act No. 15/1978 (1978), DOALOS website, available at www.un.org/Depts/los/LEGISLATIONANDTREATIES/PDFFILES/ESP_1978_Act.pdf
Economic Zone Decree (1977), DOALOS website, available at www.un.org/Depts/los/LEGISLATIONANDTREATIES/PDFFILES/PRK_1977_Decree.pdf
Economic Zone Decree of the Presidium (1984), DOALOS website, available at www.un.org/Depts/los/LEGISLATIONANDTREATIES/PDFFILES/RUS_1984_Decree.pdf
Exclusive (Marine) Economic Zone Law (1995), DOALOS website, available at www.un.org/Depts/los/LEGISLATIONANDTREATIES/PDFFILES/UKR_1995_Law.pdf
Exclusive Economic Zone (Establishment) Act (1999), DOALOS website, available at www.un.org/Depts/los/LEGISLATIONANDTREATIES/PDFFILES/NLD_1999_Act.pdf
Exclusive Economic Zone Act (1978), DOALOS website, available at www.un.org/Depts/los/LEGISLATIONANDTREATIES/PDFFILES/VEN_1978_Act.pdf
Exclusive Economic Zone Act (1992), DOALOS website, available at www.un.org/Depts/los/LEGISLATIONANDTREATIES/PDFFILES/ZAR_1992_Act.pdf
Exclusive Economic Zone Act (1993), Estonia legislation database, available at www.riigiteataja.ee/en/eli/ee/520012015003/consolide
Exclusive Economic Zone Act (2004), 57 Law of the Sea Bulletin 106 (2005)
Exclusive Economic Zone Act No. 33 (1991), DOALOS website, available at www.un.org/Depts/los/LEGISLATIONANDTREATIES/PDFFILES/JAM_1991_Act.pdf
Exclusive Economic Zone Act No. 5151 (1996), DOALOS website, available at www.un.org/Depts/los/LEGISLATIONANDTREATIES/PDFFILES/KOR_1996_EEZAct.pdf
Exclusive Economic Zone Act No. 9/84, DOALOS website, available at www.un.org/Depts/los/LEGISLATIONANDTREATIES/PDFFILES/GAB_1984_Act.pdf
Exclusive Economic Zone Act, 1984, Act No. 311, DOALOS website, available at www.un.org/Depts/los/LEGISLATIONANDTREATIES/PDFFILES/MYS_1984_Act.pdf
Exclusive Economic Zone and Continental Shelf (Environmental Effects) Act (No. 72, 2012), FAOLEX database, available at http://extwprlegs1.fao.org/docs/pdf/nze115256.pdf
Exclusive Economic Zone and Continental Shelf (Environmental Effects) Amendment Act 2013, FAOLEX database, available at http://extwprlegs1.fao.org/docs/pdf/nze151614.pdf
Exclusive Economic Zone and Continental Shelf Act (1998), DOALOS website, available at www.un.org/Depts/los/LEGISLATIONANDTREATIES/PDFFILES/chn_1998_eez_act.pdf

Exclusive Economic Zone and the Continental Shelf Laws (2004 and 2014), FAOLEX database, available at http://extwprlegs1.fao.org/docs/pdf/cyp159196.pdf
Exclusive Economic Zone Decree No. 142 (1986), DOALOS website, available at www.un.org/Depts/los/LEGISLATIONANDTREATIES/PDFFILES/ROM_1986_Decree.pdf
Exclusive Economic Zone Decree No. 28 of 5 October 1978, DOALOS website, available at www.un.org/Depts/los/LEGISLATIONANDTREATIES/PDFFILES/NGA_1978_Decree.pdf
Exclusive Economic Zone Law (2004), DOALOS website, available at www.un.org/Depts/los/LEGISLATIONANDTREATIES/PDFFILES/cyp_2004_eez_proclamation.pdf
Exclusive Economic Zone Presidential Proclamation 5030 (1983), DOALOS website, available at www.un.org/Depts/los/LEGISLATIONANDTREATIES/PDFFILES/USA_1983_Proclamation.pdf
Exclusive Economic Zone Proclamation (1994), DOALOS website, available at www.un.org/Depts/los/LEGISLATIONANDTREATIES/PDFFILES/deu_1994_eez_proclamation.pdf
Exclusive Economic Zone Royal Decree No. 236/2013 (2013), DOALOS website, available at www.un.org/Depts/los/LEGISLATIONANDTREATIES/PDFFILES/ESP_2013_Decree_eng.pdf
Exclusive Economic Zone Royal Proclamation (1981), DOALOS website, available at www.un.org/Depts/los/LEGISLATIONANDTREATIES/PDFFILES/THA_1981_Proclamation.pdf
Exclusive Economic Zones Act No. 411 (1996), DOALOS website, available at www.un.org/Depts/los/LEGISLATIONANDTREATIES/PDFFILES/DNK_1996_Act.pdf
Executive Order No. 48 (10 January 2013), Extension of Executive Order No. 39 Delimiting the Maritime Zones of the Republic of Liberia, DOALOS website, available at www.un.org/Depts/los/LEGISLATIONANDTREATIES/PDFFILES/LBR_10Jan2013_Act_EO48.pdf
Federal Act on the exclusive economic zone (1998), DOALOS website, available at www.un.org/Depts/los/LEGISLATIONANDTREATIES/PDFFILES/RUS_1998_Act_EZ.pdf
Federal Act relating to the Sea, 8 January 1986, DOALOS website, available at www.un.org/Depts/los/LEGISLATIONANDTREATIES/PDFFILES/MEX_1986_Act.pdf
Federal Law No. 19 (1993), DOALOS website, available at www.un.org/Depts/los/LEGISLATIONANDTREATIES/PDFFILES/ARE_1993_Law.pdf
Federal Law on the Continental Shelf of the Russian Federation, adopted by the State Duma on 25 October 1995, DOALOS website, available at www.un.org/Depts/los/LEGISLATIONANDTREATIES/PDFFILES/RUS_1995_Law.pdf
Fisheries Protection Zone Declaration (2005), A/60/68, available at https://documents-dds-ny.un.org/doc/UNDOC/GEN/N05/293/85/PDF/N0529385.pdf?OpenElement
Fisheries Resources (Jurisdiction and Conservation) Act, 1977, No. 13 of 16 June 1977, DOALOS website, available at www.un.org/Depts/los/LEGISLATIONANDTREATIES/PDFFILES/BHS_1977_13.pdf
Fishing Zone, Act 87–27 (1987), DOALOS website, available at www.un.org/Depts/los/LEGISLATIONANDTREATIES/PDFFILES/SEN_1987_Act.pdf
Harry S. Truman, "Proclamation 2667 – Policy of the United States with Respect to the Natural Resources of the Subsoil and Sea Bed of the Continental Shelf", 28 September 1945
Law 66–07 (2007), 65 Law of the Sea Bulletin 18 (2007)
Law concerning the extension of the Territorial Sea and the establishment of a Contiguous Economic Zone (1978), DOALOS website, available at www.un.org/Depts/los/LEGISLATIONANDTREATIES/PDFFILES/SUR_1978_Law.pdf
Law No. 1/98 (1998), DOALOS website, available at www.un.org/Depts/los/LEGISLATIONANDTREATIES/PDFFILES/STP_1998_Law.pdf
Law No. 18.565 (1986), DOALOS website, available at www.un.org/Depts/los/LEGISLATIONANDTREATIES/PDFFILES/CHL_1986_18565.pdf
Law No. 2000–2 (2000), available at http://oceansbeyondpiracy.org/sites/default/files/Cameroon_Delimitation_of_Waters_Law_2000.pdf

Law No. 21/92 (1992), DOALOS website, available at www.un.org/Depts/los/LEGISLATIONANDTREATIES/PDFFILES/AGO_1992_Law21.pdf
Law No. 2289/1995, as amended by Law No. 4001/2011, DOALOS website, available at www.un.org/Depts/los/LEGISLATIONANDTREATIES/PDFFILES/GRC_2011_Law.pdf
Law No. 30/76 relating to the Exclusive Economic Zone (1976), DOALOS website, available at www.un.org/Depts/los/LEGISLATIONANDTREATIES/PDFFILES/MDV_1976_Law30.pdf
Law No. 41 of 1 June 1979 concerning the Territorial Sea, the Economic Zone and the Continental Shelf, DOALOS website, available at www.un.org/Depts/los/LEGISLATIONANDTREATIES/PDFFILES/ISL_1979_Law.pdf
Law No. 5 dated 26 January 1989, as mentioned in Maritime Delimitation in the Indian Ocean (Somalia v. Kenya), Application Instituting Proceedings, ICJ (28 August 2014), at para. 7
Law No. 5 dated 26 January 1989, available at https://wwwex.ilo.org/dyn/natlex2/natlex2/files/download/108745/SOM108745.pdf (text in Somali, unofficially translated)
Law No. 52/AN/78 (1979), DOALOS website, available at www.un.org/Depts/los/LEGISLATIONANDTREATIES/PDFFILES/DJI_1979_Law.pdf
Law No. 60/IV/92 (1992), DOALOS website, available at www.un.org/Depts/los/LEGISLATIONANDTREATIES/PDFFILES/CPV_1992_Law.pdf
Law No. 76–655 of 16 July 1976 relating to the Economic Zone off the coasts of the territory of the Republic, DOALOS website, available at www.un.org/Depts/los/LEGISLATIONANDTREATIES/PDFFILES/FRA_1976_Law.pdf
Law No. 77–926 delimiting the Maritime Zones placed under the National Jurisdiction of the Republic of Ivory Coast of 17 November 1977, DOALOS website, available at www.un.org/Depts/los/LEGISLATIONANDTREATIES/PDFFILES/CIV_1977_Law.pdf
Law No. 8.617 of 4 January 1993, on the territorial sea, the contiguous zone, the exclusive economic zone and the continental shelf(1), DOALOS website, available at www.un.org/Depts/los/LEGISLATIONANDTREATIES/PDFFILES/BRA_1993_8617.pdf
Law No. 82–005 (1982), DOALOS website, available at www.un.org/Depts/los/LEGISLATIONANDTREATIES/PDFFILES/COM_1982_Law.pdf
Law of the Republic of Indonesia about the Sea, no. 32 (2014), available at http://extwprlegs1.fao.org/docs/pdf/ins161826.pdf
Law on Environment, No. 4 (1994), available at http://extwprlegs1.fao.org/docs/pdf/egy4984E.pdf
Law On the Continental Shelf and the Exclusive Economic Zone (1998)
Law on the Exclusive Economic Zone and the Continental Shelf (Act No. 140 of 1996), 33 Law of the Sea Bulletin 36 (1997)
Law on the Exclusive Economic Zone and the Continental Shelf (Law No. 74 of 1996), 35 Law of the Sea Bulletin 94 (1997)
Legislative Decree No. 2 (1977), DOALOS website, available at www.un.org/Depts/los/LEGISLATIONANDTREATIES/PDFFILES/CUB_1977_Decree2.pdf
Legislative Decree No. 20–76 (1976), DOALOS website, available at www.un.org/Depts/los/LEGISLATIONANDTREATIES/PDFFILES/GTM_1976_Decree.pdf
Lei no. 34/2006, available at https://dre.pt/application/file/a/539336 [Portuguese]
Marine and Coastal Access Act (2009), DOALOS website, available at www.legislation.gov.uk/ukpga/2009/23/pdfs/ukpga_20090023_en.pdf
Marine Areas Act (1993), DOALOS website, available at www.un.org/Depts/los/LEGISLATIONANDTREATIES/PDFFILES/IRN_1993_Act.pdf
Marine Boundaries and Jurisdiction Act (1978), DOALOS website, available at www.un.org/Depts/los/LEGISLATIONANDTREATIES/PDFFILES/BRB_1978_3.pdf
Marine Environment Protection and Management Law (2010), FAOLEX database, available at http://extwprlegs1.fao.org/docs/pdf/lat172860.pdf
Marine Pollution (Ships and Installations) Act, No. 34 (2013), available at http://extwprlegs1.fao.org/docs/pdf/png148580.pdf

Marine spaces Act, No. 18 (1977), as amended by the Marine Spaces (Amendment) Act, No. 15 (1978), Pacific Islands Legal Information Institute, available at www.paclii.org/fj/legis/consol_act_OK/msa132/
Marine Zones (Declaration) Act 1984, DOALOS website, available at www.un.org/Depts/los/LEGISLATIONANDTREATIES/PDFFILES/MHL_1984_Act.pdf
Marine Zones (Declaration) Act, 1983, DOALOS website, available at www.un.org/Depts/los/LEGISLATIONANDTREATIES/PDFFILES/KIR_1983_Act.pdf [repealed by 2011 law]
Marine Zones (Declaration) Act, 2011, DOALOS website, available at www.un.org/Depts/los/LEGISLATIONANDTREATIES/PDFFILES/KIR_2011_Act.pdf
Maritime Areas Act (1991), DOALOS website, available at www.un.org/Depts/los/LEGISLATIONANDTREATIES/PDFFILES/POL_1991_Act.pdf
Maritime Areas Act (1996), FAOLEX database, available at http://extwprlegs1.fao.org/docs/pdf/jam7862.pdf
Maritime Areas Act (No. 15, 1983), DOALOS website, available at www.un.org/Depts/los/LEGISLATIONANDTREATIES/PDFFILES/VCT_1983_Act.pdf
Maritime Areas Act 1992, as amended by the Maritime Areas (Amendment) Act 2019, DOALOS website, available at www.un.org/Depts/los/LEGISLATIONANDTREATIES/PDFFILES/MAA1992_2019.pdf
Maritime Areas Act No. 18 (1982), DOALOS website, available at www.un.org/Depts/los/LEGISLATIONANDTREATIES/PDFFILES/ATG_1982_18.pdf
Maritime Areas Act No. 6 (1984), DOALOS website, available at www.un.org/Depts/los/LEGISLATIONANDTREATIES/PDFFILES/LCA_1984_Act.pdf
Maritime Areas Law (2009), FAOLEX database, available at http://extwprlegs1.fao.org/docs/pdf/con96746E.pdf
Maritime Boundaries Act, 1977, Act No. 10 of 30 June 1977, DOALOS website, available at www.un.org/Depts/los/LEGISLATIONANDTREATIES/PDFFILES/GUY_1977_Act.pdf
Maritime Code, 2004, 56 Law of the Sea Bulletin 60 (2004)
Maritime Jurisdiction (Boundaries of Exclusive Economic Zone) Order 2014, DOALOS website, available at www.un.org/Depts/los/LEGISLATIONANDTREATIES/PDFFILES/IRL_2014_Order86.pdf
Maritime Space, Inland Waterways and Ports Act (2000), DOALOS website, available at www.un.org/Depts/los/LEGISLATIONANDTREATIES/PDFFILES/BGR_2000_Act-.PDF
Maritime Zone Act 2005 (Act No. 2 of 2005) 62 Law of the Sea Bulletin 52 (2006)
Maritime Zones (Amendment) Act (No. 6, 2012), FAOLEX database, available at http://extwprlegs1.fao.org/docs/pdf/mat116801.pdf
Maritime Zones (Delimitation) Law, 1986, DOALOS website, available at www.un.org/Depts/los/LEGISLATIONANDTREATIES/PDFFILES/GHA_1986_Law.pdf
Maritime Zones Act (2017), DOALOS website, available at www.un.org/Depts/los/LEGISLATIONANDTREATIES/PDFFILES/DEPOSIT/sur_mzn131_2018.pdf
Maritime Zones Act (No. 6, 2010), FAOLEX database, available at http://extwprlegs1.fao.org/docs/pdf/van99597.pdf
Maritime Zones Act 1977 (Act No. 13 of 3 June 1977), DOALOS website, available at www.un.org/Depts/los/LEGISLATIONANDTREATIES/PDFFILES/MUS_1977_Act.pdf
Maritime Zones Act 1999, FAOLEX database, available at http://extwprlegs1.fao.org/docs/pdf/sam35516.pdf
Maritime Zones Act 2012, FAOLEX database, available at http://extwprlegs1.fao.org/docs/pdf/tuv126505.pdf
Maritime Zones Act 2013 (No. 323 of 2013), FAOLEX database, available at http://extwprlegs1.fao.org/docs/pdf/niu136342.pdf
Maritime Zones Act No. 1 (2018), FAOLEX database, available at http://extwprlegs1.fao.org/docs/pdf/cok183766.pdf
Maritime Zones Act No. 10 (2009), Pacific Agricultural Policy Programme website, available at https://pafpnet.spc.int/attachments/article/648/Tonga%20Maritime%20Zones%20Act%202009.pdf

Maritime Zones Act No. 15 (1977), DOALOS website, available at www.un.org/Depts/los/LEGISLATIONANDTREATIES/PDFFILES/SYC_1977_Act.pdf

Maritime Zones Act No. 18 (2010), FAOLEX database, available at http://extwprlegs1.fao.org/docs/pdf/guy141190.pdf

Maritime Zones Act No. 47 (2015), FAOLEX database, available at http://extwprlegs1.fao.org/docs/pdf/png188723.pdf

Maritime Zones Act, 1999 (Act No. 2 of 1999), DOALOS website, available at www.un.org/Depts/los/LEGISLATIONANDTREATIES/PDFFILES/SYC_1999_Act2.pdf

Maritime Zones Act, No. 15 of 1994, DOALOS website, available at www.un.org/Depts/los/LEGISLATIONANDTREATIES/PDFFILES/ZAF_1994_Act.pdf

Maritime Zones Declaration Act (P.L. 2016–5) (2016), FAOLEX database, available at http://extwprlegs1.fao.org/docs/pdf/mas158412.pdf

Maritime Zones Law No. 22 of 1 September 1976, DOALOS website, available at www.un.org/Depts/los/LEGISLATIONANDTREATIES/PDFFILES/LKA_1976_Law.pdf

Maritime Zones of Maldives Act No. 6/96, DOALOS website, available at www.un.org/Depts/los/LEGISLATIONANDTREATIES/PDFFILES/MDV_1996_Act.pdf

Mining Act 2003 (translation), available at www.nlog.nl/sites/default/files/2018-11/2018-11-04%20%20Translation%20MBW%20English%20%20MINING%20ACT%20OF%20THE%20NETHERLANDS%20PDF.pdf

National Parliament, Law No. 7/2002, Maritime Borders of the Territory of the Democratic Republic of Timor-Leste, FAOLEX database, available at http://extwprlegs1.fao.org/docs/pdf/tim39858.pdf

Oceans Act of 18 December 1996, DOALOS website, available at www.un.org/Depts/los/LEGISLATIONANDTREATIES/PDFFILES/CAN_1996_Act.pdf

Official Proclamation (1957), DOALOS website, available at www.un.org/Depts/los/LEGISLATIONANDTREATIES/PDFFILES/IRQ_1957_Proclamation.pdf

Offshore Petroleum and Greenhouse Gas Storage Act 2006, Vol. 1, FAOLEX database, available at http://extwprlegs1.fao.org/docs/pdf/aus64464volume1.pdf

Offshore Petroleum and Greenhouse Gas Storage Act 2006, Vol. 2, available at www.legislation.gov.au/Details/C2015C00159/Html/Volume_2#_Toc416691713

Order No. 16/2012/L-CTN on the promulgation of the Law of the Sea of Vietnam No. 18/2012/QH13, FAOLEX database, available at http://extwprlegs1.fao.org/docs/pdf/vie124619.pdf

Ordinance 88–120 (1988), DOALOS website, available at www.un.org/Depts/los/LEGISLATIONANDTREATIES/PDFFILES/MRT_1988_Ordinance.pdf

Ordinance No. 24 (1977), DOALOS website, available at www.un.org/Depts/los/LEGISLATIONANDTREATIES/PDFFILES/TGO_1977_Ordinance.pdf

Ordinance No. 85–013 determining the limits of the maritime zones (territorial sea, continental shelf and exclusive economic zone) of the Democratic Republic of Madagascar, 16 September 1985, as amended and ratified by Law No. 85–013 of 11 December 1985), DOALOS website, available at www.un.org/Depts/los/LEGISLATIONANDTREATIES/PDFFILES/MDG_1985_Ordinance.pdf

Outer Continental Shelf Lands Act (1953), DOALOS website, available at www.un.org/Depts/los/LEGISLATIONANDTREATIES/PDFFILES/USA_1953_Act.pdf

Outer Continental Shelf Lands Act Amendments (1978), Congress website, available at www.congress.gov/bill/95th-congress/senate-bill/9?q=%7B%22search%22%3A%5B%22continental+shelf%22%5D%7D&r=11&s=4

Outer Limits Decree (2010), DOALOS website, available at www.un.org/Depts/los/LEGISLATIONANDTREATIES/PDFFILES/NLD_EEZ_decree2010.pdf

Petroleum Regulations of the Republic of Equatorial Guinea (2013), available at https://egronda.com/oilandgas/docs/petroleum_regulations_egronda_eng.pdf

Pollution Act (No. 6, 1981) (translate), FAOLEX database, available at www.fao.org/faolex/results/en/#querystring=JmVuZHN0cmluZz0x

Presidential Decision No. 1051 (1958), DOALOS website, available at www.un.org/Depts/los/LEGISLATIONANDTREATIES/PDFFILES/EGY_1958_Decision.pdf

Presidential Decree No. 1599 of 11 June 1978 establishing an Exclusive Economic Zone and for other purposes, DOALOS website, available at www.un.org/Depts/los/LEGISLATIONANDTREATIES/PDFFILES/PHL_1978_Decree.pdf
Presidential Decree No. 18–96 (2018), DOALOS website, available at www.un.org/Depts/los/LEGISLATIONANDTREATIES/PDFFILES/DZA_2018_Decree_1896_en.pdf
Presidential Decree No. 781, 1947, DOALOS website, available at www.un.org/Depts/los/LEGISLATIONANDTREATIES/PDFFILES/PER_1947_Decree.pdf
Presidential Regulation on Prevention of Oil Spill in the Sea, No. 109 (2006), available at http://extwprlegs1.fao.org/docs/pdf/ins72643.pdf
Proclamation by the President of the Federal Republic of Somalia (2014), FAOLEX database, available at http://extwprlegs1.fao.org/docs/pdf/som158857.pdf
Public Notice 2237, Exclusive Economic Zone and Maritime Boundaries; Notice of Limits, Federal Register Vol. 60, No. 163 (1995), available at www.un.org/Depts/los/LEGISLATIONANDTREATIES/PDFFILES/USA_1995_eez_public_notice.pdf
Regulation of safety zones in the CS in Malta, Continental Shelf Regulations, L.N. 235 (2015), FAOLEX database, available at http://extwprlegs1.fao.org/docs/pdf/mlt147865.pdf
Resolution No. 1597 concerning limits of the maritime zones (2004), 61 Law of the Sea Bulletin 17 (2006)
Royal Decree (1963), DOALOS website, available at www.un.org/Depts/los/LEGISLATIONANDTREATIES/PDFFILES/NOR_1963_Decree.pdf
Royal Decree concerning the territorial sea, continental shelf and exclusive economic zone, 1981, DOALOS website, available at www.un.org/Depts/los/LEGISLATIONANDTREATIES/PDFFILES/OMN_1981_Decree.pdf
Royal Decree of 7 June 1963 concerning the exercise of Danish sovereignty over the Continental Shelf, DOALOS website, available at www.un.org/Depts/los/LEGISLATIONANDTREATIES/PDFFILES/DNK_1963_Decree.pdf
Royal Decree on Measures to Protect Navigation, Sea Fishing, the Environment and Other Essential Interests in the Exploration and Exploitation of the Mineral and Other Non-living Resources of the Sea-Bed and Subsoil in the Territorial Sea and on the Continental Shelf, 1974 as amended by the Royal Decree (1983), DOALOS website, available at www.un.org/Depts/los/LEGISLATIONANDTREATIES/PDFFILES/bel_1983_protection_decree.pdf
Royal Decree, No. M-27 (1968), DOALOS website, available at www.un.org/Depts/los/LEGISLATIONANDTREATIES/PDFFILES/SAU_1968_Decree.pdf
Sea Boundaries Act (No. 16, 1997), FAOLEX database, available at http://extwprlegs1.fao.org/docs/pdf/nau28262.pdf
Sea Law 4/96 (1996), FAOLEX database, available at http://extwprlegs1.fao.org/docs/pdf/moz22054.pdf
Seas and Submerged Lands Act 1973 (including amendments up to 2019), FAOLEX database, available at http://extwprlegs1.fao.org/docs/pdf/aus5017.pdf
Seas and Submerged Lands Act 1973, as amended by the Maritime Legislation Amendment Act 1994, DOALOS website, available at www.un.org/Depts/los/LEGISLATIONANDTREATIES/PDFFILES/aus_1994_sea_act.pdf
Statement Issued by the Spokesman of the Ministry of Foreign Affairs (1978), DOALOS website, available at www.un.org/Depts/los/LEGISLATIONANDTREATIES/PDFFILES/KHM_1978_Statement.pdf
Statement on the Territorial Sea, the Contiguous Zone, the Exclusive Economic Zone and the Continental Shelf (1977), DOALOS website, available at www.un.org/Depts/los/LEGISLATIONANDTREATIES/PDFFILES/VNM_1977_Statement.pdf
Statute of Maritime Delimitation of the Kingdom of Saudi Arabia (Royal Decree No. 6, 2011), FAOLEX database, available at http://extwprlegs1.fao.org/docs/pdf/sau158713.pdf
Territorial Sea and Exclusive Economic Zone Act 1977, Act No. 28 of 26 September 1977 as amended by Act No. 146 of 1980, DOALOS website, available at www.un.org/Depts/los/LEGISLATIONANDTREATIES/PDFFILES/NZL_1980_Act.pdf

Territorial Sea and Exclusive Economic Zone Act, 1989, DOALOS website, available at www.un.org/Depts/los/LEGISLATIONANDTREATIES/PDFFILES/TZA_1989_Act.pdf

Territorial Sea and Exclusive Economic Zone Act, No. 16 (1977), DOALOS website, available at www.un.org/Depts/los/LEGISLATIONANDTREATIES/PDFFILES/COK_1977_Act16.pdf [repealed by 2018 law]

Territorial Sea and Exclusive Economic Zone of Namibia, Act No. 3 of 1990, 30 June 1990, DOALOS website, available at www.un.org/Depts/los/LEGISLATIONANDTREATIES/PDFFILES/NAM_1990_Act.pdf

Territorial Sea and Maritime Boundaries Act No. 25 (1989), DOALOS website, available at www.un.org/Depts/los/LEGISLATIONANDTREATIES/PDFFILES/grd_act_25_1989.pdf

Territorial Sea and Maritime Zones Law (Pyidaungsu Hluttaw Law No. 14, 2017), DOALOS website, available at www.un.org/Depts/los/LEGISLATIONANDTREATIES/PDFFILES/Myanmar_MZL_2017.pdf

Territorial Sea and Maritime Zones Law, Pyithu Hluttaw Law No. 3 of 9 April 1977, available at www.un.org/Depts/los/LEGISLATIONANDTREATIES/PDFFILES/MMR_1977_Law.pdf

Territorial Sea, Contiguous Zone, and Exclusive Economic Zone Act (1977), as amended in 2005, available at www.legislation.govt.nz/act/public/1977/0028/latest/whole.html

Territorial Sea, Contiguous Zone, Exclusive Economic and Fishery Zones Act, No. 26 (1981), DOALOS website, available at www.un.org/Depts/los/LEGISLATIONANDTREATIES/PDFFILES/DMA_1981_Act.pdf

Territorial Sea, Continental Shelf, and the Exclusive Economic Zone Law No. 28 (2003), FAOLEX database, http://extwprlegs1.fao.org/docs/pdf/syr53778E.pdf

Territorial Waters and Continental Shelf Act, 1970, DOALOS website, available at www.un.org/Depts/los/LEGISLATIONANDTREATIES/PDFFILES/SDN_1970_Act.pdf

Territorial Waters and Maritime Zones Act 1974, Act No. XXVI of 1974, DOALOS website, available at www.un.org/Depts/los/LEGISLATIONANDTREATIES/PDFFILES/BGD_1974_Act.pdf

Territorial Waters and Maritime Zones Act, 1976 (of 22 December 1976), DOALOS website, available at www.un.org/Depts/los/LEGISLATIONANDTREATIES/PDFFILES/PAK_1976_Act.pdf

The Delimitation of Marine Waters Act, No. 32 (1978), DOALOS website, available at www.un.org/Depts/los/LEGISLATIONANDTREATIES/PDFFILES/SLB_1978_Act.pdf

The Maritime Areas Act (No. 3, 1984), DOALOS website, available at www.un.org/Depts/los/LEGISLATIONANDTREATIES/PDFFILES/KNA_1984_Act.pdf

The Maritime Code (1994), DOALOS website, available at www.un.org/Depts/los/LEGISLATIONANDTREATIES/PDFFILES/HRV_1994_Code.pdf

The Maritime Zones (Establishment) Decree, 1996, DOALOS website, available at www.un.org/Depts/los/LEGISLATIONANDTREATIES/PDFFILES/SLE_1996_Decree.pdf

The Petroleum Act, RPPL 8–37 (2011), Pacific Islands Legal Information Institute, available at www.paclii.org/cgi-bin/sinodisp/pw/legis/num_act/tpaotropr8372011417/tpaotropr8372011417.html?stem=&synonyms=&query=continental%20shelf

The Territorial Sea and Exclusive Economic Zone Act, Act No. 30 of 23 October 1978, as amended by Act No. 19 of 1989, DOALOS website, available at www.un.org/Depts/los/LEGISLATIONANDTREATIES/PDFFILES/TON_1989_Act.pdf

The Territorial Waters, Continental Shelf, Exclusive Economic Zone and other Maritime Zones Act, 1976, Act No. 80 of 28 May 1976, DOALOS website, available at www.un.org/Depts/los/LEGISLATIONANDTREATIES/PDFFILES/IND_1976_Act.pdf

United States Code of Federal Regulations, Title 33, Chapter I, Subchapter N, Part 147, available at www.ecfr.gov/cgi-bin/text-idx?SID=2961df533a6e9c56e8a73fcb5c1c7e91&mc=true&node=pt33.2.147&rgn=div5

Documents

Argentines' Note Verbale to the Commission, no, N.U. No. 290/09/600, available at www.un.org/Depts/los/clcs_new/submissions_files/gbr45_09/arg_re_gbr_clcs_2009e.pdf
Argentina's Note Verbale, available at www.un.org/Depts/los/clcs_new/submissions_files/arg25_09/arg25_arg_2012e.pdf
Argentina's Note Verbale no. ENAUN No. 899/2022, available at www.un.org/depts/los/clcs_new/submissions_files/chl_89_2022/20221101ArgNvUn001Eng.pdf
Argentine's submission to the Commission, available at www.un.org/Depts/los/clcs_new/submissions_files/arg25_09/arg2009e_summary_eng.pdf
Articles concerning the Law of the Sea with commentaries, YILC, Vol. II, 8th Sess, ILC Doc A/CN.4/SER.A/1956/Add.1 (1956)
Australia's submission to the Commission, available at www.un.org/Depts/los/clcs_new/submissions_files/aus04/Documents/aus_doc_es_web_delivery.pdf
Bahamas's submission to the Commission, available at www.un.org/Depts/los/clcs_new/submissions_files/bhs71_14/BHS-ES-DOC.pdf
Bangladesh's Note Verbale no. PMBNY/67/UNCLOS/2012, available at www.un.org/depts/los/clcs_new/submissions_files/mmr08/2012_09_30_BGD_NV_UN.pdf
Bangladesh's Note Verbale no. PMBNY-UNCLOS/2009, available at www.un.org/Depts/los/clcs_new/submissions_files/mmr08/clcs16_2008_mmr_bgd_e.pdf
Bangladesh's Note Verbale no. PMBNY-UNCLOS/2009-, available at www.un.org/depts/los/clcs_new/submissions_files/ind48_09/bgd_re_ind_clcs48_2009e.pdf
Bangladesh's submission to the Commission, Executive Summary, available at www.un.org/Depts/los/clcs_new/submissions_files/bgd55_11/Executive%20summary%20final.pdf
Bangladesh's Note Verbale, no. PMBNY/CLCS/2021, available at www.un.org/Depts/los/clcs_new/submissions_files/bgd55_11/20210506BgdNvUn009.pdf
Bangladesh's Note Verbale, no. PMBNY/CLCS/2021, available at www.un.org/Depts/los/clcs_new/submissions_files/bgd55_11/20210913BgdNvUn010.pdf
Canada's Note Verbale, available at www.un.org/Depts/los/clcs_new/submissions_files/can70_13/2014_09_03_can_nv_un_001.pdf
Canada's notification to the CLCS, DOALOS website, available at www.un.org/Depts/los/clcs_new/submissions_files/rus01/CLCS_01_2001_LOS__CANtext.pdf
Canada's partial submission to the Commission concerning the Atlantic Ocean (2013), available at www.un.org/Depts/los/clcs_new/submissions_files/can70_13/es_can_en.pdf
Canada's partial submission to the Commission concerning the Arctic Ocean (2019), available at www.un.org/Depts/los/clcs_new/submissions_files/can1_84_2019/CDA_ARC_ES_EN_secured.pdf
China's Note Verbale no. CML/2/2009, available at www.un.org/depts/los/clcs_new/submissions_files/jpn08/chn_6feb09_e.pdf
China's Note Verbale no. CML/001/2013, available at www.un.org/Depts/los/clcs_new/submissions_files/chn63_12/chn_re_jpn07_01_2013e.pdf
China's Note Verbale no. CML/017/2013, available at www.un.org/Depts/los/clcs_new/submissions_files/chn63_12/chn_re_clcs63_08_2013_e.pdf
China's Note Verbale no. CML 11/2020, available at www.un.org/Depts/los/clcs_new/submissions_files/mys_12_12_2019/China_Philippines_ENG.pdf
China's Note Verbale no. CML 42/2020, available at www.un.org/Depts/los/clcs_new/submissions_files/mys_12_12_2019/2020_04_17_CHN_NV_UN_003_EN.pdf
China's Note Verbale no. CML 46/2020, available at www.un.org/Depts/los/clcs_new/submissions_files/mys_12_12_2019/2020_06_02_CHN_NV_UN_eng.pdf
China's Note Verbale no. CML 54/2020, available at www.un.org/Depts/los/clcs_new/submissions_files/mys_12_12_2019/20200729_CHN_NV_UN_e.pdf
China's Note Verbale no. CML 32/2021, available at www.un.org/Depts/los/clcs_new/submissions_files/mys_12_12_2019/20210816ChnNvUNen.pdf
CLCS, 3rd Sess, UN Doc CLCS/7 (15 May 1998)

CLCS, 10th Sess, UN Doc CLCS/32 (12 April 2002)
CLCS, 11th Sess, UN Doc CLCS/34 (1 July 2002)
CLCS, 14th Sess, UN Doc CLCS/42 (14 September 2004)
CLCS, 15th Sess, UN Doc CLCS/44 (3 May 2005)
CLCS, 19th Sess, UN Doc CLCS/54 (27 April 2007)
CLCS, 20th Sess, UN Doc CLCS/56 (4 October 2007)
CLCS, 21st Sess, UN Doc CLCS/58 (25 April 2008)
CLCS, 22nd Sess, UN Doc CLCS/60 (26 September 2008)
CLCS, 23rd Sess, UN Doc CLCS/62 (20 April 2009)
CLCS, 24th Sess, UN Doc CLCS/64 (1 October 2009)
CLCS, 26th Sess, UN Doc CLCS/68 (17 September 2010)
CLCS, 27th Sess, UN Doc CLCS/70 (11 May 2011)
CLCS, 28th Sess, UN Doc CLCS/72 (16 September 2011)
CLCS, 29th Sess, UN Doc CLCS/74 (30 April 2012)
CLCS, 31st Sess, UN Doc CLCS/78 (1 April 2013)
CLCS, 32nd Sess, UN Doc CLCS/80 (24 September 2013)
CLCS, 34th Sess, UN Doc CLCS/83 (31 March 2014)
CLCS, 35th Sess, UN Doc CLCS/85 (24 September 2014)
CLCS, 38th Sess, UN Doc CLCS/90 (1 October 2015)
CLCS, 40th Sess, UN Doc CLCS/93 (18 April 2016)
CLCS, 41st Sess, UN Doc CLCS/95 (21 September 2016)
CLCS, 45th Sess, UN Doc CLCS/101 (15 December 2017)
CLCS, 46th Sess, UN Doc CLCS/103 (6 April 2018)
CLCS, 47th Sess, UN Doc CLCS/105 (13 September 2018)
CLCS, 50th Sess, UN Doc CLCS/50/2 (5 September 2019)
CLCS, 57th Sess, UN Doc CLCS/57/2 (3 April 2023)
Colombia, Costa Rica and Panama objections, Note Verbale, available at www.un.org/Depts/los/clcs_new/submissions_files/nic66_13/col_cri_pan_re_nic_2014_02_05_e.pdf
Consultations by the President of the Tribunal with representatives of Ghana and Cote d'Ivoire, under article 3 of annex VII to the United Nations Convention on the Law of the Sea, available at www.itlos.org/fileadmin/itlos/documents/cases/case_no.23_merits/pleadings/C23_Special_Agreement.pdf
Continental shelf submission of Namibia, Executive Summary, available at www.un.org/Depts/los/clcs_new/submissions_files/nam50_09/nam2009executivesummary.pdf
Continental Shelf Submission of Norway in respect of areas in the Arctic Ocean, the Barents Sea and the Norwegian Sea, Executive Summary, available at www.un.org/Depts/los/clcs_new/submissions_files/nor06/nor_exec_sum.pdf
Cook Islands' Note Verbale no. 108/2016–17, 30 November 2016, DOALOS website, available at www.un.org/Depts/los/clcs_new/submissions_files/cok23_09/2016_11_30_COK_NV_UN_037_16-00919.pdf
Declarations upon signing or ratifying UNCLOS, available at https://treaties.un.org/doc/Publication/CN/2009/CN.890.2009-Eng.pdf
Declarations upon signing or ratifying UNCLOS, available at https://treaties.un.org/doc/Publication/CN/2014/CN.568.2014-Eng.pdf
Ecuador and Peru's Joint Declaration (2012), DOALOS website, available at www.un.org/Depts/los/LEGISLATIONANDTREATIES/PDFFILES/TREATIES/ECU_PER_1617143(E).pdf
Fiji's Note Verbale, available at www.un.org/Depts/los/clcs_new/submissions_files/fji24_09/fji24_fji4apr15.pdf
France's Note Verbale, available at www.un.org/Depts/los/clcs_new/submissions_files/can70_13/1467831E.pdf
France's partial submission to the Commission in respect of Saint-Pierre-et-Miquelon, available at www.un.org/Depts/los/clcs_new/submissions_files/fra72_14/SPM_Summary_EN_April2014.pdf

Guyana's Note Verbale, available at www.un.org/Depts/los/clcs_new/submissions_files/guy57_11/clcs57_2011_guy_e2012.pdf

ICJ, Rules of Court (1978)

ILC, Law of the sea – régime of the high seas, Summary record of the 69th Mtg, UN Doc A/CN.4/SR.69, YILC vol. I (1950)

ILC, Law of the sea – régime of the high seas, Summary record of the 131st Mtg, UN Doc A/CN.4/L.27, YILC vol. I (1951)

ILC, Draft conclusions on identification of customary international law, with commentaries, A/73/10 (2018)

IMO document, LEG/MISC.8 (30 January 2014), available at https://wwwcdn.imo.org/localresources/en/OurWork/Legal/Documents/LEG%20MISC%208.pdf

IMO, Resolution A.671(16) concerning Safety Zones and Safety of Navigation Around Off-shore Installations and Structures (1989)

India's Communications received regarding the submission made by Indonesia to the Commission, available at www.un.org/Depts/los/clcs_new/submissions_files/idn08/clcs12_2008_ind_e.pdf

India's Note Verbale no. 55/DPR/PMI/NY-2022, available at www.un.org/depts/los/clcs_new/submissions_files/lka43_09/20221025IndNvUn002.pdf

Indonesia's Note Verbale, available at www.un.org/Depts/los/clcs_new/submissions_files/submission_idn.htm

International Law Commission, Responsibility of States for Internationally Wrongful Acts, 2001, Supplement No. 10 (A/56/10)

International Law Commission, Report of the Study Group on Fragmentation of International Law: Difficulties Arising from the Diversification and Expansion of International Law, A/CN.4/L.644 (18 July 2003)

International Law Commission, Fragmentation of International Law: Difficulties arising from the Diversification and Expansion of International Law, Report of the Study Group of the International Law Commission, Finalized by Martti Koskenniemi, A/CN.4/L.682 (2006)

International Tribunal for the Law of the Sea, Rules of the Tribunal, ITLOS/8, 25 March 2021

Ireland's submission to the CLCS concerning Hatton-Rockall Area, available at www.un.org/Depts/los/clcs_new/submissions_files/irl09/irl09_exsum.pdf

Japan's Note Verbale no. SC/09/108, available at www.un.org/Depts/los/clcs_new/submissions_files/jpn08/jpn_25mar09.pdf

Japan's Note Verbale no. PM/09/735, available at www.un.org/Depts/los/clcs_new/submissions_files/jpn08/jpn_26aug09.pdf

Japan's Note Verbale no. SC/11/233, available at www.un.org/Depts/los/clcs_new/submissions_files/jpn08/jpn_09aug11.pdf

Japan's Note Verbale no. SC/11/239, available at www.un.org/Depts/los/clcs_new/submissions_files/jpn08/jpn_15aug11.pdf

Japan's Note Verbale no. PM/12/078, available at www.un.org/Depts/los/clcs_new/submissions_files/jpn08/jpn_09apr12.pdf

Japan's note to the Commission concerning the Australian submission, available at www.un.org/Depts/los/clcs_new/submissions_files/aus04/clcs_03_2004_los_jap.pdf

Japan's note to the Commission concerning New Zealand's submission, available at www.un.org/Depts/los/clcs_new/submissions_files/nzl06/japan_e.pdf

Joint Submission by the French Republic and the Republic of South Africa: General Principles of Natural Prolongation, DOALOS website, available at www.un.org/Depts/los/clcs_new/submissions_files/frazaf34_09/frazaf_clcs34_2018.pdf

Kenya's Note Verbale no. 12/34, available at www.un.org/Depts/los/clcs_new/submissions_files/ken35_09/ken_2013_10_29.pdf

Kenya's Note Verbale no. 586/14, available at www.un.org/Depts/los/clcs_new/submissions_files/ken35_09/ken_2014_10_24.pdf

Korea's Note Verbale no. MUN/230/11, available at www.un.org/depts/los/clcs_new/submissions_files/jpn08/kor11aug11.pdf

Korea's Note Verbale no MUN/022/13, available at www.un.org/Depts/los/clcs_new/submissions_files/kor65_12/kor_re_jpn_23_01_2013.pdf
Korea's Note Verbale no. MUN/191/13, available at www.un.org/Depts/los/clcs_new/submissions_files/kor65_12/kor_re_jpn_26_08_2013.pdf
Liberia's submission to the Commission, available at www.un.org/Depts/los/clcs_new/submissions_files/lib81_18/es_lib81_18.pdf
Madagascar's submission to the Commission, Executive Summary, available at www.un.org/Depts/los/clcs_new/submissions_files/mgd56_11/MDG-DOC-002_EXECUTIVE_SUMMARY_Updated.pdf
Malaysia's Note Verbale no. HA 24/09, available at www.un.org/Depts/los/clcs_new/submissions_files/mysvnm33_09/mys_re_chn_2009re_mys_vnm_e.pdf
Malaysia's Note Verbale no. HA 41/09, available at www.un.org/Depts/los/clcs_new/submissions_files/mysvnm33_09/mys_re_phl_2009re_mys_vnm_e.pdf
Malaysia's Note Verbal no. HA 30/20, available at www.un.org/Depts/los/clcs_new/submissions_files/mys_12_12_2019/2020_08_27_MYS_NV_UN_003.pdf
Micronesia's Note Verbale, no. FSMUN 07–2022, available at www.un.org/Depts/los/clcs_new/submissions_files/fsm67_13/20220426FsmNvUn006.pdf
Micronesia's submission to the Commission concerning the Eauripik Rise, available at www.un.org/Depts/los/clcs_new/submissions_files/fsm67_13/FSM_EAU_Executive_Summary.pdf
Mozambique's submission to the Commission, available at www.un.org/Depts/los/clcs_new/submissions_files/moz52_10/moz_2010_es.pdf
New Zealand's Note Verbale to the Commission, available at www.un.org/Depts/los/clcs_new/submissions_files/nzl06/nzl_2008_e.pdf
New Zealand Submission to the Commission on the Limits of the Continental Shelf, Executive Summary, available at www.un.org/Depts/los/clcs_new/submissions_files/nzl06/nzl_exec_sum.pdf
Nicaragua's Note Verbale, available at www.un.org/Depts/los/clcs_new/submissions_files/nic66_13/nic_2013_12_20_001.pdf
Nicaragua's Note Verbale no. MINIC-NU-047–13, available at www.un.org/Depts/los/clcs_new/submissions_files/nic66_13/nic_2013_12_20_002.pdf
Nicaragua's Note Verbale no. MINIC-NU-048–13, available at www.un.org/Depts/los/clcs_new/submissions_files/nic66_13/nic_2013_12_20_004.pdf
Nicaragua's Note Verbale no. MINIC-NU-049–13, available at www.un.org/Depts/los/clcs_new/submissions_files/nic66_13/nic_2013_12_20_005.pdf
Nicaragua's Note Verbale no. MINIC-NU-050–13, available at www.un.org/Depts/los/clcs_new/submissions_files/nic66_13/nic_2013_12_20_006.pdf
Nigeria's 1965 declaration recognizing as compulsory the jurisdiction of the International Court of Justice, in conformity with Article 36, paragraph 2, of the Statute of the International Court of Justice, 544 UNTS 113, available at https://treaties.un.org/doc/Publication/UNTS/Volume%20544/v544.pdf
Norway's Diplomatic Note, DOALOS website, available at www.un.org/Depts/los/clcs_new/submissions_files/nor06/note28march2007.pdf
Note Verbale no. 08/11, 11 January 2011, DOALOS website, available at www.un.org/Depts/los/clcs_new/submissions_files/gbr08/gbr_nv_11jan2011.pdf
Note Verbale no. 270/2017, 13 September 2017, DOALOS website, available at www.un.org/Depts/los/clcs_new/submissions_files/zaf31_09/2017_09_14_zaf_nv_un_030_17_00683.pdf
Oman's submission to the Commission, available at www.un.org/Depts/los/clcs_new/submissions_files/omn78_17/omn_es.pdf
Pakistan's Note Verbale, available at www.un.org/Depts/los/clcs_new/submissions_files/pak29_09/2014_10_09_PAK_NV_UN_003_14-00794.pdf
Pakistan's submission to the Commission, available at www.un.org/Depts/los/clcs_new/submissions_files/pak29_09/pak2009executivesummary.pdf

Palau's Note Verbale, available at www.un.org/Depts/los/clcs_new/submissions_files/plw41_09/clcs_41_2009_los_plw.pdf

Panama's Note Verbale to the Commission no. DGPE/DG/665/22013, DOALOS website, available at www.un.org/Depts/los/clcs_new/submissions_files/nic66_13/pan_re_nic_2013_09_30e.pdf

Panama's Note Verbale to the Commission no. DGPE/FRONT/082/14, DOALOS website, available at www.un.org/Depts/los/clcs_new/submissions_files/nic66_13/pan_re_nic_2014_02_03_e.pdf

Partial revised Submission by Brazil in respect of the Brazilian Oriental and Meridional Margin, available at www.un.org/Depts/los/clcs_new/submissions_files/bra02_rev18/BR-OMM-ExecutiveSummary.pdf

Partial Revised Submission of the Russian Federation in respect of the Continental Shelf of the Russian Federation in the Arctic Ocean, available at www.un.org/Depts/los/clcs_new/submissions_files/rus01_rev15/2015_08_03_Exec_Summary_English.pdf

Partial Submission of the Government of the Kingdom of Denmark together with the Government of the Faroes to the Commission concerning The Northern Continental Shelf of the Faroe Islands (2009), available at www.un.org/Depts/los/clcs_new/submissions_files/dnk28_09/dnk2009executivesummary.pdf

Partial Submission of the Government of the Kingdom of Denmark together with the Government of the Faroes to the Commission concerning The Southern Continental Shelf of the Faroe Islands (2010), available at www.un.org/Depts/los/clcs_new/submissions_files/dnk54_10/SFM-Executive_Summary_secure.pdf

Partial Submission of the Government of the Kingdom of Denmark together with the Government of Greenland to the Commission concerning the Southern Continental Shelf of Greenland, available at www.un.org/Depts/los/clcs_new/submissions_files/dnk61_12/DNK2012_EX_SUM_S_GREENLAND.pdf

Partial Submission of the Government of the Kingdom of Denmark Together with the Government of Greenland to the Commission concerning the North-Eastern Continental Shelf of Greenland, available at www.un.org/Depts/los/clcs_new/submissions_files/dnk68_13/DNK2013_ES.pdf

Portugal's Note Verbale, available at www.un.org/Depts/los/clcs_new/submissions_files/prt44_09/prt_re_esp_2013_09_06_13_14_21_886.pdf

Portugal's 2009 submission to the Commission, Executive Summary, available at www.un.org/Depts/los/clcs_new/submissions_files/prt44_09/prt2009executivesummary.pdf

Portugal's 2017 submission to the Commission, Executive Summary, available at www.un.org/Depts/los/clcs_new/submissions_files/prt44_09/prt2017executivesummary.pdf

Position Paper of the Government of the People's Republic of China on the Matter of Jurisdiction in the South China Sea Arbitration Initiated by the Republic of the Philippines, 7 December 2014, available at www.fmprc.gov.cn/mfa_eng/wjdt_665385/2649_665393/201412/t20141207_679387.html

Report of the US embassy in Phnom Penh concerning the 1969 declaration on territorial sea and continental shelf, available at www.cia.gov/library/readingroom/docs/CIA-RDP08C01297R000100230010-7.pdf

Rules of Procedure for Meetings of States Parties, UN Doc SPLOS/2/Rev.5 (7 May 2020)

Rules of Procedure of the Commission on the Limits of the Continental Shelf, CLCS, 21st Sess, UN Doc CLCS/40/Rev.1 (17 April 2008)

Russian Federation's note to the Commission concerning the Australian submission, available at www.un.org/Depts/los/clcs_new/submissions_files/aus04/clcs_03_2004_los_rus-siantext.pdf

Somalia's Note Verbale, available at www.un.org/Depts/los/clcs_new/submissions_files/ken35_09/2014_09_02_SOM_LET_UN_004_14-00700.pdf

South Africa's submission to the Commission, available at www.un.org/Depts/los/clcs_new/submissions_files/zaf31_09/zaf2009executive_summary.pdf

South Africa's submission to the Commission, available at www.un.org/Depts/los/clcs_new/submissions_files/zaf31_09/zaf2013_amended_executive_summary.pdf
Spain's Note Verbale no. 064 MPbcm, available at www.un.org/Depts/los/clcs_new/submissions_files/esp77_14/prt_re_esp77_en.pdf
Spain's Note Verbale no. 076 MP/bcm, available at www.un.org/Depts/los/clcs_new/submissions_files/esp77_14/2015_04_22_ESP1_NV_UN_004_15-00366.pdf
Special Agreement and Notification of 24 September 2019, ITLOS website, available at www.itlos.org/fileadmin/itlos/documents/cases/28/C28_Special_Agreement.pdf
SPLOS, 1st Mtg, UN Doc SPLOS/3 (28 February 1995)
SPLOS, 2nd Mtg, UN Doc SPLOS/4 (26 July 1995)
SPLOS, 3rd Mtg, UN Doc SPLOS/5 (22 February 1996)
SPLOS, 5th Mtg, UN Doc SPLOS/14 (20 September 1996)
SPLOS, 6th Mtg, UN Doc SPLOS/20 (20 March 1997)
SPLOS, 7th Mtg, UN Doc SPLOS/21 (9 May 1997)
SPLOS, 7th Mtg, UN Doc SPLOS/24 (12 June 1997)
SPLOS, 8th Mtg, UN Doc SPLOS/27 (23 April 1998)
SPLOS, 8th Mtg, UN Doc SPLOS/31 (4 June 1998)
SPLOS, 9th Mtg, UN Doc SPLOS/48 (15 June 1999)
SPLOS, 10th Mtg, UN Doc SPLOS/60 (22 June 2000)
SPLOS, 11th Mtg, UN Doc SPLOS/63 (6 April 2001)
SPLOS, 11th Mtg, UN Doc SPLOS/73 (14 June 2001)
SPLOS, 12th Mtg, UN Doc SPLOS/91 (13 June 2002)
SPLOS, 13th Mtg, UN Doc SPLOS/103 (25 June 2003)
SPLOS, 14th Mtg, UN Doc SPLOS/119 (23 July 2004)
SPLOS, 15th Mtg, UN Doc SPLOS/135 (25 July 2005)
SPLOS, 16th Mtg, UN Doc SPLOS/140 (19 May 2006)
SPLOS, 16th Mtg, UN Doc SPLOS/148 (28 July 2006)
SPLOS, 17th Mtg, UN Doc SPLOS/164 (16 July 2007)
SPLOS, 18th Mtg, UN Doc SPLOS/183 (20 June 2008)
SPLOS, 18th Mtg, UN Doc SPLOS/184 (21 July 2008)
SPLOS, 19th Mtg, UN Doc SPLOS/199 (6 July 2009)
SPLOS, 19th Mtg, UN Doc SPLOS/INF/22/Corr.1 (1 July 2009)
SPLOS, 19th Mtg, UN Doc SPLOS/203 (24 July 2009)
SPLOS, 20th Mtg, UN Doc SPLOS/218 (13 July 2010)
SPLOS, 21st Mtg, UN Doc SPLOS/225 (5 May 2011)
SPLOS, 21st Mtg, UN Doc SPLOS/231 (29 June 2011)
SPLOS, 22nd Mtg, UN Doc SPLOS/245 (1 May 2012)
SPLOS, 23rd Mtg, UN Doc SPLOS/259 (1 April 2013)
SPLOS, 23rd Mtg, UN Doc SPLOS/263 (8 July 2013)
SPLOS, 24th Mtg, UN Doc SPLOS/270 (14 April 2014)
SPLOS, 24th Mtg, UN Doc SPLOS/277 (14 July 2014)
SPLOS, 25th Mtg, UN Doc SPLOS/287 (13 July 2015)
SPLOS, 26th Mtg, UN Doc SPLOS/303 (2 August 2016)
SPLOS, 27th Mtg, UN Doc SPLOS/316 (10 July 2017)
SPLOS, 28th Mtg, UN Doc SPLOS/319 (2 April 2018)
SPLOS, 28th Mtg, UN Doc SPLOS/324 (9 July 2018)
Submission by the Republic of Kenya, Executive summary, available at www.un.org/Depts/los/clcs_new/submissions_files/ken35_09/ken2009_executivesummary.pdf
Submission by the Republic of Seychelles to the Commission concerning the Northern Plateau Region, Executive Summary, available at www.un.org/Depts/los/clcs_new/submissions_files/syc39_09/syc2009executivesummary.pdf
Tanzania's partial submission to the Commission, available at www.un.org/Depts/los/clcs_new/submissions_files/tza59_12/Executive%20Summary_%20URT-DOC-001_18-01-2012.pdf

The Gabonese Republic's Note Verbale, available at www.un.org/Depts/los/clcs_new/submissions_files/ago69_2013/gab_re_ago_2014_05_30.pdf
The Government of the Democratic Republic of the Congo's note verbale, DOALOS website, available at www.un.org/Depts/los/clcs_new/submissions_files/ago69_2013/1430662E.pdf
The Government of the Democratic Republic of the Congo's note verbale, DOALOS website, available at www.un.org/Depts/los/clcs_new/submissions_files/ago69_2013/cod_re_ago_oct_2015e.pdf
The Icelandic Continental Shelf – Partial Submission, available at www.un.org/Depts/los/clcs_new/submissions_files/isl27_09/isl2009executivesummary.pdf
The Maldives Note Verbale no. 2022/UN/N/25, available at www.un.org/depts/los/clcs_new/submissions_files/mus2_2022/PICLCSMauritius.pdf
Tonga's Note Verbale to the Commission, available at www.un.org/Depts/los/clcs_new/submissions_files/nzl06/tonga_e.pdf
Tonga's Partial Submission of Data and Information on the Outer Limits of the Continental Shelf Executive Summary, available at www.un.org/Depts/los/clcs_new/submissions_files/ton46_09/ton2009executive_summary.pdf
Trinidad and Tobago's submission to the Commission, available at www.un.org/Depts/los/clcs_new/submissions_files/tto49_09/tto2009executive_summary.pdf
UN press release, UN Doc SEA/2047 (6 March 2017)
UNCLOS I, Vol. VI, 4th Committee (Continental Shelf): Summary Records, 26th-30th Mtg, UN Doc A/CONF.13/C.4/SR.26–30 (24 February-27 April 1958)
UNCLOS III, 1st Sess, 1st Plen Mtg, UN Doc A/CONF.62/SR.1 (3 December 1973)
UNCLOS III, 1st Sess, 2nd Plen Mtg, UN Doc A/CONF.62/SR.2 (7 December 1973)
UNCLOS III, 2nd Sess, 17th Plen Mtg, UN Doc A/CONF.62/SR.17 (26 June 1974)
UNCLOS III, 2nd Sess, 21st Plen Mtg, UN Doc A/CONF.62/SR.21 (28 June 1974)
UNCLOS III, 2nd Sess, 22nd Plen Mtg, UN Doc A/CONF.62/SR.22 (28 June 1974)
UNCLOS III, 2nd Sess, 23th Plen Mtg, UN Doc A/CONF.62/SR.23 (1 July 1974)
UNCLOS III, 2nd Sess, 29th Plen Mtg, UN Doc A/CONF.62/SR.29 (4 July 1974)
UNCLOS III, 2nd Sess, 30th Plen Mtg, UN Doc A/CONF.62/SR.30 (4 July 1974)
UNCLOS III, 2nd Sess, 33rd Plen Mtg, UN Doc A/CONF.62/SR.33 (9 July 1974)
UNCLOS III, 2nd Sess, 2nd Committee, 5th Mtg, UN Doc A/CONF.62/C.2/SR.5 (16 July 1974)
UNCLOS III, 2nd Sess, 1st Committee, 7th Mtg, UN Doc A/CONF.62/C.1/SR.7 (17 July 1974)
UNCLOS III, 2nd Sess, 3rd Committee, 9th Mtg, UN Doc A/CONF.62/C.3/SR.9 (19 July 1974)
UNCLOS III, UN Doc A/CONF.62/C.2/L.17 (23 July 1974)
UNCLOS III, UN Doc A/CONF.62/L.4 (26 July 1974)
UNCLOS III, 2nd Sess, 2nd Committee, 16th Mtg, UN Doc A/CONF.62/C.2/SR.16 (26 July 1974)
UNCLOS III, 2nd Sess, 2nd Committee, 17th Mtg, UN Doc A/CONF.62/C.2/SR.17 (26 July 1974)
UNCLOS III, 2nd Sess, 3rd Committee, 10th Mtg, UN Doc A/CONF.62/C.3/SR.10 (26 July 1974)
UNCLOS III, 2nd Sess, 2nd Committee, 18th Mtg, UN Doc A/CONF.62/C.2/SR.18 (29 July 1974)
UNCLOS III, 2nd Sess, 1st Committee, 10th Mtg, UN Doc A/CONF.62/C.1/SR.10 (30 July 1974)
UNCLOS III, 3rd Sess, 3rd Committee, 19th Mtg, UN Doc A/CONF.62/C.2/SR.19 (30 July 1974)
UNCLOS III, 2nd Sess, 2nd Committee, 22th Mtg, UN Doc A/CONF.62/C.2/SR.22 (31 July 1974)
UNCLOS III, 1st Committee, UN Doc A/CONF.62/C.1/L.3 (5 August 1974)

UNCLOS III, 2nd Sess, 2nd Committee, 25th Mtg, UN Doc A/CONF.62/C.2/SR.25 (5 August 1974)
UNCLOS III, 2nd Sess, 2nd Committee, 26th Mtg, UN Doc A/CONF.62/C.2/SR.26 (5 August 1974)
UNCLOS III, 2nd Sess, 1st Committee, 11th Mtg, UN Doc A/CONF.62/C.1/SR.11 (6 August 1974)
UNCLOS III, 2nd Sess, 2nd Committee, 30th Mtg, UN Doc A/CONF.62/C.2/SR.31 (7 August 1974)
UNCLOS III, UN Doc A/CONF.62/C.2/L.47 (8 August 1974)
UNCLOS III, 2nd Sess, 2nd Committee, 41st Mtg, UN Doc A/CONF.62/C.2/SR.41 (16 August 1974)
UNCLOS III, 2nd Committee, UN Doc A/CONF.62/C.2/L.82 (26 August 1974)
UNCLOS III, 2nd Committee, UN Doc A/CONF.62/C.2/L.86 (28 August 1974)
UNCLOS III, UN Doc A/CONF.62/L.8/REV.1 (17 October 1974)
UNCLOS III, 3rd Sess, UN Doc A/CONF.62/WP.8/PART II
UNCLOS III, 3rd Sess, UN Doc A/CONF.62/C.2/L.89/Rev.1 (15 July 1975)
UNCLOS III, 4th Sess, UN Doc A/CONF.62/WP.8/REV.1/Part II
UNCLOS III, 4th Sess, 57th Plen Mtg, UN Doc A/CONF.62/SR.57 (15 March 1976)
UNCLOS III, 4th Sess, 58th Plen Mtg, UN Doc A/CONF.62/SR.58 (5 April 1976)
UNCLOS III, 4th Sess, 59th Plen Mtg, UN Doc A/CONF.62/SR.59 (5 April 1976)
UNCLOS III, 4th Sess, 60th Plen Mtg, UN Doc A/CONF.62/SR.60 (6 April 1976)
UNCLOS III, 4th Sess, 61st Plen Mtg, UN Doc A/CONF.62/SR.61 (6 April 1976)
UNCLOS III, 4th Sess, 62nd Plen Mtg, UN Doc A/CONF.62/SR.62 (7 April 1976)
UNCLOS III, 4th Sess, 63rd Plen Mtg, UN Doc A/CONF.62/SR.63 (8 April 1976)
UNCLOS III, 4th Sess, 65th Plen Mtg, UN Doc A/CONF.62/SR.65 (12 April 1976)
UNCLOS III, 5th Sess, UN Doc A/CONF.62/L.17 (16 September 1976)
UNCLOS III, 6th Sess, 2nd Committee, 50th Mtg, UN Doc A/CONF.62/C.2/SR.50 (23 June 1977)
UNCLOS III, 6th Sess, UN Doc A/CONF.62/WP.10 (15 July 1977)
UNCLOS III, 7th Sess, 2nd Committee, 53rd Mtg, UN Doc A/CONF.62/C.2/SR.53 (17 April 1978)
UNCLOS III, 7th Sess, 2nd Committee, UN Doc A/CONF.62/C.2/L.98 and ADD.1–3 (18 April 1978)
UNCLOS III, 7th Sess, 103rd Plen Mtg, UN Doc A/CONF.62/SR.103 (18 May 1978)
UNCLOS III, 7th Sess, 105th Plen Mtg, UN Doc A/CONF.62/SR.105 (19 May 1978)
UNCLOS III, 7th Sess, 106th Plen Mtg, UN Doc A/CONF.62/SR.106 (19 May 1978)
UNCLOS III, 8th Sess, 2nd Committee, UN Doc A/CONF.62/C.2/L.99 (9 April 1979)
UNCLOS III, 8th Sess, 2nd Committee, 57th Mtg, UN Doc A/CONF.62/C.2/SR.57 (24 April 1979)
UNCLOS III, 8th Sess, 2nd Committee, 58th Mtg, UN Doc A/CONF.62/C.2/SR.58 (24 April 1979)
UNCLOS III, 8th Sess, 112th Plen Mtg, UN Doc A/CONF.62/SR.112 (25 April 1979)
UNCLOS III, 8th Sess, UN Doc A/CONF.62/L.37 (26 April 1979)
UNCLOS III, 8th Sess, UN Doc A/CONF.62/WP.10/REV.1 (28 April 1979)
UNCLOS III, Resumed 8th Sess, UN Doc A/CONF.62/91 (19 September 1979)
UNCLOS III, 9th Sess, UN Doc A/CONF.62/L.47 (24 March 1980)
UNCLOS III, 9th Sess, UN Doc A/CONF.62/L.51 (29 March 1980)
UNCLOS III, 9th Sess, 125th Plen Mtg, UN Doc A/CONF.62/SR.125 (2 April 1980)
UNCLOS III, 9th Sess, 126th Plen Mtg, UN Doc A/CONF.62/SR.126 (2 April 1980)
UNCLOS III, 9th Sess, 127th Plen Mtg, UN Doc A/CONF.62/SR.127 (3 April 1980)
UNCLOS III, 9th Sess, 128th Plen Mtg, UN Doc A/CONF.62/SR.128 (3 April 1980)
UNCLOS III, 9th Sess, UN Doc A/CONF.62/WS/4 (10 April 1980)
UNCLOS III, 9th Sess, UN Doc A/CONF.62/WS/6 (10 April 1980)
UNCLOS III, 9th Sess, UN Doc A/CONF.62/WP.10/Rev.2 (11 April 1980)
UNCLOS III, 9th Sess, UN Doc A/CONF.62/WP.10/Rev.2/Corr.2 (9 May 1980)

UNCLOS III, Resumed 9th Sess, 130th Plen Mtg, UN Doc A/CONF.62/SR.130 (28 July 1980)
UNCLOS III, Resumed 9th Sess, 135th Plen Mtg, UN Doc A/CONF.62/SR.135 (25 August 1980)
UNCLOS III, Resumed 9th Sess, 136th Plen Mtg, UN Doc A/CONF.62/SR.136 (26 August 1980)
UNCLOS III, Resumed 9th Sess, 138th Plen Mtg, UN Doc A/CONF.62/SR.138 (26 August 1980)
UNCLOS III, Resumed 9th Sess, 139th Plen Mtg, UN Doc A/CONF.62/SR.139 (27 August 1980)
UNCLOS III, Resumed 9th Sess, 140th Plen Mtg, UN Doc A/CONF.62/SR.140 (27 August 1980)
UNCLOS III, Resumed 9th Sess, UN Doc A/CONF.62/WS/11 (2 October 1980)
UNCLOS III, Resumed 9th Sess, UN Doc A/CONF.62/WS/14 (3 October 1980)
UNCLOS III, 10th Sess, UN Doc A/CONF.62/L.76 (18 August 1981)
UNCLOS III, 11th Sess, 159th Plen Mtg, UN Doc A/CONF.62/SR.159 (30 March 1982)
UNCLOS III, 11th Sess, 165th Plen Mtg, UN Doc A/CONF.62/SR.165 (1 April 1982)
UNCLOS III, 11th Sess, 166th Plen Mtg, UN Doc A/CONF.62/SR.166 (1 April 1982)
UNCLOS III, 11th Sess, 168th Plen Mtg, UN Doc A/CONF.62/SR.168 (15 April 1982)
UNCLOS III, 11th Sess, 170th Plen Mtg, UN Doc A/CONF.62/SR.170 (16 April 1982)
UNCLOS III, Resumed 11th Sess, UN Doc A/CONF.62/121 (27 October 1982)
UNCLOS III, Resumed 11th Sess, 193th Plen Mtg, UN Doc A/CONF.62/SR.193 (10 December 1982)
UNCLOS III, NG7/2, UNCLOS official records, Platzoder, vol. IX 399 (1986)
UNCLOS official records, Platzoder, vol. IX (1986)
UNGAOR, 25th Sess, UN Doc A/RES/2749 (XXV) (1970)
UNGAOR, 49th Sess, UN Doc A/49/631 (16 November 1994)
UNGAOR, 68th Sess, UN Doc A/68/741 (7 February 2014)
UNGAOR, 69th Sess, UN Doc A/69/429 (8 October 2014)
United Kingdom's note verbale to the Commission, no. 84/09, available at www.un.org/Depts/los/clcs_new/submissions_files/arg25_09/clcs_45_2009_los_gbr.pdf
United Kingdom's Note Verbale no. 095/22, available at www.un.org/depts/los/clcs_new/submissions_files/chl_89_2022/20220422GbrNvUn001.pdf
United Kingdom's Note Verbale no. 004/23, available at www.un.org/depts/los/clcs_new/submissions_files/mus2_2022/UKNVCSN19012023.pdf
Unites States' note to the Commission concerning the Australian submission, available at www.un.org/Depts/los/clcs_new/submissions_files/aus04/clcs_03_2004_los_usatext.pdf
Vanuatu's note verbale, DOALOS website, available at www.un.org/Depts/los/clcs_new/submissions_files/fra07/van_0701306.pdf
Vanuatu's Note Verbale no. PMV/MDB/NY/0712/01, available at www.un.org/depts/los/clcs_new/submissions_files/fji24_09/clcs_24_2009_los_vut2.pdf
Viet Nam's Note Verbale no. 77/HC-2009, available at www.un.org/Depts/los/clcs_new/submissions_files/mysvnm33_09/vnm_2011_re_phlchn.pdf
Viet Nam's Note Verbale no. 86/HC-2009, available at www.un.org/Depts/los/clcs_new/submissions_files/mysvnm33_09/vnm_chn_2009re_mys_vnm_e.pdf
Viet Nam's Note Verbale no. 240/HC-2009, available at www.un.org/Depts/los/clcs_new/submissions_files/mysvnm33_09/vnm_re_phl_2009re_mys_vnm_e.pdf
Yearbook of the International Law Commission, 8th Sess, UN Doc. A/CN.4/102/Add.1, II. (United Nations, New York, 1956)

Books

Aaron X. Fellmeth and Maurice Horwitz, Guide to Latin in International Law (2009)
Alan Boyle and Christine Chinkin, The Making of International Law (2007)
Alexander Wendt, Social Theory of International Politics (1999)

Andreas Hasenclever, Peter Mayer and Volker Rittberger, Theories of International Regimes (1997)
Barbara Woodward, Global Civil Society in International Lawmaking and Global Governance: Theory and Practice (2010)
Barry Buzan, The Logic of Anarchy: Neorealism to Structural Realism (1993)
Barry Buzan, From International to World Society?: English School Theory and the Social Structure of Globalisation (2004)
Bhaso Ndzendze and Tshilidzi Marwala, Artificial Intelligence and International Relations Theories (2023)
Chinese Society of International Law, The South China Sea Arbitration Awards: A Critical Study (2018)
D. P. O'Connell, The International Law of the Sea, Vol. 1 (I.A Shearer (ed.), 1982).
Georg Sørensen, Jørgen Møller and Robert H. Jackson, Introduction to International Relations: Theories and Approaches (2022)
Gerard J. Tanja, The Legal Determination of International Maritime Boundaries (1990).
James Crawford, The Creation of States in International Law (2nd ed., 2006)
James Harrison, Making the Law of the Sea, A Study in the Development of International Law (2011)
James K. Sebenius, Negotiating the Law of the Sea (1984)
Jan Klabbers, An Introduction to International Institutional Law (2nd ed. 2009)
Katrin Fenrich, The Evolving International Procedural Capacity of Individuals (2019)
Lawrence Juda, International Law and Ocean Use Management, The Evolution of Ocean Governance (1996).
Malcolm N. Shaw, International Law (9th ed., 2021)
Massimo Lando, Maritime Delimitation as a Judicial Process (2019)
Max Weber, Essays in Economic Sociology (Richard Swedberg (Ed.), 1999)
Michael Zürn, A Theory of Global Governance: Authority, Legitimacy, And Contestation (2018)
Moshe Hirsch, Invitation to the Sociology of International Law (2015)
Natalie Klein, Dispute Settlement in the UN Convention on the Law of the Sea (2005)
Oran R. Young, International Governance: Protecting The Environment in A Stateless Society (1994)
Oran R. Young, Governance in World Affairs (1999)
Oran R. Young, Institutional Dynamics: Emergent Patterns in International Environmental Governance (2010)
Øystein Jensen, The Commission On The Limits of the Continental Shelf, Law and Legitimacy (2014)
Robin Churchill, Vaughan Lowe and Amy Sander, The Law of the Sea (4th ed, 2022)
Rozemarijn Roland Holst, Change in the Law of the Sea: Context, Mechanisms and Practice (2022)
Signe Veierud Busch, Establishing Continental Shelf Limits Beyond 200 Nautical Miles By The Coastal State (2016)
Stephan Walt, The Origins of Alliances (1987)
Stephen Fietta and Robin Cleverly, A Practitioner's Guide to Maritime Boundary Delimitation (2016)
Suezett V. Suarez, The Outer Limits of the Continental Shelf, Legal Aspects of their Establishment (2008)
Susan T. Fiske and Shelley E. Taylor, Social Cognition: From Brain to Culture (3rd ed., 2017)
Thomas Cottier, Equitable Principles of Maritime Boundary Delimitation: The Quest for Distributive Justice in International Law (2015)
Tomer Broude and Yuval Shany, Multi-Sourced Equivalent Norms in International Law (2011)
Torsten Stirner, The Procedural Law Governing Facts and Evidence in International Human Rights Proceedings (2021)

Vasco Becker-Weinberg, Joint Development of Hydrocarbon Deposits in the Law of the Sea (2014)
Vaughan Lowe, International Law (2007)
Victor Alencar Mayer Feitosa Ventura, Environmental Jurisdiction in the Law of the Sea, The Brazilian Blue Amazon (2020)
Yoshifumi Tanaka, The International Law of the Sea (3rd ed., 2019)
Youri Van Logchem, The Rights and Obligations of States in Disputed Maritime Areas (2021)
Ziva Kunda, Social Cognition: Making Sense of People (2nd ed., 2000)

Book Chapters

Alan Boyle, *Protecting the Marine Environment from Climate Change, The LOSC Part XII Regime*, *in* The Law of the Sea and Climate Change 81 (Elise Johansen, Signe Veierud Busch and Ingvild Ulrikke Jakobsen (eds.), 2020)
Alex G. Oude Elferink, Tore Henriksen, and Signe Veierud Busch, *The Judiciary and the Law of Maritime Delimitation: Setting the Stage*, *in* Maritime Boundary Delimitation: The Case Law: Is It Consistent and Predictable? 1 (Alex G. Oude Elferink, Tore Henriksen and Signe Veierud Busch (eds.), 2018)
Alexander Proelss, *The Contribution of the ITLOS to Strengthening the Regime for the Protection of the Marine Environment*, in Interpretations of the United Nations Convention on the Law of the Sea By International Courts and Tribunals 93 (Angela Del Vecchio and Roberto Virzo (eds.), 2019)
Andrea Insolia, *The Law of Maritime Delimitation in the Croatia/Slovenia Final Award*, *in* Interpretations of the United Nations Convention on the Law of the Sea by International Courts and Tribunals 225 (Angela Del Vecchio and Roberto Virzo (eds.), 2019)
Anne-Marie Slaughter, *International Law and International Relations Theory: A Prospectus*, *in* The Impact of International Law on International Cooperation: Theoretical Perspectives 16 (Eyal Benvenisti and Moshe Hirsch (eds.), 2009)
Anthony McGrew, *Globalization and Global Politics*, *in* The Globalization of World Politics, An Introduction to International Relations 19 (John Baylis, Steve Smith and Patricia Owens (eds.), 8th ed., 2020)
Barbara Koremenos, *Institutionalism and International Law*, *in Interdisciplinary Perspectives on International Law and International Relations: The State of the Art* 59 (Jeffrey L. Dunoff and Mark A. Pollack (eds.), 2013)
Catherine Redgwell, From Permission to Prohibition: The 1982 Convention on the Law of the Sea and Protection of the Marine Environment, in The Law of the Sea: Progress and Prospects 180 (David Freestone, Richard Barnes and David Ong (eds.), 2006)
Clive Schofield and Chris Carleton, *Technical Considerations in Law of the Sea Dispute Resolution*, *in* Oceans Management in the 21st Century: Institutional Frameworks and Responses 231 (A.G. Oude Elferink and D.R. Rothwell (eds.), 2004)
Constantinos Yiallourides and Natalia Ermolina, *States' Environmental Obligations in Disputed Maritime Areas and the Limits of International Law*, in Comparative Law Yearbook of International Business 125 (Christian Campbell (ed.), 2021), available at https://ssrn.com/abstract=3184800
Daniel Bodansky, *Legitimacy in International Law and International Relations*, *in* Interdisciplinary Perspectives on International Law and International Relations: The State of the Art 321 (Jeffrey L. Dunoff and Mark A. Pollack (eds.), 2013)
David M. Ong, *Towards an International Law for the Conservation of Offshore Hydrocarbon Resources within the Continental Shelf?*, *in* The Law of the Sea: Progress and Prospects 93 (David Freestone, Richard Barnes and David Ong (eds.), 2006)
Davor Vidas, *The Delimitation of the Territorial Sea, the Continental Shelf, and the EEZ: A Comparative Perspective*, *in* Maritime Boundary Delimitation: The Case Law: Is

It Consistent and Predictable? 33 (Alex G. Oude Elferink, Tore Henriksen and Signe Veierud Busch (eds.), 2018)

Donald R. Rothwell and David L. VanderZwaag, *The Sea Change towards Principled Ocean Governance*, *in* Towards Principled Ocean Governance, Australian and Canadian Approaches and Challenges 1 (Donald R. Rothwell and David L. VanderZwaag (eds.), 2006)

Eyal Benvenisti, *Customary International Law as a Judicial Tool for Promoting Efficiency*, *in* The Impact of International Law on International Cooperation: Theoretical Perspectives 85 (Eyal Benvenisti and Moshe Hirsch (eds.), 2009)

Francesca Romanin Jacur, *Formalism and Law-making in Treaty-based Ocean Governance: Limits and Challenges*, *in* Regime Interaction in Ocean Governance 156 (Seline Trevisanut, Nikolaos Giannopoulos and Rozemarijn Roland Holst (eds.), 2020)

Gemma Andreone, *The Exclusive Economic Zone*, *in* The Oxford Handbook of the Law of the Sea 159 (Donald R. Rothwell, Alex G. Oude Elferink, Karen N. Scott and Tim Stephens (eds.), 2015)

Glossary of Technical Terms, *in* Continental Shelf Limits, The Scientific and Legal Interface 321, 329 (Peter J. Cook and Chris M. Carleton (eds.), 2000)

James N. Rosenau, *Governance, Order, and Change in World Politics*, *in* Governance Without Government: Order and Change in World Politics 1 (James N. Rosenau and Ernest-Otto Czempiel (eds.), 1992)

Jeffrey L. Dunoff and Mark A. Pollack, *International Law and International Relations: Introducing an Interdisciplinary Dialogue*, *in* Interdisciplinary Perspectives on International Law and International Relations: The State of the Art 3 (Jeffrey L. Dunoff and Mark A. Pollack (eds.), 2013)

John W. Donaldson, *Oil and Water: Assessing the Link Between Maritime Boundary Delimitation and Hydrocarbon Resources*, *in* The Limits of Maritime Jurisdiction 127 (Clive H. Schofield, Seokwoo Lee and Moon-Sang Kwon (eds.), 2014)

Joost Pauwelyn and Manfred Elsig, *The Politics of Treaty Interpretation: Variations and Explanations Across International Tribunals*, *in* Interdisciplinary Perspectives on International Law and International Relations: The State of the Art 445 (Jeffrey L. Dunoff and Mark A. Pollack (eds.), 2013)

Judith Levine and Garth L. Schofield, *Navigating Uncharted Procedural Waters in a Rising Sea of Cases at the Permanent Court of Arbitration*, *in* Stress Testing The Law of the Sea 95 (2018)

K.J. Holsti, *Governance Without Government: Polyarchy in Nineteenth-century European International Politics*, *in* Governance Without Government: Order and Change in World Politics 30 (James N. Rosenau and Ernest-Otto Czempiel (eds.), 1992)

Kal Raustiala, *Institutional Proliferation and the International Legal Order*, *in* Interdisciplinary Perspectives on International Law and International Relations: The State of the Art 293 (Jeffrey L. Dunoff and Mark A. Pollack (eds.), 2013)

Karen J. Alter, *The Multiple Roles of International Courts and Tribunals: Enforcement, Dispute Settlement, Constitutional and Administrative Review*, *in* Interdisciplinary Perspectives on International Law and International Relations: The State of the Art 345 (Jeffrey L. Dunoff and Mark A. Pollack (eds.), 2013)

Kenneth W. Abbott and Duncan Snidal, *Law, Legalization, and Politics: An Agenda for the Next Generation of IL/IR Scholars*, *in* Interdisciplinary Perspectives on International Law and International Relations: The State of the Art 33 (Jeffrey L. Dunoff and Mark A. Pollack (eds.), 2013)

Leonardo Bernard and Clive Schofield, *Disputes Concerning the Delimitation of the Continental Shelf beyond 200 Nautical Miles*, *in* New Knowledge and Changing Circumstances in the Law of the Sea 157 (Tomas Heidar (ed.), 2020)

Malcolm D. Evans, *Maritime Boundary Delimitation*, *in* The Oxford Handbook of the Law of the Sea 254 (Donald R. Rothwell, Alex G. Oude Elferink, Karen N. Scott and Tim Stephens (eds.), 2015)

Malcolm Evans, *Relevant Circumstances*, *in* Maritime Boundary Delimitation: The Case Law: Is It Consistent and Predictable? 222 (Alex G. Oude Elferink, Tore Henriksen and Signe Veierud Busch (eds.), 2018)

Marcel Brus, *Bridging the Gap Between State Sovereignty and International Governance: The Authority of Law*, *in* State, Sovereignty, and International Governance 3 (Gerard Kreijen, Marcel Brus, Jorri Duursma, Elisabeth De Vos and John Dugard, (eds.), 2002)

Maria Gavouneli, *The Environmental Parameters of Maritime Security: The Case of Energy Installations*, *in* Droit De La Mer Et Droits De L'homme: Enjeux Et Perspectives, Liber Amicorum Haritini Dipla, (Laurence Boisson de Chazournes, Emmanuela Doussis, Gemma Andreone, Antonia Zervaki (eds.), 2020) [Forthcoming], available at https://ssrn.com/abstract=3519806

Mario Gervasi, *The Interpretation of the United Nations Convention on the Law of the Sea in the Chagos Marine Protected Area Arbitration: The Influence of the Land Sovereignty Dispute, in* Interpretations of the United Nations Convention on the Law of the Sea by International Courts and Tribunals 191 (Angela Del Vecchio and Roberto Virzo (eds.), 2019)

Mark W. Zacher, *The Decaying Pillars of the Westphalian Temple: Implications for International Order and Governance*, *in* Governance Without Government: Order and Change in World Politics 58 (James N. Rosenau and Ernest-Otto Czempiel (eds.), 1992)

Michael Barnett, *Social Constructivism*, *in* Globalization of World Politics, An Introduction to International Relations 192 (John Baylis, Steve Smith and Patricia Owens (eds.), 8th ed., 2020)

Michael Byers and Andreas Østhagen, *Settling Maritime Boundaries: Why Some Countries Find It Easy, and Others Do Not*, *in* The Future of Ocean Governance and Capacity Development 162 (The International Ocean Institute-Canada (ed.), 2018)

Moshe Hirsch, *Compliance with International Norms in the Age of Globalization: Two Theoretical Perspectives*, *in* The Impact of International Law on International Cooperation: Theoretical Perspectives 166, 168 (Eyal Benvenisti and Moshe Hirsch (eds.), 2009)

Natalie Klein, *Meaning, Scope, and Significance of Informal Lawmaking in the Law of the Sea*, *in* Unconventional Lawmaking in the Law of the Sea 3 (Natalie Klein (ed.), 2022)

Nele Matz-Lück, *Norm Interpretation across International Regimes: Competences and Legitimacy*, *in* Regime Interaction in International Law: Facing Fragmentation 201 (Margaret A. Young (ed.), 2012)

Nicholas A. Ioannides, *Rights and Obligations of States in Undelimited Maritime Areas: The Case of the Eastern Mediterranean Sea*, *in* Stress Testing The Law of the Sea 311 (Stephen Minas and Jordan Diamond (eds.), 2018)

Niels M. Blokker, *Governance of the International Tribunal of the Law of the Sea: The Role of the Meeting of States Parties to the Law of the Sea Convention*, *in* Interpretations of the United Nations Convention on the Law of the Sea by International Courts and Tribunals 81 (Angela Del Vecchio and Roberto Virzo (eds.), 2019)

Nuno Marques Antunes and Vasco Becker-Weinberg, *Entitlement to Maritime Zones and Their Delimitation: In the Doldrums of Uncertainty and Unpredictability*, in *Maritime Boundary Delimitation: The Case Law: Is It Consistent and Predictable*? 62 (Alex G. Oude Elferink, Tore Henriksen and Signe Veierud Busch (eds.), 2018)

Oran R. Young, *The Effectiveness of International Institutions: Hard Cases and Critical Variables, in* Governance Without Government: Order and Change in World Politics 160 (Rosenau, James N. and Ernst-Otto Czempiel (eds.), 1992)

Otto Spijkers, *Non-participation in Arbitral Proceedings Under Annex VII United Nations Convention on the Law of the Sea: Arctic Sunrise and South China Sea Compared, in* Interpretations of the United Nations Convention on the Law of the Sea by International Courts and Tribunals 171, 173 (Angela Del Vecchio and Roberto Virzo (eds.), Springer, 2019)

Øystein Jensen, *The Delimitation of the Continental Shelf beyond 200 nm: Substantive Issues*, *in* Maritime Boundary Delimitation: The Case Law: Is It Consistent and Predictable? 351 (Alex G. Oude Elferink, Tore Henriksen and Signe Veierud Busch (eds.), 2018)

Patricia Owens, John Baylis, and Steve Smith, *Introduction: From International Politics to World Politics, in* The Globalization of World Politics, An Introduction to International Relations 5 (John Baylis, Steve Smith and Patricia Owens (eds.), 8th ed., 2020)

Riccardo Pisillo-Mazzeschi, *The Due Diligence Rule and the Nature of the International Responsibility of States, in* State Responsibility in International Law 97 (René Provost (ed.), 2016)

Richard Little, *International Regimes, In* The Globalization of World Politics, An Introduction to International Relations 299 (Baylis John and Steve Smith (eds.), 2001)

Robert W. Smith and George Taft, *Legal Aspects of the Continental Shelf, in* Continental Shelf Limits, The Scientific and Legal Interface 17 (Peter J. Cook and Chris M. Carleton (eds.), 2000)

Roberto Virzo, *The 'General Rule of Interpretation' in the International Jurisprudence Relating to the United Nations Convention on the Law of the Sea, in* Interpretations of the United Nations Convention on the Law of the Sea by International Courts and Tribunals 15 (Angela Del Vecchio and Roberto Virzo (eds.), 2019)

Robin R. Churchill, *The 1982 United Nation Convention on the Law of the Sea, in* The Oxford Handbook of the Law of the Sea 24 (Donald R. Rothwell, Alex G. Oude Elferink, Karen N. Scott and Tim Stephens (eds.), 2015)

Saul Roux and Catherine Horsfield, *Review of National Legislations Applicable to Seabed Mineral Resources Exploitation, in* The Law of the Seabed 287 (Catherine Banet (ed.), 2020)

Sean D. Murphy, *Obligations of States in Disputed Areas of the Continental Shelf, in* New Knowledge and Changing Circumstances in The Law of the Sea 183 (Tomas Heidar (ed.), 2020)

Shirley V. Scott, *The LOS Convention as a Constitutional Regime for the Oceans, in* Stability and Change in The Law of the Sea 9 (Alex G. Oude Elferink (ed.), 2005)

Shunmugam Jayakumar, *The Continental Shelf Regime under the UN Convention on the Law of the Sea: Reflections After Thirty Years, in* The Regulation of Continental Shelf Development, Rethinking International Standards 1 (Myron H. Nordquist, John Norton Moore, Aldo Chircop and Ronán Long (eds.), 2013)

Signe Veierud Busch, *Law of the Sea Responses to Sea-level Rise and Threatened Maritime Entitlements, Applying an Exception Rule to Manage an Exceptional Situation, in* The Law of the Sea and Climate Change 309 (Elise Johansen, Signe Veierud Busch and Ingvild Ulrikke Jakobsen (eds.), 2020).

Signe Veierud Busch, *More Disputes Ahead for the CLCS? CLCS Practice on Rule 46 of Its Rules of Procedure, in* New Knowledge and Changing Circumstances in the Law of the Sea 232 (Tomas Heidar (ed.), 2020)

Signe Veierud Busch, *The Delimitation of the Continental Shelf beyond 200 nm: Procedural Issues, in* Maritime Boundary Delimitation: The Case Law: Is It Consistent and Predictable? 319 (Alex G. Oude Elferink, Tore Henriksen and Signe Veierud Busch (eds.), 2018)

Ted L. McDorman, *The Continental Shelf, in* The Oxford Handbook of the Law of the Sea 181 (Donald R. Rothwell, Alex G. Oude Elferink, Karen N. Scott and Tim Stephens (eds.), 2015)

Tim Dunne, *Liberalism, in* Globalization of World Politics, An Introduction to International Relations 116 (John Baylis, Steve Smith and Patricia Owens (eds.), 7th ed., 2017).

Tullio Scovazzi, *Maritime Accidents with Particular Emphasis on Liability and Compensation for Damage from the Exploitation of Mineral Resources of the Seabed, in* International Disaster Response Law 287 (Andrea de Guttry, Marco Gestri and Gabriella Venturini (eds.), 2012)

Tullio Treves, *Historical Development of the Law of the Sea, in* The Oxford Handbook of the Law of the Sea 1 (Donald R. Rothwell, Alex G. Oude Elferink, Karen N. Scott and Tim Stephens (eds.), 2015)

Tullio Treves, *Law and Science in the Jurisprudence of the International Tribunal for the Law of the Sea, in* Science, Technology, And New Challenges to Ocean Law 13 (Harry N. Scheiber, James Kraska and Moon-Sang Kwon (eds.), 2015)

Vasco Becker-Weinberg, *Seabed Activities and the Protection and Preservation of the Marine Environment in Disputed Maritime Areas of the Asia-Pacific Region, in* Proceedings From The 2012 Losi-Kiost Conference On Securing The Ocean for the Next Generation 1 (Harry N. Scheiber and Moon Sang Kwon (eds.), 2012)

Yoshifumi Tanaka, *State Responsibility for Marine Pollution from Seabed Activities within National Jurisdiction in the Marine Arctic, in* Responsibility and Liability for Commercial Activity in the Arctic, The Example of Greenland 93 (Vibe Ulfbeck, Anders Møllmann and Bent Ole Gram Mortensen (eds.), 2016)

Articles

A. V. Lowe, *The International Seabed and the Single Negotiating Text*, 13 San Diego L. Rev. 489 (1976)

Alex G. Oude Elferink, *The Continental Shelf of Antarctica: Implications of the Requirement to Make a Submission to the CLCS under Article 76 of the LOS Convention*, 17(4) Int. J. Marine & Coastal L. 485 (2002)

Alex G. Oude Elferink, *Meeting of States Parties to the UN Law of the Sea Convention*, 23 Int. J. Marine & Coastal L. 769 (2008)

Alex G. Oude Elferink, *The Arctic Sunrise Incident: A Multi-faceted Law of the Sea Case with a Human Rights Dimension*, 29 Int. J. Marine & Coastal L. 244 (2014)

Alex G. Oude Elferink and Constance Johnson, *Outer Limits of the Continental Shelf and "Disputed Areas": State Practice Concerning Article 76(10) of the LOS Convention*, 21(4) Int. J. Marine & Coastal L. 461 (2006)

Alexander Wendt, *The Agent-Structure Problem in International Relations Theory*, 41(3) Int Org. 335 (1987)

Allen Buchanan and Robert O. Keohane, *The Legitimacy of Global Governance Institutions*, 20(4) Ethics & Int. Aff. 405 (2006)

Andreas Hasenclever, Peter Mayer and Volker Rittberger, *Interests, Power, Knowledge: The Study of International Regimes*, 40(2) Mershon Int. Stud. Rev. 177 (1996)

Andreas Motzfeldt Kravik, *An Analysis of Stagnation in Multilateral Law-making – And Why the Law of the Sea Has Transcended the Stagnation Trend*, 34(4) Leiden J. Int. Law 935 (2021)

Andreas Østhagen and Andreas Raspotnik, *Crab! How a Dispute Over Snow Crab Became a Diplomatic Headache Between Norway and the EU*, 98 Marine Policy 58 (2018)

Andreas Zimmermann, *Business as Usual? The International Court of Justice's 2012 Judicial Practice: Facing New Procedural and Jurisdictional Questions*, 4(3) J. Int. Dispute settlement 521 (2013)

Anna Cavnar, *Accountability and the Commission on the Limits of the Continental Shelf: Deciding Who Owns the Ocean Floor*, 42(3) Cornell Int l. J. 387 (2009)

Anne-Marie Slaughter-Burley, Andrew S. Tulumello and Stepan Wood, *International Law and International Relations Theory: A New Generation of Interdisciplinary Scholarship*, 92(3) Am. J. Int. Law 367 (1998)

Arie M. Kacowic, *Regional Governance and Global Governance: Links and Explanations* 24 Glob. Gov. 61 (2018)

Barbara Koremenos, Charles Lipson and Duncan Snidal, *The Rational Design of International Institutions*, 55(4) Int Org. 761 (2001)

Barbara Kwiatkowska, *Creeping Jurisdiction beyond 200 Miles in the Light of the 1982 Law of the Sea Convention and State Practice*, 22 Ocean Dev. & Int. Law 153 (1991)

Barry Buzan, *Negotiating by Consensus: Developments in Technique at the United Nations Conference on the Law of the Sea*, 75 Am. J. Int. Law 324 (1981)

Bernard H. Oxman, *A Tribute to Louis Sohn – Is the Dispute Settlement System under the Law of the Sea Convention Working*, 39 Geo. Wash. Int L. Rev. 655 (2007)

Bernard H. Oxman, *The Third United Nations Conference on the Law of the Sea: The 1976 New York Sessions*, 71(2) Am. J. Int. Law 247 (1977)

Bernard Oxman, *The Third United Nations Conference on the Law of the Sea: The Eighth Session (1979)*, 74 Am. J. Int. Law 1 (1980)

Brendan Plant, *Expert Evidence and the Challenge of Procedural Reform in International Dispute Settlement*, 9 J. Int. Dispute Settlement 464 (2018)

Christopher Mirasola, *Historic Waters and Ancient Title: Outdated Doctrines for Establishing Maritime Sovereignty and Jurisdiction*, 47 J. Mar. L. & Com. 29 (2016)

Clive R. Symmons, *The Irish Partial Submission to the Commission on the Limits of the Continental Shelf in 2005: A Precedent for Future Such Submissions in the Light of the "Disputed Areas" Procedures of the Commission?*, 37 Ocean Dev. & Int. Law 299 (2006)

Constantinos Yiallourides, *Joint Development of Seabed Resources in Areas of Overlapping Maritime Claims: An Analysis of Precedents in State Practice*, 31 U.S.F. Mar. L. J. 129 (2018)

Daniel Drezner, *The Power and Peril of International Regime Complexity*, 7(1) Perspect Politics 65 (2009)

Daniel M. Bodansky, *The Legitimacy of International Governance: A Coming Challenge for International Environmental Law?* 93 Am. J. Int. Law 596 (1999)

David A. Colson, *The Delimitation of the Outer Continental Shelf between Neighboring States*, 97(1) Am. J. Int. Law 91 (2003)

Donald K. Anton, *The Principle of Residual Liability in the Seabed Disputes Chamber of the International Tribunal for the Law of the Sea: The Advisory Opinion on Responsibility and Liability for International Seabed Mining (ITLOS Case No. 17)*, 7 McGill Int J. Sust. Dev. L. & Pol'y 241 (2012)

Donald R. Rothwell, *Issues and Strategies for Outer Continental Shelf Claims*, 23 Int. J. Marine & Coastal L. 185 (2008)

Douglas Guilfoyle, *The South China Sea Award: How Should We Read the UN Convention on the Law of the Sea?*, 8 Asian J. Int. Law 51 (2018)

Edwin E. Egede and Lawrence Apaalse, *Dispute Concerning Delimitation of the Maritime Boundary between Ghana and Cote D'Ivoire in the Atlantic Ocean – Lessons from Another Maritime Delimitation Case Arising from the African Region*, 29 Ind. Int & Comp. L. Rev. 55 (2019)

Emanuel Adler, *Seizing the Middle Ground: Constructivism in World Politics*, 3(3) Eur. J. Int. Relat. 319 (1997)

Etty R. Agoes, *Indonesia and the LOS Convention: Recent Developments in Ocean Law, Policy and Management*, 15(2) Marine Policy 122 (1991)

F. M. Auburn, *The 1973 Conference on the Law of the Sea in the Light of Current Trends in State Seabed Practice*, 50 Can. B. Rev. 87 (1972)

Giorgio Gaja, *Assessing Expert Evidence in the ICJ*, 15 Law Pract. Int. Courts Trib. 409 (2015)

Giovanny Vega-Barbosa, *The Admissibility of Outer Continental Shelf Delimitation Claims before the ICJ Absent a Recommendation by the CLCS*, 49(2) Ocean Dev. & Int. Law 103 (2018)

H. Gary Knight, *Issues Before the Third United Nations Conference on the Law of the Sea*, 34 LA. L. Rev. 155 (1974)

Helmut Tuerk, *Questions Relating to the Continental Shelf Beyond 200 Nautical Miles: Delimitation, Delineation, and Revenue Sharing*, 97 Int. Law Stud. 232 (2021)

Ioannis Konstantinidis, *Between Villa Schröder (ITLOS) and the Peace Palace (ICJ): Diverging Approaches to Continental Shelf Delimitation Beyond 200 Nautical Miles*, 3(2) J. Territorial Marit. Stud. 28 (2016)

Jean-Frédéric Morin and Laura Gomez-Mera, *The Evolution of Governance Systems: The Case of the Trade Regime*, 22 Int. Stud. Rev. 1022 (2020)

Jianjun Gao, *The Delimitation Method for the Continental Shelf Beyond 200 Nautical Miles: A Reflection on the Judicial and Arbitral Decisions*, 51(2) Ocean Dev. & Int. Law 116 (2020)

Joan E. Donoghue, *Expert Scientific Evidence in a Broader Context*, 9 J. Int. Dispute Settlement 379 (2018)

Joanna Mossop, *Protecting Marine Biodiversity on the Continental Shelf Beyond 200 Nautical Miles*, 38 Ocean Dev. & Int. Law 283 (2007)

Joanna Mossop, *Protests against Oil Exploration at Sea: Lessons from the Arctic Sunrise Arbitration*, 31 Int J. Marine & Coastal L. 60 (2016)

Joanna Mossop, *The Relationship Between the Continental Shelf Regime and a New International Instrument for Protecting Marine Biodiversity in Areas Beyond National Jurisdiction*, 75(1) ICES J. Mar. Sci. 444 (2018)

Jochen von Bernstorff, *Procedures of Decision-Making and the Role of Law in International Organizations*, 9(11) German Law J. 1939 (2008)

John C. Cruden, Steve O'Rourke and Sarah D. Himmelhoch, *The Deepwater Horizon Oil Spill Litigation: Proof of Concept for the Manual for Complex Litigation and the 2015 Amendments to the Federal Rules of Civil Procedure*, 6 Mich. J. Envtl. & Admin. L. 65 (2016)

John E. Noyes, *Judicial and Arbitral Proceedings and the Outer Limits of the Continental Shelf*, 42 Vand. J. Transnat'l L. 1211 (2009)

John Gerard Ruggie, *Global Governance and "New Governance Theory": Lessons from Business and Human Rights*, 20 Glob. Gov. 5 (2014).

John R. Stevenson and Bernard H. Oxman, *The Preparations for the Law of the Sea Conference*, 68 Am. J. Int. Law 1 (1974)

John R. Stevenson and Bernard H. Oxman, *The Third United Nations Conference on the Law of the Sea: The 1974 Caracas Session*, 69 Am. J. Int. Law 1 (1975)

John R. Stevenson and Bernard H. Oxman, *The Third United Nations Conference on the Law of the Sea: The 1975 Geneva Session*, 69(4) Am. J. Int. Law 763 (1975)

Jonathan I. Charney, *United States Interests in a Convention on the Law of the Sea: The Case for a Continued Efforts*, 11 Vand. J. Transnat'l L. 39 (1978)

Jonathan I. Charney, *Progress in International Maritime Boundary Delimitation Law*, 88(2) Am. J. Int. Law 227 (1994)

Jonathan W. Kuyper, *Global Democratization and International Regime Complexity*, 20(3) Eur. J. Int. Relat. 620 (2014)

Jose E. Alvarez, *Are International Judges Afraid of Science?: A Comment on Mbengue*, 34 Loy. L.A. Int & Comp. L. Rev 81 (2011)

José Juste-Ruíz, *Compensation for Pollution Damage Caused by Oil Tanker Accidents: From "Erika" to "Prestige"*, 1 Aegean Rev. Law Sea 37 (2010)

Judith Goldstein, Miles Kahler, Robert Keohane and Anne-Marie Slaughter, *Introduction: Legalization and World Politics*, 54(3) Int. Org. 385 (2000)

Julia Lisztwan, *Stability of Maritime Boundary Agreements*, 37 Yale J. Int. L. 153 (2012)

Kai-chieh Chan, *The ICJ's Judgement in Somalia v. Kenya and Its Implications for the Law of the Sea*, 34 Utrecht J. Int. & Eur. L. 195 (2018)

Kal Raustiala and David G. Victor, *The Regime Complex for Plant Genetic Resources*, 58(2) Int. Org. 277 (2004)

Kamrul Hasan Arif, *Bangladesh-Myanmar Maritime Boundary Delimitation in the Bay of Bengal: An Analysis on the Development of International Law*, 6 Kathmandu Sch. L. Rev. 53 (2018)

Karen A. Cerulo, *Mining the Intersections of Cognitive Sociology and Neuroscience*, 38 Poetics 115 (2010)

Karen J. Alter, *The Promise and Perils of Theorizing International Regime Complexity in an Evolving World*, 17 Rev. Int. Organ. 375 (2022)

Karen J. Alter and Sophie Meunier, *The Politics of International Regime Complexity*, 7(1) Perspect Politics 13 (2009)

Kenneth W. Abbott and Duncan Snidal, *Hard and Soft Law in International Governance*, 54(1) Int. Org. 421 (2000)

Kenneth W. Abbott and Duncan Snidal, *International "Standards" and International Governance*, 8(3) J. Eur. Public Policy 345 (2001)
Kenneth W. Abbott, Jessica F. Green and Robert O. Keohane, *Organizational Ecology and Institutional Change in Global Governance*, 70(2) Int. Org. 247 (2016)
Kenneth W. Abbott, Robert O. Keohane, Andrew Moravcsik, Anne-Marie Slaughter and Duncan Snidal, *The Concept of Legalization*, 54(3) Int. Org. 401 (2000)
Klaus Dingwerth and Philipp Pattberg, *Global Governance as a Perspective on World Politics*, 12 Glob. Gov. 185 (2006)
L. D. M. Nelson, *The Emerging New Law of the Sea*, 42(1) Mod. L. Rev. 42 (1979)
Lucas Carlos Lima, *The Evidential Weight of Experts before the ICJ: Reflections on the Whaling in the Antarctic Case*, 6 J. Int. Dispute Settlement 621 (2015)
Maiko Meguro, *Litigating Climate Change through International Law: Obligations Strategy and Rights Strategy*, 33 Leiden J. Int. Law 933 (2020)
Makane Moise Mbengue, *International Courts and Tribunals as Fact-Finders: The Case of Scientific Fact-Finding in International Adjudication*, 34 Loy. L.A. Int. & Comp. L. Rev. 53 (2011)
Marc A. Levy, Oran R. Young and Michael Zurn, *The Study of International Regimes*, 1(3) Eur. J. Int. Relat. 267 (1995)
María Carolina Romero Lares, *International Regime or Regional Solution? An Overview of the Current State of Affairs of Pollution Liabilities Resulting from Offshore Oil Exploration and Exploitation Activities in Seabed Areas of National Jurisdiction*, IMSC 1 (2013)
Mark B. Feldman, Sang-Myon Rhee, Jonathan I. Charney and Ted L. Stein, *ICJ Decision in the Libya-Tunisia Continental Shelf Case*, 76 Proceedings of the Asil Annual Meeting 150 (1982)
Massimo Lando, *Stability of Maritime Boundaries and the Challenge of Geographical Change: A Reply to Snj'olaug Árnad'ottir*, 35(2) Leiden J. Int. Law 379 (2022)
Mehdi D. Piri and Michael Faure, *The Effectiveness of Cross-Border Pipeline Safety and Environmental Regulations (under International Law)*, 40(1) N. C. J. Int. Law & Com. Reg. 55 (2014)
Michael Barnett and Liv Coleman, *Designing Police: Interpol and the Study of Change in International Organizations*, 49 Int. Stud. Q. 593 (2005)
Mikhail Kashubsky and Anthony Morrison, *Security of Offshore Oil and Gas Facilities: Exclusion Zones and Ships' Routeing*, 5(1) Aust. J. Marit. & Ocean Aff. 1 (2013)
Neil B. Nucup, *Infallible or Final?: Revisiting the Legitimacy of the International Court of Justice as the "Invisible" International Supreme Court*, 18 Law Prac. Int. Courts Trib 145 (2019)
Nikolaos Giannopoulos, *International Protection of Foreign Investments in Offshore Energy Production and Marine Environmental Protection: Birds of a Feather or Frenemies Forever?*, 68 Neth. Int. Law Rev. 249 (2021)
Offshore and Out of Sight: The Ran in the North Arabian Gulf, 6 Semaphore (2008), available at www.navy.gov.au/sites/default/files/documents/Semaphore_2008_6.pdf [publication of the Australian Navy, Department of Defence, Australia]
Oran R. Young, *Regime Dynamics: The Rise and Fall of International Regimes*, 36(2) Int. Org. 277 (1982)
Oran R. Young, *Review: International Regimes: Toward a New Theory of Institutions*, 39(1) World Politics 104 (1986)
Øystein Jensen and Nigel Bankes, *Compulsory and Binding Dispute Resolution under the United Nations Convention on the Law of the Sea: Introduction*, 48(3–4) Ocean Dev. & Int. Law 209 (2017)
Paul DiMaggio, *Culture and Cognition*, 23 Annual Review of Sociology 263 (1997)
Paula M. Vernet, *The Work of the Commission on the Limits of the Continental Shelf: Current Accomplishments and Challenges on the Verge of Its 20th Anniversary*, 20(1) Max Planck Unyb 36 (2017)

Penelope Simoes Ferreira, *The Role of African States in the Development of the Law of the Sea at the Third United Nations Conference*, 7 Ocean Dev. & Int. Law 89 (1979).
Randa Salama, *Fragmentation of International Law: Procedural Issues Arising in Law of the Sea Disputes*, 19 Austl. & N.Z. Mar. L. J. 24 (2005)
Reynaldo Galindo Pohl, *Latin America's Influence and Role in the Third Conference on the Law of the Sea*, 7 Ocean Dev. & Int. Law 65 (1979)
Robert Beckman and Leonardo Bernard, *Framework for the Joint Development of Hydrocarbon Resources*, 22 Asian Y.B. Int. Law 86 (2018)
Robert Beckman, *The UN Convention on the Law of the Sea and the Maritime Disputes in the South China Sea* 107 Am. J. Int. Law 142 (2013)
Robert Keohane and David Victor, *The Regime Complex for Climate Change*, 9(1) Perspectives on Politics 7 (2011)
Robert Keohane, *International Institutions: Can Interdependence Work?*, 110 Foreign Policy 82 (1998)
Robert O. Keohane, *The Demand for International Regimes*, 36(2) Int. Org. 325 (1982)
Robert Powell, *Anarchy in International Relations Theory: The Neorealist-Neoliberal Debate*, 48(2) Int. Org. 313 (1994)
Roger K. Smith, *Explaining the Non-Proliferation Regime*, 41(2) Int. Org. 253 (1987)
Ron Macnab, *Third-Party Reactions to Continental Shelf Submissions, and their Treatment by the CLCS*, Law of the Sea Conference, Trinity College Dublin 1 (2010)
Sandrine W. De Herdt and Tafsir Malick Ndiaye, *The International Tribunal for the Law of the Sea and the Protection and Preservation of the Marine Environment: Taking Stock and Prospects*, 57 The Canadian Yearbook of International Law 353 (2019)
Sebastian tho Pesch, *Coastal State Jurisdiction around Installations: Safety Zones in the Law of the Sea*, 30 Int. J. Marine & Coastal L. 512 (2015)
Sergey M. Punzhin, *Procedural Normative System of the International Court of Justice*, 30 Leiden J. Int. Law 661 (2017)
Shane Bosma, *The Regulation of Marine Pollution Arising from offshore Oil and Gas Facilities – An Evaluation of the Adequacy of Current Regulatory Regimes and the Responsibility of States to Implement a New Liability Regime*, 26 Austl. & N.Z. Mar. L. J. 89 (2012)
Shani Friedman, *The Concept of Entitlement to an Exclusive Economic Zone as Reflected in International Judicial Decisions*, 53(1) ISR. Law Rev. 101 (2020)
Snjólaug Árnadóttir, *Provisional Boundaries and Alternative Solutions to Maritime Delimitation*, 35(2) Leiden J. Int. Law 397 (2022)
Stephen D. Krasner, *Structural Causes and Regime Consequences: Regimes as Intervening Variables*, 36(2) Int. Org. 185 (1982)
Surabhi Ranganathan, *Decolonization and International Law: Putting the Ocean on the Map*, 23 J. Hist. Int. Law 161 (2021)
Ted L. McDorman, *Global Ocean Governance and International Adjudicative Dispute Resolution*, 43 Ocean Coast. Manag. 255 (2000)
Ted L. McDorman, *The Continental Shelf beyond 200 nm: Law and Politics in the Arctic Ocean*, 18(2) J. Transnat'l Law & Pol. 155 (2009)
Ted L. McDorman, *The Role of the Commission on the Limits of the Continental Shelf: A Technical Body in a Political World*, 17(3) Int. J. Marine & Coastal L. 301 (2002)
Thomas Gehring and Benjamin Faude, *The Dynamics of Regime Complexes: Microfoundations and Systemic Effects*, 19 Glob. Gov. 119 (2013)
Thomas M. Franck and Evan R. Chesler, *An International Regime for the Sea-Bed Beyond National Jurisdiction*, 13(2) Osgoode Hall L. J. 579 (1975)
Timothy Dunne, *The Social Construction of International Society*, 1(3) Eur. J. Int. Relat. 367 (1995)
Tommy T. B. Koh, *Negotiating a New World Order for the Sea*, 24 Va. J. Int. L. 761 (1984)
Tuillio Treves, *Coastal States' Rights in the Maritime Areas under UNCLOS*, 12 Braz. J. Int. L. 40 (2015)

Tyler Pratt, *Deference and Hierarchy in International Regime Complexes*, 72 Int. Org. 561 (2018)
Valentin J. Schatz and Dmytro Koval, *Russia's Annexation of Crimea and the Passage of Ships Through Kerch Strait: A Law of the Sea Perspective*, 50 Ocean Dev. & Int. Law 275 (2019)
Wylie Spicer, *Canada, the Law of the Sea Treaty and International Payments: Where Will the Money Come from?*, 31(8) University of Calgary, The School of Public Policy, Spp Research Papers 8 (2015)
Xuexia Liao, *Evaluation of Scientific Evidence by International Courts and Tribunals in the Continental Shelf Delimitation Cases*, 48(2) Ocean Dev. & Int. Law 136 (2017)
Yunus Emre Acikgonul, *Reflections on the Principle of Non-Cut Off: A Growing Concept in Maritime Boundary Delimitation Law*, 47(1) Ocean Dev. & Int. Law 52 (2016)
Yurika Ishii, *Relevant Coasts and Relevant Area in the Maritime Delimitation of the EEZ and Continental Shelf*, 51(4) Ocean Dev. & Int. Law 307 (2020)
Zhang Hua, *The Development of International Law of the Sea by International Courts and Tribunals, A Case Study of Due Diligence Obligation*, 9 Korean J. Int. & Comp. L. 132 (2021)
Zou Keyuan, *Historic Rights in International Law and in China's Practice*, 32(2) Ocean Dev. & Int. Law 149 (2001)

Websites

American Petroleum Institute Website, available at www.api.org/oil-and-natural-gas/wells-to-consumer/exploration-and-production/offshore/offshore-production-facilities
Arbitration Between the Republic of Croatia and the Republic of Slovenia, PCA website, available at https://pca-cpa.org/en/cases/3
Australian Government, Department of Agriculture, Water and the Environment Website, available at www.environment.gov.au/marine/marine-pollution/montara-oil-spill
Australian Government, Department of Foreign Affairs and Trade, available at www.dfat.gov.au/geo/timor-leste/Pages/joint-communique
Bureau of Safety and Environmental Enforcement website, available at www.bsee.gov/newsroom/library/offshore-incident-archive
Business and Human Rights Resource Center Website, available at www.business-humanrights.org/en/latest-news/shell-lawsuit-re-oil-pollution-in-nigeria/
Canada's page, DOALOS website, available at www.un.org/Depts/los/LEGISLATIONANDTREATIES/STATEFILES/CAN.htm
CBD, UN Treaty Collection (UNTC) Website, available at https://treaties.un.org/pages/ViewDetails.aspx?src=TREATY&mtdsg_no=XXVII-8&chapter=27
Christoph Saake, A Straight Line Towards the Sea, A Comment on the Judgment in the case of Maritime Delimitation in the Indian Ocean (Somalia v. Kenya), voelkerrechtsblog (18 October 2021), available at https://voelkerrechtsblog.org/a-straight-line-towards-the-sea/
CIA's World Factbook, Maritime Claims, available at www.cia.gov/the-world-factbook/field/maritime-claims/
David Testa, Comments on Coastal and Flag State Jurisdiction in the M/T "San Padre Pio" Dispute, EjilTalk! (September 3, 2019), available at www.ejiltalk.org/comments-on-coastal-and-flag-state-jurisdiction-in-the-m-t-san-padre-pio-dispute/
Declarations made upon signature, ratification, accession, succession, or anytime thereafter, DOALOS website, available at www.un.org/depts/los/convention_agreements/convention_declarations.htm
Declarations Recognizing as Compulsory the Jurisdiction of the International Court of Justice under Article 36, paragraph 2, of the Statute of the Court, UN Treaty Collection Website, available at https://treaties.un.org/pages/ViewDetails.aspx?src=TREATY&mtdsg_no=I-4&chapter=1&clang=_en

Division for Ocean Affairs and the Law of the Sea (DOALOS) Website, Submissions to the Commission on the Limits of the Continental Shelf, pursuant to article 76, paragraph 8, available at www.un.org/Depts/los/clcs_new/commission_submissions.htm

FAOLEX database, available at www.fao.org/faolex/results/details/en/c/LEX-FAOC003534

Gabon Page, DOALOS website, available at www.un.org/Depts/los/LEGISLATIONANDTREATIES/STATEFILES/GAB.htm

India's legislation database, available at www.indiacode.nic.in/handle/123456789/1484?view_type=search&sam_handle=123456789/1362

www.internationallawoffice.com/Newsletters/Energy-Natural-Resources/Africa/Herbert-Smith/Congo-Brazzaville-New-Legislation-Concerning-the-Dismantling-of-Oil-Installations#

ITLOS Website, available at www.itlos.org/en/main/cases/list-of-cases/

James Crawford, Articles on Responsibility of States for Internationally Wrongful Acts, 2001 (2012), Audiovisual Library of International Law, UN website, available at https://legal.un.org/avl/ha/rsiwa/rsiwa.html

Joint Submission by Malaysia and the Socialist Republic of Viet Nam, DOALOS website, available at www.un.org/Depts/los/clcs_new/submissions_files/submission_mys-vnm_33_2009.htm

Law of the Sea, A Policy Primer, Presented by The Fletcher School's LL.M. Program in International Law & Maritime Studies Program, Tufts University (2017), available at https://sites.tufts.edu/lawofthesea/chapter-seven/

"Legislation Malta" website, available at https://legislation.mt

Malcolm D. Evans and Nicholas A. Ioannides, A Commentary on the 2023 Nicaragua v Colombia Case, EJIL:Talk! (4 August 2023)

http://maritime-connector.com/wiki/platforms/

Maurice Blackburn Lawyers Website, available at www.mauriceblackburn.com.au/class-actions/current-class-actions/montara-oil-spill-class-action/

New-Zealand legislation website, available at www.legislation.govt.nz/act/public/1964/0028/latest/LMS304788.html?search=qs_act%40bill%40regulation%40deemedreg_continental+shelf+1964_resel_25_h&p=1

New-Zealand legislation website, available at www.legislation.govt.nz/all/results.aspx?search=qs_act%40bill%40regulation%40deemedreg_continental+shelf_resel_25_h&p=2

Nicholas A. Ioannides and Constantinos Yiallourides, A Commentary on the Dispute Concerning the Maritime Delimitation in the Indian Ocean (Somalia v Kenya), EJIL:Talk! Blog (22 October 2021), available at www.ejiltalk.org/a-commentary-on-the-dispute-concerning-the-maritime-delimitation-in-the-indian-ocean-somalia-v-kenya/

OSPAR Website, available at www.ospar.org/convention

Palau's Page, DOALOS website, available at www.un.org/Depts/los/LEGISLATIONANDTREATIES/STATEFILES/PLW.htm

Partial Submission by Malaysia in the South China Sea, DOALOS website, available at www.un.org/Depts/los/clcs_new/submissions_files/submission_mys_12_12_2019.html

Permanent Court of Arbitration Website, available at https://pca-cpa.org/en/cases/141/

Spain's Page, DOALOS website, available at www.un.org/Depts/los/LEGISLATIONANDTREATIES/STATEFILES/ESP.htm

"Stare Decisis", Merriam-Webster Dictionary, available at www.merriam-webster.com/dictionary/stare%20decisis

Submission by Angola, DOALOS website, available at www.un.org/Depts/los/clcs_new/submissions_files/submission_ago_69_2013.htm

Submission by the Argentine Republic, DOALOS website, available at www.un.org/Depts/los/clcs_new/submissions_files/submission_arg_25_2009.htm

Submission by Australia, DOALOS website, available at www.un.org/Depts/los/clcs_new/submissions_files/submission_aus.htm

Submission by Ireland, DOALOS website, available at www.un.org/Depts/los/clcs_new/submissions_files/submission_irl1.htm

Submission by the Commonwealth of the Bahamas, DOALOS website, available at www.un.org/Depts/los/clcs_new/submissions_files/submission_bhs_71_2014.htm

Submission by the Federal Republic of Somalia, DOALOS website, available at www.un.org/Depts/los/clcs_new/submissions_files/submission_som_74_2014.htm

Submission by the French Republic, DOALOS website, available at www.un.org/Depts/los/clcs_new/submissions_files/submission_fra_72_2014.htm

Submission by the Kingdom of Denmark, DOALOS website, available at www.un.org/Depts/los/clcs_new/submissions_files/submission_dnk_54_2010.htm

Submission by the Kingdom of Norway, DOALOS website, available at www.un.org/Depts/los/clcs_new/submissions_files/submission_nor_30_2009.htm

Submission by the People's Republic of China, DOALOS website, available at www.un.org/Depts/los/clcs_new/submissions_files/submission_chn_63_2012.htm

Submission by the Republic of India, DOALOS website, available at www.un.org/Depts/los/clcs_new/submissions_files/submission_ind_48_2009.htm

Submission by the Republic of Kenya, DOALOS website, available at www.un.org/Depts/los/clcs_new/submissions_files/submission_ken_35_2009.htm

Submission by the Republic of Korea, DOALOS website, available at www.un.org/Depts/los/clcs_new/submissions_files/submission_kor_65_2012.htm

Submission by the Republic of Nicaragua, DOALOS website, available at www.un.org/Depts/los/clcs_new/submissions_files/submission_nic_66_2013.htm

Submission by the Republic of Palau, DOALOS website, available at www.un.org/Depts/los/clcs_new/submissions_files/submission_plw_41_2009.htm

Submission by the Socialist Republic of Viet Nam, DOALOS website, available at www.un.org/Depts/los/clcs_new/submissions_files/submission_vnm_37_2009.htm

Submission by the United Kingdom of Great Britain and Northern Ireland, DOALOS website, available at www.un.org/Depts/los/clcs_new/submissions_files/submission_gbr1.htm

Submission by the United Kingdom of Great Britain and Northern Ireland, DOALOS website, available at www.un.org/Depts/los/clcs_new/submissions_files/submission_gbr_45_2009.htm

Table recapitulating the status of the Convention and of the related Agreements, DOALOS website, available at www.un.org/depts/los/reference_files/status2019.pdf

The International Oil Pollution Compensation Funds Website, available at https://iopcfunds.org/about-us/legal-framework/

UN Goals, available at https://sdgs.un.org/goals

UNEP website, available at www.unep.org/unepmap/who-we-are/contracting-parties/offshore-protocol

United Nations Convention on the Law of the Sea, Chapter XXI, UN Treaty Collection website, available at https://treaties.un.org/pages/ViewDetailsIII.aspx?src=TREATY&mtdsg_no=XXI-6&chapter=21&Temp=mtdsg3&clang=_en

Viet Nam's Independent Submission to the Commission, DOALOS website, available at www.un.org/Depts/los/clcs_new/submissions_files/submission_vnm_37_2009.htm

Index

Made in the USA
Las Vegas, NV
24 October 2026

14bbfad3-1c75-4076-96b0-91bcc87c70beR01